WITHDRAWN

A Study of Thinking

A WILEY PUBLICATION IN PSYCHOLOGY

HERBERT S. LANGFELD

Advisory Editor

A Study of Thinking

JEROME S. BRUNER

JACQUELINE J. GOODNOW

the late GEORGE A. AUSTIN

With an Appendix on Language
by ROGER W. BROWN

A Publication of the Harvard Cognition Project

NEW YORK · JOHN WILEY & SONS, INC.

London

Sixth Printing, July,1962

Copyright © 1956, by John Wiley & Sons, Inc.

Library of Congress Catalog Card Number: 56-7999

Printed in the United States of America

24479

In Memory
of
Egon Brunswik

Preface

The past few years have witnessed a notable increase in interest in and investigation of the cognitive processes—the means whereby organisms achieve, retain, and transform information. This increase in interest and effort should, we suppose, be counted as a "revival," since there was an earlier time (the years before the first World War), when the Higher Mental Processes constituted a core topic within psychology.

One need not look far for the origins of the revival. Partly, it has resulted from a recognition of the complex processes that mediate between the classical "stimuli" and "responses" out of which stimulus-response learning theories hoped to fashion a psychology that would by-pass anything smacking of the "mental." The impeccable peripheralism of such theories could not last long. As "S-R" theories came to be modified to take into account the subtle events that may occur between the input of a physical stimulus and the emission of an observable response, the old image of the "stimulus-response bond" began to dissolve, its place being taken by a mediation model. As Edward Tolman so felicitiously put it some years ago, in place of a telephone switchboard connecting stimuli and responses it might be more profitable to think of a map room where stimuli were sorted out and arranged before ever response occurred, and one might do well to have a closer look at these intervening "cognitive maps."

Information theory is another source of the revival. Its short history in psychology recapitulates the fate of stimulus-response learning theory. The inputs and outputs of a communication system, it soon became apparent, could not be dealt with exclusively in terms

vii

of the nature of these inputs and outputs alone nor even in terms of such internal characteristics as channel capacity and noise. The coding and recoding of inputs—how incoming signals are sorted and organized—turns out to be the important secret of the black box that lies athwart the communication channel. Those who would apply information theory to psychological phenomena are, then, similarly faced squarely with the problems of mediating cognition.

Finally, the revival has been stimulated by deep and long-term changes in personality theory. Freud's brilliant insights at the turn of the century focussed attention on what might appropriately be called the motivational economy of man's adjustment: the expression of inner drives and the resolution of such drives when they conflict. His formulations and their later extension were, in considerable measure, a revolt against the excessive rationalism of the 19th century. Cognitive activity was at first of interest to the personality theorist only to the degree that it illustrated the manner in which "rational" processes could be made captive of imperious drives and defenses. Here too there has been a significant change. Psychoanalysis and personality theory generally have become increasingly interested in what has come to be called "ego psychology," and the so-called synthetic functions of the ego grow more and more central. Perhaps the change can even be dated to the publication of two books in the late 1930's, one psychoanalytic, the other not: Anna Freud's *The Ego and the Mechanisms of Defense,* and Gordon W. Allport's *Personality.* In any case, as the ego came out of hiding, the interest in cognitive functioning came with it. If the work that came to be called the "New Look" in perception started off searching for manifestations of autism in perceiving, it soon became transformed into a search for links between general laws of perception and cognition on one side and general laws of personality functioning on the other.

This book is an effort to deal with one of the simplest and most ubiquitous phenomena of cognition: categorizing or conceptualizing. On closer inspection, it is not so simple. The spirit of the inquiry is descriptive. We have not sought "explanation" in terms of learning theory, information theory, or personality theory. We have sought to describe and in a small measure to explain what happens when an intelligent human being seeks to sort the environment into significant classes of events so that he may end by treating discriminably different things as equivalents. In dealing with the problem, we have found ourselves travelling far afield.

What we have to record in these pages is the outcome of a five-year program of research, part of the Cognition Project in the Laboratory of Social Relations at Harvard University. The work has been made possible by grants from the Laboratory, from the Rockefeller Foundation, and from the Behavioral Sciences Division of the Ford Foundation, and we are greatly indebted to each of them for their support.

The work began in 1951 when two of us spent a year free of teaching duties at the Institute for Advanced Study and we gladly acknowledge our debt to its Director, Dr. J. Robert Oppenheimer, both for providing the opportunity and for giving us much good advice and helpful encouragement. He once expressed the view that units of analysis in science usually turn out to be much larger and more inclusive than one at first expects. As our own work has progressed from initial concern with the number of bits of information assimilated from single encounters with events to an ultimate concern with the informational properties of long sequences of acts called strategies, we recognize the appropriateness of his remark.

Empirical research began the next year at Harvard, and as is so often the case in psychology, the plans and formulations of the first year of thinking underwent some drastic changes when translated into experiments. Dr. Robert V. Seymour, whose doctoral thesis was one of the first efforts at such translation, contributed greatly then and on subsequent occasions to our understanding of the conceptualizing process. It was he who first saw the way in which conceptualizing behavior could be treated as a strategy problem. Chapter 4 of this book is largely based on his efforts. A doctoral research in the following year had much the same energizing effect on our efforts, the work of Dr. Robert E. Goodnow. His exploration of the manner in which human beings deal with and use uncertain cues provides much of the basis for Chapter 7.

Throughout, we have had the good fortune of being goaded and contained by research collaborators and assistants who have contributed materially to the design of research and its interpretation, and to the climate of thought in which we have worked. Claire Zimmerman, Jean Matter, Donald O'Dowd, Elise Bartholomew, William Hull, Mary Potter, Michael Maccoby, Malcolm Jeeves, George Talland, Michael Wallach, and Lotte Bailyn have all carried a share of the effort and we are indebted to them. Lotte Bailyn began the unravelling of the problem of how "either-or" concepts are handled in thinking, an account of which is to be found in Chapter 6, and Mary Potter contributed to the design and execution of research reported in various parts of the book.

The program of research and the subsequent stages of analysis and writing were greatly aided by our regular but unofficial Thursday afternoon seminars, attended by research students, assistants, and an occasional colleague engaged in allied work. The kind of seminar that is nourished by work in progress, we discovered, is the best seminar of all. We hope this book does justice to the hotbed of ideas that flourished in Bow Street on Thursday afternoons.

Many colleagues have given us valuable comment and criticism at various stages of our work, both at Harvard and on the occasions when we have presented parts of the present book to colloquia at Yale, California, Swarthmore, Duke, Wellesley, and Clark. None of the studies reported in these pages has been published before; our colleagues and colloquia were the principal means of getting the necessary corrective. The late Professor Egon Brunswik, both through his writings and through personal conversation, has contributed much to our thinking. It is a privilege to offer this book in his memory. We have also gained much from our colleagues Professor George Miller, Professor Frederick Mosteller, and Professor Roger Brown who has written an appendix to this book on applications to psycholinguistics. There are many others to be thanked, but we particularly wish to single out Professors Carl Hovland, Robert Bush, Clyde Kluckhohn, John Whiting, Ray Hyman, Renato Tagiuri, and Evon Vogt. We are also indebted to Professor Herbert S. Langfeld for his helpful suggestions.

Finally, we are grateful for the patient editorial and secretarial efforts of Miss Sally Cheng, and for the labors of Michael Wallach in preparing the index.

George Austin, our friend and collaborator, died in his thirty-second year, in December, 1955. The death of one so young, so courageous, and so promising is a loss to his friends and to learning.

JEROME S. BRUNER
JACQUELINE J. GOODNOW

Cambridge, Mass.
May, 1956

Contents

"We may insist as much as we like that the human intellect is weak. . . . But nevertheless there is something peculiar about this weakness. The voice of the intellect is a soft one, but it does not rest until it has gained a hearing. Ultimately, after endlessly repeated rebuffs, it succeeds."

S. Freud
The Future of an Illusion
p. 93

CHAPTER 1

Introduction

We begin with what seems a paradox. The world of experience of any normal man is composed of a tremendous array of discriminably different objects, events, people, impressions. There are estimated to be more than 7 million discriminable colors alone, and in the course of a week or two we come in contact with a fair proportion of them. No two people we see have an identical appearance and even objects that we judge to be the same object over a period of time change appearance from moment to moment with alterations in light or in the position of the viewer. All of these differences we are capable of seeing, for human beings have an exquisite capacity for making distinctions.

But were we to utilize fully our capacity for registering the differences in things and to respond to each event encountered as unique, we would soon be overwhelmed by the complexity of our environment. Consider only the linguistic task of acquiring a vocabulary fully adequate to cope with the world of color differences! The resolution of this seeming paradox—the existence of discrimination capacities which, if fully used, would make us slaves to the particular—is achieved by man's capacity to categorize. To categorize is to render discriminably different things equivalent, to group the objects and events and people around us into classes, and to respond to them in terms of their class membership rather than their uniqueness. Our refined discriminative activity is reserved only for those segments of the environment with which we are specially concerned. For the rest, we respond by rather crude forms of categorial placement. In place of a color lexicon of 7 million items, people in our society get along with a dozen or so commonly used color names. It suffices to note that the book on the desk has a "blue" cover. If the task calls for finer discrimination, we may narrow the category and note that it is in the class of things called "medium blue." It is rare indeed that we are ever called upon to place the book in a category of colors comprising *only* the unique hue-brightness-saturation combination it presents.

The process of categorizing involves, if you will, an act of invention. This hodgepodge of objects is comprised in the category "chairs," that assortment of diverse numbers is all grouped together as "powers of 2," these structures are "houses" but those others are "garages." What is unique about categories of this kind is that once they are mastered they can be used without further learning. We need not learn *de novo* that the stimulus configuration before us is another house. If we have learned the class "house" as a concept, new exemplars can readily be recognized. The category becomes a tool for further use. The learning and utilization of categories represents one of the most elementary and general forms of cognition by which man adjusts to his environment. It was in this belief that the research reported in this volume was undertaken. For it is with the categorizing process and its many ramifications that this book is principally concerned.

IDENTITY AND EQUIVALENCE CATEGORIES

The full moon, the moon in quarter, and the crescent moon all evoke the same nominative response, "moon." From a common response made by a person to an array of objects we infer that he "has" an equivalence or identity category. The similar responses from which we draw such an inference need not be verbal. An air-raid siren, a dislodged piton while climbing, and a severe dressing-down by a superior may all produce a common autonomic response in a man and by this fact we infer that they are all grouped as "danger situations." Indeed, the person involved may not be able to verbalize the category. While this is in itself interesting, it is not crucial to our point, which is simply that an equivalence range is inferred from the presence of a common response to an array of discriminably different events. This leaves many technical questions unsettled (cf. Klüver, 1933), but it serves to get the inquiry under way.

Two broad types of categorizing responses are obviously of interest. One of them is the identity response, the other the equivalence response, and each points to a different kind of category.

Without belaboring the obvious, identity categorization may be defined as classing a variety of stimuli as *forms of the same thing*.

What lies behind the identity response is not clear, save that it is obviously a response that is affected by learning. It does not do to say simply that an object is seen as the identical object on a later encounter if it has not "changed its characteristics too much." The moon in its phases varies from a sliver to a circle, in color from luminous white to the bronzed hunter's moon. Sheldon (1950) collected a series of photographs of the same individual over a period of 15 years, the person standing in the same position against a uniform background. The photographs span the period from early boyhood to full manhood. As one riffles through the stack, there is a strong and dramatic impression of the identical person in the process of growth. Yet the pictures go through a drastic metamorphosis. Because such identity responses are ubiquitous and because they are learned very early in life, we tend to regard them somehow as a different process from other forms of categorizing—the recognition of two different people as both being people. Yet both depend upon what Michotte (1950) speaks of as the presence of a *cachet spécifique* or essential quality. They are both forms of categorizing. What differs is the nature of the inference: in the one case we infer "identity" from the presence of the *cachet,* in the other case "equivalence."

How one comes to learn to categorize in terms of identity categories is, as we have said, little understood. Too often we have succumbed to the Kantian heritage and taken identity categories as given. Piaget's recent work (1953) and the work of Michotte (1946) leave the question open. Piaget speaks of the learning of identity as corresponding to the mastery of a principle of conservation as in the conservation of energy in physics. At certain stages of development, an object passed behind a screen is not judged by the child to be the same object when it emerges on the other side. Hebb (1949) proposes that certain forms of neural growth must precede the capacity for the maintenance of identity. Whether the capacity is "innate" and then developed by being extended to new ranges of events or whether the capacity to recognize identity is itself learned is not our concern here. It suffices to note that its development depends notably upon learning.

That there is confusion remaining in the adult world about what constitutes an identity class is testified to by such diverse proverbs as *plus ça change, plus la même chose* and the Heraclitan dictum that we never enter the same river twice. Indeed, in severe psychotic turmoil one sometimes notes an uncertainty about the identity category that is the "self" in states of depersonalization, and a rather poignant reminder that the identity of self is even equivocal in normal states is provided by the sign behind a bar in the Southwest:

> I ain't what I've been.
> I ain't what I'm going to be.
> I am what I am.

We speak of an equivalence class when an individual responds to a set of discriminably different things as the *same kind of thing* or as *amounting to the same thing*. Again we depend for our knowledge of the existence of a category upon the presence of a common response. While there is a striking phenomenological difference between identity and equivalence, both depend upon the acceptance of certain properties of objects as being criterial or relevant—again Michotte's *cachet spécifique*—and others as being irrelevant. One may distinguish three broad classes of equivalence categories, each distinguished by the kind of defining response involved. They may be called *affective, functional,* and *formal* categories.

Certain forms of grouping appear to depend very heavily upon whether or not the things placed in the same class evoke a common affective response. A group of people, books, weather of a certain kind, and certain states of mind are all grouped together as "alike," the "same kind of thing." Further inquiry may reveal that all of them were experienced during a particularly poignant summer of childhood. What holds them together and what leads one to say that some new experience "reminds one of such and such weather, people, and states" is the evocation of a defining affective response.

Characteristically, categories marked by an affective defining response are not amenable to ready description in terms of the properties of the objects comprising them. The difficulty appears to lie in the lack of correspondence between affective and linguistic categories. As Schachtel (1947) and McClelland (1951) have suggested, categories bound together by a common affective response frequently go back to early childhood and may resist conscious verbal insight by virtue of having been established before the full development of language. For categorizing activity at the preverbal stage appears to be predominantly nonrepresentational, depending not so much on the common external properties of objects as on the relation of things encountered to internal needs, to follow Piaget's argument (1951), or, to follow Schachtel's, on idiosyncratic and highly personalized impressions. Dollard and Miller (1950) argue persuasively that much of psychotherapy consists of the verbal labelling and resorting of such preverbal categories, so that they may become more accessible to the forms of symbolic or linguistic manipulation characteristic of adult problem-solving. Indeed, it is not difficult to imagine that the effectiveness of poetry often rests on its ability to cut across our conventional linguistic categories in a way evocative of more affective categorizations. Archibald MacLeish (1939) catches well this esthetic need for freedom from conventional verbal categories in his lines,

> A poem should be palpable and mute
> As a globed fruit
> Dumb
> As old medallions to the thumb
> Silent as the sleeve-worn stone
> Of casement ledges where the moss has grown—
> A poem should be wordless
> As the flight of birds.

The problems of specifying the properties of objects that mediate a common categorizing response become less arduous when the category is a functional or utilitarian one. Rather than an internal state rendering a group of things equivalent, now equivalence is based on an external function. The objects of a functional category fulfill a concrete and specific task requirement—"things large enough and strong enough to plug this hole in the dike." Such forms of defining response almost always have, as Bartlett (1951) suggests, a specific interpolative function ("gap filling") or a specific extrapolative function ("how to take the next step"). The experiments by Maier (1930, 1931, 1945) represent an outstanding instance of research on the conditions which facilitate and inhibit the recognition of "requirements" necessary for correct identification of an object as fulfilling specific functions in a particular task situation, such situations, for example, as how to bridge a gap between two objects given certain limits and certain properties in the materials provided.

Formal categories are constructed by the act of specifying the intrinsic attribute properties required by the members of a class. Such categories have the characteristic that one can state reliably the diacritica of a class of objects or events short of describing their use. The formal properties of science are a case in point. Oftentimes the careful specification of defining properties even requires the constructions of special "artificial" languages to indicate that common-sense functional categories are not being used. The concept "force" in physics and the word standing for the functional class of events called "force" in common sense do not have the same kind of definition. What is accomplished in effect by formal categories is that one is able to devise classes whose defining properties are not determined by the suitability of objects to a specific task. The emphasis of definition is placed more and more on the attribute properties of class members and less and less on "utilitanda properties," to borrow a term from Tolman (1932). The development of formalization is gradual. From "things I can drive this tent stake with" we move to the concept "hammer" and from there to "mechanical force," each step being freer of definition by specific use than the former.

The development of formal categories is, of course, tantamount to science-making and we need not pause here to discuss this rather impenetrable problem. It suffices to note that formal categories and formal category systems appear to develop concurrently with methods for representing and manipulating them symbolically. What impels one to formalization we cannot say. That the urge is strong is unquestionable. Indeed, it is characteristic of highly elaborated cultures that symbolic representations of formal categories and formal category systems are eventually developed without reference to the classes of environmental events that the formal categories "stand for." Geometry provides a case in point, and while it is true that its original development was contingent upon the utilitarian triangulation systems used for redividing plots after floods in the Nile Valley, it is now the case that geometers proceed without regard for the fit of their formal categories to specific empirical problems.

It is obvious that there are close relationships between affective, functional, and formal categories and that they are often convertible one into the other. About the conversion of functional categories into formal ones—finally rendering the category of "things good for postpartum mothers" such as ground bone and certain chalks into the formal class "calcium"—we have already taken some notice. It is interesting that the gifted mathematician often speaks of certain formal categories in terms that are also affective in nature. G. H. Hardy in his delightful "apology" (1940) speaks of the class of things known as "elegant solutions" and while these may have formal properties they are also marked by the fact that they evoke a common affective response. The distinction between the three types is, we would suggest, a useful one and it may well be that the process whereby they are learned is informatively different. It is suggestive, for example, that the brain-injured patients described by writers like Goldstein (1940) and Head (1926) seem quite capable of utilizing functional categories but are precipitated into a crisis when faced with the need of locating or forming or using categories divorced from the immediate function to be served by their exemplars.

THE INVENTION OF CATEGORIES

To one raised in Western culture, things that are treated as if they were equivalent seem not like man-made classes but like the products of nature. To be sure, the defining criteria in terms of which equivalence classes are formed exist in nature as potentially discriminable. Rocks have properties that permit us to classify them as rocks, and some human beings have the features that permit us to categorize them as handsome. But there exists a near infinitude of ways of grouping events in terms of discriminable properties, and we avail ourselves of only a few of these.

Our intellectual history is marked by a heritage of naive realism. For Newton, science was a voyage of discovery on an uncharted sea. The objective of the voyage was to discover the islands of truth. The truths existed in nature. Contemporary science has been hard put to shake the yoke of this dogma. Science and common-sense inquiry alike do not discover the ways in which events are grouped in the world; they invent ways of grouping. The test of the invention is the predictive benefits that result from the use of invented categories. The revolution of modern physics is as much as anything a revolution against naturalistic realism in the name of a new nominalism. Do such categories as tomatoes, lions, snobs, atoms, and mammalia exist? In so far as they have been invented and found applicable to instances of nature, they do.° They exist as inventions, not as discoveries.

Stevens (1936) sums up the contemporary nominalism in these terms: "Nowadays we concede that the purpose of science is to invent workable descriptions of the universe. Workable by whom? By us. We invent logical systems such as logic and mathematics whose terms are used to denote discriminable aspects of nature and with these systems we formulate descriptions of the world as we see it and according to our convenience. We work in this fashion because there is no other way for us to work" (p. 93). Because the study of these acts of invention is within the competence of the psychologist, Stevens calls psychology "the propadeutic science."

The recognition of the constructive or invented status of categories changes drastically the nature of the equivalence problem as a topic for psychological research. The study of equivalence becomes, essentially, a study of coding and recoding processes employed by organisms who have past histories and present requirements to be met.

° See Burma and Mayr (1949) for an enlightening discussion of the "reality" of the species concept in systematic zoology.

The implicit assumption that psychological equivalence was somehow determined by the "similarity" or "distinctive similarity" of environmental events is replaced by the view that psychological equivalence is only limited by and not determined by stimulus similarity. The number of ways in which an array of events can be differentiated into classes will vary with the ability of an organism to abstract features which some of the events share and others do not. The features available on which to base such categorial differentiation, taken singly and in combination, are very numerous indeed. As Klüver (1933) so well put it more than two decades ago, the stimulus similarity that serves as a basis for grouping is a selected or abstracted similarity. There is an act of rendering similar by a coding operation rather than a forcing of equivalence on the organism by the nature of stimulation.

Two consequences immediately become apparent. One may ask first what are the preconditions—situational and in the past history of the organism—that lead to one kind of grouping rather than another. The characteristic forms of coding, if you will, now become a dependent variable worthy of study in their own right. It now becomes a matter of interest to inquire what affects the formation of equivalence classes or systems of equivalence coding. The second consequence is that one is now more tempted to ask about systematic individual and cultural difference in categorizing behavior. In so far as each individual's milieu and each culture has its own vicissitudes and problems, might one not expect that this would reflect itself in the characteristic ways in which members of a culture will group the events of their physical and social environment? And, moreover, since different cultures have different languages, and since these languages code or categorize the world into different classes, might it not be reasonable to expect some conformance between the categories normally employed by speakers and those contained in the language they use?

Consider now the scope of the problem, the generality of categorizing, and the benefit to be derived from studying its various manifestations.

THE GENERALITY OF CATEGORIZING

The first benefit to be derived from a closer study of categorizing behavior is a gain in generality for psychological theory. Categorizing is so ubiquitous that an understanding of its psychological nature cannot help but shed light on a wide range of problems within psychology. Most of the examples we have given thus far have, perhaps for simplicity's sake, been drawn from the field of perception. This is misleading. For the act of categorizing, operationally defined in the manner discussed in the foregoing, may occur in a perceptual situation or one not involving the presence of stimulus objects. Logically speaking, there is no distinction between them save in the sense that the materials categorized differ. Categorization at the perceptual level consists of the process of identification, literally an act of placing a stimulus input by virtue of its defining attributes into a certain class. An object of a certain color, size, shape, and texture is seen as an apple. The act of identification involves a "fit" between the properties of a stimulus input and the specifications of a category. Categorization of "conceptual objects" also involves the fit of a set of objects or instances to the specifications of a category. We categorize, say, Whig and Tory statesmen of the first half of the 19th century in terms of whether each instance of the class had certain characteristics of allegiance, belief, etc. Or we class together all prime numbers by virtue of whether they meet the criterion of nondivisibility.

One of the principal differences between the two forms of categorization—the "perceptual" on the one hand and the "conceptual" on the other—is the immediacy to experience of the attributes by which their fitness to a category is determined. In the perceptual case, the relevant attributes are more immediately given by which we judge the categorial identity of an object, at least in simple perceptual situations. At the other end, the attainment of knowledge about the attributes that are relevant may require a difficult strategy of search as, for example, in the field of art history when one seeks to identify a painting as, say, a Massaccio or a product of one of his students, or as in science when by the use of the Ascheim-Zondek test one seeks to classify a woman two weeks after her last menstruation as pregnant or not. There are, of course, steps in between the two extremes where the relevant cues to categorization are only "moderately immediate" and in which some strategy of search behavior is required of the subject, a striking experimental example being the behavior of subjects attempting to identify tachistoscopically presented material or material presented peripherally or at low illumination or with a high noise background.

We have lingered on the continuity. of categorization at the perceptual and conceptual levels not so much to insist upon the identity of all categorization behavior—for there are striking differences in the behavior of subjects operating with conceptual and perceptual categories as we can see in examining the experimental literature—but rather to urge the importance of the economy gained by treating the underlying process as common in the two activities and in the phenomena that lie between. Undoubtedly some people show preferences for the extreme of utilizing perceptually immediate attributes in their categorizing while others are more "conceptual" or "abstract," which we know from the important work of Hanfmann and Kasanin (1937, 1942), Goldstein and Scheerer (1941), and others who have studied sorting behavior systematically. Our objective is to show that the basic processes of categorization are the same, even though operating under different conditions of attribute immediacy and under different conditions of life history in the organism.

One final point on the relationship between conceptual and perceptual categorization is worth attention. It is frequently the case that people develop means of altering conceptual categories into categories that can be utilized with more immediate perceptual cues. One example will suffice, one that is fairly common in the act of differential diagnosis in medicine. It is the pride of the good diagnostician that with practice he no longer needs elaborate laboratory tests to determine the nature of a patient's syndrome, that frequently he can "spot" the case by the time the patient has walked across the consultation room and taken his seat by the physician. Immediate features of gait, complexion, posture, and the like come to serve for the act of categorization that had formerly to depend upon highly mediate cues gleaned from laboratory tests.

In the most general sense, then, any cognitive operation involving the grouping and regrouping of materials into equivalence classes is rendered more comprehensible once one has a better grasp of the nature of categorizing. Judgment, memory, problem-solving, inventive thinking, and esthetics—not to mention the more conventional areas of perception and concept formation—all involve such operations.

There is a more extended sense in which categorizing is ubiquitous. To this we turn next.

LANGUAGE, CULTURE, AND CATEGORIZING

The categories in terms of which man sorts out and responds to the world around him reflect deeply the culture into which he is born. The language, the way of life, the religion and science of a people: all of these mold the way in which a man experiences the events out of which his own history is fashioned. In this sense, his personal history comes to reflect the traditions and thought-ways of his culture, for the events that make it up are filtered through the categorial systems he has learned. The typologies into which kinds of people are sorted, as, for example, witches and nonwitches among the Navaho; the manner in which kin are categorized in societies with and without primogeniture rules; the classification of women into "sisters" and "eligibles" described by Hallowell (1951); the categorization of certain acts as friendly and others as hostile: all of these are projections of deep cultural trends into the experience of individuals. The principal defining attribute of an "intelligent man" for the Navaho is, according to one informant, a man who has seen a great many different things and travelled much. The word *yaigeh* which denotes this type of intelligent man does not include a man who, say, is noted for his domestic wisdom. It is difficult to determine whether there is a unitary category for "general intelligence" in Navaho. The first category used by our informant in specifying intelligence is especially interesting. The Navaho were historically a nomadic people who, though geographically no longer mobile, continue to show a great interest in distant things and events.*

The example just cited immediately suggests the controversial theories of Benjamin Lee Whorf (1940) and brings into question the relation between the lexical categories of a language and the customary cognitive categories in terms of which the speakers of a language sort their worlds. We shall not pause here to attempt a resolution of the two extreme views, the "cloak theories" and the "mold theories," the one holding that language is a cloak conforming to the customary categories of thought of its speakers, the other that it is a mold in terms of which thought categories are cast. The resolution will obviously have great bearing on theories of categorizing and on the issues involved in understanding the relation between culture and personality. These are problems the reader will find discussed in the appendix to this book prepared by Dr. Roger W. Brown.

In fine, we would note only that problems of how categories are formed and used are relevant not only to classical problems within psychology, but also to the sciences of culture, notably anthropology and linguistics.

THE ACHIEVEMENTS OF CATEGORIZING

What does the act of rendering things equivalent achieve for the organism? It is a good preliminary question, like the functional query of the biologist: "What is accomplished by digestion?" The

---

* We are greatly indebted to Professors Evon Vogt and John Roberts, both of whom have discussed with us at length the cognitive characteristics of Navaho and Zuni society. Professor Vogt also made it possible for one of the authors (J.S.B.) to get some sense of the cross-cultural importance of categorizing phenomena on an all-too-brief visit to New Mexico in the summer of 1954.

answer provides only a prolegomenon to further inquiry, for if we reply, "Digestion serves to convert external substances into assimilable materials that can then enter into the metabolic process," the next question is bound to be "How is this accomplished?" But the functional question is clearly important, for unless it is fruitfully posed, the later questions about "how" must surely miscarry. So long as the nervous system was conceived of as something that cooled the humors, it served little purpose to ask how this was accomplished.

A first achievement of categorizing has already been discussed. By categorizing as equivalent discriminably different events, the organism *reduces the complexity of its environment.* It is reasonably clear "how" this is accomplished. It involves the abstraction and use of defining properties in terms of which groupings can be made and much will be said of these things later.

A second achievement has also been mentioned: categorizing is the *means by which the objects of the world about us are identified.* The act of identifying some thing or some event is an act of "placing" it in a class. Identification implies that we are able to say either "There is thingumbob again" or "There is another thingumbob." While these identifications may vary in the richness of their elaboration, they are never absent. A certain sound may be heard simply as "that sound which comes from outdoors late at night." Or it may be heard as "those porcupines chewing on that old tree stump." When an event cannot be thus categorized and identified, we experience terror in the face of the uncanny. And indeed, "the uncanny" is itself a category, even if only a residual one.

A third achievement, a consequence of the first, is that the establishment of a category based on a set of defining attributes *reduces the necessity of constant learning.* For the abstraction of defining properties makes possible future acts of categorizing without benefit of further learning. We do not have to be taught *de novo* at each encounter that the object before us is or is not a tree. If it exhibits the appropriate defining properties, it "is" a tree. It is in this crucial aspect, as we mentioned earlier, that categorizing differs from the learning of fiat classes. Learning by rote that a miscellany of objects all go by the nonsense name BLIX has no extrapolative value to new members of the class.

A fourth achievement inherent in the act of categorizing is the *direction it provides for instrumental activity.* To know by virtue of discriminable defining attributes and without need for further direct test that a man is "honest" or that a substance is "poison" is to know *in advance* about appropriate and inappropriate actions to be

taken. Such direction is even provided when we come up against
an object or event which we cannot place with finality. To the
degree the new object has discriminable properties and these properties have been found in the past to be relevant to certain categories,
we can make a start on the problem by a procedure of "categorial
bracketing." The object appears to be animate; what does it do if
it is poked? It stands on two legs like a man; does it speak? Much
of problem-solving involves such repeated regrouping of an object
until a pragmatically appropriate grouping has been found. In short,
such successive categorizing is a principal form of instrumental
activity.*

A fifth achievement of categorizing is the opportunity it permits
for *ordering and relating classes of events.* For we operate, as noted
before, with category *systems*—classes of events that are. related to
each other in various kinds of superordinate systems. We map and
give meaning to our world by relating classes of events rather than
by relating individual events. "Matches," the child learns, will
"cause" a set of events called "fires." The meaning of each class of
things placed in quotation marks—matches, causes, and fires—is given
by the imbeddedness of each class in such relationship maps. The
moment an object is placed in a category, we have opened up a
whole vista of possibilities for "going beyond" the category by virtue
of the superordinate and causal relationships linking this category
to others.

In speaking of achievements we have not, perhaps, placed enough
stress on the anticipatory and exploratory nature of much of our
categorizing. In the case of most categorizing, we attempt to find
those defining signs that are as *sure* as possible as *early* as possible to
give identity to an event. At the barest level of necessity, this is
essential to life. We cannot test the edibility of food by eating it
and checking the consequence. We must learn ways of anticipating
ultimate consequences by the use of prior signs. In simpler organisms than man, one often finds that there is a built-in mechanism for
response to such anticipatory signs. The greylag gosling, observed
by Tinbergen (1948), responds with a flight reaction to a hawk-like
silhouette drawn on a wire across its pen. The young of the black-
headed gull responds to a red spot on the side of its mother's bill
with a "begging response" for food and the mother responds to the
open bill of the young by inserting food. Lashley's description
(1938) of the response of cyclostoma to anticipatory danger signs by

---

* The instrumental role of categorizing is treated in detail in Chapter 3.

the mobilization of stinging nettles provides an example at an even simpler phyletic level. Anticipatory categorizing, then, provides "lead time" for adjusting one's response to objects with which one must cope.

It is this future-oriented aspect of categorizing behavior in all organisms that impresses us most. It is not simply that organisms code the events of their environment into equivalence classes, but that they utilize cues for doing so that allow an opportunity for prior adjustment to the event identified. We are especially impressed with the anticipatory nature of categorizing when we consider the phenomenon of the "empty category."

This is the process whereby defining attributes are combined to create fictive categories: classes of objects that have not been encountered or are clearly of a nature contrary to expectancy. The empty category is a means whereby we go beyond the conventional groupings we impose on the segments of nature we have encountered. It is a way of going beyond the range of events one encounters to the sphere of the possible or even, in the phrase of the philosopher Nelson Goodman (1947), to the "counterfactual conditional"—events that could be but which are contrary to experience. This surely is one of the principal functions of categorizing.

Two cases may be given to illustrate the uses of such categories in the cognitive economy of man. One is the class of creatures known as centaurs, half man, half horse. The other is the class of "female Presidents of the United States, past, present, and future." The first example illustrates the use of the empty category as the currency of art, fantasy, and dream; perhaps it is a vehicle for exploring the ambiguous interstices of experience. The second example of an empty category is from the sphere of problem-solving and thinking. Hypotheses in problem-solving often take the form of creating new categories by the combining of potential defining attributes. The physicist says, "Consider the possibility of a nuclear particle whose orbit is a spiral." Indeed, the neutrino in nuclear physics was postulated first as an empty category on logical grounds, and only when appropriate measures became available was it "found." So too Neptune. Working from data on the perturbation of Uranus, Bessel reached the conclusion that a trans-Uranian planet must exist. Adams and LeVerrier computed possible orbits for the as yet undiscovered planet. It was only then that the planet was "found" by observation at the Berlin Observatory in 1846, 23 years after Bessel's conclusion.

To a certain extent, the foregoing discussion of the achievements of categorial activity almost precludes the necessity for discussing the problem of "cognitive motivation." What is served by postulating categorizing motives beyond saying such things as "The person strives to reduce the complexity of his environment," or "There is a drive to group things in terms of instrumental relevance?" We would argue that the postulation of motives to correspond to achievements of functioning is an empty procedure. But there are problems of motivation involved in categorizing behavior over and beyond this level of discourse, and to these we turn next.

THE MOTIVE TO CATEGORIZE

There are three ways in which cognitive motives in general may be conceived. The first is to postulate need processes assumed to be at the basis of cognitive activities. Bartlett (1932), for example, speaks of "effort after meaning" and Tolman (1951) of a "placing need" to account for the push that impels people to categorize, identify, and place things. Hilgard (1951) postulates two goals of perception: the goal of stability and the goal of clarity or definiteness. These take on the function of guiding and impelling perceptual and cognitive behavior. One can justify the positing of such needs or goal strivings only on the ground that they are frustratable, satiable, and to a certain degree specific with respect both to appropriate initiators and gratifiers. The difficulty with all such conceptions to date, whether in the general forms of "cognitive need" or in the more restricted form of Woodworth's will to perceive (1947), is that they have no specifications about the conditions that arouse the need, gratify it, frustrate it, or satiate it. To the extent that this is true, such theories serve no purpose save to equate cognitive achievements with a motive to achieve.

We believe, however, that there are clear signs now present in the psychological literature whereby it is possible to construct a theory of cognitive needs that goes beyond this general form. Experiments by Wyatt and Campbell (1951) and Postman and Bruner (1948) indicate that the presentation of objects to be recognized under difficult or stressful conditions of viewing leads to categorizing or identification behavior that varies in a systematic way from the behavior prevailing under normal perceptual conditions. The latter experiments show that, when the completion of categorizing is blocked by the introduction of almost impossible viewing conditions, the effect is to produce "reckless" identification behavior on subsequent opportunities for perceiving, reckless in the sense that abortive identification occurs in the absence of adequate cues. The result, as Wyatt and Campbell point out, is to "saddle" the perceiver with an inappropriate categorization which must then be disconfirmed by subsequent stimulation before pragmatically adequate, "correct" recognition can occur. Here then is a first step toward specifying some of the effects of frustration of a "placing need." The McGill studies of perceptual deprivation (Bexton, Heron, and Scott, 1954) provide another example of systematic study of the "placing need." Deprivation in the form of being barred from perceptual commerce with the normally rich world of objects appears to have the temporary effect of disrupting the smooth sequential flow of cognitive activities normally involved in problem-solving and may indeed even disrupt the normal constancy processes so basic to object perception and object recognition. In so far as studies establish the nature of antecedent conditions affecting the operation of cognitive needs, to that extent do notions about "needs for clarity and stability" become theoretically viable. Short of this the postulation of cognitive needs is little more than a restatement of the fact that cognitive activity achieves something for the organism.

Uudoubtedly one of the conditions affecting the manner in which we categorize the objects around us is the need-state of the organism. For cognition is also instrumental activity geared to other forms of goal striving. This is not to say that, were it not for "primary" needs like hunger or "secondary" needs like the desire for prestige, cognitive processes would be as idle as a lawn mower when the grass is not in need of cutting. Perhaps the most thoroughgoing exposition of cognition as instrumental activity is to be found in McDougall's general theory (1926), but he too had to postulate a primary need or "propensity" called curiosity to keep his organism from falling into a vegetative state in the absence of other needs. Such "directive state" theories of cognition, to use F. H. Allport's term (1955), have recently come much into vogue in the implicit assumptions underlying much of the "New Look" work in perception and have clearly proved to be fruitful in stimulating research on the relationship between need-states in general and perceptual selectivity. But it is quite apparent that cognitive activity is not entirely a handmaiden of other drives. There is some process of "decentration," to use Piaget's term (1951), that frees our cognitive activity from such domination and makes it possible for us eventually to play chess or be abstractly curious without being driven to do so by hunger, anger, etc.

One characteristic of cognitive activity, whether at the level of instrumental activity or in the playful realms of chess, is that it has associated with it some rather unique affective states. The sense of tension that occurs when we cannot "place" somebody, the frustration we have been able to induce in subjects serving in tachistoscopic experiments when exposure levels were too low, the malaise of the trained mind faced with a seemingly causeless effect— all of these are as characteristic of frustrated cognitive activity as desire is of blocked sexual activity. There is also the phenomenology of the Eureka experience: the "Aha, *Erlebnis*," or the "That's it!" feeling. Reports of such experiences have, of course, been used as a basis for inferring the presence of a generalized cognitive need, be it called "effort after meaning" or what not.

We have seen our subjects going through agonies of frustration with difficult problems and experiencing "Eureka!" when they thought (often wrongly) that they had found a solution, and we have wondered what function was served by such an affect. Perhaps none, or perhaps even our question is meaningless. We have the impression that such an affect provides a kind of feedback which regulates the flow of problem-solving behavior. Cognitive frustra- tion, within tolerable limits, helps keep search-behavior going. The "insight" experience leads to new bursts of testing activity. We are completely without evidence for such assertions or even without proposals as to how one might gather evidence.

ON THE VALIDATION OF CATEGORIZING

Categorizing an event as a member of a class and thereby giving it identity involves, as we have said, an act of inference. Whether one is deciding what the blob was that appeared for a few milliseconds in a tachistoscope or what species of bird it is that we have our binoculars trained on or what Pueblo period this potsherd belongs to, the basic task is not only to make an inference but to make the "right" inference. Is the blob a face, the bird a scissor-tailed flycatcher, the potsherd from Pueblo II? How can we be sure? Let it be clear that we are not asking philosophical questions. We want to know, simply, how people make sure (or make sur*er*) that they have placed an event in its proper identity niche.

There appear to be four general procedures by which people re- assure themselves that their categorizations are "valid." The first is *by recourse to an ultimate criterion*, the second is *test by consistency;* the third, *test by consensus* and the fourth, *test by affective congru- ence*. Consider each in turn.

Recourse to an Ultimate Criterion. A simple functional category provides an example. By means of such defining properties as color, size, and shape, mushrooms are divisible into a class of edible mushrooms and a class of inedible ones. A mushroom fancier, out in the woods picking mushrooms, must decide whether a particular mushroom is or is not edible. To the extent that the defining properties are not masked, he is able to make a preliminary categorization: he calls it inedible. If you should ask him how he can be sure, he would doubtless tell you that the way to be absolutely sure is to eat it. If it makes you sick or kills you, then his categorization was "right" or "valid."

The example chosen is perhaps too simple. For there are many categories where it is difficult to specify *the* ultimate criterion against which to check the adequacy of the defining attributes. But the simplification will serve us for the while.

When recourse to an ultimate criterion for defining a category is of grave consequence, the culture may take it upon itself to invent labels or signs by which examplars of the category can be spotted in sufficient time for appropriate avoidance. The custom of putting a red skull and crossbones on bottles of poison, the use of red color on dangerous industrial machinery, stop signs at dangerous intersections—all of these are examples of the artificial creation of anticipatory defining attributes that in effect save one an encounter with a dangerous ultimate criterion.

Test by Consistency. Perhaps the simplest example one can give of such testing is the perception of speech. One is "surer" that one identified a word correctly if the word fits the context of what has gone before. Since the categorization of events usually takes place in a context which imposes constraints on what a particular event can be, there is more often than not the possibility of validation by consistency.

Some listeners to the famous Orson Welles broadcast of *The War of the Worlds,* faced with the choice of deciding whether the Martian invasion was "real" or "theatrical," used a consistency criterion determined by the set of beliefs that had already been established in their past lives. "We have found that many of the persons who did not even try to check the broadcast had preexisting mental sets that made the stimulus so understandable to them that they immediately accepted it as true. Highly religious people who believed that God willed and controlled the destinies of man were already furnished with a particular standard of judgment that would make an invasion of our planet and a destruction of its members an 'act of God.' This was particularly true if the religious frame of reference was of the eschatological variety providing the individual with definite attitudes or beliefs regarding the end of the world. Other people we found had been so influenced by the recent war scare that they believed an attack by a foreign power was imminent and an invasion—whether it was due to the Japanese, Hitler, or Martians—was not unlikely" (Cantril, 1940, p. 191).

Validation by consistency is perhaps nowhere better illustrated than in modern taxonomic research. At the lowest level, so-called alpha taxonomy, one seeks to differentiate as many species as possible in terms of whatever defining properties are visible. Such a technique leads to vast multiplication of categories. There are now about a third of a million species of plants, and each year about 5,000 are added. There are about 2 million species and subspecies of animals and it is estimated that new ones are being added at the rate of 10,000 per year. Some estimates of the number of insect species run as high as 3 million (Silvestri, 1929), and given new radiological methods of producing mutations, the possible number of virus types seems almost unlimited. As far as identification is concerned, the modern taxonomist readily agrees (Mayr, 1952) that species are not "discovered" but "invented." The principal problem of "validation" at this level is to establish the "existence" of a category, which means, essentially, that other investigators can distinguish the same grouping if they follow directions for finding it.

It is at the next level of taxonomy, beta taxonomy, that the criterion of consistency becomes critical, for now the task is to order the bewildering array of species into a *system* of classification. Whether or not one's grouping of a series of species into genera and then into a phylum is "valid" or not depends upon whether the properties of the grouped species are consistent with one's conception of evolution. The correctness of the grouping "elasmobranchs" as distinguished from "teleostean fishes" depends upon whether the defining morphological properties of the two classes fit a consistent pattern of development as formulated in evolutionary theory. Teleostean fishes are more "evolved" or "higher than" sharks because of the consistent differences in skeletal system, renal system, circulatory system, etc. What makes the classification valid is that it is explicable in terms of a more general theory about the changes in morphology and physiology that characterize the evolution of animal life. If one would seek to establish the validity of considering a certain group of animals as constituting a phylum, the test would be by consistency with the requirements of the theory governing classification not only of this new phylum but of phyla generally.

Test by Consensus. Such categories as "good citizen" or "decent person" are often in effect consensually validated. Because the defining properties are vague and disjunctive, there is often uncertainty about the status of instances. In consequence, to validate our categorization of a man as a "decent fellow" we may turn to the categorizations made by people with whose values we identify—what a number of sociologists call a *reference group* (cf. Merton and Kitt, 1950). Under other circumstances, we may turn simply to those individuals who happen to be in the immediate vicinity when a categorial decision must be made. We see two men fighting on the street: "Who started it?" we ask a man on the edge of the crowd that has collected, in an attempt to categorize the guilty member. In deciding whether the Welles broadcast was "real" or a play, many victims were determined in their categorization by the fact that others were treating the broadcast as "news" rather than "entertainment."

Where the placement process has marked consequences for the society and when the criteria to be used are ambiguous in nature, virtually every culture has devised a process whereby an official decision can be provided. In our own society, the courts and the judicial process provide this means. Whether or not a man is a felon is decided by specialists in such matters, working with the guide of official definitions embodied in a legal code. Due process of law involves a careful inspection of the degree to which an individual and his acts "fit" the defining properties of a thief or an embezzler. We also create official definitions of a more positive type. Working with a highly ambiguous set of standards, the French Academy makes the decision whether or not a given Frenchman is "an immortal"; or a special body weighs the scientific products of a man and decides whether he should be "starred" in *American Men of Science* or be entitled to the distinction of wearing the initials "F.R.S." after his name. Establishment of consensus by official action is effective to the degree that people will give precedence to the official decisions made. If validation by either direct test, consistency, or unofficial consensus is given precedence, then official methods of categorizing may be at odds with what generally prevails as categorization in a society.

Test by Affective Congruence. While this is a special case of test by consistency, it merits treatment on its own. It is best described as an act of categorizing or identifying an event that carries with it a feeling of subjective certainty or even necessity. Such subjective certainty may also characterize an act whose validation rests on other forms of validating test. But we refer here to the pure case: the unjustifiable intuitive leap buttressed by a sense of conviction. One infers the existence of God, for example, from the overwhelming beauty of a mountain scene: "Such beauty could be produced neither by man nor by the random force of nature." God's presence is there-after inferred from the experience of beauty. There is buttressing both by consistency and by consensus, but what provides the basic validating criterion is the affective component in the act of categorizing.

Such acts, because they are particularly inaccessible to disproof, are of special interest to the student of nonrational behavior. What seems especially interesting about acts of categorization of this sort is that they seem to be inaccessible in proportion to the strength of certain inner need systems whose fulfillment they serve. "The more basic the confirmation of a hypothesis is to the carrying out of goal striving activity, the greater will be its strength. It will be more readily aroused, more easily confirmed, less readily infirmed," (Bruner, 1951, p. 127). In its most extreme pathological form, validation by affective congruence makes it possible for the paranoid to construct a pseudo-environment in which the random noises about him are categorized as words being spoken against him. At the level of normal functioning, it permits the acceptance of such unknowable absolutes as God, the Dignity of Man, or Hell.

LEARNING TO CATEGORIZE

Much of our concern in subsequent chapters will be with the "attainment of concepts," the behavior involved in using the discriminable attributes of objects and events as a basis of anticipating their significant identity. We can take as a paradigm the behavior of a young gourmet who is determined to gather his own mushrooms in the conviction that the wild varieties are far more worthy of his cooking skills that the cultivated types available in the market. His first aim is to discriminate between edible and nonedible mushrooms. If he were really starting from scratch, he would have two sources of information. On the one hand, he would be able to note the characteristics of each mushroom or toadstool he picked. He could note its color, shape, size, habitat, stalk height, etc. He would also know whether each mushroom, fully described as we have noted, made him ill or not when eaten. For the sake of the inquiry, we endow our man with considerable enthusiasm and sufficient sense so that he eats only a small enough portion of each mushroom to allow him to determine edibility without being killed by the adventure. His task is to determine which discriminable attributes of the mushrooms he tries out lead with maximum certainty to the inference that the type is edible.

Note that our man already knows of the existence of the two classes of mushroom in terms of the ultimate criterion of edibility. He is seeking defining attributes that will distinguish exemplars of these two classes. In this sense, we speak of his task as one of concept *attainment* rather than concept *formation*. If his task were that of attempting to sort mushrooms into some meaningful set of classes, *any* meaningful set of classes in the interest of ordering their diversity, then we might more properly refer to the task as concept formation. Concept formation is essentially the first step en route to attainment. In the case of mushrooms, the formation of the hypothesis that *some* mushrooms are edible and *others* are not is the act of forming a concept. *Attainment refers to the process of finding predictive defining attributes that distinguish exemplars from nonexemplars of the class one seeks to discriminate.*

There are two ways of asking questions about the searcher in this example of concept attainment. The first asks, "What is the best, the most rational way for him to proceed?" At this level, we are dealing with the analysis of ideal strategies, a topic that will concern us centrally in subsequent chapters. A second question is, "How does he in fact proceed?" The first question is, if you will, a question of the logic of science or of "operations research" and its answer will be based on a consideration of how the searcher for defining attributes can most rapidly or most safely or most stylishly or most joyfully learn which attributes to trust. We shall ask both questions, for our interest lies in the relation between ideal performance and actual performance. How one proceeds in this way will presently be told.

PLAN OF THE BOOK

The book is divided into three sections. In the first section, comprising the first three chapters, including the present one, discussion centers on the nature of categorizing activity and its relation to inferential activity in general. In Chapter 2 the nature of various psychological and formal kinds of equivalence classes is discussed and also the manner in which they depend upon the utilization of cues or defining attributes that vary in validity and preferential value. Chapter 3 deals with the factors involved in learning how to sort the environment into functionally significant equivalence classes. How do subjects achieve, retain, and transform information useful for such "environmental sorting"? How describe the sequence of acts whereby a person comes to know what features of the environment are relevant to his categorizing objective? What kinds of contingencies does the person encounter in trying to "make sense" of a jumble of unsorted events in his world? What are some of the factors, informational and motivational and situational, that alter the way in which the person searches for groupings in his environment? What is the relative role of "thinking" as compared to "external testing" in finding out what cues are relevant? What are the conflicting goals in categorial problem-solving that force the adoption of "compromise" strategies? These are some of the questions to which the third chapter is addressed. The reader will find threads of game theory and the theory of communication in our treatment of these problems, but they are incidental to the general attempt to describe the systematics of categorizing and conceptualizing.

Part II of the book, comprising five chapters, is monographic in intent. In the first four chapters we describe a series of some 20 experiments on concept attainment under a variety of conditions—concept attainment here described as the process of learning what features of the environment are relevant for grouping events into externally defined classes. These chapters contain applications of the theory presented in the first part of the book to a set of richly varied empirical data. The aim of these experiments and their discussion is not so much to do an exhaustive job of describing how people attain concepts as it is to describe and illustrate a general approach to this cognitive problem. In Chapter 8 an effort is made to bring together the theoretical issues raised in the book and to evaluate them in terms of experiments reported.

Part III comprises an appendix written by Dr. Roger W. Brown, applying the theory of categorizing to phenomena of psycholinguistics. It is concerned with classical problems of language coding as well as with the vexing question of the role of language in the patterning of thought.

To the reader conversant with contemporary American psychology, the book will appear singularly lacking in the more familiar forms of theoretical discourse. Neither the language of learning theory, of Gestalt theory, nor of psychoanalysis will be evident save in the form of incidental reference. For our objective has not been to extend reinforcement theory or the theory of traces or any other prepared psychological position to the problems of categorizing. We have not ignored the rich theoretical backgrounds of contemporary theory. Rather, we have come gradually to the conclusion that what is most needed in the analysis of categorizing phenomena—as represented by studies of concept attainment, generalization, and abstraction—is an adequate analytic description of the actual behavior that goes on when a person learns how to use defining cues as a basis for grouping the events of his environment. With this objective in mind, we have also made no attempt to give a systematic review of the literature of concept formation and generalization, a decision made much easier by the recent appearance of reviews by Vinacke (1951, 1952), Johnson (1955), Leeper (1951), and Humphrey (1951). We have benefited from these excellent synoptic accounts and been encouraged by them to move in the direction of a more analytic approach.

CHAPTER 2

On attributes
and concepts

What is it that one learns when one learns a "concept"? In the last chapter, we discussed the means whereby an individual learns to match his personal category to a category as it is officially or pragmatically defined and, in the course of this discussion, the question of validation of inference was also brought under examination. It is necessary now to consider in more detail what is involved in drawing an inference from a defining attribute to the class membership or identity of an object. What do we mean by attributes? What are the various forms of relationship between a defining attribute and a class; what are, if you will, the different ways in which a cue or a set of cues can signal the identity of an object? What makes some attributes important and others irrelevant from either a logical or a psychological point of view? It is with such problems as these that the present chapter is concerned.

ATTRIBUTES AS SIGNALS

In the preceding chapter much was made of the anticipatory nature of cognitive activity. We constantly "go beyond the information given." We hear a familiar voice in the passage and call out "Hello, Bill." We find signs of severe confabulation in a patient's thinking and classify him as a schizophrenic. We select certain attributes and use them as a basis for inference. What is an attribute? Boring (1942) puts the matter well, "A stone is shape, color, weight, and kind of substance in complicated relation. When such descriptive ultimates are general properties which can vary continuously or discretely, when they are, in short, parameters, they may, if one chooses, be called attributes of the object described" (p. 19). In this sense, the "beauty" and the "throwability" of the stone are as much attributes as are its weight and size. An attribute, in brief, is any discriminable feature of an event that is susceptible of some discriminable variation from event to event. Indeed, if it did not vary it would very likely not be discriminable in any case—"the fish will be the last to discover water."

When some discriminable feature of the environment is used as a basis for "going beyond" by inference, it serves as a signal. When such a discriminable feature is used as a means of inferring the identity of something, we speak of it as a *criterial attribute*, a term about which much more will be said later. Let it be clear that any attribute "varying continuously or discretely" from event to event can be used as a criterial attribute in this sense.

When we say that any attribute may vary, we imply that any attribute represents a dimension along which one may specify values. The attribute of color may be represented by the values red, violet, blue, green, etc., and there are continuous gradations along it. Other attributes, those that vary discretely, have no such continuity. The simplest discrete attribute dimension is, of course, a binary one and this type is very common. A woman is married or not married, she is dead or alive, and in the eyes of the law she is sane or not sane. A young man is or is not a member of this college, he is or is not on the Dean's List, he is legally in good standing or not in good standing. There are special problems involved in utilizing attributes of either the discrete or continuous variety and these will concern us betimes. For the moment, all that need be considered is that so long as an attribute has more than a single value it can serve in a criterial status: an object that exhibits one value (a *positive* value) *may* be a member of one equivalence category; an object exhibiting a second value (a *negative* value, e.g., the absence of the first one) *may not* belong.

Now it is also the case that a *range of values* may serve to define exemplars of a category. For example, one of the defining attributes of the fruit orange is color, and the positive value of the attribute is a range of colors from orange-yellow through red-orange. There are many discriminable hues that are "acceptable" as signals that the round object before one is an orange and is thus discriminable from such other classes of things as lemons and grapefruits. The width of the range of positive values of an attribute that an individual will accept as a basis for categorization is determined by several factors and no discussion of the nature of attributes as signals is complete without consideration of these.

The first of these factors is the conditions under which the person learned to utilize the attribute in discriminating exemplars from nonexemplars of a class. The problems involved here are the same as those involved in the formation of a so-called generalization gradient. One of the training conditions is the nature of the discrimination practice given to the individual. Take our example: if a person were trained to discriminate oranges from nonoranges with all the instances of the fruit at a middle orange (as this is defined in our color nomenclature) and with the nonexemplars varying all over the color continuum, then the range of acceptable colors of oranges would be small. If learning were such that exemplars varied within a wide range from yellow-orange to orange-red, then the range would be larger. These are fairly obvious matters at a common-sense level, although it would be helpful indeed if there were corroborative research available to check. All that can be said with any degree of assurance is that the range of positive defining values of an attribute used by a person in making inferences will reflect the range on which he obtained discrimination training.

Two things are known, neither with elaboration, about the effects of learning to categorize with few as compared with many variations in the positive values of a defining attribute. The first is that it is more difficult to learn to categorize when such variations are present during learning (e.g., Wolfle, 1936 and Grether and Wolfle, 1936). In the Grether and Wolfle study, for example, the speed of learning a brightness discrimination was greater for rats who were not exposed to variations in the brightness of the stimuli. The second finding, reported by Luborsky (1945), is that training with variation in the exemplars encountered leads to a broader range of values being acceptable. Learning to identify a type of aircraft by exposure to five different training silhouettes leads to readier recognition of new silhouettes of this type of plane than does training on but three kinds of silhouettes. This finding indeed suggests the range-broadening effect of variability in values during training. Wolfle (1936) suggests that for purposes of training efficiency it is best to employ variation in values during categorization training. "The optimal range of variation to employ during training is unknown, but well worth investigating. Until experimental results provide information, it is probably safe to advise variation over a major portion—but not over the entire extent nor at every point within it—of the range within which generalization is desired" (p. 1274).

A second factor is the number of categorial discriminations the individual must make on the basis of variations in an attribute's values. If, for example, the color continuum from yellow through red had to be used for making several categorial discriminations—distinguishing the peels of lemons, tangerines, navel oranges, Temple oranges, kumquats, etc.—the range of admissible colors for any one of the categories would very likely narrow down. Everything we know about the method of single stimuli in psychophysics points to this type of "narrowing" as a function of the requirements of discrimination. If sample weights in the range from 50 to 150 grams have to be judged in terms of "heavy," "*medium*," and "light," the middle category will be broader than if the subject is required to use five categories of discrimination: "very heavy," "moderately heavy," "*medium*," "moderately light," and "very light."

The range of acceptable or positive attribute values varies as a function of stage of category learning. Evidence of stimulus generalization based on original training with a single-value stimulus, such as a dog learning to anticipate the coming of food upon the presentation of a signal, indicates that early in learning a broader generalization range prevails than later in the training (Beritoff, 1924).

There are other factors besides learning conditions which affect the range of attribute values that an individual will regard as criterial of a given category. One of these seems to be something of a personological order. An unpublished experiment by Bruner and Rodrigues in 1951 serves as an illustration. A group of 40 subjects were set the task of adjusting the values of various attributes with the instruction that, for example, they indicate on an oscillator the highest pitch of a female singing voice they would be likely to encounter, the lowest pitch, and the "average" pitch. They were then asked to do this for a series of other categories. The brightest, average, and darkest color of an overcast sky; the reddest, most average, and yellowest orange (fruit); the longest, most average, and shortest dog; the highest, most average, and lowest male singing voice; the tallest, most average, and shortest normal man, etc. Seven such tasks were given. After conversion of each of the attributes into subjective scale units (e.g., the mel scale for pitch), the value ranges employed by each subject (the number of scale units between "highest" and "lowest" setting) were rank-ordered for the subjects. It was found that subjects were consistent in width of their ranges from task to task as indicated by a measure of concordance (Kendall's measure, W). Rather interestingly, the "range consistency" of subjects tended to be more striking when those attributes with which the subjects had most experience were not included. Pettigrew (1955) has shown similar results using a paper and pencil version of this procedure.

Finally, cultural usage is obviously a factor determining ranges of attribute values. Whoever has troubled to examine color nomenclature in different cultures knows the extraordinary variability in the width of such color categories as "blue" and "green." For a more extended discussion of cultural factors, the reader may turn to the appendix.

One cannot think long about the problem of acceptable attribute ranges without considering the important related problem of the nature of the transition in attribute values as one moves from exemplars to nonexemplars of a class. There are some categories where the defining attributes as officially stated are highly precise. Those who are eligible for being called for selective service must, in terms of the defining attribute of age, be at least 18 years of age, and the 18th birthday is the sharp cutting point. But what is accepted as the cutting point between "adolescent" and "adult"? The defining attribute of age in such a case is divided into positive and negative values by a fuzzy band and the most appropriate answer we can give to the question "Is this 19-year-old an adolescent?" is "Maybe he is or maybe he isn't." So too with the category of colors to be called "red" and the class of human beings called "good athletes": the defining attributes that discriminate them from other categories have fuzzy transition zones. Lenneberg (1955) has suggested that one of the reasons children have such difficulty in learning to apply color names correctly lies in these transition zones. And Frenkel-Brunswik (1949) cites research indicating that the ethnocentric personality has difficulties in changing his categorization under conditions where attribute values are changing from a positive to a negative value gradually. The stimulus array was a series of pictures of a dog gradually changing into a cat. "The prejudiced group tended to hold on longer to the first object and to respond more slowly to the changing stimuli. There was greater reluctance to give up the original object about which one had felt relatively certain and a tendency not to see what did not harmonize with the first set as well as shying away from transitional solutions" (p. 128). This is one aspect, of course, of what Frenkel-Brunswik calls "intolerance of ambiguity." In Chapter 7 we shall have occasion to look again at the manner in which the objectives of one's categorizing efforts affect the handling of fuzzy transitions in defining attributes.

What needs saying in conclusion is, simply, that very little is known about the conditions that lead certain people to adopt relatively large or relatively small ranges of values indicative of the identity of objects. What is abundantly clear to those who have scanned the psychological literature for material relevant to the problem is that the present literature on stimulus generalization and equivalence—the closest approaches to the matter—is not sufficient to our needs. The investigation of attribute ranges in categorizing requires more elaborated paradigms than that provided by the simple generalization study which seeks to answer the question, "Given positive training on one value of an attribute, how many other values will elicit the same response and with what frequency or amplitude?"

DEFINING AND CRITERIAL ATTRIBUTES

There are two ways in which the signalling value of attributes can be specified. One of them is in terms of an external statement of the defining properties of a class as given by a legal code, by scientific convention, or by the statement of the degree of correlation between an attribute and an ultimate criterion. There is an official definition of a felon, for example, and this definition provides the *defining attributes* of those who are to be included in the class. The official definition may not be in accord with the definition as employed by a particular individual. On a particular type of highway, one official *defining attribute* of "safe driving" may be speed, the appropriate value range being any speed up to and including 50 miles an hour. For a particular driver, unconstrained by the presence of highway police, the *criterial attribute* of the class of activity called "safe driving" may be whether or not the car "feels" under control. Learning to obey the law or the process of "socialization" involves the matching of criterial to defining attributes: the former being the attributes used by a particular individual, the latter being the official defining attributes specified officially.

It may also happen that there will be disagreement not between official defining and psychologically criterial *attributes,* but in the *range of values* operative in each case. Both the law and the driver may accept "speed" as the attribute. The law may specify that speeds up to 50 miles per hour are safe and permissible. The driver may include speeds up to 60 miles per hour. The socializing agent again is the highway police.

The distinction between defining attributes and criterial attributes is essential to all of the discussion that is to follow. For it permits us to think of categorizing as a process of achievement: discovering the defining attributes of the environment so that they may serve with their proper values as the criteria for making judgments about identity. In research on concept attainment, what is involved is learning to isolate and use the defining attributes of positive instances of a concept as these are specified by the experimenter. One makes the defining attributes one's own criterial attributes. In the process of attaining veridical perception, as when one must recognize correctly what is being presented in a tachistoscope, the problem is the same. And indeed, if one looks at scientific endeavor, the object there is still the same: to utilize defining attributes that predict with maximal correctness certain classes of consequent events: to predict, for example, that a class of behavior known and agreed upon as "extinction" will occur when certain antecedent attributes have been present, such as the withholding of "reinforcements." Wherever an individual must adjust to the categories held by others or specified by code, or wherever an individual must make his categorial discriminations conform to a pragmatic criterion as in discriminating edible from nonedible mushrooms, it is necessary to make a distinction between defining and criterial attributes and to examine the degree to which the two conform.

A general definition of what is meant by a criterial attribute of a given concept or category is readily stated. Take the category of things called "apples" by some particular person. We are interested in those attributes that affect the probability of our person calling an object an apple. For simplicity's sake we will give our person only visual access to the objects we will place before him. It is fairly likely that such things as color, size, texture, and shape will affect the likelihood of any object being called an apple. But the matter can be put more precisely than this. In so far as *changes in the values of any particular attribute* do not produce changes in the probability of the object being called an apple, we call that attribute noncriterial. Any attribute which when changed in value alters the likelihood of an object being categorized in a certain way is, therefore, a criterial attribute for the person doing the categorizing. Obviously the extent to which an attribute's values affect the likelihood of categorization is a measure of its *degree of criteriality.* Conceive, for example, of an attribute with two values. When one value is present, an object exhibiting it is called "X" with a probability of 1.0; when the other value is present, the probability drops to 0.0. This is an oversimplification, but it serves to illustrate what is meant by *maximum criteriality. Zero criteriality* is the case in which there is *no* difference in likelihood of categorization in the presence of the two attribute values.

Much the same sort of thing can be said about the nature of a defining attribute, save for the fact that one is not concerned with the categorizations of a particular person or of a sample of persons chosen randomly. Rather, the categorizing decision which interests us in this case is that provided by "official" sources. The degree of definingness of an attribute can be stated as the extent to which a change in attribute value alters the likelihood of the "code book" classifying an object as belonging or not belonging in a class. The legal case is perhaps the most clear-cut. There are certain defining attributes of the legal class "citizen of the United States" and alterations along any of these attribute dimensions drastically affect whether or not a person is so considered in a court of law. But let it be said immediately that the legal case is seldom as clear as this, and definitions depending on either consensus or upon some ultimate pragmatic consequence virtually never are. If we take the "community definition" of a "good family man" we will find that attributes also vary in their degree of definingness. Obviously the attribute "goodness as a provider" will be consensually defining in terms of altering the likelihood of a man being included in the class. But in certain groups it will very likely not affect consensual categorization as much as the attribute "marital fidelity." So too with pragmatic consequence as a basis of definition. Take the earlier example of the mushroom. By careful sampling, we may find that a certain color range predicts with a probability of 0.6 that mushrooms exhibiting a color within the range are in the edible class. Colors outside the range indicate edibility with a probability of only 0.2. Such an attribute would be considered more defining than, let us say, the presence of single versus multiple stalks, which, let us assume, differentiate only at the level of 0.5 and 0.4 respectively. In sum, one specifies definingness in much the same terms as one specifies criteriality of an attribute, the critical difference being that in the former case one refers to an "official" categorization and in the latter to the categorizations made by a given individual or sample of individuals.

But the most important reason for keeping clearly in mind the distinction between defining and criterial attributes is that the two differ markedly in the conditions determining their status. In a later section, we shall examine in detail the determinants of criteriality. This will perforce be a psychological discussion and the inquiry will center upon such matters as the role of frequency of association, vividness, and other important factors that lead an individual to rely upon an attribute in making categorial inferences. The moment we speak of the determinants of "definingness," of why a particular attribute or attribute value is defining of a certain class of events, we are out of psychology and into the realm either of law, custom, logic, or formal science. That a prime number is logically defined as a number divisible only by itself and by unity is a fact or a convention of mathematics. That an individual is more prone to judge an odd number to be prime than an even number is a statement out of psychology. How oddness-evenness got to be a critical attribute for the categorization of primeness is a concern of psychologists. Why primeness is mathematically defined as it is is referable only to the field of mathematics or to its history.

THE DEFININGNESS OR VALIDITY OF ATTRIBUTES

Tolman and Brunswik (1935) speak of the "causal texture of the environment" to refer to the probability with which cues or signals point to their referents. A black door in a discrimination apparatus "leads to" food with a probability of 1.0, to take an example. Information theorists speak of causal texture as the redundancy of an input and speak of the transitional or contingent probability that characterizes the occurrence of two stimulus events (e.g., Miller, 1953). It is this "causal texture" that must be learned and dealt with when a person masters a task of categorizing in which the identity of an object or event is inferred from some of its attributes. Since we shall be deeply involved later in examining the process by which people do indeed learn such relations, we must consider here the nature of "causal texture."

Consider the relationships that can hold between a single two-value attribute exhibited by an array of instances and the class membership of the instances. For illustration, the attribute will be body temperature, its two values being "normal" and "abnormal." To what extent does abnormal body temperature indicate the presence of an infectious disease (and let us assume that there is a simple method of establishing whether or not an individual has an infectious disease). More properly, we should ask to what extent does body temperature permit an inference of the presence or absence of an infectious disease.

The simplest case is one that may be represented in a fourfold table as follows:

		Temperature	
		Abnormal	Normal
Disease	Present	50	0
	Absent	0	50

Assuming for a moment that the 50 cases with normal temperature comprise an adequate sample of the population from which they are drawn and so too the 50 abnormal cases, then four simple inferences are possible:

    a. When temperature is abnormal, disease will be present.
    b. When temperature is normal, disease will be absent.

    c. When disease is known to be present, temperature will be abnormal.
    d. When disease is known to be absent, temperature will be normal.

The first two of these inferences refer to the *ecological validity of the cue* of body temperature for making inferences about disease. The last two refer to the *ecological validity of the label*—"health" or "disease"—in making inferences about the state of body temperature. When each of the four inferences is certain, we shall call it a "certainty case."

It is of course apparent that Nature rarely provides such comforting certainties. More often, to use the phrase of Lord Keynes (1921), one must resolve "matters of opinion" and it is for such resolutions that the theory of probability has been constructed. For the inferential value or validity of both cues and labels is more frequently than not probabilistic. Consider a second possible arrangement of the relations between cues and referents, a "mixed case." Again 50 cases of normal and 50 cases of abnormal temperature are studied.

Temperature

		Abnormal	Normal
Disease	Present	40	0
	Absent	10	50

Two of the possible inferences are certain; two are probabilistic.

    a. When temperature is abnormal, disease may or may not be present.
    b. When temperature is normal, disease is absent.
    c. When disease is known to be present, temperature will be abnormal.
    d. When disease is known to be absent, temperature may or may not be normal.

Now, if a given individual were interested in finding a diagnostic sign of disease, abnormal temperature would only be a probabilistic one. If his task were to select disease-free people easily and quickly, normal temperature would be most useful to him—provided he did not mind passing up those disease-free people who were running temperatures.

There is an isomorph to this mixed case that would be more useful to the clinician, although it is formally identical to the foregoing. It is as follows:

Temperature

		Abnormal	Normal
Disease	Present	50	30
	Absent	0	20

All that differs about this mixed case is that now abnormal temperature implies disease with certainty, again assuming that one is not interested in the "typhoid Mary's" who are temperature-free but are also afflicted with disease.

Finally there is the case in which all inferences are suggestive and nothing is implied with certainty.

| | | Temperature | |
		Abnormal	Normal
Disease	Present	40	20
	Absent	10	30

One cannot make inferences from temperature to disease with certainty nor from disease to temperature with certainty. This is the "probabilistic case."

In sum, then, there are three forms of "causal" relationship between defining attributes and category membership, and in all of them it is possible to use either cues or labels as bases of inference: the certainty, mixed, and probabilistic cases. The great psychological question is the learning or utilization of these relationships.

DETERMINANTS OF ATTRIBUTE CRITERIALITY

Criteriality, as we have said, is the extent to which an individual uses the different values of an attribute for inferring the identity of objects exhibiting these values. A moment's reflection will make it clear that cues do not achieve criteriality simply on the basis of their goodness or validity for prediction. For example, if excellent course grades predict that a candidate will have a successful career in graduate school in 80% of cases encountered and not-excellent grades lead to a successful career only 40% of the time, we may nonetheless come to take this attribute as completely criterial and to depend on it in what we shall later call a "100:0" fashion. All students with excellent grades are admitted and none are admitted who have grades other than excellent. In such a case, the criteriality of grades as an attribute is higher than their defining value or ecological validity. We had best reserve the question whether such behavior is "nonrational" until later chapters. The example makes clear that there are factors other than sheer validity or "definingness" that may lead to a cue becoming highly criterial in categorizing behavior. Consider now some of the determinants of criteriality or degree of utilization.

The first of these is, of course, the capacity of the organism, be it

rat (e.g., Brunswik, 1939) or human (e.g., Goodnow, 1955), to register
upon and learn to utilize the actual probability of connection between
events in the environment. The complexities of such learning are reserved for Chapter 7. It need only be remarked here that most higher
organisms are highly sensitive to changes in the probability relations in
their environment and will tend to use any cue that does better than
chance.

But how great a reliance will be placed on a probabilistic cue—how
often it will be utilized for making a particular categorization—is determined by additional considerations to the goodness of the cues.
The most important and general of these is what we shall call the
objectives of the person's categorizing decision. These may be varied:
to save time, to be maximally correct, to conserve energy, to minimize
the number of errors, to delay making a decision until the full evidence is available, to make a decision on the minimum evidence
feasible, etc.

Where categorization must be done under time pressure or in a
manner to conserve energy, immediately available cues will become
more criterial, utilized more in making categorizations. Working in
the pressure of the induction center during the Second World War,
psychiatrists charged with the task of "screening" inductees (categorizing them into mentally fit and mentally unfit) came to rely more
and more upon immediately obtainable information which, were time
not so short, they would have utilized less freely. "Did you wet your
bed as a child?" gets information quickly and it is information that
permits inferences about maladjustment. But its ecological validity
as an attribute is clearly insufficient to justify its criteriality in a less
pressing crisis.*

The pressure of time, combined with a pressure for accuracy, may
lie behind the preference for utilizing attributes which are the least
liable to masking, interference, and distortion. For example, the tonal
attributes of loudness and pitch are more often tested as defining
attributes in identifying sounds than are volume and density. Values
of the former pair of attributes are discriminable in the usual ambient
noise encountered in the environment. Volume and density may be
more subject to masking, interference, and distortion. Indeed, so un-
used are we to attending to this potentially discriminable pair of tonal
attributes that subjects must be taught to discriminate them in a rela-

---

* Preference for immediately available cues need not, of course, depend entirely upon the objective of fast categorization. Heidbreder (1945) argues persuasively for a general preference for cues which can be directly and perceptually
apprehended (1948).

tively anechoic and noiseless laboratory situation as in the well-known experiments of Stevens (1934).

Conservation of time and energy, achieving maximum accuracy, and maximizing the general value of an outcome are only a few of the kinds of factors that may enter into determining the objectives of a person faced with a categorizing decision. In the following chapter, more will be said about the role of objectives. Our aim here has been merely to introduce the matter as one of the factors influencing the degree to which a particular attribute will be utilized by an individual faced with a categorizing decision.

Over and beyond the ecological validity of cues and the need for adjusting to the requirements of a categorizing situation, there are factors of structure and morphology that are likely to influence the degree to which an organism will utilize a cue in his reactions. At the simplest level, one finds examples of preference in cue utilization that are either innate or are developed so early in the organism's life as to be indistinguishable from innate preferences.

That cue-utilization preferences may be innate, particularly in lower organisms, is amply demonstrated in the brilliant observational studies of Tinbergen (1951), Lorenz (1952), and the "ethologists." Lorenz's observations on the strongly fixed preference of the Old World shrew for kinesthetic cues and on the virtual inability of this species to test or to utilize directional cues given by distance receptors in adapting to the environment serves as an illustration. The work of Krech, Rosenzweig, and Bennett (1955) on preference for kinesthetic or visual cues in maze learning is another example. E. D. Adrian (1947) has proposed that cortical specialization for the integration of different sensory cues varies as a function of preferential use of cues in different species. Using a technique of electrical mapping of discharges in the cortex subsequent to stimulating different receptors, he finds, for example, that man has a relatively high proportion of cortical cells given over to the integration of visual and auditory cues, that dogs show a more marked specialization for dealing with olfactory cues, and at an even more specialized level the pig exhibits a remarkably widespread electrical activity in the cortex following stimulation of tactile receptors on the snout.

There is also evidence, of course, that animals *acquire* a hierarchy of cue preference—what Lawrence (1949, 1950) has succinctly described as the "acquired distinctiveness of cues." Making a cue relevant in one situation increases the likelihood that it will be tried out hypothesiswise and used if appropriate in a new situation. Lawrence has shown that cues acquire this distinctiveness through prior use, and

common-sense observation as well as the history of science lend weight
to this finding. It is a commonplace that men can be trained to utilize
cues seldom otherwise used in "piercing" the mask of camouflage in
aerial photographs taken for military purposes. Or compare in
zoological classification the difference between Cuvier, who, with a
background of major interest in anatomy, suggested classification on
the basis of structure, and Von Baer, whose proposal to classify on a
developmental basis reflected his background of genetics.

The examples of Cuvier and Von Bair suggest that as a result
of past experience some attributes acquire criteriality by virtue
of "systematic status." To understand the manner in which people
come to utilize cues out of systematic preference requires a brief
digression into the nature of category systems. We illustrate by
taking the concept "man," *homo sapiens*. What are the diacritica of
man, the distinguishing features that differentiate him? Whether one
asks this question from the point of view of "official" defining attributes
or from the point of view of the criterial attributes that any given
person would use, the question cannot be answered unless one specifies the nature of the discrimination that must be made. If one is
seeking to isolate the distinguishing features that differentiate man
from all those things that can be grouped as nonman, one set of differentiating features will be most useful. This we may refer to as the
"A versus not-A" case. But suppose the task is to differentiate man
from anthropoid apes; then another set of attributes would be more
relevant. Here we are dealing with the "A versus B" case. The third
case is provided by the systematic task of ordering or arranging *all*
species of organism into a *set* of classes, one of which is man. In this
case, one seeks a set of differentiating characteristics that will not only
distinguish man from apes but which may also serve to distinguish
whales from fish, arachnids from insects, and even *homo sapiens* from
pithecanthropus erectus. For the object of systematic categorization
as compared with *ad hoc* categorizing is that one seeks to find a minimum set of reliable attributes capable of guiding one to a series of
categorizing decisions about many forms of identity.

When one is wedded to a set of defining attributes that have been
useful in carrying out an exhaustive task of categorizing many classes,
the attributes that have proved useful in handling part of the array of
categories will be preferred for handling the rest of the array. Contemporary developments in morphology provide a striking example.
There has in recent years been much new taxonomic work on surface
feeding and diving ducks the world over. Up to the fairly recent past,
the usual morphological differentiating features in this work were em-

ployed. Distribution of feathers, coloring, wing barring, and other such features were the conventional diacritica. There was an investment in them: they had proved useful and stable. So long as ducks showed the common morphology and a few simple behavioral signs (mode of take-off, feeding, etc.) they were grouped together. *Ipso facto* such features had high criteriality and were the ones that would be tested in the eternal search for new species. Most ornithologists of a generation ago would have scoffed at the suggestion that further differentiation of species categories could be achieved by a close study of the courting, nesting, and young-care patterns of ducks. Today, under the impact of work by Lorenz (1952), Mayr (1955), and others, instinctive behavior patterns have achieved the status of "official" defining attributes. As a result, they also have achieved far greater criteriality in influencing the tentative categorizations of taxonomists in search of new species. For they turn out to have the systematic differentiating property that predisposes the orderly taxonomist in their favor.

It is not only the orderly taxonomist who is predisposed to utilize attributes that have "systematic status." Verisimilitude is a weak form of systematic status; the attribute that has "face validity" is one which fits in with our other knowledge. In the Brunswik and Reiter (1938) study, for example, height of brow is a highly criterial cue for judging intelligence. This is an attribute that "makes sense," that fits with all we know or feel about the relevance of the brain to intelligence. Red hair as a sign of temperament, size as an indicator of strength—these are attributes which often acquire by virtue of verisimilitude a criteriality over and beyond their ecological validity.

To pursue the problem of why some stimulus properties rather than others are impressive and more preferred as bases of grouping the world would get one deep into the psychology of perception. As Köhler (1947) has persuasively argued, we do well to begin with the visual world as we find it—a world of objects and things. Our primary concern is not with what it is about an attribute which leads to its being more *eindringlich* than others but with the way in which such a property affects utilization of the attribute in categorial decisions.

Finally evidence is beginning to accumulate on one other factor that bears upon the preference for various attributes in categorizing. It is the linguistic codability of attributes and the codability of distinctions among the values of an attribute. First as to the linguistic codability of an attribute as such. There exists in commonly spoken English no single term for describing the density of a tone as density has been described by Stevens (1934). It is conceivable that there could be a linguistic community in which the specific term "density" existed outside the technical circle of acousticians and that it referred to the same attribute as the one isolated by Stevens. The difference between this community and the English-speaking community would not be in terms of the capacity to *discriminate* density from other attributes. Peoples who have but one word for green and blue are capable of discriminating the difference between the two hues, so that capacity is not in question. Indeed, it would also be possible to describe linguistically what is denoted by the word "density" in English, although it might be necessary to use a paragraph of connotative or metaphorical prose in doing so. The difference would lie, most probably, in the *habitual tendency to use the attribute* in making everyday discriminations and in searching out defining attributes.

We have perhaps been somewhat unsystematic in describing the various factors that may lead an individual to prefer to utilize certain cues in making categorial and other kinds of inference, for the subject is one that is too little explored to lend itself to ready ordering. The "rational" validity of cues, the requirements of the situation, certain forms of innate and acquired cue-preference hierarchies, systematic preference, and linguistic codability are all in need of further study as determinants of criteriality. One rather introspective point serves to conclude the discussion. However acquired, cue preference seems to be accompanied by certain subjective states often enough reported to warrant a word here. To use the term originally employed by Katz (1935) to characterize the "impressiveness" of colors, preferred cues seem to take on an *eindringlich* quality. They "look" right and they look more impressive. In concept-attainment experiments using such "meaningless" attributes as color, shape, etc., the attribute values that eventually turn out to be defining of the correct concept seem to take on an "impressive" or figural property while the others seem to "recede" in figural value. When meaningful materials are used as instances, faces varying in certain features or airplane silhouettes differing in wing, tail, and engine construction, certain properties—the human forehead, for example, and also the wings of the airplanes—appear to be more impressive even at the outset and before the concept has been attained. Analysis of cue preference in these latter experiments indicates that subjects utilize these "impressive" cues more than their ecological validity warrants. We do not pretend to know what these subjective changes in the appearance of attributes "mean" or whether they can be conceived of as anything more than the resultant of other processes, yet no account of the factors producing increased utilization of cues for inference can be complete without some mention of this interesting and admittedly puzzling introspective datum.*

CATEGORY TYPES: CONJUNCTIVE, DISJUNCTIVE, AND RELATIONAL

It is usually the case for one to infer identity or some other significate not from a single attribute exhibited by an instance but from several attributes taken together. That is to say, we do not attempt to infer illness *only* from abnormal body temperature, but from a whole set of clinical signs taken in combination. The question of how attributes or cues are combined for making inferences now concerns us. The principal distinction we wish to make is between *conjunctive, disjunctive,* and *relational* concepts, each involving a different mode of combining attributes.

To render more concrete the description of types of categories, we refer to the array of instances contained in Figure 1. Each instance is made up of figures and borders. The figures vary in shape (square, circle, or cross), in color (red, green, or black), and in number (single, double, or triple). The borders vary in number (one, two, or three). Thus, the instances comprise the combinations of four attributes, each with three values. Each instance in the array exhibits one value of each of the four attributes. We may speak of a "category" of instances or a concept in terms of the defining properties of some subset of the instances. For example, "all cards with one red figure" is a concept, so too "all cards with two figures and/or with circles," so too "all cards possessing the same number of figures and borders." The three examples turn out to be drastically different kinds of concepts, and we turn now to a consideration of their difference.

A *conjunctive category* is one defined by the *joint presence* of the appropriate value of several attributes. A typical conjunctive category in the universe of Figure 1 may be defined by the *conjunction* of three figures, redness, and circles, i.e., all cards containing three red circles. Three exemplars of this category are to be found in the figure. All others fail to qualify. Most experiments on concept attainment deal with such conjunctive categories, and procedures such as the Vigotsky Test and the Wisconsin Card Sorting Test are based on them as well.

The *disjunctive category* may be illustrated by that class of cards in Figure 1 that possess three red circles, *or* any constituent thereof: three figures, red figures, circles, three red figures, red circles, or three

---

* The closest analogue we can find in the literature on the subjective analysis of attention and "clarity" is the concept of *derived primary attention* proposed by Titchener (1915) to account for the increased subjective prominence or "attensity" of objects to which we have learned to attend habitually.

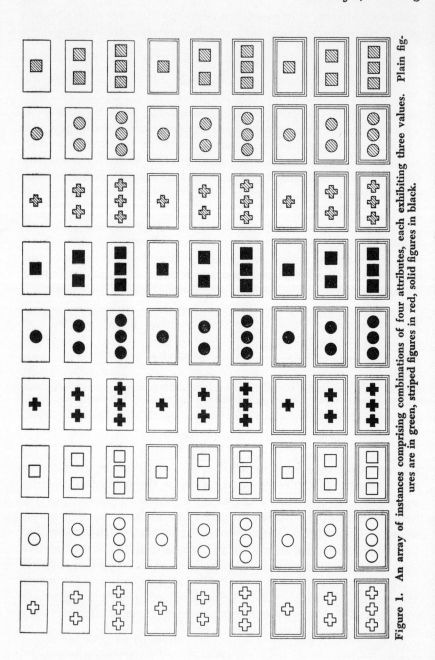

Figure 1. An array of instances comprising combinations of four attributes, each exhibiting three values. Plain figures are in green, striped figures in red, solid figures in black.

circles. The class comprises 57 instances. Any fraternal or civic organization with a membership requirement such as "Anyone residing in *or* paying taxes in Altavista shall be eligible for membership" exemplifies a disjunctive category. A strike in baseball is also disjunctive. A strike is a pitch that is across the plate and between the batter's knees and shoulders *or* it is any pitch at which the batter strikes but fails to send the ball into the field. Similarly, a "walk" occurs either when four balls have been pitched *or* when a pitched ball strikes the batter.

The difficulty with disjunctive concepts is their arbitrariness; the lack of any apparent relation between these attributes which can substitute for one another. This feeling of arbitrariness may be one source of resistance to the categories used by clinical psychologists. A concept such as "stable personality" or "serious disturbance" can only be defined disjunctively, with sometimes one set of signs serving as the cue and sometimes others. Hammond (1955) and Todd (1954) have commented on the role of such vicarious functioning of cues in clinical judgment.

The relational concept or category is one defined by a specifiable relationship between defining attributes. Thus in the universe of Figure 1, we may define as a class all those instances containing the *same* number of figures and borders, or those cards with fewer figures than borders. Income tax brackets (after deduction), each specifiable as a class, are defined in terms of the relationship between number of dependents and level of income. "Effective stimulus" is defined in psychology as an energy change at a receptor surface capable of discharging the receptor: a relationship between two states.

It is sometimes possible to describe the same grouping or class of instances in terms of two different combinations of attributes. One way of combining attributes may prove to be equivalent to another in terms of the groupings that result by use or application, i.e., it may turn out that one rule for combining attributes may prove to be equivalent to another. Such cases are of interest, particularly in the sciences where they are capable of generating theoretical controversy of the kind that produces more heat than light.

An arbitrary array of 16 instances helps to provide an illustration. The array is made up of a set of cards (they are cards used in experiments which will be considered later). Each card has on it a small figure and a large figure. The small figure may either be a triangle or a rectangle, and whichever it is, it can also be black or yellow. So too the large figure: a rectangle or a triangle, yellow or black. Thus, there are four attributes, each with two values. Each card exhibits

one value of each attribute.   The array of instances can be numbered
for convenience as follows:

	Large Figure			
	Triangle		Rectangle	
Small Figure	Yellow	Black	Yellow	Black
Triangle				
Yellow	1	2	3	4
Black	5	6	7	8
Rectangle				
Yellow	9	10	11	12
Black	13	14	15	16

Thus, instance 1 contains a large yellow triangle and a small yellow
triangle; instance 7, a large yellow rectangle and a small black triangle.

What is interesting about this array and many others as well is that
one can define the *same* subset of instances with different concepts,
indeed, different *types* of concepts.   Take, for example, the subset of
instances 2, 4, 5, 7, 10, 12, 13, 15.   This subset can be defined by five
different concepts:

1. Two figures of opposite color.
2. One yellow figure.
3. One black figure.
4. Black figure and yellow figure.
5. Small black with large yellow *or* small yellow with large black.

In this subset, each of these definitions—some conjunctive, some disjunctive, and some relational—define the same class.

What is particularly instructive about this example is that it under-
lines the "invented" or "constructed" nature of a concept or category.
For the way in which a person will categorize *new instances encountered* will depend drastically upon the type of concept he has constructed out of the instances in this array.   While it is true that all of
the concepts noted in the foregoing describe the same subset of instances, the different concepts lead to different modes of categorizing
once one gets outside this array.   A person operating with the concept "two figures of different color" would consider an instance containing a green circle and a purple circle to be an exemplar of the concept.   None of the other concepts would lead to the inclusion of such
an instance.   Indeed, each of the concepts listed would at one point
or another diverge from the others in dealing with new kinds of instances.

We may conclude, then, by noting that when one learns to categorize a subset of events in a certain way, one is doing more than simply learning to recognize instances encountered. One is also learning a rule that may be applied to new instances. The concept or category is, basically, this "rule of grouping" and it is such rules that one constructs in forming and attaining concepts. In this sense, conjunctive, disjunctive, and relational categories are different types of rules for grouping a set of attribute values for defining the positive or exemplifying instances of a concept.

PROBLEMS IN HANDLING MULTIPLE-SIGNAL ATTRIBUTES

In preceding pages we have dealt with a variety of the properties of attributes and attribute combinations that affect the manner in which they may be used as a basis for inferring the categorial identity of things. The defining and criterial status of attributes, their immediacy and proneness to masking, their linguistic codability, the nature of their ranges and transition values, and finally the manner in which they may be combined: all of these have concerned us in turn. We come now to the problem of the number of attributes that are exhibited by an array of instances to be categorized and the number of attribute values that are actually used by an individual in discriminating one class of objects from another.

The number of criterial attributes affecting categorization makes a difference in two ways. The first is with respect to *learning* a category, and the second is in *utilizing* the category after it has been learned. The former problem must be postponed for a moment because it involves other considerations shortly to be introduced. The latter is a matter of immediate concern. If there are a dozen criterial attributes affecting one's categorization of a class of objects, the process of scanning the values of each attribute prior to reaching an inferential decision about the identity of the object would be both a strain and time-consuming regardless of how the attributes were combined in terms of a concept type. In the ordinary behavior of a person, there is likely to be a tendency toward the reduction of such strain since time pressures usually are operative. Under pressure of time or under conditions of stress, the individual will not "attend to" or take into consideration all of the attributes that might be considered under more leisurely conditions.

There appear to be two principal ways in which the strain of weighing many attributes can be reduced. One is by reduction in the number of attributes considered; the other by a process of combining or recoding attributes into attribute configurations.

Consider first *attribute reduction*. The individual can "fall back" on the most criterial attributes, whatever the basis of their criteriality may be, and base his categorization on them. Or, as in the case of subjects in the stress experiment of Postman and Bruner (1948), he may fall back on those attributes most immediately discriminable; and this is likely to be the case where time pressure is operative. He may "regress" to the attribute on which he first focused in the process of learning the category. He may base his categorization on that attribute some value of which has been found highly predictive of the presence of appropriate values of other criterial attributes. In short, there are various ways in which attribute reduction can occur. We know attribute reduction has occurred when it can be shown that attributes that were formerly criterial no longer make a difference for a person's categorizations.

The extent to which attribute reduction occurs under different conditions reflects various requirements placed on the individual in the categorizing situation. For example, if the consequence of miscategorization are severe, it seems likely that attribute reduction will not be very marked as long as error can be reduced by taking into account the values of many attributes. Where the consequences of error are not great but where time pressure is great, we would expect to find notable attribute reduction. Where the array of cues to be used in categorization are all relatively low in validity, again one would expect to find less reduction than under conditions where some of the cues available are highly predictive and others not.

The development of configurational attributes is best illustrated by a concrete example. The student being introduced for the first time to microscopic techniques in a course in histology is told to look for the *corpus luteum* in a cross-sectional slide of rabbit ovary. He is told with respect to its defining attributes that it is yellowish, roundish, of a certain size relative to the field of the microscope, etc. He finds it. Next time he looks, he is still "scanning the attributes." But as he becomes accustomed to the procedure and to the kind of cellular structure involved, the *corpus luteum* begins to take on something classically referred to as a *Gestalt* or configurational quality. Phenomenologically, it seems that he no longer has to go through the slow business of checking size, shape, color, texture, etc. Indeed, "corpus luteumness" appears to become a property or attribute in its own right.

What is happening here is a recoding of the stimulus input in terms of those features of the object perceived that make possible the reconstruction of the remainder of the object. Such reconstruction is possible because in fact the defining features of most objects and events are redundant with respect to each other. A bird has wings and bill and feathers and characteristic legs. But the whole ensemble of features is not necessary for making the correct identification of the creature as a bird. If it has wings and feathers, the bill and legs are highly predictable. In coding or categorizing the environment, one builds up an expectancy of all of these features being present together. It is this unitary conception that has the configurational or Gestalt property of "birdness." Indeed, once a configuration has been established and the object is being identified in terms of configurational attributes, the perceiver will tend to "rectify" or "normalize" any of the original defining attributes that deviate from expectancy. Missing attributes are "filled in" (Bruner and Minturn, 1955), reversals righted (Postman, Bruner, and Walk, 1951), colors assimilated to expectancy (Bruner, Postman, and Rodrigues, 1951). When the conception is well enough established, it takes on the property of being able to serve as a discriminable and seemingly irreducible attribute of its own. One can array things in the degree of their birdlikeness in much the same way as one can array lengths, a presumably less complex attribute. The tachistoscopic recognition of words provides an interesting case in point. At first one attempts to perceive words in terms of their letters, but with practice one is able to perceive them as wholes, reconstructing the letters by virtue of having learned the redundancy of the features that make up the word. Attneave (1954) has proposed an ingenious way in which one may analyze simple visual figures in terms of the redundancy contained in their pattern and his basic reasoning is much the same as in the example of word perception.

It is probably in this way that many "good Gestalten" are established, Gestalten which were anything but good at the outset. The point is one grievously overlooked in much of the writing of Gestalt theorists, but this is not our concern here. What is important to note here is that such establishment of configurational attributes provides one of the chief techniques of reducing the strain of attribute scanning in the utilization of categories.*

Now the question of learning a concept and the effect of the number of attributes on it. In later chapters, several studies will be reported dealing with the question of the number of defining attributes

* The writers are indebted to Egon Brunswik with whom the idea of configurational attributes was first discussed in the summer of 1954 and whose proposal of a "smearing mechanism" as a basis for Gestalt formation served as our taking-off point.

and the number of nondefining attributes displayed by an array of objects which a person must learn to categorize into exemplars and nonexemplars of a concept. Take a scientist trying to discover what kinds of cells are and are not cancer prone. He knows that some are and some are not and he is trying to find out what characteristics of cells lead to cancer proneness. There are thousands of discriminable attributes exhibited by the cells to be studied: all their chemical components, their size, weight, stainability by different dyes, etc. Any one of these may in fact be defining of the class "cancer prone." Obviously, the larger the number of discriminable attributes, the more arduous the job of testing them. It has been shown in various studies that the technique one employs for testing attributes will change as the arduousness of the task increases. Reed (1946b) has found, for example, that when the complexity of the materials used in a concept-attainment experiment is great (many discriminable attributes), subjects tend to revert to rote-memory techniques for trying to learn which are exemplars and which nonexemplars of the concept they are seeking. If the complexity is less, the subject will more likely attempt to extract the common attributes of exemplars and learn the concept in this way. More generally, the task of a person faced with many attributes to be tested is to limit somehow the strain on memory or "bookkeeping" that is involved.

Trying to keep track of which attribute values and which combination of attribute values are correlated with some criterion—which properties of cells increase cancer susceptibility, for example—may require extraordinary measures. The statistician develops such special techniques as multiple correlation and the analysis of variance to reduce the strain of dealing with a large number of attributes. The ordinary problem-solver also has measures he can employ and we shall deal with these in later chapters.

Here it becomes necessary to introduce a distinction between two types of attributes that eventually turn out to be nondefining of a concept: the distinction between *noisy* and *quiet* nondefining attributes. If one were learning to distinguish different makes of motor cars by their appearance, the color of cars would be a noisy nondefining attribute; it varies from instance to instance and thus requires testing as a possibly relevant attribute but is not defining. Any attribute that has a single value across the whole array of instances to be tested we term a quiet nondefining attribute. All cars have some metal parts: an irrelevant attribute but one that needs no testing for it does not vary from instance to instance. In brief, any attribute whose testing distracts or delays the discovery of a set of defining attributes is a noisy attribute. North and Leedy's experiment (1952) is an excellent example of the way in which noisy attributes encountered early in concept attainment can have just this delaying effect.

The extent to which the number of discriminable and varying attributes in an array of instances affects the task of concept attainment will of course depend upon the nature of the concept to be attained. It can readily be seen that conjunctive, disjunctive, and relational concepts—since they require different methods of combining the positive values of defining attributes—will generate different requirements for scanning. Given an array of instances exhibiting six attributes each with five discriminable values, the number of combinations to be tested if one is looking for a conjunctive concept will be different from the number if one is operating on the hunch that the concept is relational. These are matters that will be discussed in considerable detail in later chapters when we deal with strategies for attaining concepts. We mention the problem here to alert the reader to one of the massively important consequences ensuing when one generalizes from a simple to a complicated universe of instances that must be tested for their possible grouping into conceptual classes.

We turn now to an examination of the problems involved in the process of attaining a concept.

CHAPTER 3

The process
of concept attainment

It is curiously difficult to recapture pre-conceptual innocence. Having learned a new language, it is almost impossible to recall the undifferentiated flow of voiced sounds that one heard before one learned to sort the flow into words and phrases. Having mastered the distinction between odd and even numbers, it is a feat to remember what it was like in a mental world where there was no such distinction. In short, the attainment of a concept has about it something of a quantal character. It is as if the mastery of a conceptual distinction were able to mask the preconceptual memory of the things now distinguished. Moreover, the transition experience between "not having" the distinction and "having it" seems to be without experiential content. From the point of view of imagery and sensory stuff the act of grasping a conceptual distinction is, if not *unanschaulich* or impalpable, to use the language of the Wurzburg investigators, at least unverbalizable. It is, if you will, an enigmatic process and often a sudden process. The psychologist's "aha experience" singles out this suddenness as does the literary man's "shock of recognition." Something happens quickly and one thinks one has found something. Concept attainment seems almost an intrinsically unanalyzable process from an experiential point of view: "Now I understand the distinction, before there was nothing, and in between was only a moment of illumination."

It is perhaps because of the inaccessibility of reportable experience that psychologists have produced such a relatively sparse yield of knowledge when they have sought to investigate concept attainment and the thought processes by techniques of phenomenological analysis. To say, as Graham Wallas (1926) did a generation ago, that thinking or invention is divided into the four stages of "preparation," "incubation," "illumination," and "verification" is helpful only in so far as it serves to indicate that while the experience of "grasping" (illumination or insight) is sudden, it is imbedded in a longer process —still to be described in analytic terms. We do well to heed the lesson of history and look to sources of data additional to the report of direct experience as a basis for understanding what is the process of concept attainment.

The remainder of this volume is in large measure given over to the study of how people come to grasp conceptual or categorial distinctions. One may state these guiding questions. How do people *achieve* the information necessary for isolating and learning a concept? How do they *retain* the information gained from encounters with possibly relevant events so that it may be useful later? How is retained information *transformed* so that it may be rendered useful for testing an hypothesis still unborn at the moment of first encountering new information? People do manage these vastly complex tasks of achieving, retaining, and transforming information and they do so without exceeding the relatively narrow limits of human cognitive capacity. They do it in a manner that reflects with nicety the requirements of speed, accuracy, and the like that are imposed upon them by circumstances. We look about us and we see people constantly engaged in picking up and using information that enables them to make conceptual distinctions on the basis of appropriate defining attributes, doing it in such a way that they seem neither overwhelmed by the complexity of the task nor much endangered by maladaptive slowness or by reckless speed. People learn to distinguish conceptually between daylight color film and indoor color film, between different cuts of meat, between fresh vegetables and stale ones, between policemen and subway guards, between detergents and soap flakes, between honest and crooked politicians, between bashful children and less timid ones, between a flow of traffic that permits crossing the street safely and a flow that one should not risk. How may one go about analyzing the learning process that leads to such rational behavior?

THE INVESTIGATION OF CONCEPT ATTAINMENT

It is more than a casual truism of the operational behaviorist that in order to study a psychological process one must externalize it for observation. Concept attainment is not an exception. How get it externalized into observable behavior? Verbal report, as we have noted, provides insufficient data for making generalizations about it. What then?

Consider the chain of events leading up to the learning of a concept, and we purposely choose an example from everyday life. Our hypothetical subject is a foreigner who has arrived in town and is being introduced around by an old resident who is a trusted friend of his. The people to whom he is being introduced are the instances. After each encounter with a new person—an "instance," in the jargon of concept studies—his friend remarks either, "He's an influential person" or "He's a nice fellow but not very influential." Our subject has reason to respect his friend's judgment and is, more or less intentionally, trying to learn the basis of his friend's distinction between "influential" people and "nice but not influential" people. Looked at more precisely, he encounters instances and then has them labelled categorywise as in one class or another by his tutor-friend. The instances that he encounters vary in the myriad of attributes by which human beings are marked. Some are more educated than others, better travelled, more facile conversationally, richer, more forceful, etc. His task is to determine which attributes lead reliably to membership in the class "influential people." Note one thing. Very early in the round of visits, our subject begins to make tentative judgments of his own, prior to his friend's advice, as to whether the person he is meeting is influential or not, perhaps on the basis of attributes that he would have difficulty in describing even to himself. With respect to these tentative hypotheses, several contingencies may arise: he may consider a person influential and have his judgment confirmed or infirmed by his friend, or he may consider a person not influential with the same two possible outcomes. And, of course, the tutor-friend can also resolve cases of doubt for him. If the friend were also able to give him the proper advice about the defining attributes of the class, the task would be finished. But let us assume that this is not to be the case, that the tutor-friend is somehow reticent on this score.

Our subject as we have described him thus far exists in something of a privileged enclave in which he is protected from the consequences of his own tentative judgments. This is how it is, of course, in most concept-attainment studies—whether a particular Chinese figure is called a CIV or a DAX by a subject is seemingly without consequence, save that miscalling may hurt one's self-esteem. But it is conceivable that our man may have to act on the basis of his tentative categorization before getting his friend's guidance, and his action may have serious consequences. To what extent will this lead to constant errors in his placement of people and in the tentative hypotheses he develops? Our man's position is privileged too in the sense that there is no limit of time on his learning activity. Suppose that his tutor-friend were only going to be in town for a few days and in that time he had to learn to recognize examples of the category "influential people" in order to carry out his future business. To what extent would this influence his approach to learning?

We must also ask a question about record-keeping. How does the person keep track? Each instance he encounters exhibits many attributes, and our man notes the value of some of these and not others upon encountering exemplars and nonexemplars of the class "influential people": that more of the "influentials" were rich than poor, but not that more of them were tall rather than short. He may also want to keep track of the fate of those tentative hypotheses that were checked and found wanting on subsequent encounters. Is the record-keeping (whether in his head or in a ledger) of such a kind that it ensures the ready utilization of information encountered?

Finally, how does the person know when he has learned the concept in a serviceable way? This is a deceptively simple question. The first thing that may come to mind is that the person knows he has learned the concept when he feels he is able to predict the status of new instances with a sufficiently high degree of certainty. But what is a "sufficiently high degree of certainty" when a person is working with a probabilistic concept where cues do not yield complete prediction of identity? We will find that some people will continue to explore obvious attributes and abstract not obvious ones to explore so long as they are not able to categorize perfectly. Others will stabilize in their behavior and will base their categorizations exclusively on partially predictive cues without any further effort to try out new, possibly relevant attributes. Even when a subject is working with a simple conjunctive concept whose defining attributes predict perfectly the status of all instances encountered, he may not be sure that he "has" the concept even though he is performing perfectly. He will go on testing new instances, "just to be sure." We do not mean to obscure what may seem to be a simple matter, but in fact it is very difficult to describe what it is that leads a subject to state that he has now learned the concept. For simplicity's sake, it is often better to by-pass the question and to ask instead whether the attributes that are criterial for the subject in his categorizing judgment are also the attributes that are defining of the concept. Let it be clear, however, that some people require many more encounters beyond this point before they feel any degree of certainty; others reach the stage of certainty before their behavior meets this criterion.

The first and most notable thing about the sequence of events set forth is that it can be described as a series of decisions. At the very outset, even before the person has so much as encountered a single instance, he must make a decision about the nature of the task. Will he try to learn the concept "influential people" or will he concentrate on remembering in rote fashion which people he met were and which people were not "influential"? There are then decisions to be made, important ones from the point of view of efficiency, as to which attributes and how many attributes he should attend to in attempting to find out how to spot an influential person without having to ask his friend or going through the difficult business of observing the exercise of influence in the community. And should a tentative hypothesis prove wrong, his next decision is how to change it. Indeed, if his hypothesis is correct on one encounter, should he hold to it *in toto?* The decisions, moreover, are always contingent on the consequences he foresees and he must also make decisions about what consequences seem reasonable. If you will, then, the steps involved in attaining a concept are successive decisions, earlier ones of which affect the degrees of freedom possible for later decisions.

In studying concept attainment, then, it has been our aim to externalize for observation as many of the decisions as could possibly be brought into the open in the hope that regularities in these decisions might provide the basis for making inferences about the processes involved in learning or attaining a concept. These regularities in decision-making we shall call *strategies*.

The phrase "strategies of decision-making" is not meant in a metaphoric sense. A strategy refers to a pattern of decisions in the acquisition, retention, and utilization of information that serves to meet certain objectives, i.e., to insure certain forms of outcome and to insure against certain others. Among the objectives of a strategy are the following:

   a. To insure that the concept will be attained after the minimum number of encounters with relevant instances.
   b. To insure that a concept will be attained with certainty, regardless of the number of instances one must test *en route* to attainment.
   c. To minimize the amount of strain on inference and memory capacity while at the same time insuring that a concept will be attained.
   d. To minimize the number of wrong categorizations prior to attaining a concept.

Other objectives can be stated and will concern us in later sections of the book. These suffice to illustrate what is intended by the objectives of a strategy.

Let it be said at the outset that a strategy as we are using the term here does not refer to a conscious plan for achieving and utilizing information. The question whether a person is or is not conscious of his strategy, while interesting, is basically irrelevant to our inquiry. Rather, a strategy is inferred from the pattern of decisions one observes in a problem-solver seeking to attain a concept. What instances does he seek to test, what hypotheses does he construct, how does he change these when he meets certain contingencies? These are the data from which strategies are inferred. The manner in which one proceeds in analyzing a strategy can only be described here in general terms: the specifics require the type of concrete analysis of behavior with which the four following chapters are concerned. Essentially, what is required is that one construct an ideal strategy or a set of ideal strategies that have the formal properties necessary to meet certain demands or objectives with "maximum rationality." Such ideal strategies can be stated in quite strict logical terms. For any given concept-attainment task, for example, there is an ideal strategy that can be constructed having the property that by following it one can attain a concept with a minimum number of encounters—but without regard to the cognitive strain involved. There are other ideal strategies having the property of minimizing cognitive strain, but they often are wasteful of the number of instances one must encounter en route to solution. And, indeed, there are also ideal compromise strategies that serve both the purposes of cognitive economy and rapid solution. To put the matter perhaps too simply, the analysis of performance strategy consists in comparing the actual performance of a subject with a set of rational or ideal strategies and determining a best fit. We ask then which ideal strategy does the subject's performance conform to most closely.

Obviously, strategies as employed by people are not fixed things. They alter with the nature of the concept being sought, with the kinds of pressures that exist in the situation, with the consequences of behavior, etc. And this is of the essence. For what is most creative about concept-attainment behavior is that the patterning of decisions does indeed reflect the demands of the situations in which the person finds himself. We do not know how strategies are learned, and the matter does not concern us for the present. Presumably they are learned. "What" is learned, however, is not of the order of a set of simple responses. For the systematic behavior of subjects attaining concepts is a highly patterned, skilled performance. If contemporary theories of learning are to deal with such performances, it is our feeling that the unit of analysis now called the "response" will have to be broadened considerably to encompass the long, contingent sequence of acts that, more properly speaking, can only be called a "performance." But such matters are not, as we have said, within the scope of this book. Our effort is directed to locating strategies for dealing with information and trying to understand the manner in which they reflect the person's adjustment to the complex environment in which he must move.

CONDITIONS AFFECTING CONCEPT-ATTAINMENT BEHAVIOR

The pattern of decisions involved in attaining a concept is affected by a host of factors. Without doing too much violence to this diversity of determinants, it is possible to group them under several rather broad headings.

1. *The definition of the task.* What does the person take as the objective of his behavior? What does he think he is supposed to do?

2. *The nature of instances encountered.* How many attributes does each exhibit, and how many of these are defining and how many noisy? Does he encounter instances at random, in a systematic order, and does he have any control over the order in which instances will be tested? Do instances encountered contain sufficient information for learning the concept fully?

3. *The nature of validation.* Does the person learn each time an instance is encountered whether it is or is not an exemplar of the concept whose definition he is seeking? Or is such validation only available after a series of encounters? Can hypotheses be readily checked or not?

4. *The consequences of specific categorizations.* What is the price of categorizing a specific instance wrongly and the gain from a correct categorization? What is the price attached to a wrong hypothesis? And do the various contingencies—rightness or wrongness of a categorization of "X" and "not-X"—have a different price attached to them?

5. *The nature of imposed restrictions.* Is it possible to keep a record of instances and contingencies? Is there a price attached to the testing of instances as a means of finding out in which category they belong? Is there pressure of time to contend with, a need for speedy decisions?

Consider each of these matters in turn.

The Definition of the Task. The first consideration here is whether or not the person is consciously or "reportedly" seeking to attain a concept. Consider our hypothetical subject mentioned in the preceding section. It makes a vast difference in behavior whether he is "set" to find out the extrapolatable properties of the class of people who are influential or whether he is merely trying to remember in rote fashion which of the people he met were and which were not influential. Many of the classic experiments in concept attainment, beginning with Hull's famous study (1920), have employed rote-memory instructions, leading their subjects to believe that their task was to memorize the labels of different figures presented to them rather than to seek to discover what were the defining properties of instances bearing the same labels. Yet we know from the careful studies of Reed (1946a) that this prior set of the subject makes a considerable difference, even when the concepts to be attained are simple in nature. When a subject is set only to learn names, the rate of success in discovering the basis for grouping was 67%; with instructions to discover the basis for grouping, the figure increased to 86%—and this, let it be noted, with very simple concepts.

In the appendix, Roger Brown proposes that one of the functions of words is to alert people to the possibilities of concept attainment. We say to a class of students in biological chemistry, "Consider now the substance *histamine*." The function of such a word is to suggest that a concept is about to be presented and that one must be alert to the possible defining attributes in terms of which its exemplars can be differentiated from other things in the world. It may well be, as Goldstein (1940) has so vigorously and persuasively suggested, that people are differentially set to handle the events they encounter, some seeking constantly to form conceptual groupings, others to deal with events concretely in terms of simple identity categories, "This thing in all its appearances," rather than "This thing as a member of the class of things alpha." There are many deep and unsolved problems surrounding the question of what it is that alerts people to conceptualizing activity, and it is clear that the full picture of concept-attainment behavior will not emerge until these problems are solved.

A second question concerning the definition of the task is the person's expectancies concerning the nature of the concept with which he must deal. In Chapter 6, it will be abundantly clear that people in our culture dislike .and do not have much skill in dealing with disjunctive concepts—a class of events defined by the presence of the appropriate values of one attribute *or* another attribute *or* both in conjunction. Some of our own studies have indicated that, when the nature of the concept to be sought is not specified, subjects will tend to assume that they are looking for a simple conjunctive concept of the certainty type. Is it indeed the case, as the late Alfred Korzybski (1951) urged, that Western man is burdened down by a preference for conjunctive classification stemming from the tradition of so-called Aristotelian logic? Does the difficulty of dealing with disjunctive,

relational, and probabilistic concepts reflect the difficulty of such concepts or does the difficulty perhaps reflect certain cultural biases in
problem-solvers?

These are questions that cannot presently be answered. Certainly,
there are cultural factors at work, or subcultural ones. The organic
chemist, if organic chemistry can be treated as a subculture, develops
a taste for relational groupings, at least during his working hours.
Benzene rings, for example, are essentially relational groupings. Presumably, the physicist who works in quantum mechanics and nuclear
theory will develop a taste for probabilistic concepts by the very
nature of the discipline he must use. Though the generalization requires a leap, it is probably the case that most modern science is moving in the direction of probabilistic-relational concepts: classes of
events defined in terms of the probability that certan attribute values
will represent a kind of relation to each other. In economics, one
classes nations over a period of years in terms of an average state of
their balance of payments, whether favorable or unfavorable. Botany,
a field in which conjunctive classificatory schemata have been classical,
now deals with concepts such as a habitat's "balance," or with approximations to certain forms of "climax" in which a special variety of soil,
climate, and flora are in a quasi-stationary equilibrium.

Still another feature of "defining the task," already alluded to earlier,
is the predilection for criterial attributes that a person brings to the
task of concept attainment. This is particularly the case when the
task is one of constructing a series of systematic categories for continuing use as in geology, zoology, or anthropology. What is striking
about such "attribute-predilection" (and the Latin origin, *praedilegere*,
"to choose in advance," is indeed the proper word) is that one finds
both in the behavior of subjects and of scientists that preferred but
nondefining attributes are not readily given up even when one's encounter with instances proves them to be noisy and useless. In so far
as people define the task of attaining a concept as one of proving
that their prior hunches about defining attributes were right, it will be
reflected in the pattern of decisions about changes in one's hypotheses
in the face of infirming contingencies.

One hidden feature of the definition of a task—one of the skeletons
in the psychologist's closet—needs some publicity, for it most certainly
affects the manner in which people in experiments go about the task
of attaining a concept. It is the "two-man game" feature of most experimental research on the thought processes. Subjects in psychological experiments tend to define the task as one in which their abilities
are under test. As a result, "error" may come to have a consequence

that is different from and perhaps more severe than what usually prevails in more private cognitive activity. The effect may be to lead the subject to play safe in his choice of hypotheses or in the instances he chooses for testing. One countervailing factor, however, may make such a hedgehog strategy less attractive. For the subject in approaching a task also may operate on the assumption that the experimenter would not have chosen an easy task for testing his abilities. So one often finds subjects trying complicated approaches to a problem when easy ones would have served them better, and admitting it sheepishly after they discover that the task was simpler than they thought. We cannot settle this vexing problem here, but wish only to point it out as a ubiquitous and important factor in determining the behavior of subjects in experiments on the thought processes.

One last point about the subject's definition of the task: his expectations about what constitutes successful solution or successful progress in a problem-solving task. Simmel (1953) reports that one of the subjects in her problem-solving experiment asked to be allowed to keep going after he had attained solution on the grounds that his solution was "inelegant." At the other extreme, Smedslund (1955) tells of one of his subjects in a multiple-cue probability experiment who was doing badly and showing no improvement. When queried, he replied that his "system" was quite satisfactory and that he was "performing as well as one could possibly do under the given circumstances, and that he was not responsible for his failures because they were unavoidable" (p. 39). The two contrasting cases illustrate nicely the extent to which the objectives of the systematic behavior adopted by a subject will differ as a function of how he defines his task. In one case, the subject wants an "elegant solution," in the other he wants to do only somewhat better than chance. What is interesting about these levels of aspiration is that they determine in considerable measure when the person will cease trying, where he will stabilize and end the strainful process of searching out relevant attributes and relations. Thus all the factors that have to do with the setting of the level of aspiration—situational and personological alike—will in some measure affect the definition of a task and in so doing affect the objectives that go into the forming of a behavior strategy.

One other feature of "aspiration level" is the depth of understanding that the subject seeks to achieve in his solution. We single out this point because it has special relevance to the matter of "knowing" a concept behaviorally and "knowing" it at the level of verbal report. The world of mathematics is rife with examples of people who could come up with correct solutions before ever they were able to describe the steps used in attaining them. Many experiments in concept attainment, including our own, have shown that subjects are able to distinguish correctly exemplars from nonexemplars of a concept before being able to name the defining features on which their judgments are based. The studies of Hull (1920), Smoke (1932), and Walk (1952) all provide examples. Indeed, Adkins and Lyerly (1951) indicate that different factors contribute to success on two forms of the Progressive Matrices Test, one form requiring the subject to recognize the answer, the other to furnish it. We do not know whether there is a difference in behavior that results when one sees one's task as "behavioral attainment" in contrast to "verbal attainment" of a concept. There is evidence, however, that the two forms of attainment come at different points in a sequence of behavior and that "good" problem-solvers show this separation more markedly than poor ones.. At least Thurstone (1950) suggests, on the basis of Bouthilet's study (1948), that creative problem-solving may express itself in this way, with the more imaginative problem-solver being the one whose actual performance runs well ahead of his ability to state verbal justifications for it. It remains to be seen whether patterns of decisions in problem-solving reflect this kind of difference.

The Nature of Instances Encountered. Return for a moment to the hypothetical foreign visitor seeking to discover the defining attributes of an influential person. At the outset, he is armed with a certain amount of wisdom. While it is possible for him to distinguish many possible attributes of the people-instances he encounters, he is wise enough to know that certain of these are more likely to be important than others and will not waste his time considering whether shoe size is something worth attending to. But even after he strips the situation down to the most likely factors—factors, of course, that had proved useful in making distinctions between influential and other people in his own country—the number that remain to be tested will make a great deal of difference in terms of the nature of the task and, indeed, in the strategy he will adopt. First, in terms of the number of possible hypotheses he may entertain about the correct basis for inferring the influence of a person. Suppose, for argument's sake, that there were four likely attributes, each with three discriminable values. Let us say one is *age* (under 35, 35–50, over 50), *economic status* (high, medium, and low), *religion* (Catholic, Jew, Protestant), and *apparent aggressiveness* (high, medium, low). Assuming (quite in the manner of an Aristotle-ridden Western man!) that the concept "influential people" is conjunctive, the four attributes each with their three values could be compounded in a frighteningly large number of ways. For example, the influential people could be defined in terms of the values of all *four* attributes and include all those who are:

Over 50, rich, Protestant, and moderately aggressive.

Or they could be defined by values of only *two* attributes:

Rich and Protestant.
Rich and moderately aggressive.
Over 50 and highly aggressive, etc.

The larger the number of attributes exhibited by instances and the larger the number of discriminable values they exhibit, the greater will be the number of hypotheses to be entertained. This is the first constraining factor imposed on problem-solving by the nature of instances encountered.

Here we may foreshadow the next chapter and note that one of the principal differences between various strategies is the rate with which they eliminate alternative hypotheses about which attribute values are relevant for identifying exemplars of a concept. Moreover, the larger the number of attributes being considered, and therefore the larger the number of alternative hypotheses to be eliminated, the greater will be the necessity for adopting a "quick elimination" strategy if time is short or if the number of encounters permitted is limited by their costliness. In sum, the number or richness of the attributes to be dealt with almost inevitably introduces a factor to be dealt with in attaining concepts.

The nature of the instances that one must bring under conceptual grouping may also vary in terms of the *kinds* of attributes they exhibit: their immediacy, their familiarity, their status as good systematic differentia, and their value in past conceptualizing. We remarked, for example, that our hypothetical foreigner in search of the defining attributes of "influence" would adopt certain "reasonable" attributes as good places for starting his search. This is indeed a rational procedure, although we shall see in the following chapter that the road to failure in concept attainment is often marked by a sense of verisimilitude created by past experience. These matters have already been discussed and all that need be said at this point is that they make a systematic difference to be considered empirically in later chapters.

The manner and order of encounter with instances is another factor in determining the behavior of subjects. Does the effort to isolate a conceptual grouping begin with a positive instance or exemplar of the concept being sought? If the concept to be discovered is conjunctive, then from a sheer informational point of view the problem-solver is in a position, if he knows how to utilize the information contained in this instance, to eliminate a very great majority of the possible hypotheses that were entertainable before such an encounter. If the concept is disjunctive, a first positive instance often proves the occasion for adopting an altogether incorrect approach to the problem (cf. Chapter 6). Hovland (1952) has provided an excellent analysis of the potential information to be gained from positive and negative instances of a conjunctive concept when such instances appear at different places in a series of encounters and we shall have occasion to look at the matter in some detail in the three following chapters.

The sheer frequency of positive and negative instances, whatever the order in which they are encountered, also governs the likelihood of encountering certain contingencies with respect to the tentative hypotheses one is trying out. That is to say, one may encounter positive or negative instances and each of these is capable of confirming or infirming an hypothesis the problem-solver may have tentatively developed concerning the correct concept. If, for example, one encounters a red instance at a time when one is considering the hypothesis that "red" is the correct basis for grouping, and if the instance encountered is positive or exemplifying of the concept, then we speak of this as a positive confirming contingency. Each contingency encountered requires an act of decision on the part of the problem-solver. Shall he maintain the hypothesis that he is holding tentatively or shall he change it, and if he changes it, how shall this be done? Now, a high proportion of negative instances (at least where conjunctive concepts are concerned) inevitably places a strain on inference capacity whether the instance confirms or infirms the hypothesis in force. (Lest the reader be puzzled, a negative instance, one not exemplifying the concept being sought, is confirming when it is predicted to be negative by the hypothesis in force.) And in so far as negative instances are infirming of an hypothesis, the change that is required in the hypothesis entails considerable strain on memory for reasons that will be apparent presently. Thus a long series of encounters with negative instances often requires the person to adopt modes of solution that are predominantly devoted to reduction on memory strain.

Smoke (1933) has made much of the role of negative instances in concept attainment. He contrasted the performance of subjects who worked with a series of instances composed half of positive and half of negative instances in contrast to subjects working with positive instances alone. Success in attainment did not seem affected by these two conditions, a questionable finding since the two series were not equated for the amount of information they contained, but a finding that has been properly established by the better controlled experiment of Hovland and Weiss (1953). Smoke makes an exceedingly interesting point about the subjects in the two groups. "There is a tendency for negative instances to discourage 'snap judgments.' . . . The subjects . . . tended to come to an initial wrong conclusion less readily and to subsequent wrong conclusions less frequently, than when they were learning from positive instances alone," (p. 588). This finding suggests that negative instances play some role, yet to be ascertained, in determining the feeling of confidence that leads the subject to believe he has attained the concept.

Are encounters with instances orderly or haphazard? Consider the matter in terms of our useful hypothetical foreigner. Suppose his friend had introduced him to residents of the community in a prearranged order somewhat as follows. He begins by meeting people who are rich, over 50, and Protestant, and who differ only in terms of aggressiveness. He then moves on to people who are rich, over 50, Catholic, and again only differing in aggressiveness, etc., until he has had a chance to sample each attribute systematically and see its relationship to influence in the community. A properly conscientious guide, if he were of an orderly turn of mind, would doubtless do something like this in educating his friend. If he did, he would find that his pupil arrived far more easily at the correct solution. For the patterns of solution that people adopt in attempting to attain concepts reflect very sensitively the order inherent in the instances they meet. Where order is systematic, the objective of minimizing memory strain becomes notably less, and with a reduction of strain, new modes of attack begin to appear.

The question of the orderliness of encounter and the effort to reduce cognitive strain brings us to a more general problem, one that has to do with methods of reducing disorder and confusion used by a subject in attaining or utilizing concepts. The reader will very soon become aware of the importance of what we will later call a "focus": an exemplar of a concept that the problem-solver uses as a reference point or *pied-à-terre*. Virtually all the effective strategies for attaining concepts depend upon the use of some sort of initial focus. Recall your own efforts in learning to distinguish prime numbers from other numbers. It is likely that you will recall the number 3 as your first association, and this number is very likely the focus point from

which you began exploring other exemplars of that interesting class
of integers divisible only by themselves and unity. So, too, we
would expect that our hypothetical foreign visitor would be likely to
take the first "positive instance" encountered of an influential person
and use him as a basis for comparison with new members of the class.
The use of such foci in concept attainment—usually positive instances
although not universally so—represents one of the most direct and
simple ways of reducing strain on memory and on inference. "Reference backward" to the focus is perhaps what suggests that under
certain circumstances the attaining of a concept is like the construction of a composite photograph, although the image connoted is, we
believe, a highly misleading one.

Indeed, *after* a concept has been attained, the process of keeping
order continues by the use of two processes. One of them is represented by the phenomenon of the adaptation level: the formation of
a "typical instance" of the category. This consists essentially of
"summarizing" all exemplars of a class that have been encountered
in terms of typical or average values of each of the defining attributes
of the class. For example, the subjects in the experiment of Bruner
and Rodrigues previously described found no difficulty in setting a
color wheel to the typical color of an eating orange, less trouble,
indeed, than they had in setting the extremes of the acceptable range.
A typical instance of a category is, then, the adaptation level of the
values of the defining attributes of the class, whether computed as a
weighted geometric mean of instance values as Helson (1948) proposes or in some other way. A "typical orange," for example, has
a typical color, typical size, typical shape, etc. As Helson suggests,
such an adaptatation level or typical instance permits one to evaluate
exemplars in terms of their "fitness" in the category.*

Another order-preserving device used after a concept has been
attained, akin in some respects to the typical instance, is the "generic
instance," a representation of the concept in terms of idealized
values of the defining attributes and stripped of all noisy attributes.
It is perhaps the kind of schematized imagery that Fisher (1916)
reports developing in her subjects as they move toward concept

---

* An interesting study by D. R. Brown (1953) indicates the importance of
identifying an instance as a member of a class of relevant instances as a condition for its affecting the adaptation level or typical instance of a category.
Making a weight distinctively separate from a class of weights being judged by
a subject reduces significantly its effect as an anchor on the series or its contribution to the adaptation level of the series. The role of categorial identity as
a factor in adaptation level phenomena is discussed in Brown's paper.

attainment. Often they become highly conventionalized, as, for example, the images of the different types of levers described by Archimedes which are represented by idealized fulcra, levers, and weights. The usual isosceles right-angled triangle that one thinks of when the class "right-angled triangle" is mentioned is another case in point. It is highly doubtful whether the average right-angled triangle we see is indeed marked by two equal sides around the right angle. The function of the generic instance beyond its use as an ordering or simplifying device is obscure, but it may well be that it is used as a search model in problem-solving behavior when a subject is considering what classes of things would be relevant to fill a gap in an unsolved problem.

Another feature of the sequence of instances encountered now needs consideration. There is a specifiable point in any sequential array of information that, formally speaking, can be regarded as "informationally sufficient." One can illustrate this by reference to the amount of information necessary for deciding whether A is equal to, greater than, or smaller than C. The informationally sufficient array of information is

$$A > B$$
$$B > C$$

and any further data or any repetitions of these data would be redundant. The mystery story writer, Ellery Queen, uses the same technique when he informs the reader that at a certain point all the clues necessary are available if the reader wishes to solve the mystery. One can specify the minimum array of instances necessary in order for our hypothetical foreigner to solve the problem of who is influential. But however convincing this may sound as a logical matter, it is grossly misleading from a psychological point of view. Redundancy thus defined has very little to do with psychological redundancy. The point of *psychological* informational sufficiency depends upon the strategy of information utilization a person has adopted, and upon the manner and rate at which he is using the information contained in instances he is encountering. Since more than a few psychological experiments on concept attainment utilizing instances with multiple attributes have failed to take into account either the formal or the psychological point of informational sufficiency, the matter is worth noting in passing. For the way in which people will operate when insufficient information is provided them is not of the same order as their behavior when a sufficient series of instances has been permitted them, as will be seen in the following chapter.

A critical question in determining the kind of strategies that may be employed is whether or not the person can control the order of instances he will encounter or whether they come to him under the control either of chance factors or of some external agency. The difference can be caricatured as similar to that which separates the clinician and the experimentalist. Let us say that each is interested in finding out what areas of the brain mediate (i.e., are defining attributes of) intact pattern vision. The experimentalist goes systematically about the task of extirpating now this area, now that, all in a manner dictated by the canons of efficient experimental design, until he arrives at the point where he is ready to publish his paper. The clinician gets his cases as they come, testing for pattern vision and for brain damage. In principle (and if the clinician were patient enough and orderly enough to keep his records elegantly) there is no difference in the situations of the two men. But in fact, the difference in behavior is striking. It is not simply that the experimentalist has "cleaner data." When the data are, so to speak, "cleaned up" (as they are in Chapters 4 and 5), the difference in the kinds of decisions each must make is even more apparent. It is a matter worthy of scrutiny, and it will receive that in the appropriate place.

Another feature of "control" versus "no control" over the order of instances one encounters is whether or not one encounters instances when one is ready for them. In Hull's well-known study (1920) in which the defining attributes of the concepts to be attained were radicals imbedded in pseudo-Chinese ideograms, he contrasted two orders of presentation: one going from displays containing complex exemplars to ones with simple exemplars, the other from simple to complex. Simple and complex are defined by the number of what we have called "noisy attributes" contained in exemplars to be grouped. When subjects were allowed only a short and specified time to examine each exemplar, there was no difference in success rates for the two procedures. But if subjects were allowed to proceed at their own pace, "if each individual experience in the series is continued until the reaction to it is just perfected before passing on to the next, there is a distinct advantage in favor of the simple-to-complex method," (p. 38). We shall see in Chapter 5 that the result of "readiness for the next instance" is not simply that one succeeds more readily, but that it also affects the manner in which a subject goes about the decisions required in his task.

One can go on almost endlessly about the critical role of the nature and order of instances encountered, and more will be said about the problem in later chapters—for example, of the effect of successive encounters with instances as compared with simultaneous encounter with an array of instances that are either laid out in an orderly or in a random fashion. These are problems that are not simply technical in nature. They critically affect the manner in which concept-attainment behavior unfolds and they have notable implications for teaching practice as well. How, for example, should one expose a student to the bewildering array of instances that must be categorized in terms of the concepts of geology or botany or any of the other classificatory sciences? And with respect to the conduct of scientific research, when the scientist has control over the instances being scrutinized or must depend on a random intake as the clinician must, what is the optimal way of ordering one's contact with instances so that one can test them for defining attributes? When a neuroanatomist, using techniques of electrophysiology, attempts to collate the data on localization in order to map those brain areas associated with different behavioral processes, how shall he proceed? One neurologist, Karl Pribram (1953), proposes that one pay attention only to "positive instances," reported instances where a given area has been found to be related to the presence of a particular kind of behavior—related either by the evidence of extirpation or the evidence of electrophysiological activity. Is this the best procedure? The evidence to be presented in later chapters indicates that it may not always be so.

The Nature of Validation. We have already had occasion in Chapter 1 to examine the various sources of validation of one's categorizations: by reference to a pragmatic criterion, by "official" or consensual validation, by consistency, etc. Now we must introduce the question of *opportunity* for validation in the course of attaining a concept: the frequency of validation, how soon it occurs after a tentative categorization has been made, the ambiguity of validation (since it is not always clear whether we are "right" or "wrong"), and the extent to which the validation is direct or indirect.

Usually in psychological experiments we give subjects (be they animal or human) full knowledge of results. In a typical discrimination learning experiment, an animal must learn to make a distinction between, say, black doors and white doors in terms of the pragmatic criterion of whether they are in the class "go-throughable" or "blocked." If the correction method is used, the animal learns which door is correct and may also have an opportunity for checking the wrong door if he happens to try it first. Where noncorrection procedures are followed, the animal at least gets a chance to test one instance for its positive or negative status. So too in concept-attainment experiments. The subject is shown an instance, may be asked to give his best guess about its category membership (usually to be indicated by a label of some sort), and then told the correct label. Only in the test trials is validation withdrawn. To test the animals' conceptual learning, new instances are introduced, say, a light gray and a dark gray door, in place of the black and white ones, and both doors are left unlatched to see whether the animal has learned the relational concept of going to the darker (or the lighter) door. In concept-attainment experiments, the same procedure is followed. Instances other than those used in the original learning are introduced and these the subject must label without benefit of feedback from the experimenter who now changes his role from tutor to that of tester.

Much the same type of procedure prevails when the young child is being taught to distinguish the conceptual entities of the environment. At first, the word "cat" is uttered each time the child is exposed to this animal. Then there is a stage at which the child is asked to name it and if he is correct we validate by approbation; if not we correct him. Eventually, the child comes to operate on his own and validation by an external source is given only on an intermittent basis.

But there are many cases in everyday life where the course of validation is neither so regular, so benign, nor so well designed to help the struggling attainer of concepts. Validation may be absent, may in fact be prevented; it may be greatly delayed and frequently is. Indeed, it is often indirect and ambiguous as well. The pattern of validating clearly, immediately, frequently, and directly, so typical of psychological experimentation, does not by any means heed the *caveat* of Brunswik (1947) that psychological research designs be representative of the life situations to which their results will be generalized.

One feature of opportunity for validation is simply the frequency with which validation is available. Infrequent opportunity for validation may have the effect of increasing the reliance on preferred cues that are considerably less than certain. If in learning to categorize aircraft silhouettes attempted identifications are not frequently checkable against external information, the effect may be to lead the learner to utilize excessively some cues that have permitted him to make a few successful identifications in the past. One may under conditions of restricted opportunity for validation stabilize one's cue utilization too soon and end with a level of performance that is less efficient than warranted by the goodness of cues available. Or with reduced opportunity, one may turn to some other external criterion for checking one's categorizations. Experiments by Asch (1951) and Crutchfield (1954) indicate that, if correction is not readily available, subjects will turn to the group consensus as a basis for validation, even though the subject may be utilizing better bases for categorization than can be found in the consensus. In the Asch experiment, for example, the subject is asked to categorize the length of lines in terms of their height. Given no validation by the experimenter and given the fact that the group of which he is a member consists of "stooges" who are all primed to call out the wrong categorizing answer, the beleaguered subject soon comes to adopt the group norm as the basis of validation and begins to change his own pattern of calls. To be sure, Asch notes that few subjects were tricked to the extent of "seeing" length of lines in this distorted way. But the fact of the matter is that the actual categorizations made do suffer a marked change under these conditions. If external validation on the actual length of lines had been provided regularly, it is dubious indeed that the effect could have been produced, although Crutchfield's research indicates that even with some external validation, susceptibility to consensual pressures varies widely from subject to subject.

Frequency is only one feature of validation. Immediacy is another. In human relationships one quite often learns to make and continues to make groupings of people and events in the environment with considerably delayed validation. Consider such categorizations of other people as "honest" or "of high integrity" or as a "promising young man." Perhaps under the tutelage of parents and peers, we early learn to classify people as, say, "honest," "somewhat shifty," and "downright crooked" on the basis of a minimum number of defining attribute values. We are often a long time finding out the validity of such categorizations if indeed we ever fully do. "He seemed like an honest man from all I could tell, and I must say I'm suprised that . . ." The "seeming" and the validation may be years apart.

It is likely that long delay in the validation of one's categorial inferences also leads to undue reliance on those few cues that have in the past paid off predictively or to reliance upon consensus in much the same manner discussed in connection with reduced frequency of validation. If we are unable to check immediately our bases for classification against a good external criterion, we are readier to use the vicarious criterion of consensus or to rely on rather nonrational cues.

It may also be characteristic of delayed validation that one reconstructs backward from the validation to possible defining attributes that "might have been." A man is suddenly found to be an embezzler who for the last ten years has been accepted as a pillar of the community. Immediately the "search backward" begins as we try to "recall" signs that might have led us to infer correctly that the man was going to behave in this way. The eventual effectiveness of the "search backward" will depend of course on what was called in the last chapter the ecological validity of labels. More likely than not, the cues that are honored in the consensus of folklore will be "found." "He did, after all, have shifty eyes," or "He did act rather too piously and one does well to suspect that sort of thing." Or a factor of vividness will operate. "That facial tic probably indicated a not very balanced person."

It is rather unfortunate that one must treat the subject of delayed validation by reference to intuitive examples from everyday life, for it seems apparent that it is a rich area for systematic psychological inquiry. The psychological literature yields little on the subject.

The same complaint can be made about work on the ambiguous validation of categorial inference. Everyday life abounds with examples, yet a literature of experimentation on the subject is virtually nonexistent. Without meaning to be flippant in illustration, we may take the heavily magical sphere of angling as a prime starting ground of examples. Consider the fly fisherman who is "learning" a stream, one of the principal components of which is learning to sort his flies into those that are "takers" on this stream and those that are not. His testing of instances consists of making a series of casts and determining whether the particular fly he is using will or will not raise a fish. If he is serious about his sport, his objective in learning is to be able to emerge with knowledge such as "a small pattern, tied sparsely, of a dark color, cast slightly upstream" will take fish (the presumed criterion) on Yellowjacket Brook. Consider what is involved in validation and what makes for ambiguous validation. There are some days when fish will rise to anything up to and including a discarded cigarette butt. There are other days when fish will rise for nothing that is offered. Somewhere between there are days when, to use the conventional phrase, the fish are "feeding selectively." Validation under these variable circumstances is hard to estimate. Is failure to get a strike on a particular fly an indication that the fly is inappropriate or simply that no fish are feeding that day? Does a strike mean that the fly used is in the category of "takers" or simply that the fish are striking at everything offered?

The essence of ambiguous validation is that the validating criterion provides uncertain information as in the example just cited. This may come about in one of two ways. The first is that the validating criterion—whether a pragmatic one, an official one, or what not—itself turns out to have a probabilistic relationship to the concept. Take the category "mentally ill" as a case in point. We seek prognostic signs of mental illness that may prove useful in predicting mental breakdown. Part of the difficulty in fixing upon useful anticipatory attributes of this sort is the difficulty of finding a validating criterion. Admission to a mental hospital? Clearly not, since many severe neurotics spend their lives without going into a mental hospital. Going to a psychiatrist for treatment? Again, the validating criterion is not certain, for many people seek the aid of a psychiatrist in times of personal troubles without being seriously ill and a good many neurotics avoid the psychiatrist on principle. Under these circumstances, one is faced with a category that is clearly accepted as "existing" by the society at large but about which there is a lack of full agreement concerning a properly valid criterion. As frequently happens, the consequences of the decision as to whether a particular person is or is not mentally ill are extremely grave, as in establishing responsibility for crimes or when it must be decided whether a will is valid or not. Under these circumstances societies maintain official organs for deciding. One must have recourse to a court of law.

A second condition of ambiguous validation is when the validating criterion is itself equivocal in the sense that it may not be clear whether it indicates one way or the other. The angling example given a moment ago is a sufficient illustration of this case. Does a strike or the absence of a strike provide sure information on whether or not a particular fly is a "taker"?

The effect of ambiguous validation on the process of concept attainment and concept utilization seems to be much as we have described it under conditions of reduced opportunity for or delay in validation. Quips about the fisherman being the easiest thing to catch are not without justification and the multimillion-dollar fishing-tackle industry is a tribute to the range of nonrational factors that affect the fisherman. The contending claims of laymen and experts alike concerning the predisposing factors leading to mental ailments bespeak the same type of failure to pin down the defining conditions associated with a category whose validating criterion is itself ambiguous.

One last matter remains in considering validation. It has to do with "direct" and "indirect" validation. By direct test we mean the chance to test one's hypothesis about what an exemplar of a category *is*. The child is seeking to find out what is meant by the concept "cat." An animal comes along. The child says, "That's a cat." The parent says either "yes" or "no." In either case, a direct test of the hypothesis has been made. An indirect test, of course, is the case in which the same child says, "Oh, that's not a cat." Again the parent will answer in the affirmative or negative. But the child's hypothesis about what a cat *is* will not be tested directly, only his residual hypothesis about what a cat *is not*. Note that this is not a matter of positive and negative instances. It refers to the direct or indirect test of an hypothesis, regardless of the negative or positive status of the instance that occurs.

Consider a simple experimental procedure used by Goodnow (1955a) in which the subject must bet either on the left key or the right key of a "two-armed bandit." He has an hypothesis that the right key will pay off. Each time, one or the other key pays off, so that which ever way he bets, he will know which one was correct. The subject has an hypothesis that the right key will pay off on the next trial. Under these circumstances, subjects prefer to "act out" their hypothesis by a choice of the right key, even though in doing so they risk losing by virtue of the fact that they have learned the left key does in fact pay off 70% of the time. To bet on the left and find that the right key paid off "does not give you the same information" as a straight choice of right, as one subject put it. We suspect that such indirect validation is more difficult for the subject because it requires transformation of information and risks the making of errors. Though the transformation is not great, the urge to avoid indirect tests may often lead to risk in the interest of making more direct tests. We will see later, particularly in Chapter 7, that under many conditions this feature of validation can be a critical factor in determining decisions about what instances to test next.

So much, then, for problems raised by the nature of validation. We turn next to the critical question of the consequences of categorizing events in one class or in another while one is in process of learning a category and after learning has been completed and the category is being used for grouping the environment.

The Anticipated Consequences of Categorizing. The point has already been made that learning a new category can be fruitfully conceived of as the making of a series of interrelated sequential decisions. These decisions include such matters as what instance to test next, or what hypothesis to adopt next. It is in decisions such as these that the anticipated consequences become of major importance.

We begin by stating some of the assumptions we make about the relations between decisions and their expected consequences. The first assumption, already implicit in much of the previous discussion, is that each step in a performance can be usefully regarded as a choice or decision between alternative steps. The second assumption is that in analyzing the expected consequences of a decision it is necessary to consider the expected consequences not only of the step taken by the decision-maker but also of the step he did *not* take. The third assumption is that the expected consequences of a decision can be analyzed into two components. The first is the *estimated likelihood of occurrence of alternative outcomes*. The second is the *value* placed by the decision-maker on anticipated outcomes. So much by way of introduction. We turn now to the application of these notions, taken principally from outside psychology, to the process of categorization.*

Consider first the question: what are the outcomes which have value for an individual in a concept-attainment situation? And how does the individual's performance reflect the value to him of certain kinds of outcome rather than others?

Which particular outcomes are valued depends essentially upon the objectives of the individual. Take as an example the objective of attaining a concept after encountering as few instances as possible. This is a common objective guiding subjects in their decisions about instances to test and hypotheses to try out. We may deliberately set this objective before them by insisting that the concept must be attained within a limited number of choices. Or we may say to a subject, often without realizing the consequences, "Try to discover the nature of the concept as quickly as you can." By either procedure we are telling the subject that *each encounter with an instance matters* and that as much information as possible must be extracted from each.

Suppose one is testing instances to find out whether or not they are exemplars of the concept one is trying to learn, as for example in the Vigotsky Test or the procedures used in the experiments to be considered in later chapters. One chooses an instance at the outset that turns out to be positive. It exhibits values of, say, six attributes. The next decision to be made by the person is: "What kind of instance to test next?"

This decision is informationally a crucial one. Concretely, shall the person choose an instance that is drastically different from the first positive instance encountered, or shall he choose one that differs only slightly? If our by now somewhat overworked foreigner had met first an influential person who was over 50, rich, Protestant, and aggressive, should he now ask to meet one who is over 50 but poor, Catholic, and meek? Or shall he choose a second case for testing who

---

* The reader familiar with economic theory will see immediately that there is a fair similarity between the assumptions made here and those made in many economic theories of choice (cf. Arrow, 1951). We have in fact derived much stimulation from such theories and especially from the arguments of Knight (1921), Shackle (1949), and Marschak (1950, 1954), who appear to us to be most aware of the psychological features of choice and decision-making.

differs in only one respect from the original influential person encountered? Let us suppose the individual chooses as his second instance one who differs in all respects save one from the previous positive instance. This is a desperate measure in the sense that, should the instance chosen turn out to be negative, it will provide the individual with little or no information. He will not know which one or ones of the many attributes changed made the instance negative. If, however, the instance chosen turns out to be positive, then in one fell swoop the individual will have learned that only the one attribute left unchanged really mattered as far as influence is concerned—a very big yield indeed.

In contrast, what are the consequences if the individual chooses as the second instance to test one which differs in only one respect from the previous positive instance? Whether it turns out to be positive or negative, one is assured of being able to use the information it provides. If positive, the one attribute changed does not matter; if negative, the one attribute changed does matter. Whatever the result, however, only one attribute will have been checked. If there are six or more attributes which may be defining, the task of solution will barely have begun.

Faced with the need to attain the concept within a limited number of instances encountered, which step will the individual take? Shall he choose as his next instance one which differs in all respects save one from the previous positive instance, or one which differs in only one respect? In other words, will he take a chance or adopt the slow-but-sure method?

Presented with such a question, the reader will surely demur: "It all depends upon whether the individual expects the next instance to turn out to be positive or negative." If he thinks the instance is more likely to be positive, then he will be more prone to take a chance and choose a second instance which differs a great deal from the previous positive one. But if he thinks it is very likely to be negative, then he will be more prone to take the surer step and choose an instance which differs little from the previous positive instance. As we shall see in the next chapter, this is how our subjects do decide between alternative steps. The precise results can be ignored for the moment. We wish in this chapter simply to make the point that the step taken or the decision made rests upon a resolution of expectations about the values of positive and negative outcomes and the likelihood of occurrence of each of these.

We have introduced this discussion of anticipated consequences and of expected values and likelihoods by reference to a concrete problem.

We wish now to talk about consequences in a more general and somewhat more formal manner. As our context, we take the case where the individual is presented with a choice of placing an object or event in one category or another under conditions of uncertainty, and we consider the consequences of placing the object or event in each category and being right or wrong in one's placement.

The basic device in such analysis is the *payoff matrix*. Suppose we start with as simple an example as possible: a psychophysical experiment in which a series of lines is being presented, each to be categorized as "long" or "short." The subject at the outset is given a reference line, 10 inches in length, all lines longer than which are to be called "long," all lines shorter to be called "short." The subject is told to be as careful as possible. He is told, moreover, that for every four short lines presented, there will be six long lines. The matrix can be specified as follows:

Anticipated Events and Outcome Values

Decision Alternatives	Longer Than 10 Inches	Shorter Than 10 Inches
Categorize as "long"	Good	Bad
Categorize as "short"	Bad	Good
Estimated likelihood of events	0.60	0.40

In this "accuracy" matrix, the outcome values of placement in either category are balanced. Categorizing correctly a line as "short" is as good as correctly categorizing it as "long." Both correct categories are equally valued, and both incorrect placements are equally negatively valued. Since the outcome values are balanced, we would expect to find that estimates of event probability would be the major factor biasing judgment whenever there is uncertainty. We would expect the subject in case of doubt to favor calls of "long," since he has been told that long lines are the more likely.

The fact of the matter is that the accuracy matrix with its balanced outcome values is only one of several highly interesting matrices that may govern categorizing decisions. Let us consider what the problems are like when the outcome values of placement in either category are not equal. There is, for example, a matrix that we have come to call a "sentry matrix" because it is so well illustrated by the plight of a sentry in a combat zone. A sentry is standing at his post. It is his task to categorize oncoming figures in the dark as friend or foe.

Enemy intelligence and reconnaissance have been so good that enemy and friend alike now know the password and it can no longer be used as a basis of discrimination. The sentry estimates that the chances of any given figure being friend or foe are 50:50. Two alternatives are available to him. He may categorize the approaching figure as a foe and open fire. Or he may categorize it as a friend and hold fire. We represent the matrix as follows:

Anticipated Events and Outcome Values

Decision Alternatives	Foe	Friend
Categorize "foe" and fire	Alive and highly regarded	Alive, regretful, but duty fulfilled
Categorize "friend" and not fire	Dead or wounded	Alive, but feels both lucky and neglectful
Estimated likelihood of events	0.50	0.50

This is a matrix where the events being equally likely we can expect the decisions to be biased by the unequal outcomes of placement in the two categories. If the sentry categorizes an approaching figure as foe and is correct, the outcome is highly favorable (alive and highly regarded); if incorrect, the outcome is not too bad (alive, regretful, but duty fulfilled). If the sentry categorizes an approaching figure as friend and is correct, the outcome is middling in value (alive, feels both lucky and neglectful); if incorrect, the outcome is highly unfavorable (dead or wounded). The outcome values are all in favor of categorizing an uncertain figure as foe and acting accordingly. It is small wonder that sentries are regarded as so dangerous to men returning from patrol.

We have chosen so far two simple cases of categorizing decision: one where the expected outcome values are balanced, and where the differences in expected event probabilities sway decision; the other, where expected event probabilities are balanced, and where differences in outcome values bias decision. One need not be limited to such simple cases. In general, the argument can be made that, when outcome values are equal for placement in one category or another, categorizing decisions will correspond to the expected event probabilities; and when outcome values are not equal, categorizing decisions will be biassed in the direction of the most favorable alternative. Experimental studies supporting this argument will be found in Chapter 7.

It must be noted, however, that we are always limited to statements about the *direction* that bias will take as long as we remain on the descriptive level. We can make no predictions about the *amount* of bias or departure from expected event probabilities that will occur. Predictions of amount call first for replacing our descriptive statements of value with numerical statements. Once such numerical values have been assigned, one can follow the traditional mathematical technique of multiplying outcome values by probability estimates to obtain a measure of "expected utility," and one can also argue for a general principle such as "maximizing utility" to determine which alternative should be chosen. There are, however, a number of problems in determining how the expected values of an outcome for any given individual can be quantitatively stated. Again, these questions are more fully discussed in Chapter 7. For the moment, we wish to anticipate the discussion only to the extent of stating our general conclusion. This is that we are not prepared to develop or to utilize as yet any formal or mathematical model to predict the effect of anticipated consequences on categorizing judgments. We have chosen to be satisfied with less precise prediction and to concern ourselves with the psychological questions which must eventually underlie any model. The most important of these questions concern the objectives determining outcome values and the conditions affecting an individual's estimate of event probability.

For all its present limitation, the concept of a payoff matrix is a useful and a suggestive one. In the first place, it suggests problems that have far too long been overlooked. Psychophysics, concerned as it is with the categorization of magnitudes, could well be reexamined for the manner in which outcome values and likelihood estimates affect categorizing behavior. It could, we believe, thereby be brought much closer to the judgmental behavior of people in everyday situations.

Analysis of the effects of anticipated consequences in terms of payoff matrices may also serve as a link between motivational states and judgmental behavior. Specifically, one's set in judging is partially describable in such terms. Again we may benefit by examining the judging acts that prevail in everyday life. One example is the personnel officer who must categorize applicants into "acceptable" and "unacceptable" groups and who is punished only when his incorrect categorization takes the form of classing as acceptable a man who later fails. The practices of the progressive school provide another example: there the child is rewarded for his correct categorizations only, the others being overlooked. The situation in the basic training camp is yet another example: only errors are noted and punished, correct acts are overlooked. Each time a subject walks into an experimental room, he imposes a payoff matrix on the situation the experimenter presents to him and often the experimenter needs to set him straight.*

The Nature of Imposed Restrictions. We end with what may seem like a trivial problem in comparison with the one just discussed: the restrictions imposed upon concept-attainment strategies by the nature of one's working conditions. But in fact, the topic is anything but trivial. Concretely, for example, does the individual have to work toward concept attainment without such external aids as paper and pencil? Does he encounter instances visually and concretely or must he work entirely from verbal descriptions of instances? Are the instances with which he must cope concrete and palpable such as the stimulus cards of the psychologist, or are they abstract and only to be inferred like the data of the modern physicist? These are among the things that comprise the conditions of work that impose restrictions on the manner of attaining a concept.

A few words about the problems involved will suffice to introduce the subject and to foreshadow later chapters. In so far as one is forced to operate entirely "in the head" in solving a concept—on a "mental problem" rather than one in which concrete instances must be sorted— one's method of proceeding may have to take into account the added strain in some way or other. One may literally have to throw away information and proceed more slowly if one is to succeed at all. Indeed, there are certain strategies of concept attainment that are "informationally wasteful" but which make it possible to work under a restricting work condition and we shall turn to these shortly. It has been our experience in studying the behavior of our subjects that people who have been trained in mathematics and theoretical physics, where systems of condensed notation make easy the task of carrying along a lot of information, frequently attempt solutions to conceptual problems that, while excellent in principle, cannot succeed because of the impositions they make upon memory.

More often, to be sure, ineffectiveness in concept attainment derives from the use of techniques that are too wasteful of information and do not utilize fully enough the cognitive capacities of our subjects. The

---

* An interesting example is provided in a recently reported experiment by Green (1955). His subjects operated in a kind of Skinner-box situation where, when a positive exemplar of a concept appeared, they were to hit a key as often as they could get points. The experimenter soon discovered that subjects had to be warned not to hit the key when a nonexemplar was shown. So long as there was no penalty for doing so they operated on the principle of not taking any chances: one *might* be wrong about an instance that seemed like a nonexemplar.

use of the dramatic instance as a basis for arriving at the definition of a concept, overextrapolation of attributes found useful in the past with a failure to adopt an adequate information-gathering strategy—these and various other lapses from cognitive rigor are more notable.

In the end, the question reduces to one of choosing a mode of attack that is appropriate to the restrictions imposed by the conditions of work provided. The point is a simple one and an obvious one. Its importance for conceptual activity will be apparent.

THE FOLLOWING CHAPTERS

We have perhaps strained the reader's patience by lingering so long in these opening chapters on the various ramifications and the conditions affecting the process of categorial inference. Our justification is threefold. Firstly, we wished to make it as clear as possible that the task of isolating and using a concept is deeply imbedded in the fabric of cognitive life; that indeed it represents one of the most basic forms of inferential activity in all cognitive life. Secondly, it was our wish to develop in some detail the great functional utility of this type of activity in the adjustment of organisms to their environment: the role of categorizing in the economy of knowing one's environment. And finally, perhaps of most importance, our object has been to sketch in outline some of the processes involved in pragmatically *rational* or *effective* behavior. Organisms do group the objects and events of their world into pragmatically useful concepts and they do so with regard to reality constraints. Psychology has been celebrating the role of "emotional factors" and "unconscious drives" in behavior for so long now that man's capacity for rational coping with his world has come to seem like some residual capacity that shows its head only when the irrational lets up. To account for the exquisite forms of problem-solving that we see in everyday life and may see in our laboratories any time we choose to give our subjects something more challenging than key-pressing to perform, highly simplified theories of learning have been invoked. One learns concepts by the association of external stimuli with internal mediating stimuli either by some simple law of frequency or contiguity or by a rather circular and overbegged law of effect. If we have at times portrayed conceptual behavior as perhaps overly logical, we will perhaps be excused on the ground that one excess often breeds its opposite. Man is not a logic machine, but he is certainly capable of making decisions and gathering information in a manner that reflects better on his learning capacity than we have been as yet ready to grant.

In the following four chapters our concern will center on a series of several dozen experimental studies of concept attainment and concept utilization, the result of a three-year program of experimentation constructed to help us understand what is involved when a person learns to group discriminably different things in his environment into equivalence classes and to recognize new members of these classes without any further learning.

CHAPTER **4**

Selection strategies
in concept attainment

Whenever one seeks to "find out some-
thing," one is immediately faced with deciding upon the order in
which to make one's inquiries. It is commonplace to remark that
some orders of inquiry are better than others. We say of a scientist's
research that it is a beautiful series of experiments, or of a lawyer that
he has mastered the art of asking questions. It is with the ordering of
inquiry, the steps in research or testing, that the present chapter is
concerned.

We begin with an example. A neurologist is interested in the
localization of pattern vision in monkeys. More specifically, he is
interested in six cortical areas and their bearing on pattern vision. He
knows that, with all six areas intact, pattern vision is unimpaired.
With all six areas destroyed, pattern vision is absent. His technique
of research is extirpation. In planning his research, how shall he
proceed? Destroy one area at a time? All but one at a time? In
what order shall he do his successive experiments?

The prime question is "What is to be gained by choosing one order
as compared to another order of testing instances?"

The first thing to be gained is, of course, an opportunity to *obtain
information appropriate to the objectives of one's inquiry*. One may
wish to choose an instance at any given point in concept attainment
that can tell one the most about what the concept might be. One
may seek to avoid redundant instances, or may want such an instance
for reassurance. It also happens that at different points in the choice
sequence negative and positive instances have different informative
value. By choosing instances in a certain order, it is possible for a
person to increase the chances of encountering a negative or a positive
instance when he needs them. This may seem at first to be absurd,

for how can a person choose a positive or a negative instance before he knows what the concept really is? Later, we will see that certain strategies guarantee that *within a set of choices* a person can assure such an encounter. To sum up, controlling the sequence of instances allows the person to ensure that the instances before him *contain appropriate information.*

A second benefit inherent in controlling the order of instances tested is *to increase or decrease the cognitive strain involved in assimilating information.* Ideally, instances should be chosen for test in such an order that whatever their potential informational value and whatever their status, whether positive or negative, their information can be assimilated without undue strain on memory or inference. There are several ways, as we shall see, in which the assimilability of information may be controlled by choosing instances in a certain order. A well-contrived order of choice—a good "selection strategy"—makes it easier to *keep track* of what hypotheses have been found tenable or untenable on the basis of information encountered. We shall have a great deal to say in later sections about this feature of selection strategies.

A third advantage is not at first obvious. By following a certain order of selecting instances for testing one *controls the degree of risk involved.* There are conservative orders and highly speculative ones. One may test instances in such an order as to guarantee that the concept will definitely be attained after a certain number of choices. But one may also choose instances in an order such that there is either the chance of very rapid attainment with good luck, or very slow attainment with bad. "Taking a flier" is within the power of the person who controls the order in which he will select instances. And by the same token, a safe course may be chosen.

In sum, selection strategies bestow three potential benefits upon their users:

   a. They increase the likelihood that instances encountered will contain appropriate information.
   b. They render less strainful the task of assimilating and keeping track of information.
   c. They regulate the amount of risk one will undergo in attaining a correct solution within a limited number of choices.

Before turning to an examination of the conditions that affect the adoption of various selection strategies, we must first examine four ideal selection strategies with respect to their usefulness in achieving the benefits just described.

IDEAL SELECTION STRATEGIES AND THEIR BENEFITS

We concentrate in this chapter on conjunctive concepts. Let us set before a subject all of the instances representing the various combinations of four attributes, each with three values—specifically, all the instances illustrated in Figure 1—an array of 81 cards, each varying in shape of figure, number of figures, color of figure, and number of borders. We explain to the subject what is meant by a conjunctive concept—a set of the cards that share a certain set of attribute values, such as "all red cards," or "all cards containing red squares and two borders"—and for practice ask the subjects to show us all the exemplars of one sample concept. The subject is then told that we have a concept in mind and that certain cards before him illustrate it, others do not, and that it is his task to determine what this concept is. We will always begin by showing him a card or instance that is illustrative of the concept, a positive instance. His task is to choose cards for testing, one at a time, and after each choice we will tell him whether the card is positive or negative. He may hazard an hypothesis after any choice of a card, but he may not offer more than one hypothesis after any particular choice. If he does not wish to offer an hypothesis, he need not do so. He is asked to arrive at the concept as efficiently as possible. He may select the cards in any order he chooses. That, in essence, is the experimental procedure.

There are four discernible strategies by which a person may proceed in this task. These we label the *simultaneous-scanning strategy*, the *successive-scanning strategy*, the *conservative-focusing strategy*, and the *focus-gambling strategy*. Let us describe each of these briefly and consider the manner in which each bestows upon its users the three benefits mentioned previously.

Simultaneous Scanning. In the present array (Figure 1), composed of instances that may exhibit any of three values of four different attributes, there are 255 possible ways of grouping instances into conjunctive concepts. A first positive card *logically* eliminates 240 of these, and the informational value of any other positive or negative card thereafter presented can similarly be described in terms of the remaining hypotheses that it logically eliminates. Now, simultaneous scanning consists in essence of the person using each instance encountered as an occasion for deducing which hypotheses are tenable and which have been eliminated. This is a highly exacting strategy, for the subject must deal with many independent hypotheses and carry these in memory. Moreover, the deductive process is exacting.

If the subject is able to follow the strategy successfully, his choice of next instances to test will be determined by the objective of eliminating as many hypothetical concepts as possible per instance chosen. Suppose, for example, that a subject in our experiment has narrowed the possible concepts down to three: the concept must either be all *red* cards, all cards with *circles,* or all cards with *red circles.* Prior choices have eliminated all other hypotheses. Since we are dealing with an ideal strategy here, let us also assume an ideal subject: a subject with perfect rationality and perfect discriminative capacities. Such a subject would certainly know how to avoid choosing redundant instances that eliminated no hypotheses. By choosing a card for testing that contained at least one of the two features, circles or red color, he would guarantee that the next instance encountered contained appropriate information. He would have to decide whether to choose an instance containing *one* of the relevant features or *both* of them: the next instance will contain a circle and no other relevant feature, contain red and no other relevant feature, or it will contain red circles. Consider now the consequences of each of these decisions for each of the three possible concepts:

Properties of Instance Chosen for Testing	If Correct Concept Is:		
	Red Only	Circle Only	Red Circle
Red only	Instance positive Eliminates: circle red circle	Instance negative Eliminates: red	Instance negative Eliminates: red
Circle only	Instance negative Eliminates: circle	Instance positive Eliminates: red red circle	Instance negative Eliminates: circle
Red and circle	Instance positive Eliminates: nothing	Instance positive Eliminates: nothing	Instance positive Eliminates: nothing

Such an analysis of the nine possible outcomes should suggest to the subject that his next choice should contain only one of the relevant attributes; at the least, such a choice will eliminate one hypothetical concept, at best two of them. To choose a card containing both relevant attribute values means that no information will be obtained regardless of what the correct concept is.

Now, if the subject can figure out the nine possible outcomes (and has enough time to do so), he will be able to make a wise decision about how next to proceed. The decision is important, for it will determine whether he will be able to solve the problem with one more choice; if these were expensive experiments rather than simple tests of the status of instances, the difference might be critical. But it is quite obvious that most human beings cannot or will not go through such an elaborate analysis of the situation in order to determine their best next step. Indeed, if there had been ten hypotheses still remaining in our example, the paper and pencil work involved in assessing next moves would have been prohibitive. So we can sum up by remarking that while it is possible in principle for the person using simultaneous scanning to plan the best next step, the task of guaranteeing *maximum* informativeness of a next choice is in practice too difficult to accomplish.

With respect to rendering easier the assimilation and retention of information contained in instances encountered, simultaneous scanning has little to recommend it. After each choice the subject must go through the difficult process of deducing which hypothetical concepts have been eliminated and carrying the result of these deductions in memory. There appears to be no means whereby simultaneous scanning can reduce this heavy load on inference and memory.

Nor does simultaneous scanning provide a way of regulating the riskiness of one's next choices—no practical way, at least. We shall leave the matter at that, hoping that it will become much clearer in a later section. The best one can do is to compute the riskiness of a choice by the method just outlined.

Successive Scanning. This strategy consists in testing a single hypothesis at a time. The subject has the hypothesis that *red* is the feature common to all correct cards, and chooses instances containing red in order to test whether they are positive instances. He goes on testing hypotheses until he hits the correct concept. The typical successive scanner then *limits his choices to those instances that provide a direct test of his hypothesis.*

Now it is quite apparent that such a technique for choosing instances cannot assure that the person will encounter instances containing the maximum information possible. That is to say, since instances are chosen only to test one hypothesis at a time, one is likely to choose logically redundant cards some feature of which has been used before to test some previous hypothesis. On this point more will be said later, for it is evident that this is much like discontinuity in learning.

It also follows that the strategy has little worth from the point of view of regulating risk. There is little the user can do either to take bigger gambles or lesser gambles in his choice of instances. His only possible maneuver here is a rather far-fetched one, but one that subjects nonetheless indulge in. This consists really of playing a guessing game with the experimenter in choosing an order of hypotheses to test. For example, subjects will often operate on the assumption that the experimenter is out to "trick" them and that, therefore, the correct concept cannot be a "simple" one, namely, that it will not be a single-attribute concept like "red" or "circles." In consequence, users of successive scanning begin, more frequently than would be expected by chance, by "guessing" that the hypothesis is defined by more than one attribute and choose cards to test such multiattribute hypotheses.

What then is served by the use of successive scanning? The gain is nearly all in the relief of cognitive strain. Limited inference is required and the principal strain on memory is to keep track of what hypotheses have already been tested and found wanting.

A closer examination of the manner in which strain on inference is reduced brings us directly to a most characteristic feature of cognitive activity which we shall encounter on subsequent occasions in analyzing the behavior of subjects in probability situations. It is this. Human subjects—and the same may be true of other species as well—prefer a direct test of any hypothesis they may be working on. To recall the meaning of direct test, a subject is faced with deciding whether a white door or a black door is the correct entrance to a reward chamber and adopts the hypothesis that the white door is correct. There are two ways of testing this hypothesis. The *direct way* is to try the white door. The *indirect way* is to try the black door. In a direct test, as we have noted, the knowledge obtained needs no further transformation for testing the hypothesis. White is either correct or incorrect. The indirect test requires a transformation: if the black door is correct, then the white door was not correct and therefore the hypothesis is wrong; if the black door is wrong then the white door must have been correct and the hypothesis is right. It may be that the reason for the preference for direct test is in the interest of cognitive economy: saving the person from having to transform his knowledge. Another possible explanation, one which does not preclude the first, is that we do not fully accept the possibilities of correctness and incorrectness being mutually exclusive. We have a backlog of experience in which it has not always followed that if white is correct black is wrong or vice versa. We have also experienced situations where more than two alternatives were possible, and only a direct test would be effective.*

In any case, when a subject behaves in the typical manner of the successive scanner and limits himself to testing instances directly related to his hypothesis, his behavior appears to follow the principle of direct test. In sum, then, successive scanning has little utility either in guaranteeing maximum informativeness of one's choices or in regulating risk. Its chief benefit is in the reduction of cognitive strain by limiting its user to direct test of hypotheses. As such, its principal utility may be as a procedure that is useful when the cognitive going gets rough or when one has good reason to believe that a particular hypothesis will turn out to be correct.

Conservative Focussing. In brief, this strategy may be described as finding a positive instance to use as a focus, then making a sequence of choices each of which alters but one attribute value of the first focus card and testing to see whether the change yields a positive or a negative instance. Those attribute values of the focus card which, when changed, still yield positive instances are *not* part of the concept. Those attribute values of the focus card that yield negative instances when changed *are* features of the concept. Thus, if the first positive card encountered contains three red circles with two borders (3RO2b), and if the concept is "red circles," the sequence of choices made would be as follows, each choice changing a *single* attribute value of the focus card:

3RO2b (+) focus card†
2RO2b (+) first choice: eliminate "three figures" as a relevant attribute value
3GO2b (−) second choice: retain "red" as a relevant attribute value
3R✚2b (−) third choice: retain "circle" as a relevant attribute value
3RO1b (+) fourth choice: eliminate "two borders" as a relevant attribute value

Ergo: concept is "red circles."

Note one thing. When a subject has changed an attribute value of the focus card and the new card chosen turns out to be positive, this result logically eliminates the attribute in question from consideration. *No* value of such an attribute can be relevant to the concept. The subject need not sample any further values of it.

Several other features of this strategy are especially noteworthy.

---

* It is of interest that the first experiment which drew attention to a preference for direct test—in the form of participant behavior—used a situation where more than two alernatives were possible (Heidbreder, 1924).

† The symbol (+) denotes a positive instance; (−) a negative instance.

From the point of view of guaranteeing that each instance encountered be informative, the strategy does just that. By following it, redundancy can be completely avoided. The strategy guarantees, moreover, that each instance be encountered will contain a "safe maximum" of information, as we will see when the risk-regulating property of the strategy is examined below.

The benefits in cognitive economy to be gained by using this strategy are striking. The first of these is that by its use the subject is enabled to disregard completely the bewildering business of eliminating possible hypotheses from the domain of 255 possible concepts in terms of which he may group instances. For in fact, the technique is designed to *test the relevance of attributes*. Given an initial positive card, his choices are designed to consider the four attribute values of the focus card one at a time to see which of these may be eliminated. In the present example there are four single attribute values to be considered, much less than the 15 rather complex hypotheses that would have to be considered in simultaneous scanning. A second contribution of this strategy to cognitive economy is that it guarantees that the relevance of all attribute values in the focus card will be *tested relatively directly*. If a change in an attribute value of the focus instance makes a difference, then that attribute value of the focus is relevant; if not, it is irrelevant. A third benefit is more subtle. By choosing a particular positive instance as a focus, the person *decreases the complexity and abstractness of the task* of keeping track of information he has encountered. All subsequent choices and their outcomes can be referred back to this focus instance much as if it were a score card. The attributes of the focus card are ticked off on the basis of subsequent tests.

There is one notable disadvantage to the strategy from the point of view of cognitive economy. Unless the universe of instances to be tested is arrayed in an orderly fashion so that a particular instance may be easily located on demand, the task of search imposed on the user of conservative focussing may become rather severe. We shall see examples of this disadvantage later.

Now for risk regulation. The expression "conservative focussing" has been chosen with good reason. Every choice is safe, safe in the sense that it logically guarantees the presence of information in the instance chosen for testing. This guaranteed information is not the maximum possible. On the other hand, the choice never carries the risk of yielding *no* information. We have already noted that by following the strategy, the subject will never choose a redundant instance, one that carries no new information. To understand fully why it is that a chosen instance almost never contains the maximum amount of information possible, we must turn to a consideration of focus gambling.

Focus Gambling. The principal feature of this strategy is that the subject uses a positive instance as a focus and then changes *more than one* attribute value at a time. In the present array (Figure 1) from which our examples are drawn, the subject might change two or three attribute values at once. This may not seem very different from conservative focussing, but a closer examination will make clear that it is. In particular, several features of focus gambling are of interest from the point of view of the risk-regulating nature of a strategy, and these we shall consider first.

In most tasks involving concept attainment, whether in the laboratory or in everyday life, one objective is to get the job done in as few choices or tests as possible, particularly if choices or tests are costly. It is always possible, given the use of conservative focussing, to complete the job with only as many tests as there are attributes to be tested. Focus gambling provides a way of attaining the concept in *fewer* trials than this limit. But in doing so it also imposes a risk. The risk is this. By using the strategy, one *may* succeed in attaining the concept in fewer test choices than required by conservative focussing. But the strategy also *may* require many more test choices than this. If one is in a position to take such a risk—the risk that solution may be very fast, very slow, or in between—then focus gambling is an admirable procedure. Such a position would be one where, presumably, quick solution paid off very handsomely compared to the losses to be suffered by slow solution.

It can readily be seen how the gambling feature is built into this interesting strategy. Again consider an example. Our subject as before takes as his focus the first positive card given him as an example: three red circles with two borders (3RO2b). Rather than change only *one* attribute value of this focus, he will take a flier and change *three* of them. Let us say then that his next choice is 3G✛1b. Now, if the change should "make no difference," i.e., if the instance chosen is still positive, then the concept must be that attribute value shared by the positive focus card and the next card chosen (also positive): namely, "three figures." In one fell swoop, the user of this strategy has eliminated three attributes and attained the concept. Similarly, if two attributes of the focus are changed and a positive instance still results, then the two changed attributes are eliminated. So far, the strategy seems riskless enough.

The difficulty arises when a change in more than one attribute of the focus yields a *negative* instance. For when this happens, the only way in which a person can assimilate the information contained in the instance is to revert to the method of simultaneous scanning: to use the instance as an aid to eliminating possible hypotheses. This has the effect, of course, of diminishing drastically the economical nicety of a focus-gambling strategy. It is now no longer possible to proceed by testing *attributes* for their relevance. Instead, one must deal with *hypothesis elimination* by the method described in connection with simultaneous scanning or throw away the potential information contained in negative instances.

From the point of view of guaranteeing that instances chosen contain new information, focus gambling does not have the feature that makes conservative focussing notable. It does not guarantee that redundant instances will be avoided. For in so far as the person using this procedure does not use the information contained in negative instances, he is likely to, and frequently does, choose instances in the course of solution that contain the same information that might have been assimilated from such prior negative instances.

Finally, with respect to making the cognitive task of information assimilation easier, the strategy has most of the features of conservative focussing. One does not have to consider the full array of possible hypothetical concepts (unless one wishes to utilize the information of negative instances). It is geared to the testing of attributes in the focus card rather than to hypothesis elimination in the pure sense. It also provides for direct testing of hypotheses about the relevant attributes. As before, it reduces complexity by the use of a focus instance as a "score card." But it is lacking in economical benefits whenever negative instances occur. The user can do nothing with these unless he shifts strategy. And there is a temptation to do just this. Finally, the strategy also has the fault of requiring a considerable amount of search-behavior if one is to find appropriate instances to test.

CONDITIONS AFFECTING USE OF SELECTION STRATEGIES

The remainder of this chapter is given over to a series of experiments investigating the conditions that lead intelligent adult subjects to utilize variants of one or another of the four selection strategies just outlined. A word about why certain conditions were selected for investigation is in order.

Three objectives of selection strategies have been described: guaranteeing that instances chosen contain potential information to be assimilated, rendering the assimilation of this information cognitively less strainful, and regulating risk. The experiments to be presented have been designed with a view to *altering the exigency* of each of these objectives, the last two of them directly, the first indirectly.

Consider first the reduction of cognitive strain in assimilating and keeping track of information. Suppose we take a subject attempting to attain a concept with all of the instances arrayed before him in an orderly fashion so that at any time he may refer to these for orientation. Let us compare his performance when he works with an ordered array of instances always perceptually available with the condition where he must attain a concept without the array before him, i.e., do the problem "in his head." Instances are chosen in the same way, save that instead of pointing to one, the subject must name one from memory. The usual guidance is given to him with respect to whether the card he has chosen verbally is positive or negative. Now, in the first case, the strain of the task—given the constant display of the instances—is less than in the second case. The problem in the second case is for the subject to keep in mind all instances and to bear in mind which instances chosen have been positive and which negative. This task is greatly aided in the first case by having the instances there to refer to. In sum, a subject working "in his head" must find some means of reducing cognitive strain; at least this is more of a problem than it is for a subject working "on the board." It would be reasonable to expect that the strategies would differ: that those who work "in the head" will be more likely to adopt a strategy imposing minimum strain. In doing so, they may, moreover, neglect the first objective of a selection strategy: to guarantee that instances chosen be potentially informative.

Or take a second example. Suppose subjects work under one of two conditions. Either the array of instances is arranged in an orderly fashion with all like cards together, as in the tidy array of Figure 1, or the cards are arrayed in an order determined by a table of random numbers, so that any given card may be next to any other given card without respect to the attribute values they possess. Again, under these circumstances, the latter condition would be more strainful from the point of view of "keeping track" of what instances had been tested. In addition, the random order would impose difficulties in searching out specific instances to test. Again we might expect differences, those working under the second condition perhaps being more oriented to reducing both cognitive strain and the time used in the search of instances.

Or consider the difference between subjects working with abstract materials of the kind we have been describing and those working with concrete or "thematic" materials in which the task is not to group by color, shape, etc., but according to different types of human situations possessing comparable attributes. In the latter case the subject will be far likelier to have more "prepared" or conventional hypotheses about what kinds of grouping are relevant. Might one not expect that under the latter conditions subjects would be tempted to proceed by what in essence is the easy technique of successive scanning?

Turn now to the matter of risk regulation. Suppose we compare a scientist who has a permanent post and a long-range opportunity for testing out a series of ideas about some complex problem with one who has very limited time and resources and can test only a few of his ideas. It is likely that the latter will undertake more risky experiments than the former—given that the two are of equal imaginativeness and ability. A comparable case can be constructed in concept attainment. Compare two subjects attempting to solve a problem, one given an unlimited number of choices, the other drastically limited in the number of choices he can make. Will the second adopt a more risky strategy than the first?

Or suppose one could arrange to parallel the condition found in everyday life where the testing of instances on the way to solution of a conceptual problem may be costly. In any given enterprise, this testing cost is usually balanced against the gains to be achieved by final solution of the problem. This too can be paralleled. We may then pit testing cost against outcome gain and inquire about the changes in strategy that will occur. Certainly we may expect some differences in riskiness of strategy and in effectiveness.

Finally, it is a common observation that a long streak of good luck may be a fine antidote to caution. Put more formally, if a person is given a prolonged exposure to success in solving conceptual problems, will he be more likely to show an increasing tendency to attempt risky strategies?

What has been set forth in the foregoing is a summary of the experiments with which the remainder of the chapter will be concerned.

ALTERING COGNITIVE STRAIN

"In-the-Head" Versus "On-the-Board.* Twelve Harvard undergraduates served as subjects in a pilot experiment to be described here. The purpose of the study was to see how various strategies fare when they are used in situations of increasing cognitive strain.

---

* Dr. Robert V. Seymour aided in the formulation, design, and running of this experiment and furnished many of the basic ideas used in the analysis of results.

Each subject was presented a large board containing the orderly array of 81 instances shown in Figure 1. Each instance contained a value of each of the four attributes. The cards are arranged, as the reader can see, in such a way that there was no difficulty locating any particular one that the subject might wish to choose for testing. As in all of the experiments considered in this volume, no "trickery" was employed in explaining the task. The subject was told that he would be shown a particular card which would exemplify a concept that the experimenter had in mind—a positive instance of the concept. The meaning of a concept (a conjunctive concept, more precisely) was carefully explained: a way of grouping the cards in terms of some shared characteristic or characteristics like "all red cards" or "all cards with green squares." The subject was told that it was his task to pick cards one after another and after each choice we would tell him whether the card chosen was positive or negative, i.e., whether it exemplified or did not exemplify the correct concept. He was told to feel free to venture a guess about the concept any time he chose to, although we would limit him to one guess per choice. "Of course, try to go about the job as efficiently as you can," each subject was told, although no great emphasis was placed upon the matter and no further mention was made of it, except by subjects themselves who were mindful of their own efficiency.

Each subject, tested individually, was given three problems to solve. The board containing all 81 instances was before him during the first two problems, and then the board was removed and he was told that the last one would be done without it. The idea, let it be said, provoked a certain amount of groaning. As one would expect, subjects did markedly better on the average for the first two problems than for the last one. But this is a superficial observation. Let us examine the matter at a deeper level.

First as to strategies employed. The two principal modes of attack were modified forms of the conservative-focussing and the successive-scanning strategies. These modifications are quickly described and are interesting in their own right. A principal modification of conservative focussing can be summed up in the phrase "thirst for confirming redundancy." The subject chooses a focus, then chooses alterations of it for testing. Rather than alter an attribute value of the focus only once which is all that is necessary to establish whether the attribute in question is relevant to the concept or not, subjects sometimes have a tendency to test a second alteration. For example, if the focus card has "two *red* squares with one border" the subject will first choose a card with "two *green* squares with one border" which, let us say, turns out to be positive (indicating that color is not a feature of the concept). Instead of going on to test another attribute, he may attempt to make doubly sure and on his next choice pick "two *black* squares with one border." This choice is redundant, but it is apparently comforting. The reader will readily recognize this behavior as another example of what we described earlier as the *need for direct test:* rather than discard "black" by logical elimination (an indirect method), the subject expends a choice on a redundant instance for the assurance of direct test. This feature of strategic behavior is not, however, disruptive of the strategy nor does it place any added strain on the problem-solver. If one looks at it in terms of a *quid pro quo,* the subject is willing to increase the number of tests he will make for the satisfaction he achieves in performing a direct test as a double check. As we shall see in a moment, this form of double checking may prove particularly comforting when the going gets rough.

The second modification of conservative focussing concerns a changed conception of the focus with subsequent choices. Recall that the pure form of the strategy calls for choosing cards that hold all but one of the attribute values of an initial positive card constant on each choice. In practice, this is not always done. Instead, the subject ceases to attend to those attributes of the focus card that have proved irrelevant when he makes new choices of instances to test. In choosing new instances, he does not hold these irrelevant values of the focus card constant any longer. Only those attributes that have already proved relevant or that have not yet been tested are now held constant. In a sense, this modification of the strategy consists of reducing the focus to those features of it that still count.

The chief modification in the successive-scanning strategy used by our subjects consisted in adding a memory feature to it. Instead of testing an hypothesis against chosen instances until it was found wanting and then going on to test another hypothesis *de novo* in the same way, subjects tried to remember the status of as many past instances encountered as possible so that they would not be starting from scratch in testing a second hypothesis. Thus, though they would pick cards to test the hypothesis "all red cards," they would try to remember the other values of these cards when they shifted to testing, say, "squares with two borders." In point of fact, they were combining features of simultaneous scanning and successive scanning. They were able to operate in this way with moderate effectiveness as long as the array of instances was both orderly and perceptually available.

Now we turn to the behavior of our subjects. Seven of them developed a variant of focussing strategy while working with the first two "on-the-board" problems. The remaining five adopted a variant of successive scanning with the added feature of trying to capitalize on their ability to remember the status of instances previously encountered.* Of the seven focussers, five showed no decline in effectiveness when it became necessary for them to work problems "in their head." The sixth showed the need for "direct test" in the sense of not being willing to eliminate attribute values on logical grounds but preferring to test them directly. In all six cases, performance was orderly and governed nicely by the use of a focus. The seventh case represented a typical failure of memory: forgetting what the values of the focus card were. His performance, once this failure had occurred, was a combination of hacking around for a new focus and utter confusion.

The history of the scanners was not so fortunate. The modified strategy they had developed made heavy demands upon memory in order that as much information as possible be brought to bear on each new hypothesis. Four of the five scanners came to ruin when they had to do problems "in their head." They were confused, made errors such as choosing redundant cards, and generally turned in a muddled performance. The fifth scanner discovered focussing in attempting to work the third problem in his head and turned in a faultless performance, with a pattern of choices conforming exactly to ideal focussing.

The difference between the groups—scanners and focussers—was striking from the point of view of choices required. To solve the "in-the-head" problem, scanners required a median of 13 choices; focussers only five. The median number of redundant choices made by focussers was one; by scanners six. The scanners repeated a median of four choices; the focussers only one. To understand these differences fully, they must be compared with the performance of the two groups on the second "on-the-board" problem (after they had had some experience in the situation, but with the cards arrayed before them). As we have just noted, the median number of choices

---

* A focusser was defined as a subject whose choices in the main varied only in one attribute value from those attribute values of the focus card that had been found relevant or were still untested. The only other types of choices permitted subjects in this group were redundant choices where the third value of an attribute was checked, or focus-gamble choices shown by later choices to be utilized as such. When the majority of the choices was of these types, the subject was considered a focusser. All others were treated as scanners.

required for solving the in-the-head problem was 13 for the scanners. This was an increase over the median of ten choices needed by these same subjects for solving the second problem with the cards before them. No such increase characterized the focussers. They required a median of five choices for the in-the-head problem, and five choices for the problem with cards present. The same pattern characterized the median number of redundant choices made: four and six for the second and third problems done by scanners; one and one for the focussers. Choice repetition rarely occurred in any subjects when the instances were present before them.

To sum up, modified focussing strategy is more efficient than modified scanning for attaining concepts when the instances are perceptually unavailable. Its superiority over scanning rests in its relative freedom from exacting memory and inference demands. The superiority becomes the more marked when the amount of cognitive strain inherent in the task is increased. Scanners show a decrement in quality of performance under more difficult conditions; focussers show little or no change.

The general conclusion we wish to draw is a simple one. Certain strategies are less strainful than others in terms of the demands they place on memory and upon inference. The form of modified conservative focussing used by some of our subjects makes fewer demands than the memory-dependent variant of successive scanning used by others. One can rate situations as well as strategies in terms of the general demands that they make upon the problem-solver's memory and inference capacities. Working on problems with orderly visual aids before one imposes less general strain than does work of a similar nature where there are no visual aids and everything must be done in the head. Thus we can speak of the intrinsic strain imposed by a strategy and the extrinsic strain imposed by a general working situation. The more strainful a strategy, the less good it is likely to be in a strainful situation. The strategy that works relatively well when a situation makes few general cognitive demands may prove beyond a person's capacity when the general cognitive going becomes rough.

*Ordered Versus Random Arrays.** We turn now to our next exploratory experiment on the effects of increasing the general cognitive stress imposed on a problem-solver by the nature of the situation in which he must work. The condition investigated was the orderliness

---

* The experimental findings and, in the main, the interpretations reported in this section are drawn from Robert V. Seymour (1954).

of an array of instances that a subject had to work with in attempting to attain a concept.

The experiment may be quickly summarized, for the procedures involved are similar to those already described. Two groups of 15 subjects each, advanced undergraduates and graduate students in Harvard University, were set the task of attaining concepts by the selection method. That is to say, an array of instances was placed before them and they were told that a card exemplifying a concept would be shown them. After that their task was to select cards on the board for testing. Each time a card was selected, the experimenter would tell them whether or not it exemplified the concept. Each subject, tested separately, worked four problems in this way.

The array before them was made up of instances each exhibiting one of two possible values of six attributes. Each card contained two figures, a large one on the left and a small one on the right. The six attributes and their values were as follows:

1. Shape of the large figure: rectangle or triangle.
2. Color of the large figure: yellow or black.
3. Border of the large figure: present or absent.
4. Shape of the small figure: rectangle or triangle.
5. Color of the small figure: yellow or black.
6. Border of the small figure: present or absent.

Out of these six attributes, each with two values, 64 instances could be constructed. One card, for example, might contain a large black rectangle with a border and a small yellow triangle without a border; another, a large yellow rectangle with a border and a small yellow triangle also with a border.

In carrying out his task, the subject was told that he might have as many choices as he needed and as much time as he needed, but that he should try to attain the concept in as few choices as he could. No such aids as paper and pencil were provided. The subject was told that he might venture a guess whenever he wished to about the nature of the concept but that he was allowed only one guess after each choice. After each choice, the experimenter indicated to the subject simply whether the card was "correct" or "incorrect" in the sense of exemplifying the concept or not.

The only difference between the two groups of 15 subjects was in the arrangement of the cards on the board before them. In each case, the board had the identical 64 cards laid out in eight columns and eight rows. The Random Group had the cards arranged on the board in a random manner, each card being assigned at random to one of the 64 positions on the board. In presenting the board to the subject, of course, no comment was made about the nature of its arrangement.

The arrangement of the cards for the Ordered Group was very orderly indeed. All cards with large black figures occupied the first four rows; those with large yellow figures occupied the remaining four rows. Cards with small black figures were placed in the first four columns and those with small yellow figures in the next four columns. Each shape and each kind of border were further arrayed in a prearranged pattern within this general ordering. The consequence of this ordering was that any two cards that neighbored each other on the board differed from each other in only one attribute value.

In general appearance, the ordered board was perceptually tidy; the random board resembled a rather wild patchwork quilt. However, it was no problem for the subject to tell a yellow from a black, a large figure from a small, a rectangle from a triangle, or a figure with a border from one without. All the relevant characteristics were highly visible and readily discriminable.

The question we were asking was this. What kinds of strategies would the two groups of subjects adopt? The Random Group was faced with an array of instances whose arrangement gave little or no visual support to the subjects in the task of sorting out positive from negative instances in order to attain the correct concept. One would expect that members of the Random Group might develop the least cognitively strainful strategy commensurate with the demand to acquire information efficiently. Certainly conservative focussing effects great cognitive economies and might have served well for dealing with such a random array of instances save for two disadvantages. The first of these was that focussing of any kind—whether conservative or risky—required that the subject be able to locate the specific instances needed for testing: instances that differed from the original focus card in oṇly certain attribute values. This was difficult to do on a scrambled board where any instance might appear in any of the 64 positions on the board. A second disadvantage of focussing in this situation was that it was relatively difficult to keep in mind which of the six attributes had been tested and which found relevant, for the process of scanning the board for appropriate instances to test exposed the subject to such an array of varied instances that retroactive interference might hinder remembering what he had done and found on previous choices.

There was another consideration. The demand upon the subject as far as informational efficiency was concerned was not very great in this situation. He was told that his task was to attain the concept with as few choices as possible. We shall see in a following section that his requirement for maximizing the informational yield of each choice can be made considerably more stringent. Under the circumstances of the experiment we are describing, the pressure toward efficiency might not have been great enough to lead the subject to organize his choice behavior to the point required by a focussing strategy.

Finally, the perceptual structure of the random board was not such as to lead to systematic testing of attributes. The orderly relationship between instances was not marked, and it is precisely orderly relationship that makes a focussing strategy most feasible.

A reconsideration of the "best strategy" for the Random Group does not, then, lead so readily to the conclusion that conservative focussing is ideal. Indeed, it may well be that under the circumstances imposed, a still less demanding strategy might be predicted. The only less demanding strategy is, of course, some variant of pure successive scanning with a minimum of reliance on memory for past instances. In any case, any prediction one makes cannot be rigorous save that one would expect a subject in the Random Group to adopt a less strainful strategy than a colleague in the Ordered Group.

The situation with respect to the Ordered Group was quite different. The cards were arranged to emphasize the orderly combining of attribute values. Any instance a subject chose to test could be readily found. He could easily keep tract *in spatial terms* of what instances were tested. If anything, we should expect subjects to be led into a focussing strategy.

So much for prediction. What actually happened was rather clear-cut. Members of the Ordered Group took an average of 6.1 choices to attain the correct concept, while those in the Random Group required an average of 10.4 choices per problem, a highly reliable difference. If a subject used an ideal conservative focussing strategy, he should be able to attain the concept in six choices, since there were six attributes to be tested for relevance. The score of the Ordered Group strongly suggests that conservative focussing was being used by these subjects; not so, however, in the case of subjects in the Random Group.

To be sure, all members of the Ordered Group did not complete all of their problems in precisely six choices. If we consider the average number of trials on the four problems required by each subject in this group, we find that 7 of the 15 subjects had an average of *fewer* than six trials (in no case less than 5.0). This was accounted for by the fact that subjects in this group were often able to guess successfully, or even to solve the problem logically, in fewer than the six trials required by conservative focussing. Successful guesses came about when, in using a focussing strategy, the subject would determine, say, three or four relevant attribute values of the focus and then guess these as the concept. The chances of successful guessing under the circumstances are high. Sometimes a subject was able to eliminate more than a single attribute value of the focus by recourse to focus gambling on a given choice. Both these tendencies led to attainment at a faster rate than could be achieved by ideal conservative focussing.

It is interesting that in the case of the Random Group only two subjects showed an average number of trials to attainment at, or less than, the minimum required by conservative focussing. One of these conformed fully to ideal conservative focussing; another one went so far as to try some focus gambling with some success. As for the others, their average number of choices on the four problems varied from 7.0 at the lowest to 16.2 at the highest.

The difference in strategy can be isolated in terms of several critical variables. The first of these is with reference to the first choice made by a subject following the presentation of the first positive card—the illustrative positive card given at the outset to the subject that is amenable to use as a focus. In how many attribute values did the subject's first choice differ from the first positive card shown him? In the case of the Ordered Group, the average number of attribute values distinguishing a first choice and the first positive card given was 1.1. The corresponding figure for the Random Group was 1.8. Of the 15 members of the Ordered Group 11 made a first choice that varied only one attribute from the first focus card on *all four* of their problems. The same thing was done by only one member of the Random Group: the ideal conservative focusser we have mentioned. The Ordered Group, in sum, was strongly oriented toward the first focus card, while the Random Group was considerably less so. It would be incorrect to say that they were not oriented toward this first positive card at all; chance selection of a first card would yield an average change from the focus of 3.2 attribute values.* The fact that the observed change is significantly lower is not, however, a

---

* In an array such as this one, the 63 cards left after 1 card has been indicated as an initial positive exemplar distribute as follows: 6 differ from the focus in one attribute, 15 in two, 20 in three, 15 in four, 6 in five, and 1 in six attributes.

function of focussing behavior. More likely it comes from the fact that members of the Random Group were doing successive scanning: deriving an hypothesis from the first positive card and then choosing cards to test the hypothesis directly. This means that their first choice would differ less from the first positive card than would be expected by chance.

Another measure of the difference between the groups is in the number of choices made that were more like the original focus card than like any other preceding card chosen. We may examine this by asking in each case which of the preceding cards encountered including the illustrative card has the largest number of attributes in common with a present choice. Where two preceding cards have equal similarity to a present choice, let us count the one encountered earlier as being the more similar. In ideal conservative focussing, of course, the original focus card will always be most similar to each choice.

In focus gambling, the array of choices made will not all be most similar to the original focus. Several preceding choices will share honors with this original focus card. So too in successive scanning. We may ask, on each problem, how many different preceding cards turned out to have the status of being "most similar" to subsequent choices. The more a strategy approaches ideal conservative focussing, the closer this figure will be to 1.0 per problem. Deviations in the direction of focus gambling or successive scanning will move it away from this value. The figures for the two groups—an average per problem for the four problems—were 1.7 instances for the Ordered Group, 3.6 instances for the Random Group. Perhaps a simple way of summing up the matter is to say that nine in every ten choices made by the Ordered Group had the original focus as a most similar preceding instance, whereas only three-quarters of the choices made by the Random Group could be so characterized.

The Ordered Group, in short, was sticking very closely to the original focus card in making subsequent choices. The Random Group was not. In so far as other instances than the original focus were in the position of being most similar to subsequent choices, this tended to occur in the Ordered Group by virtue of attempts at focus gambling. Most of the random subjects showed this tendency as a result of successive scanning.

With respect to redundant choices made, again a striking and reliable difference is noted between the groups. The average number of redundant choices per problem for the Ordered Group was 1.0. The corresponding figure for the Random Group was 4.1. The chief cause of redundant choice in the Ordered Group differs interestingly from that of the Random Group. In the former, redundant choices were encountered as a result of unlucky excursions into focus gambling. It comes about this way. A subject chooses a card that alters, say, two of the attributes of the focus in an effort at gambling. The instance turns out to be negative, indicating that either one or both of the attributes changed is relevant. Unless the subject uses simultaneous scanning for the rest of his choices, he cannot determine whether one, the other, or both attribute values changed are the relevant ones. So he goes back to changing *both* attribute values of the original focus one at a time. In so doing, he is logically bound to choose a redundant card. For the two-attribute change that leads to a negative instance logically contains the information that will be present in one of the two successive single-change choices of the same attribute values. A redundant choice is bound to occur. The only reason this hapless technique does not drive up the number of choices required by the Ordered Group is that likely as not the changing of more than a single attribute value at a time leads to the selection of a positive card, which allows one to eliminate *both* the attribute values changed at once. By virtue of this, one gets the problem solved in fewer choices.

The redundant choices of the Random Group are on the whole of the kind one expects from successive scanning. Instances are chosen to test an hypothesis. After the hypothesis is rejected by infirming information, a new hypothesis is adopted and instance chosen to test it. In the course of testing the second hypothesis, instances are chosen that contain no information beyond what could have been derived from the instances previously encountered. Hence the redundancy. The only way to avoid such redundancy would be to rely on the memory-and-inference pattern of simultaneous scanning. This our subjects were unable to do.

A last indication of the difference between the groups is in the number of *incorrect* hypotheses offered. The averages per problem were 0.5 per subject in the Ordered Group; 1.4 for the Random Group. The difference is also qualitative in nature. The focussers of the Ordered Group would sometimes guess incorrectly when they had limited the number of relevant attributes to what appeared a "reasonable" number. That is to say, they would determine that three particular attribute values of the focus were relevant or determine that three were irrelevant. In either case they would be tempted to guess that the three found relevant up to this point defined the concept. This is a good guess, of course, and worth the small risk of being wrong. Often, it turned out well.

In the Random Group guessing of wrong hypotheses characteristically occurred when the subject was testing an hypothesis and found that several instances in a row confirmed it. The reader will recognize that in such an array as the one employed, involving six attributes, such a procedure is not likely to lead to a very high proportion of correct guesses. It is not surprising then that the number of incorrect guesses about the concept was reliably higher in the Random than in the Ordered Group.

What may we conclude from this experiment? Perhaps the first conclusion is that the type of strategy adopted in a given situation reflects the nature of the situation. The successive scanning of the Random Group, aided by what additional remembering a subject could muster, was well suited to the requirements of the task. That is not, of course, meant as "praise" for the performance of these subjects. It is meant as a recognition of the fact that in a cognitively stressful situation, they adopted a strategy that made few additional demands on cognitive effort. By doing so, they gave up a certain degree of information-getting efficiency. Similarly, the strategy of the Ordered Group again suggests a nice adaptation to the structure and requirements of the testing situation. Strategies were used that took advantage of the orderly arrangement of instances. Indeed, the interesting mixture of conservative and risky focussing undertaken also showed a nice adaptation to the fairly ambiguous requirement that they "try to attain the concept in as few instances as they could."

Abstract and Thematic Materials.[*] Both commonplace observation and experimental studies on reasoning suggest that most human beings perform logical operations with more confidence and precision when the material about which they must reason is concrete. The often quoted studies by Wilkins (1929) and Eidens (1929) are a case in point. In these experiments, deduction tasks were set up in parallel form: one set couched in the A's and B's of the logician, the other in the concrete language of experience. Take, for example, the four following propositions which were found to yield the typical deductions noted next to each.

Proposition	Typical Deduction
If all A are B	then all B are A
If no A are B	then no B are A
If some A are B	then some B are A
If some A are not B	then some B are not A

---

[*] We are indebted to Robert V. Seymour for assistance in the experiment reported in this section.

Only the second and third deductions are, of course, correct. What is immediately quite striking is that the errors committed in the first and fourth examples seem quite unthinkable when we examine concrete instances of these propositions. It is not likely that many people would deduce from "All men are mammals" the conclusion that "All mammals are men." Nor will we be led from "Some men are not criminals" to the conclusion that "Some criminals are not men." It would appear as if the common sense embodied in language or in experience had the effect of guiding one to the reasonable conclusion—a form of guidance not present when we try to cope with the A's, B's, p's, and q's of formal logic. When we are dealing in the concrete realm, verisimilitude provides a way of checking upon validity.

But such an appearance of truth may also predispose us to accept invalid arguments. The psychological literature on thinking abounds in examples of such "biassing" of arguments. Conclusions that are preferred in the sense of being most congruent with one's own attitudes and values will often be reached in spite of the fact that they are both incorrect logically and readily detectable as such when they appear in a neutral form. The experiments of Morgan and Morton (1944), of Janis and Frick (1943), and particularly the carefully designed study of Thistlethwaite (1950) all point to this phenomenon as a general one in thinking.

What does it mean to say that, on the one hand, people escape certain logical errors when they have the guidance of common experience and, on the other, that common experience has the effect of producing certain preferential forms of error? To us, it suggests that much of human reasoning is supported by a kind of thematic process rather than by an abstract logic. The principal feature of this thematic process is its pragmatic rather than its logical structure. It consists of a tendency to work with and to prefer empirically reasonable propositions, whether as hypotheses or as conclusions. One might well call the tendency an "effort after empirical verisimilitude."

The history of science provides many rueful examples of the "logic of verisimilitude" and one of these serves us well as an introduction to the experiment to be reported in this section. The incident in question occurred in 1795, nine years after the discovery of the planet Uranus, and the principal figure involved was the great French astronomer Lalande. In that year Lalande failed to discover the planet Neptune, although the logic of events should have led him to it. Lalande was making a map of the heavens. Every night he would observe and record the stars in a small area, and on a following night would repeat the observations. Once, in a second mapping of a particular area, he found that the position of one star relative to others in that part of the map had shifted. Lalande was a good astronomer and knew that such a shift was unreasonable. He crossed out his first observation of the shifting point of light, put a question mark next to his second observation, and let the matter go. And so, not until half a century later did Neptune get added to the list of planets in the solar system. From the aberrant movement, Lalande might have made the inference not that an error had been made but that a new planet of the solar system was present. But he was reasonable. And it was more reasonable to infer that one had made an error in observation than that one had found a new planet.

Lest one be tempted to write off the episode as a historical curiosity of the remote past, it is worth remembering that the first report of atomic fission a century and a half later made by Hahn and Strassman (1939) ends with the remark, "Perhaps after all we have been deceived by a series of strange coincidences." This was in 1939. Interestingly enough, two authors in the preceding year (Curie and Savitch, 1938) had made an identical observation on the end result of bombarding uranium with neutrons and failed to achieve the discovery.

Now let us return to the more restricted realm of experiments on concept attainment. In all of the experiments thus far reported in this chapter, we have used abstract materials: forms, colors, numbers, borders, and the like. None of these materials had the property of tempting subjects toward operating by canons of verisimilitude. Indeed, because the material was "nonsense" material, subjects were possibly liberated from such tendencies. Suppose instead of using abstract material we utilized highly concrete material of the kind that might lead a person to lean more heavily on familiar or preferred ways of grouping. What might we expect?

The most reasonable expectation is that in so far as there are "preferred" or "reasonable" ways of grouping materials in an array, then the problem-solver would be likely to try out these modes of grouping; they would provide the hypotheses to be tested. If this were the case, then the strategy to be expected would be akin to successive scanning: a technique for trying out hypotheses successively. One might also expect that, since the material is meaningful, and thus more readily remembered, it should be easier to remember what hypotheses had been tested by what instances and whether or not these same instances were relevant for testing subsequent hypotheses. In short, if successive scanning is used, it should not be so discontinuous that the subject gets no benefit from past instances in shifting to new hypotheses. Thus, one might predict a strategy lying midway between successive scanning and simultaneous scanning.

Consider now the design of the experiment. Two groups were used; let us call them the Abstract and Thematic Groups. The Abstract Group comprises the same 15 subjects discussed earlier as the Ordered Group working with unlimited choice. We shall be using the same performance records discussed before. Recall that the ordered array of 64 instances with which they worked was made up of the combinations of six attributes, each with two values. Each instance consisted of a card with two figures on it, a large one and a small one. Each of these figures could vary in shape (triangle or rectangle), color (yellow or black), and border (present or absent). The orderly arrangement of the cards on a display board has already been described (see page 98).

The design of the corresponding thematic material in this experiment was governed by two requirements. The first was to parallel the structure of the abstract cards as closely as possible. The second was literally to make the instances of this array reek with meaning. To achieve the first objective, instances were again constructed of two figures: a large one and a small one, an adult human being and a child. As in the abstract material, each of these figures had three attributes varying in two values. The adult figure could be either a *man* or a *woman*. The second attribute was dress: the adult, whether man or woman, was either in *night dress* or in *day dress*. Finally, the adult figure was either *smiling and giving* a gift or was *frowning with arms clasped* behind the back. In shorthand terms, then, the adult figure varied in the three attributes of *sex*, *dress*, and *affect*. So too the child figure. It could be either a boy or girl. Whichever it was, dress was either daytime clothing or night dress. Finally, the child was either holding out its hands toward the adult figure and smiling (as if to receive) or looking down with hands clasped behind the back. The instances used were printed on cards approximately 3 by 5 inches in size. Some examples of the actual figures employed are reproduced in Figure 2.

A word should be said about the thematic material. It is characteristic of each instance in the array that it seems to be evocative of a little story or theme. Here is a figure of a father in night dress giving a little boy dressed in a bathrobe a present and the little boy has his eyes cast down and his hands behind his back. As one subject said about this instance, "It looks as if Daddy bought the wrong present for Junior." Another figure looks like a scolding mother who is fully dressed and berating her son for failure to get up and get dressed be-

Figure 2. Four instances from the thematic array.

fore coming down to breakfast. In sum, it is characteristic of instances of this sort that they have the power of evoking thematic imagery about the over-all nature of the "parent-child" situation portrayed. The purpose of the experiment was carefully explained, subjects being told what a conjunctive concept was and given some examples of possible concepts such as "all cards with a woman" or "all cards with a child in night dress."

What of performance on the two kinds of task? Recall that both groups were given four problems to solve. We shall deal with the average number of choices, etc., necessary for attainment of the concept per subject per problem. Little need be said about the problem-by-problem change in performance, for there seemed to be little in either group. First, in terms of the average number of choices per problem to attain the concept, there is a considerable and statistically significant difference between the groups. The Abstract Group required, as we may recall, an average of 6.1 choices per problem. The corresponding number of choices for the Thematic Group was 9.7—half again as many choices. The range of choices required for the Abstract Group was from 5.0 to 7.2 choices; for the subjects of the Thematic Group, from 7.0 to 11.75. The number of redundant choices for both groups fits the same pattern: 1.0 per problem for the Abstract Group, 3.9 for the Thematic Group.

As noted in connection with our previous discussion, the Abstract Group utilized primarily a conservative-focussing strategy with certain features of focus gambling. What is most striking about the performance of the Thematic Group was its relatively "continuous" successive scanning: the testing of hypotheses successively but with a seeming ability to utilize past instances to evaluate new hypotheses. The difference is illustrated by the number of incorrect hypotheses offered by the members of each group. The average number of incorrect hypotheses offered per problem by the Abstract Group was 0.5, the range being from 0.0 to 1.0. The figure for the members of the Thematic Group was 1.9, with a range from 0.25 to 5.25. It is quite evident that the latter group had "reasonable" and readily accessible hypotheses on their minds.

What can be said qualitatively about the performance observed? In the performance of the Abstract Group, subjects were relatively indifferent about attributes. In choosing cards for testing, they would as soon change one as another attribute of the original focus card. In the case of the Thematic Group, there were in all 582 card choices made by the 15 subjects, and in the course of this some 1125 changes were made in the attributes of the first positive card presented the subject (the original focus). Of these, 440 were changes in the dress of either the adult or child figure. Next came changes in the affect of the figures: 357 of these occurred. Least often changed was the sex of either figure: 328 changes occurred. Certainly there is not much difference in conspicuousness of the attributes of the thematic cards. If anything, the conspicuousness of the attributes is probably inversely related to the amount of change that occurred. For probably the sex of the figures is the most striking attribute. If one were testing instances by a focus strategy, one would expect the sex of a figure on the focus card to be changed as often as any other attribute. Instead, we find that the sex of the figures is changed the *least* often of any attribute. The indication is that the hypotheses being favored by our subjects have to do with the sex of the particular figures: it is this feature of the original focus that is most often held constant in choosing instances to test.

An analysis of the actual hypotheses offered by the Thematic subjects provides some insight into the preference pattern just mentioned. These subjects offered 113 incorrect hypotheses in the course of dealing with the 60 problems attacked by the group as a whole. The correct concept on half of these 60 problems contained a specification about the sex of the adult figure. Yet 65.5% of the *incorrect* hypotheses offered by subjects specified the sex of the adult figure. The pattern of incorrect guessing and its relation to correct concepts is in itself rather interesting:

	Adult			Child		
	Sex	Affect	Dress	Sex	Affect	Dress
Per cent correct concepts containing	50.0	50.0	45.2	53.2	38.7	35.5
Per cent incorrect hypotheses containing	65.5	55.8	43.4	55.8	32.7	38.9
Difference	+15.5	+5.8	−1.8	+2.6	−6.0	+3.4

It is difficult to interpret these figures fully, and it would be going well beyond our understanding to attempt to do so. What does seem quite apparent, however, is that there is a considerable tendency to prefer testing hypotheses about the sex of the adult figure in arriving at the concept. And sex is the attribute least often changed from the initial positive card shown the subject. Indeed, in the 582 card choices made, the initial value of adult sex is altered 26% of the time, as compared with changes in the dress of the child figure which occur in 38% of the choices made, the most frequently changed attribute.

We may conclude, then, that not only were subjects who worked with thematic materials led to utilize a somewhat continuous form of successive scanning but that in doing so they seemed to prefer hypotheses having to do with the sex of the adult figure. To put this matter in its proper perspective, we must return now to an earlier discussion of the criteriality of a concept's attributes.

In that discussion, the point was made that there were certain "nonrational" determinants of criteriality, that certain cues to the class identity of an object were preferred over and beyond their ecological validity. Certain cues are "more natural" or more impressive. In connection with probabilistic categorizing, treated in Chapter 7, much will be said about the relative weight given to such cues in identifying objects as belonging to one class or another. In the present context, two points are worth making in passing. The first has to do with the manner in which preferential tendencies show themselves, the second with the possible origin of such preference in the material used in this experiment.

The subject is presented with a first card and told that it exemplifies the correct concept. Let us say the card contains a "mother in night dress giving to a daughter in night dress who is receiving the gift" (to use the meaningful language so often employed by our subjects). Any or all of the six attribute values contained in this first positive instance might define the concept, which may be "mother" or "daughter receiving" or any combination. When a subject uses successive scanning, i.e., when he adopts an hypothesis derived from this first focal card, he must make a decision as to which of the attributes are defining and which are noisy. He is essentially making a wager on the relevance of various attributes when he formulates an hypothesis for test. Fundamentally, then, the question is this: given the appearance of six attribute values in a positive instance, which of them will be "strengthened in criteriality" most by being associated with a positive instance? In the present experiment, the single attribute most "strengthened" by the single association with an initial positive instance is, as we have seen, the sex of the adult figure.

Why? Here we can only speculate. The most obvious explanation that comes to mind has to do with the thematic nature of the cards. As remarked earlier, each card seems to evoke a theme or story. If the reader will look at an instance at random in Figure 2, he will notice that any story he makes up about it very readily casts the adult figure into the role of chief protagonist and source of action. He will also notice that the sex of the adult figure is a very important feature of the theme. Thus he may think of a story such as this: "An angry father in his bathrobe is scolding a little girl who has come in late from the street and who is downcast by the scolding she is getting." It seems not unlikely that the central position of the "father" or "mother" in the evoked theme probably predetermines the preferential criteriality attained by the attribute of the adult sex.

We may summarize the experiment briefly in the following terms. To attain concepts with materials that are meaningful and amenable to familiar forms of grouping leads to several difficulties. In the first place, the problem-solver is likely to fall back upon reasonable and familiar hypotheses about the possible groupings. In so doing, he may be led into a modified form of successive scanning: the strategy par excellence for going through a list of hypotheses. In the second place, the thematic material will, more readily than abstract material, lead certain attributes to have nonrational criteriality: the subject will "hang on" to these and will formulate hypotheses around them.

From the point of view of the reduction of cognitive strain, we would interpret these findings in much the same way as we may interpret the findings on syllogistic reasoning with which the present experiment was introduced. Where it is possible to do so, the individual will fall back on the guidance of common experience in attempting to attain a concept. As in the case of the astronomer Lalande, a cue will be used as a basis for making a familiar rather than an unfamiliar inference about the identity or "meaning" of an event. In the case of syllogisms about familiar events, habitual association may serve to override the logically necessary conclusion. In the present experiment, the familiar bases of grouping material provided in the thematic instances tend to predispose the person to "reasonable" successive hypothesis-testing and thereby predispose him away from more efficient forms of focussing strategy.

Does this in any sense serve the cognitive economy desired in problem-solving? To the extent that the environment has regularity or redundancy, one may expect that what has been familiar in the past will be relevant in the future. Certainly one of the ways of minimizing the surprise value of the environment is to operate on a principle of "persistence-forecasting"—predicting that what occurs next will be like that which occurred before. In this broader sense, reliance on familiar forms of grouping and upon their handmaiden, successive scanning, is not without adaptive benefit for the problem-solver. One may perhaps call such a tendency "rigidity," as Luchins (1942) has in discussing the so-called *Einstellung* effect. It seems more likely that in so far as the environment in which we must operate is highly regular, we do fairly well in being guided by familiar and successful past solutions. What we lose in terms of efficiency or elegance of strategies employed for testing familiar hypotheses, we probably gain back by virtue of the fact that in most things persistence-forecasting does far better for us with less effort than most other forms of problem solution. It is only in unconventional or unusual situations that such an approach proves costly.

Cognitive Strain Reconsidered. Three experiments have been described to illustrate two general points. The first of these is highly general: the utilization of a strategy is in some degree a response to the nature of the stimulus events with which one must deal. One reacts to the ordered properties of an array by utilizing these properties in making choices. If the array is such as to highlight the systematic manner in which attribute values vary, this feature seems to lead to the adoption of a strategy that makes use of it, namely, a systematic focussing strategy. If the array is a "familiar" one in which the person has expectancies concerning what might be "right" or "important," he will use these familiar features as a basis of hypotheses and adopt a scanning strategy. While this is hardly a startling finding, it does underline one way in which strain is reduced: by going along with the nature of the stimulus materials that one has before one.

The second general point is this. Where the nature of a task imposes a high degree of strain on memory and inference, the strategy used for coping with the task will tend to be less conducive to cognitive strain. To put it in terms of an analogy, if someone has to move a heavy weight, there is more likelihood that the mover will have recourse to strain-reducing techniques for carrying out his task. Some of these techniques may involve a reduction in efficiency: e.g., dividing the total weight into parcels and moving each parcel successively. Others may involve an increase in efficiency, e.g., the utilization of a lever or a dolly or some other "labor-saving" device.

But again, the meaning of efficiency cannot be understood without reference to the problem-solving task with which a person must cope. A strategy that may be efficient and relatively without strain in one situation may prove beyond one's capacities in another. Scanning is adequate if one has the support of stimulus materials before one; it may fall apart if it becomes necessary to carry information in one's head. The kind of scanning utilized by our subjects in dealing with thematic materials may be adequate in a situation where one has indeed learned what kinds of hypotheses are likely to be right. In a completely unpredictable domain, it is wasteful to be tempted by verisimilitude.

When we speak, then, of a strategy as being a move in the direction of efficient or inefficient strain reduction, such a statement must be modified to refer to particular kinds of situations. Some strategies, to be sure, will deal effectively with a wide range of situations; others will be found wanting as the cognitive going gets rough. But aside from this generalized efficiency, one must always consider the extent to which a given mode of approach meets the requirements of a task with which a person must deal here and now.

REGULATING RISK

"Suppose you, the reader, have to choose between two decisions: to build or not to build a bomb-proof shelter for you and your family. To make the example drastic, let us suppose that you are rich but that the shelter would cost you practically the whole of your fortune; and that such a shelter is both indispensable and sufficient for life preservation in the case of war. Thus your two alternative decisions and the two alternative states of the world (war or peace) combine into the following 'payoff matrix':"*

	States of the world	
Decisions	Peace	War
Build shelter	Alive and poor	Alive and poor
Don't build shelter	Alive and rich	Dead

Any decision one may make about how to solve a problem also has a characteristic risk feature. Suppose we take the case of the scientist deciding upon his next experiment, working on localization of complex pattern vision in the anthropoid brain, by extirpation techniques. The scientist, recall, is interested in six cortical areas and knows before he starts that if *all* six areas are destroyed, no pattern vision can be found; if *all* are present, pattern vision is present. What is the best way to proceed?

We see at once that we are dealing with a decision between following a conservative-focussing or focus-gambling strategy here, the brain with all six areas intact serving as a focus. Of course, the case is not so simple as this, for even if the experimenter extirpates several areas at once and destroys pattern vision thereby (i.e., changes several attributes of the focus and gets a negative instance), he will still

---

* Marschak, J. (1954, p. 3). The matrix is also taken from Marschak.

be able to extract information from his results, for simultaneous-scanning methods may also be employed. But there is an interesting point to be made here. From the point of view of the information contained in an instance, it is the case that, given an initial positive instance as a focus, the more attribute values of this instance one changes in making a next choice, the less information will it contain if it should turn out to be negative and the more information will it contain should it be positive. Information in this sense refers to the number of alternative hypotheses any chosen instance will eliminate. Thus, even if simultaneous scanning is used, the choice of a negative instance will be less valuable the more it differs from the initial positive instance.*

Given one more datum, we are in a position to specify a payoff matrix governing the decision about the next experiment to be done by our scientist. This datum is a measure of the scientist's expectancy of encountering a positive instance or negative instance on his next "try." And there are two means whereby the scientist can arrive at this estimate: by "experience" or by formal computation. If the scientist has had a long string of positive instances on the occasions when he has taken the course of changing many attributes, then he will be likely to operate on the assumption that nature is rich in positive instances. A string of negative outcomes may, on the other hand, lead him to expect few positive instances. Formal computation of the chances of encountering positive or negative instances in an array such as we have described is free of the effects of past experience. It is based on the probability with which positive and negative instances will occur given definition of the correct concept by varying numbers of attributes. It need not concern us here: all our experience indicates that subjects use an empirical rather than a formal means of estimating the likelihood of positive instances.

---

* The matter can be stated mathematically as follow. Let A equal the number of attributes in the array; in the case of our example, this would be 6 since this is the number of brain areas under consideration. Let D equal the number of attributes values in a given choice that differ from the values contained in the original positive focus. The number of hypotheses that will be eliminated after a choice that turns out to be positive is 2^D, i.e., the larger the number of value differences between focus and choice, the larger the number of hypotheses eliminated. If a negative instance is encountered on a choice, the number of eliminated hypotheses follows the function, 2^{A-D}: the greater the difference between choice and focus, the fewer the hypotheses eliminated if the chosen instance is negative. This computation is relevant only for arrays each attribute of which has but two values.

Now consider the question, after the subject has an established expectancy about positive and negative instances, whether he should follow a course of changing more than a single attribute of the focus and risking the possibility of getting either the feast of a positive instance or the famine of a negative instance. The decision, as remarked before, is one that can be described in terms of a payoff matrix.

Anticipated Events and Outcome Values

Decision Alternatives	Positive Instance	Negative Instance
Change one attribute at a time	Gain of moderate amount of information Not get very far toward complete solution	Gain of moderate amount of information Not get very far toward complete solution
Change more than one attribute at a time	Gain of considerable information Get far toward complete solution	Gain of little or no information* Make little progress toward complete solution

It is quite apparent that the decision to be made rests upon two considerations. The first of these is the estimated probability of encountering a positive instance. The more likely the person thinks he is to encounter a positive instance, the greater will be the likelihood of his making the second decision—to change many attributes of the focus. If we follow Marschak and arbitrarily assign values from 0.0 to 1.0 to the various outcomes depending upon their desirability, then we may say that the outcome, "Gain of considerable information; get far toward complete solution" has a value of 1.0; "gain little or no information; make little progress toward complete solution" has a value of 0.0; and the other two outcomes have a value of 0.5. What is called the expected utility of a decision can be computed by multiplying the estimated probability of the two events by the values assigned to their outcomes, and then summating these products. Suppose a subject had the estimate that the chance of encountering positive instances was 0.80, negative instances 0.20; then the matrix could be solved as follows:

---

* The expression "little or no information" is used here since a subject using a focus strategy would get no information from such an outcome; a subject using simultaneous scanning would get proportionally little depending on how many attributes of the original focus he had changed.

Anticipated Events

Decision Alternatives	Positive Instance	Negative Instance	Expected Utility of Decision
Change one attribute	0.5×0.80	0.5×0.20	0.50
Change many attributes	1.0×0.80	0×0.20	0.80
Estimated probabilities	0.80	0.20	

Under these circumstances, if the individual is operating on the basis of maximizing utility, then we would expect him to proceed by changing many attributes at once.

Now, if the estimate of the likelihood of a negative instance goes to 0.80, with the estimate for a positive instance at 0.20, the expected utility of decisions is reversed.

Anticipated Events

Decision Alternatives	Positive Instance	Negative Instance	Expected Utility of Decision
Change one attribute	0.5×0.20	0.5×0.80	0.50
Change many attributes	1.0×0.20	0×0.80	0.20
Estimated probabilities	0.20	0.80	

Thus, given this change in subjective likelihood estimate, a subject would be expected to use the one-change strategy, whereas before he might well have used the many-change strategy.

A prime factor in determining the value of an outcome is the number of tests that the person can make or can afford to make. The fewer the tests or experiments he can perform, the more important is it for him to get as close as possible to a complete solution with each instance tested. Given severe restriction in number of tests, it is likely that he will choose the course of changing many attributes. For though he may fail by this procedure, it is also the only procedure by which he can succeed. The greater the restriction on the number of tests, then, the higher the value of information which goes some distance towards solving the problem and the more likely it is that subjects would tend toward changing many attributes. The two experiments that follow are devoted to the two conditions we have described: change in subjective estimates of the likelihood of encountering positive instances, and change in outcome values resulting from restriction in the number of tests a person can make. To these we turn immediately.

Limitation of Choice. The experiment to be reported is a very simple one indeed.* Our only interest is in the manner in which an individual makes his first choice of an instance to test after being shown a positive card exemplifying the concept. The stimulus materials used were an array of 64 instances laid out in an orderly fashion as described earlier, with each instance exemplifying one of two possible values of six attributes. The cards and the array were identical with those described previously in connection with experiments on "orderly" and "random" arrays.

Three groups of subjects were run, about 20 in each, again students at Harvard. All of them were innocent of any knowledge about the objective of the experiment except that they knew their task was to attain a concept. Their instructions were standard. First the array was described as containing cards each of which exhibited six characteristics: the shape, color and border of a large figure; and the same characteristics of a small figure. They were then told what was meant by a concept: a group of cards sharing certain common characteristics, e.g., all the cards containing small yellow figures, or all those with large black triangles, etc. Subjects were run individually with the large display board before them. After it was ascertained that the nature of the problem was understood, subjects were told that their task was to choose cards from the board and after each choice the experimenter would tell them whether the card chosen was or was not an exemplar of the correct concept. Before beginning to choose, subjects were always shown an instance that exemplified the correct concept. At this point the treatment given the subjects diverges.

A first group was told that they should attempt to solve the problem in *as few choices as they could,* and nothing was said about the number of choices they would be allowed. It was tacitly understood that no limitation would be imposed. The second group was told that they would be allowed only *four* choices. The third group was told that they would have but *one* choice to make.

The three instructions can be likened to three situations in a football game. The first is the opening play when one's team has first gained possession of the ball after the initial kickoff and has the whole

---

* Again we are indebted to Dr. R. V. Seymour for most of the data presented in this section, although our interpretation differs from that proposed by him. Cf. R. V. Seymour, *op. cit.* Additional data were collected and further analyses carried out by Donald O'Dowd.

afternoon of plays before it. The second can be likened to gaining possession with four downs to play in the closing minute of the game. The last, of course, is the classic instance when a team that is tied with its opponent has one last play in the game before the clock runs out.

Prediction is obvious: the fewer the choices permitted, the more will the person's behavior evince risk-taking. We may examine the difference between our groups of subjects, pooling the results from the four problems done by each subject, the number of first choices which differ from the illustrative card in more than one value. The incidence of such first choices is:

> 12% in the group permitted unlimited choice.
> 33% in the group permitted only four choices.
> 72% in the group permitted only one choice.

What of the *number* of attribute values changed in this focus gambling? The difference between groups is not great. The average change from the initial positive card for the subjects with unlimited choice was 1.2; for the subjects limited to four choices, 1.5; and for the "one-shot" group, 2.1. The explanation is not hard to find. When subjects deviate from the single-change conservative-focussing strategy, they do not deviate far, particularly when they are as inexperienced in this type of problem as our subjects were. They change two or three attribute values of the original card, but rarely more. It is only with certain kinds of experience, as we shall see, that massive changes are made.

Let us sum up the matter this way. If one wishes to "break the bank" by the choice of any one instance (i.e., solve the problem completely) one has to be willing to take the risk of getting virtually no information at all from this choice. Whether one is willing to undergo the disappointment of obtaining very little information under these circumstances is a question of how urgently one feels about breaking the bank. If there is but one chance for testing, ending up with no information is a cheap price for the opportunity one has had for solving the problem completely. Indeed, it is virtually no price at all. Where is the risk? If the subject had changed only one attribute, he would have obtained a guaranteed amount of information whether the instance proved positive or negative, but in neither case would he be near solution, and worse luck too, for he has used up his only chance for testing.

The problem of risk regulation, then, seems to be essentially a problem of deciding what objective is "important" or "worth while."

When choice is limited, what becomes important is that one move *quickly* toward the solution of the problem. The importance of achieving a guaranteed intake of information on each test vanishes in value.

Now reconsider the scientist as he decides upon his next experiment. Shall he remove one area of the cortex or some greater number among the six areas that concern him? Again, the decision is about what is more important: to make a big scientific killing or to add a modest but guaranteed brick to the scientific edifice. This is the decision to be made, whether the scientist has one or many opportunities for doing experiments. If there is but one opportunity for experiment, he may still choose to do the safe and sound thing: extirpate one area and have it known for sure whether this area alone affects pattern vision. If he wants to make a complete solution and be the man who solved the problem, he could extirpate five of the six areas with the reasonable guarantee of fame should it turn out that, after so doing, pattern vision will still be intact.

In conclusion, then, the matter of risk seems to be—at least psychologically—a matter of deciding what it is that one wants to achieve. The primary question is *kind* of risk, not *amount* of risk. It is only when one has determined the objectives that impel the individual to take certain kinds of risk that one can determine the values that various outcomes have for him and begin to utilize a payoff matrix as a way of analyzing and predicting decisions.

How risk is regulated, then, depends upon the *relative psychological values* of the outcomes contained in a payoff matrix. At least this is half the matter. There is also a question of estimates of the probability of variously valued outcomes, to which we turn now.

Subjective Likelihood Estimates.* In the present experiment, we alter experimentally the subject's conception of the probability with which various outcomes or "states of the world" will occur. It is as if, to refer back to Marschak's example, we altered the person's conception of the likelihood of war or peace occurring by controlling his life history in such a way that he either experiences war as the more likely event or peace.

The design of the experiment is not without entertainment, for it involves playing a rather benign trick on the subjects. In all, 48 subjects were employed, all of them students in the Graduate Schools of Harvard University. They are, thus, relatively superior in intelligence. As in previous experiments they were tested individually.

---

* For fuller details of this experiment, see R. V. Seymour, *op. cit.*

Half of the subjects worked with an ordered array of 64 instances, identical with the one already described (page 98), which consisted of the combinations of six attributes, each of which had two values. The other half worked with a randomly arranged board made up of the same instances.

Each subject was given four successive concepts to be attained. The limited choice procedure was employed, and each subject was allowed to choose only four instances on each problem, after being shown an instance that exemplified the concept. Two kinds of treatments were used in combination for various subgroups. The first *varied the number of positive and negative instances* subjects encountered in the course of making their choices. The second *varied the number of concepts that subjects "succeeded" in attaining* in their four problems.

Two equal groups may be distinguished with respect to their "luck" in encountering positive instances on their choices. One group nearly *always* encountered positive instances; a second group practically *never* encountered positive instances. In each case this procedure was followed in such a way that the experimenter never gave inconsistent information to subjects, i.e., information about the positive or negative status of an instance that contradicted information previously given. This required a certain nimble-wittedness on the part of the experimenter that we must now describe.

Consider first the group that encountered practically all positive instances. A card is shown the subject, exemplifying the correct concept. On the basis of this one exemplar, certain concepts are ruled out as possible but 56 different concepts are still possible in a six-attribute, two-value array. So long as the subject's first choice of a card is consistent with *any* of these 56 concepts, and in every case it was, the experimenter replies, "Yes, the card chosen contains the correct concept." This chosen positive instance, taken together with the first sample card, further restricts the number of cards that can now be positive, i.e., the number of cards that now exemplify a possibly correct concept. So long as a subject picks one such card, again the experimenter replies by informing him that the instance chosen "contains the correct concept" or "is positive." Again, there was no case in which a second choice was not consistent in this sense. The same procedure was followed for third choices. These were always called positive. On the fourth choice, however, some of the subjects chose a card that could not be positive in the light of past information. Whenever this happened, the experimenter gave the subject the correct information, i.e., he told him that the card did not exemplify the concept. Of the 192 problems solved by subjects, such a contingency rose fewer than a dozen times.

A comparable regimen was followed for subjects who received all negative instances. Again, completely consistent information was given. Only in rare cases was it necessary to give a subject the information that a positive instance had been chosen.

After four choices on any given one of the four problems each subject worked on, he was asked to give his hypothesis concerning the correct concept. This hypothesis could either be consistent with the information obtained on the four prior instances or inconsistent.*

Half of the subjects, upon offering an hypothesis at the end of their four choices, were *always* told that the concept they proposed was incorrect. Thus they "failed" the four problems. The other half were always told that they were correct in their hypothesis. Before a subject had much time to consider the matter of success or failure in any great detail, the next problem was given to him, introduced always by the presentation of a card, exemplifying the new concept to be attained. This rapid transition to the next problem was just as well, for in many cases the information given the subject about the correctness of hypothesis was inconsistent with what had gone before.

There are thus four groups of 12 subjects each; they received the following treatment:

All positive instances: hypothesis always correct (positive-correct).
All positive instances: hypothesis always wrong (positive-incorrect).
All negative instances: hypothesis always correct (negative-correct).
All negative instances: hypothesis always wrong (negative-incorrect).

The procedure outlined for "failing" or "passing" subjects is something short of ideal. Fortunately for our present concern, there seems to be little effect brought about by the actual success or failure of an attempted solution. The subjects appeared to take this information in good stride, recognizing or believing that four choices was a chancy number in terms of being able to get the concept correctly or, if they

---

* By consistent we mean, of course, that the concept proposed by the subject was one that had not been infirmed by any instances previously encountered. Since our interest was primarily in the manner in which consistent strategies are affected by the treatment described above, an arbitrary rule was adopted that we would include in the study only those subjects who in at least two out of their four problems gave consistent hypotheses after four choices. All others were discarded. In selecting subjects according to this criterion, six had to be discarded from amongst those using the ordered board. Thus, all of the 48 subjects used in the experimental analysis were "correct" in proposing an *hypothesis after four choices on at least half of their problems.*

"achieved" correctness, attributing their good fortune partly to luck. The principal results with which we shall be concerned have to do with the effects of encountering positive and negative instances—with a comparison of the performance of those 24 subjects who virtually always encountered positive instances and the other 24 who encountered virtually nothing but negative instances on their choices.

What may we expect? Subjects who encounter positive instances should show an increase in their tendency to choose a first instance that differs in more than a single attribute from the initial exemplar they have been shown. For their "luck" in striking positive instances encourages them to take the risk of such a choice. What is the risk? It is essentially that if more than a single attribute is changed and a *negative* instance results, then the information contained in the instance cannot be used except by adopting exceedingly difficult simultaneous scanning. By the same token, subjects who encounter negative instances on most of their choices should develop more conservative techniques, moving in the direction of one-attribute changes. For the only kind of negative instance that can be used in a focussing strategy is one which is removed from the initial focus card by only one attribute value.

The results obtained confirm such a prediction. Consider first the number of subjects on "positive" and "negative" regimens who, on their first choice, change more than one attribute value of the first positive exemplar that has been shown them. Recall that there are 24 subjects in each group.

	Problem			
	First	Second	Third	Fourth
Encounter all positive instances	10	13	15	21
Encounter all negative instances	13	12	8	2

The same picture emerges when one considers the average number of attribute values of the initial focus that are changed by subjects in making their first choices. The figures are as follows:

	Problem			
	First	Second	Third	Fourth
Encounter all positive instances	1.54	1.79	2.00	2.67
Encounter all negative instances	1.75	1.67	1.42	1.08

Again the trends in the two groups are sharply divergent. The subjects with a history of predominantly positive instances steadily increase the number of changes made in the focus card; those with negative instances decrease until they approach the value expected from conservative focussers.

We remarked before that succeeding or failing to attain the concept seemed to make no difference in the risk-taking nature of strategies employed. If we compare the 24 subjects who attained all the concepts "correctly" with those who "failed" in all of them, no systematic difference is present. Each group is made up, of course, of equal numbers of "positive" and "negative" subjects. First, as to the number of subjects who change more than a single attribute of the initial focus on their first choice:

	Problem			
	First	Second	Third	Fourth
Attain all concepts	11	10	11	11
Fail all concepts	12	15	12	12

The number of attributes changed similarly shows no difference.

	Problem			
	First	Second	Third	Fourth
Attain all concepts	1.58	1.50	1.67	1.83
Fail all concepts	1.71	1.96	1.75	1.92

There is perhaps a slight though not significant tendency for the "failure" subjects to follow a more gamblerlike focussing strategy. It is not striking and is far short of statistical reliability. Failure to attain the concept under the chancy conditions of very limited choice appears to have little effect on this feature or, for that matter, other features of the strategy.*

Other measures could be presented showing differences between our two primary groups: those with negative and those with positive instances. Such measures would not, however, be of relevance here since they would indicate merely the manner in which subjects were responding to different amounts of information. For the fact of the matter is that in terms of the actual information contained, instances in an all-negative series do contain less information—from a formal information point of view as well as psychologically. The data presented give a sufficient picture of the one point we wish to make.

The point is this. Given a situation in which some form of focussing occurs, the extent to which the focussing will be of a gambling

---

* It is highly likely that this lack of effect would not be found had the subjects been given a sufficient number of choices to warrant their feeling that the problem was fully within their competence.

type will be adjusted to the subject's learned expectancy about the likelihood of encountering positive or negative instances. Where an expectancy about the likelihood of encountering positive instances becomes established, it becomes efficient to attempt rather freewheeling focus gambling.

What may we conclude from this experiment?

The first conclusion seems simple enough. Subjects seem to try to increase the amount of information they obtain on their four choices as they move from problem to problem. Those who encounter positive instances with high consistency achieve this by utilizing more and more frequently a focus-gambling strategy, assuring more information in the face of positive instances. Those with a high expectancy of encountering negative instances move toward conservative, one-change strategy. It is hardly relevant to ask whether our subjects are "rational" in the sense of "knowing" that their changing behavior achieves this result. Relatively few could report this in so many words. What is more important is that they behave in this fashion. They are apparently sensitive to changes in the likelihood of encountering positive or negative instances.

How shall we account for the difference between our "positive" and "negative" subjects? One can deal with the matter in terms of the expected utility model mentioned earlier. As the probability of encountering positive and negative instances alters, the expected utility of the two decisions—changing one attribute value versus changing more than one attribute value—gradually shifts position. And indeed, the model is suggestive. In a formal sense, it may be said that the subjects in this experiment were seeking to maximize the expected utility of their decisions and in this way to regulate the risk involved in their problem-solving behavior. At least, it seems evident that decisions about concept-attainment strategies alter in the face of changing probabilities of encountering different kinds of instances. An individual will increase the rate of gaining information within the limits imposed by this probability. If the chances of encountering positive instances become too slim, he will move in the direction of a safe-and-sound procedure where a guaranteed amount of information can be obtained regardless of the positive or negative status of instances encountered. If the environment becomes highly "positive," he will move to increase his informational yield by adopting a strategy that under normal circumstances would be a risky one.

At the beginning of the chapter, several ideal strategies of attaining concepts were described. The point was made that a strategy of selecting instances for testing what is relevant should have three characteristics: it should guarantee that instances chosen for test are potentially informative, that the information they contain be assimilable without undue strain, and that the strategy be capable of regulating risk. We have examined in some detail two types of experiment. In the first part of the chapter we presented several studies where cognitive strain imposed by the task was altered. The object was to determine whether strategies responded to the change in cognitive strain inherent in the problems posed for the subjects. In general, we found that strategies alter with the imposition of strain in the form of heavy memory or inference requirements. We also found that strategies alter with the nature of the risk inherent in the situation—alter in the sense of adjusting to the opportunities provided by the situation in keeping with the objectives one seeks to achieve.

The chapter has served to introduce a method of examining problem-solving behavior viewed as a sequence of decisions designed to achieve information useful in getting to a final resolution of a problem. All the experiments have had in common the fact that the subject had a great deal of freedom to test whatever features of the situation seemed relevant to him. In this sense, our subjects were put into the position of being free-lance investigators testing now this and now that feature of nature in an effort to find what it was that certain crucial events had in common, that differentiated them from other events. What was it that made certain things edible while others were inedible? Or what was it that made certain objects inflammable and others not?

In the next chapter, we look at a more restricted kind of cognitive activity. The behavior is more that of the bench-bound lecture-goer who receives information in a sequence decided upon by others than himself. Under these circumstances, how shall he discover what are the defining properties of events?

CHAPTER 5

Reception strategies
in concept attainment

Up to this point, our concern has been almost exclusively with the means whereby an individual may *select* instances in such a way as to isolate easily and efficiently the attributes that are useful for inferring a conjunctive grouping. What is perhaps most distant from life about this procedure is its Olympian quality. The universe is spread before one and one has freedom of choice as to what one will take as an instance for testing. There are perhaps times when an experimentalist in science has the good fortune to work on problems that have this feature. More likely, his plight is that he must make sense of what happens to come along, to find the significant groupings in the flow of events to which he is exposed and over which he has only partial control. *His major area of freedom is in the hypotheses he chooses to adopt, not in the manner in which he can choose instances to test.* The clinician's condition is perhaps more typical than that of the experimentalist.

Take again as an example the problems of neurophysiology, familiar from the last chapter. A clinical neurologist in the course of his practice encounters a patient with a damaged brain exhibiting the set of speech defects called aphasia. Now the concept of aphasia need not be "formed" for it already exists. The aphasia case is referred to him by an examining diagnostician. The diagnostician's statement that the case "shows aphasia" is the criterion of a positive instance. The research neurologist is now trying to find out about the neural correlates of aphasia. He must, in other words, seek the neural defining attributes of the class of patients known as aphasics. If one wishes to say that the neurologist is trying to find the "causes" of aphasia, this in no sense changes the basic problem, which is to find what neural conditions lead to the inference of aphasia with maximum certainty.

If the experimentalist were engaged in such a pursuit and could find laboratory animals capable of speech and on whom surgery might be performed, then he would be in a position to act much as our subjects of the last chapter. This would take the form of systematically removing areas of the brain in certain combinatorial orders until the answer was forthcoming. But the clinician has to take his cases as they come. He must employ a *reception strategy.*

Let us begin at the beginning of modern neurology by taking Paul Broca as our subject: a gifted neurologist of the mid-19th century.* He has a chance to carry out an autopsy on an aphasic patient. He finds massive damage in that portion of the brain at the base of the third frontal convolution (since named, in his honor, Broca's area), "the speech center." But this describes only part of the properties of the "instance." For Broca's exact description of the patient's lesion shows a softening of the brain in the left hemisphere all the way from the frontal lobe dorsally to the parieto-occipital junction, extending downward as far as the superior portion of the temporal lobe. One can sum this up more simply by saying that there is much more destroyed than Broca's area alone. It is at this point that Broca is able to exercise his major freedom: the freedom to formulate an hypothesis. He could attribute the aphasia to *all* of the destroyed areas or to any part thereof. He takes his option and proposes that aphasia is caused by damage to a speech center: the famous "Broca area." Perhaps there is reason in the fact that this is the area of most concentrated degeneration. Nonetheless, the die is cast. The neural defining attribute of aphasia is this particular "speech center."

At the other extreme we have Flourens, who adopts another option. No *specific* lesion is taken as a defining attribute of aphasia. If the aphasic's brain shows specific damage, it is the interaction of the damaged areas and the intact areas together that create the final common path of aphasia.

What is of great interest about these two innovators is that each has a line of descendants, call them the localists and the totalists. The former seek always a specific area where possible: some set of limited defining attributes, adding new attributes only when forced by the

---

* In the interest of exposition, we shall take certain liberties with the history of this complex field. If the reader finds that our historical license leads us to over-exaggeration, he will, we hope, forgive us and treat our examples as fictional rather than real figures.

burden of much evidence. The list of localists, requiring oversimplification in its compiling, includes such names as Fritsch, Hitzig,
Bianchi, Flechsig, and Adrian. The totalists have wanted to stay as
close as possible to the whole cortex as an explanation, and it is only
with the greatest reluctance that they will subtract any of its attributes
as irrelevant. Here too we find a distinguished list: Goltz, Munk,
Hughlings Jackson, Head, Goldstein, Lashley. The interesting thing
about each group is not only that they attempt to proceed as they do
but that they urge the absurdity of proceeding in any other way.

In point of fact, one could begin either way—adopting either a part
or a whole hypothesis—and arrive at the same conclusion provided
one did not become rigidified before the process of proof was completed. Here we must leave real neurology, for the issues are too
tangled. But if one works with the kind of schematization used in
the last chapter, it is possible that, when one encounters an aphasic,
one may base an hypothesis on the state of *all* areas or upon the
state of *one* particular area. What is even more important than the
starting hypothesis is what one does with it when one encounters
new instances that differ from it. For an hypothesis is not a final
declaration so much as it is something to be tried out and altered.
We shall be considering in this chapter the manner in which, in the
kinds of problems we have been discussing, hypotheses are changed
to conform to the arbitrary stream of events to which they are
exposed.

The first and obvious thing about an hypothesis is that it can have
any one of four fates when exposed to a new event to which it is
relevant. Let us bring Paul Broca back on the scene. He has de-
clared his hypothesis on the relevance of the speech center. Each
new patient he sees can have his speech center intact or destroyed.
Again, each patient he sees must either have the symptoms of aphasia
or not have them. Broca's world, then, is made up of four contingencies.

	Speech Area	Symptomatology
1.	Destroyed	Aphasia
2.	Intact	Aphasia
3.	Intact	No aphasia
4.	Destroyed	No aphasia

It is apparent that two of the contingencies confirm, or at least fail to
infirm, Broca's hypothesis. A patient with the speech center destroyed and the symptoms of aphasia confirms it. One with the center

intact and without aphasia at least fails to infirm his hypothesis. Two of the outcomes are damaging to Broca's hypothesis. A patient with speech center intact and aphasia is as infirming as one whose speech center is destroyed but who shows no sign of aphasia. Let us adopt the language of medicine, for the moment, and speak of any case as positive which shows the signs of illness we are investigating; its absence negative. Whether it is positive or negative, a case can confirm or infirm the hypothesis in force. In this fashion of speaking, then, the four contingencies that Broca can meet are:

1. Positive confirming: Aphasic with speech center destroyed.
2. Positive infirming: Aphasic with speech center intact.
3. Negative confirming: Nonaphasic with speech center intact.
4. Negative infirming: Nonaphasic with speech center destroyed.

A good reception strategy consists in being able to alter hypotheses appropriately in the face of each of these contingencies. At an even more primitive level, obviously, it consists in being able to recognize their existence and to formulate hypotheses in such a way that, whatever the contingency met, one will know how and whether to change one's hypothesis.

A PARADIGM AND TWO STRATEGIES

Three things are required to reproduce in the laboratory a task comparable to the examples we have given. *First,* one must construct an array of instances that are alike in some respects and different in others, so that there are multiple ways in which the instances in the array may be grouped. *Second,* instances must be encountered by the person in an order over which he has no control. *Third,* the subject must know whether each instance is positive or negative in the sense of exemplifying or not exemplifying a concept. *Fourth,* the subject must be given freedom to formulate and reformulate hypotheses on each encounter with an instance. Given these requisites, a task is easily set. A grouping or a concept to be attained is chosen, and the subject is shown in succession exemplars and nonexemplars of this concept. His objective is to formulate an hypothesis that will distinguish an exemplar from a nonexemplar among the instances he encounters.

We begin with instances such as those illustrated in Figure 1, composed of the combinations of three values of each of four attributes—cards each showing four properties, such as "two red squares and three borders" or "one black cross and two borders." We decide upon a "concept:" say "all black figures." We present one instance at a time to the subject, telling him whether or not it exemplifies the concept, whether it is positive or negative. After each card, the subject is asked to indicate his best hypothesis concerning the nature of the correct concept. Thus, following the presentation of any given card, he offers an hypothesis. The experimenter makes no comment. The next card the subject encounters must perforce represent one of the four possible contingencies. It may be *positive* or it may be *negative*. Whether it is one or the other, it also has the property that it *confirms* or *infirms* the subject's previously held hypothesis about the nature of the correct concept.

Before examining the behavior of subjects dealing with such problems, it is perhaps well to consider the ideal strategies that are applicable. Logically, they are identical to the strategies discussed in the last chapter. First, there is a focussing strategy which, as before, is useful both for maximizing information yield and for reducing the strain on inference and memory. The surprisingly simple rules for the alteration of hypotheses with this strategy are best presented with the aid of an illustration.

The clinician begins, let us say, with an aphasic showing a badly damaged brain—Areas I to VI destroyed. He takes as his first hypothesis that destruction in *all* six areas must be responsible for aphasia. If he should encounter a positive-confirming instance (another aphasic with like destruction), he maintains the hypothesis in force. If he should meet a negative-confirming instance (a non-aphasic with some or all of the areas intact), he still maintains his hypothesis. The only time he changes is when he meets a positive-infirming instance. An example of one such would be an aphasic with Areas I to III intact, and Areas IV to VI destroyed. Under these circumstances, he alters his hypothesis by *taking the intersect between his old hypothesis and the new instance:* those features common to the two. The features common to the old hypothesis and the new positive instance can be readily seen:

Old hypothesis: Areas I, II, III, IV, V, VI destroyed produce aphasic.
New positive instance: Aphasic with Areas I, II, III, intact; IV, V, VI destroyed.

Thus the clinician chooses as his new hypothesis: "Areas IV, V, and VI destroyed produce aphasia."

Now consider the rules in their barest form. The first one is of central importance. *Take the first positive instance and make it* in toto *one's initial hypothesis.* From here on, the rules can be simply described. They are:

	Positive Instance	Negative Instance
Confirming	Maintain the hypothesis now in force	Maintain the hypothesis now in force
Infirming	Take as the next hypothesis what the old hypothesis and the present instance have in common	Impossible unless one has misreckoned.* If one has misreckoned, correct from memory of past instances and present hypothesis

By following this procedure, the subject will arrive at the correct concept on the basis of a minimum number of events encountered. The strategy has only two rules in addition to the initial rule that one begin with a positive instance *in toto* as one's hypothesis. These two rules are:

1. Consider what is common to your hypothesis and any *positive-infirming* instance you may encounter.
2. Ignore everything else.

It is apparent, of course, that focussing in the present case is analogous to the focussing strategy under conditions where the subject chooses the order of the instances that he will consider. In both types of problems, the first positive card encountered is used *in toto* as a guide, in the reception case as the basis for all subsequent hypotheses, and in the selection case as the point of departure for all subsequent choices of instances whose positive or negative character will systematically delimit the concept. In focussing where one chooses instances, the problem-solver tests attribute values of the focus card one at a time as a means of seeing which features of the initial focus card are relevant to the concept. In the reception case, one embodies this focus card in one's initial hypothesis and then evaluates its attribute values in the light of subsequent instances encountered.

In the interest of brief nomenclature, we shall refer to the ideal strategy just described as the *wholist strategy* since it consists in the adoption of a first hypothesis that is based on the whole instance initially encountered, followed by an adherence to the rules of focussing just described. From time to time, we shall also use the expression *focussing* to describe the strategy.

---

* For a fuller exposition of this point, see pages 149–150.

As in the selection case, scanning strategies are also possible here. Again, they may take one of two forms. The first is the simultaneous process described in the last chapter where a person attempts to use each instance to make all possible inferences about the correct concept. A first positive card "eliminates these 240, and renders possible these 15 hypotheses," etc. This is the "simultaneous" form of the scanning strategy, so called because all alternative possible hypotheses are entertained simultaneously. It is of little interest to us primarily because we find no behavior conforming to it. Nor, for that matter, did we observe the kind of "lazy" successive scanning that can be described in ideal terms as formulating one hypothesis at a time and holding on to it so long as confirming instances are encountered, changing only when an infirming instance is encountered to an hypothesis not yet tested. Then one starts afresh to test the new hypothesis with no reference to instances used for the test of prior hypotheses. This of course is successive scanning in its pure, discontinuous form.

The type of scanning strategy that best describes the behavior of our subjects is, as before, a compromise between these two forms. It is a strategy that begins with *the choice of an hypothesis about part of the initial exemplar encountered. When this hypothesis fails to be confirmed by some subsequent instance, the person seeks to change it by referring back to all instances previously met and making modifications accordingly.* That is to say, he bets on *some* feature of the exemplar, choosing it as his hypothesis about why the instance is an exemplar of the category—why it is correct. So long as the next exemplars also exhibit this feature, the hypothesis is retained. Or if nonexemplars do not show it, it is also retained. But as soon as an instance infirms the hypothesis, the hypothesis is changed. The change is made with as much reference as possible to what has gone before. He now seeks to formulate an hypothesis that will be consistent with all instances thus far encountered. To do so requires either a system of note-taking or a reliance on memory. Let us look more specifically at the way contingencies are handled.

Confirming contingencies are handled as in the ideal wholist strategy. The subject maintains the hypothesis in force. The two infirming contingencies present a challenge to the strategy in that both of them require him to go back in his memory over past instances encountered.

To sum up, the rules of the scanning strategy are as follows. Begin with *part* of the first positive instance as an hypothesis. The remaining rules can be put in the familiar fourfold table.

	Positive Instance	Negative Instance
Confirming	Maintain hypothesis now in force	Maintain hypothesis now in force
Infirming	Change hypothesis to make it consistent with past instances: i.e., choose an hypothesis not previously infirmed	Change hypothesis to make it consistent with past instances; i.e., choose hypothesis not previously infirmed

For describing this procedure we shall use the expression *part-scanning strategy* or, on occasion, *part strategy*.

Let us now briefly sum up the differences between the two strategies:

1. Part-scanning obviously makes more demands on memory and inference than does the focussing strategy. The wholist's hypothesis is modified at each step to incorporate the information gained from the instances he has encountered. He need never recall either his past hypotheses or the relation between these. *For his present hypothesis is a current summary of all these.* Only when he must recover from an error is recourse to memory necessary. The part-scanner must fall back on memory or the record every time he encounters an infirming instance.

2. The scope of one's initial hypothesis—whether a part or a whole hypothesis—will alter the probability of encountering the four different contingencies. This is a straightforward matter of arithmetic that will be made clear later in the chapter. The most dramatic feature of this "arithmetical fate" of the two strategies is that a wholist who follows all the rules of his strategy will *never* encounter the most psychologically disrupting of the contingencies: the negative-infirming case.

3. To succeed, the scanner must remain alert to all the characteristics of the instances he is encountering, for he may have to revise his hypothesis in the light of these. Such a degree of alertness and spread of attention is not required of the focusser. If he stays with the rules of focussing, he need pay no heed to the characteristics of the instances encountered after he has used them to correct his hypothesis. If you will, the scanner must keep a continuing interest in nature; the focusser need only be preoccupied with his hypothesis.

So much, then, for the ideal strategies. Specifically, we have three objectives in the research to which we now turn.

1. The first is to examine the degree to which performance corresponds to the ideal strategies, the degree to which one acts like a

Broca or a Flourens from problem to problem and from contingency to contingency.

2. The second is to examine change in performance over a long series of problems varying in the cognitive strain they impose.

3. Finally, we wish to raise some questions about the effectiveness of the two strategies under varying work conditions. We know, for example, that scanning is more dependent upon memory and inference that is focussing. What difference does this make for success and failure in attaining concepts?

AN EXPERIMENTAL DESIGN

Our experimental operations can be sketched rapidly so that the present design may be contrasted with some of the classical studies. At the outset the nature of the task is fully described for the subject. As noted earlier, an array of instances is constructed. The subject is presented instances from this array one at a time, and each is designated as either positive or negative. The first instance presented is always positive. The subject is asked after each instance to state his hypothesis concerning the correct concept: what it is that the first positive card exemplifies. Instances are presented until the subject has had at least as many instances as would be required logically to eliminate all hypotheses save the correct one. At no time does he have more than one instance before him, and should he ask about instances previously encountered, the experimenter demurs. No such aids as paper and pencil are permitted him. Moreover, it is explained at the outset just what it is about the instances that need be considered: the shape of the figure they contain, the color of these figures, their number, etc.*

For the reader not well acquainted with the literature on concept attainment, we should like to point out here several crucial differences between the conduct of this experiment and of classical experiments in this field which have also used arbitrary sequences. First no effort was made to conceal the nature of the subject's task. He knew that his job was to find out the "correct concept." He knew what a concept was: a grouping of instances in terms of common properties. He knew what properties of instances were worth considering. And he knew, finally, that what he was seeking was a conjunctive concept, and that only one concept was to be attained in each problem.

---

* We are particularly indebted to Mrs. Mary Crawford Potter for aid in designing and executing this experiment as well as devising techniques of analysis for it.

In these respects, the procedure differed from the procedure originally introduced by Hull (1920). In the Hull procedure, the subject was *not* told what his task was. Rather the task was presented as a study in rote learning. The subject had the task of learning to associate names or nonsense syllables with instances that were presented to him. There might, for example, be five different concepts, illustrated by an array of instances; and the subject's task was to "learn" that particular cards were labeled "DAX," others "CIV," etc. If he did not figure it out for himself, he might never realize that "DAX" cards were so labelled because they shared certain common attribute values. The test of whether the subject had attained the concept was, at least in Hull's study, whether the nonsense syllables could be applied to a series of new cards that illustrated the various concepts but which had not been presented before. In sum, *incidental* concept attainment was being studied. William James urged that the psychology of religion begin with the investigation of "the most religious man in his most religious moment." We wanted at the outset to see concept attainment at its best.

There is one other crucial difference between our procedure here and earlier ones, a difference whose importance has already been lucidly remarked upon by Hovland (1952). In studies inspired by Hull's procedure, it was not made clear to the subjects what it was about the instances presented to them that might be relevant. The different attributes and their values were, in short, left uncontrolled. Thus, Hull used a set of pseudo-Chinese characters, a particular radical of which was the defining attribute of the correct concept. It is apparent that the number of attributes a subject might consider as possibly relevant are close to limitless: any component stroke, angularity, or curvedness of components, thickness of strokes, crowdedness of strokes, number of right angles, number of strokes, number of disconnected lines, width, length, and symmetry of characters, predominance of vertical or horizontal strokes, "movement" or "stillness" of the arrangement of strokes.

So long as the experimenter does not know to which and to how many component attributes the subject is attending, it is impossible to control or understand the amount of information being presented to the subject by any one instance or combination of instances. One cannot know when the subject has had an informationally adequate series of instances—adequate to eliminate all but one, the correct concept. Nor is it possible to study the effect of the number of defining attributes in the concept as compared to the number of noisy irrelevant attributes. To be sure, the use of such characters in concept-attainment studies provides highly useful knowledge—knowledge about the manner in which subjects abstract attributes from a complex situation. But the *process* of how concepts are attained, given the abstraction of attributes, is greatly obscured. Perhaps most serious of all, where the experimenter does not know to what attributes the subject is attending, he cannot know whether the instance he is presenting a subject is positive-confirming, positive-infirming, negative-confirming, or negative-infirming. And moreover, in order to know the contingencies with which the subject is coping, it is necessary to have the subject state his hypothesis after each instance rather than merely respond in terms of a set of labels.

These points of design reflect our concern with the necessity of externalizing the decisions a subject makes en route to the attainment of a concept, a concern discussed in Chapter 3. It was a deliberate choice on our part to use a known number of attributes, each with a known number of values—known to both the experimenter and the subject. If you will, then, this is concept attainment with the perceptual-abstraction phase by-passed.

Details of Procedure. The instances were cards containing various shapes, colors, and numbers of figures; and various kinds, colors, and numbers of borders. The six attributes and their values comprising the problems were:

> *Number of figures:* one, two, or three.
> *Kind of figures:* square, circle, or cross.
> *Color of figures:* red, blue, or green.
>
> *Number of borders:* one, two, or three.
> *Kind of borders:* solid, dotted, or wavy.
> *Color of borders:* red, blue, or green.

Subjects were run in groups of about ten. They were first shown a sample of several stimulus cards and the experimenter points out how the cards vary in their attribute values. It was then carefully explained to the subject that a concept is a combination of attribute values, e.g., "all cards containing crosses," or "all cards containing one green figure." Thus, the experimenter points out, certain cards represent positive instances of the concept. For example, the card containing "one green circle with three borders" (1G◯3b) is a positive instance of the concept "cards containing one green figure." By the same token, the subject was informed about the meaning of a negative instance as a card not exemplifying the concept.

We then said: "I will now show you a sequence of cards and tell you whether each is a positive or a negative instance of the concept I have in mind. *After each card, please write down your best guess of the concept."* Each subject was provided with a response sheet. Each problem was done on a single sheet, the last entry on the sheet being the subject's final answer. If the final answer corresponded to the correct concept, the subject was considered to have attained the concept. Cards were presented one at a time for only ten seconds. No hints were given and once a card had been shown and removed, the subject was not reminded of what it had been. The subjects were instructed to write down on their score sheets only their hypotheses and nothing else. It was not possible for them to refer back to previous hypotheses since the subjects were asked to cover them, as soon as they are written down, by a card. This covering card was also a "code card" containing abbreviations for the subjects to use in writing their response.

Sampling of Subjects and Problems. The subjects, 46 Harvard and Wellesley undergraduates, were given 14 problems to solve. The problems varied in the number of possibly relevant attributes with which the subject had to deal and in the number of attributes that defined the concept. The number of possibly relevant attributes varied from three to six and the number of attributes that actually defined the correct concepts varied from one to five.

The attributes used for any given problem were chosen at random, with the restriction that all six attributes were used equally often in the 14 problems. When, for example, a problem involved the use of three attributes, subjects were told what these were and the other attributes were kept at a constant value so as not to distract subjects from their task. The attributes that defined a concept were similarly chosen at random, with the same restriction as mentioned before.

The instances used for each problem were such as to approximate as closely as possible the following desiderata. *First,* that just enough instances be given so that the subject have sufficient information for attaining the concept with no redundant instances included in the series. *Second,* that the total number of instances presented for each problem be the same. *Third,* that the ratio of positive to negative instances presented in the various problems be the same. *Fourth,* that each problem occur equally often in the first, second, third, or fourth quarter of the series of problems. While we were able to come close to these prescriptions, it was combinatorially impossible to realize them completely. Subjects had to be divided into four subgroups and given slightly different sets of problems. The nature of the instances presented in the set of problems given to one subgroup is set forth in Table 1.

TABLE 1

The 14 Problems Given Subjects in One Subgroup

Problems

	1	2	3	4	5	6	7	8	9	10	11	12	13	14
Attr. values of concept	1	2	1	2	3	3	1	2	3	4	1	2	3	4
Total attributes in array	3	3	4	4	4	4	5	5	5	5	6	6	6	6
Informative pos. instances*	3	2	3	3	2	2	3	3	3	2	3	3	3	3
Redundant pos. instances	0	1	0	0	0	1	0	0	0	1	0	0	0	0
Informative neg. instances	1	2	2	2	3	3	2	2	3	4	1	2	3	4
Redundant neg. instances	2	1	1	1	0	0	1	1	0	0	2	1	0	0
Total instances presented	6	6	6	6	5	6	6	6	6	7	6	6	6	7

But the fit to our prescription was not bad at that. All but three of the problems in this set contained six instances, and these three were only one away from this number. Four of the problems involved instances comprising exactly one full informational cycle with no redundant instances; the others contained one positive redundant instance, and sometimes one or two negative redundant instances. The balance of positive and negative instances was practically constant throughout. Finally, nearly all the possible combinations of ratios of defining to total attributes were represented all the way from one defining attribute value for a three-attribute array to four defining attribute values for a six-attribute array.

ADHERENCE TO STRATEGY

Two ideal strategies have been described in terms of a set of rules for constructing a first hypothesis and for changing it upon encountering various contingencies. The general question we wish to ask is whether, on the whole, subjects adhere consistently to the rules of these strategies or whether, if you will, their behavior is random. The question is reminiscent of one asked years ago by Krechevsky (1932) about maze-learning in the rat: is it a chance performance or systematic, this process of finding the way to a correct solution?

Three concrete questions can be put. Problems are begun with either the "part" hypothesis of the scanner or the "whole" hypothesis of the focusser. Are subjects consistent from problem to problem in using a whole or a part initial hypothesis? Given an initial hypothesis of one or the other type, to what extent do subjects follow the remaining rules of the ideal strategy that would permit them to reach a cor-

---

* This includes the positive instance, i.e., the initial card presented.

rect solution with minimum information? Where does a subject's performance diverge from the ideal strategy?

Regarding consistency in the utilization of part and whole hypotheses on a series of problems done by a single subject, there is a very marked tendency for the subject to use one or the other approach consistently. In this type of problem, at least, people are either consistently like Broca or like Flourens. The relevant data are presented in Figure 3.

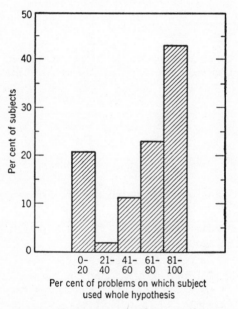

Figure 3. The percentage distribution of subjects with respect to the relative frequency with which they used initial whole hypotheses in dealing with problems.

We also see in this figure that it is the exception for subjects to use the two forms of initial hypothesis with equal frequency. It is rather interesting, too, that the whole hypothesis is preferred to the part hypothesis.* In fact, about 62% of the problems were begun with whole hypotheses. A word must be said about the strength of this preference.

Upon being shown an instance exhibiting, say, four attribute values, there are 15 opening hypotheses possible. Of these, one contains all

---

* In a partial replication of this experiment, with subjects run individually and with no time pressure, the same preference for whole hypotheses was found.

four attribute values, and 14 contain fewer than all four of these. The larger the number of attributes in an instance, the greater the number of alternative hypotheses possible. But always, there is only one of these alternatives that contains all the attribute values on the instance —the so-called whole hypothesis. Thus, the probability of choosing a whole hypothesis by chance alone diminishes as the number of attributes used increases. The best way of showing the strength of our subjects' preference for whole hypotheses is to consider the proportion of whole hypotheses actually used and the number expected by chance.

TABLE 2
Percentage of Problems Begun with Whole Hypotheses and Percentage Expected by Chance

Number of Attributes in Array	Percentage Begun with Whole Hypothesis	Percentage Expected by Chance
3	70	12
4	65	7
5	59	3
6	70	2

The first question posed was whether subjects are consistent from problem to problem in their preference for either part or whole hypotheses. The answer can be given in three parts: *a.* They are consistent from problem to problem. *b.* There is a preference for whole hypotheses far in excess of chance. *c.* Both the consistency and the preference hold for problems of varying complexity.

Why this preference for whole hypotheses? Two explanations suggest themselves. The first is that when the number of attributes to be dealt with is relatively limited, a person may be willing to deal with them all at once. Perhaps had we gone well above the subjects' immediate memory-and-attention span, there might have been a tendency to break the task down by dealing with packets of attributes. A second explanation takes us back to the preceding chapter where the role of verisimilitude was discussed. In the kind of abstract material used here, it is not likely that subjects will have any strong preferences about the relevance of particular attributes in the array. They have no favorites to ride. In consequence, there is no preformed tendency to concentrate upon any particular attribute.

So far we have concerned ourselves with the nature of the initial hypotheses adopted after presentation of the illustrative positive card. Consider now the way in which these initial hypotheses are modified in the light of contingencies subsequently encountered.

The Meeting and Handling of Contingencies: Wholists. Recall the four rules for the ideal focussing strategy, the ideal ways for a wholist to handle the four contingencies.

Contingency	Ideal procedure
Positive confirming (PC)	*Maintain* hypothesis now in force
Negative confirming (NC)	*Maintain* hypothesis now in force
Positive infirming (PI)	*Change* hypothesis to whatever the old hypothesis and the new instance have in common
Negative infirming (NI)	*Change* hypothesis on the basis of memory of past instances

How often are these rules followed by subjects who begin with a whole hypothesis—the wholists? The ideal rules are followed on:

> 54% of encounters with PC contingencies.
> 61% of encounters with NC contingencies.
> 54% of encounters with PI contingencies.
> 10% of encounters with NI contingencies.

The first three contingencies are handled ideally with a frequency far in excess of chance, and we shall return later to the question of what constitutes chance performance. But ideal handling of the negative-infirming contingency is strikingly rare. Why?

For the wholist to deal with the negative-infirming contingency, he must change his hypotheses on the basis of his memory of past instances encountered. In short, he must backtrack. This is the only contingency where focussers must use memory in this rote way. In practice, wholists do attempt to remember past instances when they meet a negative-infirming contingency, but to remember correctly and to extract the implications from what they have remembered is a task most often beyond them. Actually, the contingency should never arise—if the other rules are followed. Since focussing does not tend to orient the person toward literal remembering of past instances, it is not surprising that the contingency is only dealt with successfully in about 10% of encounters. The scanner, whose behavior we shall examine in detail shortly, is more memory-oriented. He deals successfully with this contingency on 26% of his encounters with it.

The focusser's departure from the rule for handling positive-infirming contingencies takes a simple form. The contingency is ideally met with the intersect rule: take that which is common to the old hypothesis and the infirming positive instances before one. On occasions, subjects are tempted to ignore this rule and to maintain their old hypotheses unchanged. More often, they "underintersect." Underintersecting consists in using for one's new hypothesis only *some* of the features common to the old hypothesis and the new infirming positive instance.

The lack of complete adherence to the ideal rules for handling confirming instances (either positive or negative) brings to light an intriguing feature of subjects' performance. The rule for both confirming contingencies is: "Maintain unchanged the hypothesis in force." The fact is that for some subjects at least it is difficult to maintain hypotheses in their present state when new instances come along. The involved subject often feels that he is making progress only when he changes his hypothesis in response to new instances. Maintenance seems to be equated with "no progress." He is, if you will, too "participant," too devoted to the idea that change is progress.

Consider now the frequency with which wholists actually encounter the various contingencies *en route* to attainment. The average problem contained five contingencies: five instances encountered after the initial illustrative card. Of these,

> 0.3 were PC contingencies.
> 3.0 were NC contingencies.
> 1.6 were PI contingencies.
> 0.1 were NI contingencies.

It is quite evident, then, that the principal contingencies to be coped with are negative confirming and positive infirming, constituting 4.6 of the average of 5 instances encountered on each problem.

To determine which of these two important contingencies—positive infirming and negative confirming—created more trouble for users of the wholist strategy, the following analysis was carried out. Problems handled by the wholist strategy are separable into four types:

a. Those in which *both* contingencies were handled appropriately.
b. Those where *neither* was handled appropriately.
c. Those where PI contingencies *were* handled appropriately, but NC not.
d. Those where NC contingencies *were* handled appropriately, but PI not.

Table 3 sets forth the number of problems of each type and the proportion of each type successfully solved. In brief summary, handling both contingencies appropriately leads to virtually certain success. Handling neither appropriately always leads to failure. If one does not handle the positive infirming contingency properly, failure is as likely as if one violated both critical contingencies. Such a violation is far worse than improper handling of a negative confirming contingency, after a violation of which recovery and success follow half the time.

TABLE 3

Handling of PI and NC Contingencies by Focussers

Response to Contingencies	Number of Problems	Per Cent Solved
Both contingencies always handled appropriately	103	97
Neither contingency ever handled appropriately	160	20
PI appropriate; NC not	54	48
NC appropriate; PI not	37	22

In brief, then, the handling of the positive infirming contingency by the intersect rule is the heart of the wholist strategy, for it is by this rule that the subject is enabled to alter his hypotheses in a manner such that it summarizes and keeps current all the information he has encountered to date.

The Meeting and Handling of Contingencies: Partists. How do scanners fare when they meet the various contingencies? The rules of the ideal scanning strategy are as follows:

Contingency	Ideal procedure
PC	*Maintain* hypothesis now in force
NC	*Maintain* hypothesis now in force
PI	*Change* to a hypothesis consistent with memory of past instances
NI	*Change* on same basis as for positive infirming

How often do partists follow these rules? They follow them on:

> 66% of encounters with PC contingencies.
> 52% of encounters with NC contingencies.
> 50% of encounters with PI contingencies.
> 26% of encounters with NI contingencies.

As with the wholists, the widest divergence from the rule comes in dealing with the taxing contingency of a negative infirming instance. Consider, as we did before in the case of the wholists, how the partists come to deviate from the ideal strategy.

Faced with confirming contingencies, either positive or negative, a subject should maintain his hypothesis unchanged. As with the wholists, however, many partists find it difficult to maintain a hypothesis unchanged in the presence of a new instance. They too feel that change is progress, that use should be made of each instance presented them.

Why is a negative-infirming contingency so difficult to deal with for a partist? Adherence to the ideal rule is not striking: 26% as against 50% for an infirming positive instance. For one thing, a negative infirming contingency contains a "double negative." The card illustrates what the concept is *not*, and it also tells you that your present hypothesis is *not* right. In this sense, a negative infirming contingency provides highly indirect information. Furthermore, such an instance provides one with no new base on which to ground a new hypothesis. A positive infirming contingency provides at least a set of attribute values upon which a new hypothesis can be formed.

Consider now the frequency with which scanners encounter the various contingencies en route to attainment. The average problem contains five contingencies. Of these:

> 0.6 were PC contingencies.
> 2.7 were NC contingencies.
> 1.3 were PI contingencies.
> 0.4 were NC contingencies.

As with the focussing strategy, the contingencies most frequently encountered are negative confirming and positive infirming, constituting 4.0 of the average of 5 contingencies met per problem per subject.

To determine which of these contingencies was the more crucial for users of the scanning strategy, we again divided problems into the four familiar groups:

  a. Those in which *both* contingencies were handled appropriately.
  b. Those where *neither* was handled appropriately.
  c. Those where PI contingencies *were* handled appropriately, but NC *not.*
  d. Those where NC contingencies *were* handled appropriately, but PI *not.*

Table 4 sets forth the number of problems of each type met and the proportion of each successfully solved.

TABLE 4

Handling of PI and NC Contingencies by Scanners

Response to Contingencies	Number of Problems	Per Cent Solved
Both contingencies always handled appropriately	22	73
Neither contingency ever handled appropriately	85	8
PI appropriate; NC not	52	31
NC appropriate; PI not	29	7

In sum, handling both of these two contingencies appropriately is associated with a high rate of success. Handling neither appropriately almost always leads to failure. If one does not handle the positive infirming contingency appropriately, failure is as likely as if neither contingency had been appropriately responded to.

Once again it is the handling of the positive infirming contingency that is the heart of the strategy. For the focusser, its handling in terms of the intersect rule was the way in which he could so modify his hypotheses that each hypothesis was a summary of the information encountered up to that point. For the scanner, the use of the positive infirming contingency is equally crucial: it provides a base on which to build a new hypothesis and a score card against which memory of past instances can be checked.

THE EFFECTIVENESS OF THE TWO STRATEGIES

Which strategy leads more often and more efficiently to success? Complete adherence to the ideal rules of either, of course, leads with inevitability to success. But there are deviations from the ideal rules: all wholists do not always adhere to the rules of focussing, nor partists to scanning.

If one can compare the success of partists and wholists, taking their strategic behavior as we find it, the advantage lies with the wholists. But the real question is: *which strategy is the more effective under what conditions?* Does the effectiveness of each strategy vary with the over-all difficulty of the problem to which it is applied, and is there a difference between the two in this effectiveness? Recall that the problems given to subjects varied in difficulty: difficulty depending upon the number of attributes to which one had to attend. For the larger the number of attributes represented by instances to be dealt with, the larger the number of hypothetical concepts in terms of which the instances may be grouped. If A attribute values are present in a first positive instance presented, the number of possible hypotheses about the correct concept will equal the sum of A values taken one at a time (for one-value hypotheses), taken two at a time (for two-value hypotheses), up to A at a time (for A-value hypotheses). The number of possible concepts for each case used, then, is:[*]

> Three-attribute problems = 7 possible concepts.
> Four-attribute problems = 15 possible concepts.
> Five-attribute problems = 31 possible concepts.
> Six-attribute problems = 63 possible concepts.

---

[*] The formula for the number of hypotheses after a first positive instance is:

$$H = \sum_{i=1}^{A} \binom{A}{i},$$ where H is the number of hypothetical concepts possible after a first positive instance and A is the number of attributes in the array.

It is quite evident that the task of keeping track of possible hypotheses increases considerably in difficulty with an increase in the number of attributes in the array.

Figure 4 indicates that the number of attributes in a problem is indeed a source of increasingly difficulty. It is not surprising that the wholists were more effective with problems at *all* levels of difficulty. The fact of the matter is that it is easier for a subject to follow all the rules of focusing, and the superiority of the wholist does indeed derive from this kind of total adherence. For all levels

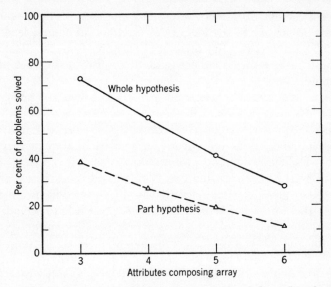

Figure 4. The percentage of problems begun with whole and with part hypotheses that are solved as a function of the number of attributes represented in the problem.

of difficulty, there were more people who seemed able to adhere to all the rules of focussing than those able to follow through with memory-bound scanning. The only explanation we can give as to why the partists who relied on scanning did not "fall apart" faster when problems grew more difficult than did wholist focussers was that the pace of the experiment was too fast. With an increased number of attributes in the instances, and with instances coming one after the other at a rapid rate, the focusser was as likely to get confused in remembering his hypothesis as the scanner was in recalling past instances. We have no direct evidence in support of the explanation, but it seems reasonable.

Under what conditions would one expect wholist focussing to show marked superiority to partist scanning? The results thus far presented indicate a general superiority of the former over the latter. It seems reasonable, does it not, that the more difficult one made the task of remembering instances, the more marked would this superiority be. Take, for example, the "time strain" imposed by the ten-second presentations used in the experiment just described. What if the subjects had been run individually and had been allowed to get instances for testing at their own pace and with as much time registering on instances as they wished? An exploratory study of just this kind has been done (Austin, Bruner, and Seymour, 1953). The same strategies emerge, the same proportion of wholists and partists, although the degree of adherence to ideal strategy is greater under these relaxed conditions. It is interesting to compare the behavior of subjects in this experiment with that of the time-pressured subjects with whose behavior we have been principally concerned in this chapter. Consider the effectiveness of wholists and partists on comparable three- and four-attribute problems. *Without time pressure and proceeding at their own pace, wholists and partists do equally well:* 80% of problems done by wholists were solved correctly; 79% done by partists. But *with time pressure,* 63% of problems done by wholists were solved; 31% done by partists. In short, time pressure has a relatively small deleterious effect on the success of focussing, but a major effect on the success of scanning—literally halving its effectiveness.*

The reasonable conclusion, akin to the conclusion of the preceding chapter, is that the more a task increases the strain inherent in a strategy, the more hazardous will such a strategy become. If one increases the number of alternatives to be kept in mind (e.g., Bruner, Miller, and Zimmerman, 1955), or cuts down redundancy, or increases stress and time pressures, it seems reasonable to expect that a strategy requiring feats of memory and inference will suffer more than one not requiring such feats.

STRATEGIES AS DESCRIPTIVE OF BEHAVIOR

Early in the chapter the point was made in passing that the behavior of our subjects conformed moderately well to the ideal strategies we had described and that, moreover, the degree of conformance

---

* There are several small differences between the major study where time pressure was applied and the pilot study without time pressures: principally that the problems worked under time pressure had fewer redundant instances than the leisurely problems. This probably contributed additionally to the differential effectiveness of the two strategies.

found was massively in excess of what one would expect by chance. It is to this question that we must finally return. How well is behavior described by referring it to the yardstick of ideal strategies?

The first and most obvious point to be made is that the ideal strategies that have served us so steadily in this chapter are essentially refined versions of what we have observed our subjects doing. They were not invented by us in an *a priori* manner. Our description of ideal strategies is a description of what, it seemed to us, our subjects were trying to "bring off."

There are sources of evidence that are considerably stronger than this mild "intuitive" point. The first has to do with the agreement that exists between the theoretical frequencies with which various contingencies should be encountered if subjects are conforming to ideal strategies and the actual frequencies with which contingencies were encountered. The second is the analysis of *total adherence* to ideal strategy: the number of cases in which ideal strategies were followed in their entirety, and the likelihood that such adherence could have occurred by chance.*

Expected and Observed Encounters With Contingencies. For purposes of discussion, we shall concentrate on a problem in which the instances presented the subject contain four attributes, each of them capable of exhibiting one of three possible values. Let us say that the four attributes are number, color, and shape of figures and number of borders. Given a first positive instance on a problem, one may choose as an hypothesis one, two, three, or four values of the initial positive card. In this experiment the correct concept may in fact be defined by any one, two, or three of these values. No concept is defined by all the attribute values in the initial illustrative card. We know, of course, that the larger the number of values defining a concept, the fewer the positive cards. In our present array, 27 of the 81 cards would be positive if the correct concept were defined, say, by the single value "red." Only 3 cards in the 81 possible would be positive if three values defined the concept.

Now the question to be examined is how many instances representing the four contingencies would be expected by chance, given the adoption of an initial hypothesis marked by different numbers of attribute values, when the correct concept itself is defined by dif-

---

* The data presented in this section are taken from the previously mentioned study by Austin, Bruner, and Seymour (1953) in which subjects were allowed to proceed at their own pace and without time pressure. It is with this study that we began our investigation of reception strategies in concept attainment.

ferent numbers of attribute values. More concretely, what contingencies should a wholist or partist encounter? There may be one-, two-, three-, and four-value hypotheses in the face of one-, two-, or three-value concepts. Begin with the presentation of a first instance, a positive card exhibiting one of three possible values of each of four attributes. The correct concept, let us say, is defined by one of the attribute values on the first card. The first card is "2R◯1b" and it exemplifies the concept "R." Suppose the subject now adopts a one-value hypothesis consistent with the first instance. This could be either "2," "R," "◯," or "1b." Now we ask, what is the chance that a next card, chosen at random from the array of possible instances, will be positive confirming, positive infirming, negative confirming, or negative infirming? We know that one-third or 27 of the cards in the array are positive, i.e., contain a red figure. Now the chance that any of these will be positive *and confirming* will be as follows. If the subject has the right hypothesis, "R," all 27 positive instances will be confirming. If he has any of the three wrong one-value hypotheses, say "1b," only nine of these will be confirming: the nine instances that contain both "R" and "1b." Thus, the average theoretical frequency of positive confirming encounters on the first instance after the illustrative card is:

$$\frac{9 + 9 + 9 + 27}{4} = 13.5$$

It is in this way that the values contained in Table 5 are computed. They represent the average theoretical frequency with which a second instance in a series will fall into one of the contingencies when this second instance has been picked at random from the array of 81 possible instances.

It can readily be seen from this table that there is *no* chance of encountering a negative infirming contingency on the second instance if one begins by adopting a four-value hypothesis (a whole hypothesis). The smaller the number of values in one's initial hypothesis, the greater the likelihood that the next card will be negative infirming. This is true regardless of the number of values actually defining the concept. Contrariwise, the likelihood of encountering a negative confirming instance increases as the number of values in one's hypothesis increases.

If we now examine the behavior of our subjects, it will be apparent that partists do encounter more negative *infirming* instances than wholists, and that wholists meet more negative *confirming* instances. Similarly, wholists will show a higher ratio of positive infirming to posi-

TABLE 5

Number of Instances in the 81-Card Array That Will on the Average Fall Into Each of the Four Contingencies When the Subject Has Adopted Different Numbers of Values of the Initial Positive Card as His Hypothesis

Attribute Values Defining Correct Concept	Contingency	Attribute Values in Hypothesis			
		1	2	3	4*
1	PC	13.5	6.0	2.0	1.0
	PI	13.5	21.0	25.0	26.0
	NC	40.5	51.0	53.5	54.0
	NI	13.5	3.0	0.5	0.0
2	PC	6.75	4.0	2.0	1.0
	PI	2.25	5.0	7.0	8.0
	NC	51.0	66.7	71.0	72.0
	NI	21.0	5.3	1.0	0.0
3	PC	2.5	2.0	1.5	1.0
	PI	0.5	1.0	1.5	2.0
	NC	53.5	71.0	76.5	78.0
	NI	24.5	7.0	1.5	0.0

tive confirming contingencies than will partists. Table 6 shows the average number of different contingencies encountered by subjects on problems begun with whole or with part hypotheses.

TABLE 6

Average Contingencies Encountered per Problem by Subjects Beginning With Whole and Part Hypotheses†

Contingency	Initial Whole Hypothesis	Initial Part Hypothesis
PC	0.7	1.0
PI	1.3	1.0
NC	3.4	2.8
NI	0.4	1.0
Total contingencies	5.8	5.8

In general, there is quite fair agreement between the incidence of contingencies we would expect to occur if subjects followed the two ideal strategies and the incidence we observe to occur in the problems begun with part and whole hypotheses.

The major difference lies in the expected and observed frequency of encountering a negative infirming contingency after starting with

---

* For this array adoption of a four-attribute hypothesis constitutes the wholist approach.

† Based on 355 problems begun with whole hypotheses; 214 begun with part hypotheses.

a whole hypothesis. If the wholist strategy is fully followed, negative infirming contingencies cannot occur. But they are encountered on an average of 0.4 times per problem per subject. These negative infirming contingencies arise from subjects' occasionally departing from the rules of the strategy. Outside of this one discrepancy between the general observed and expected incidences of contingency encounters, the agreement is more than sufficient to demonstrate the utility of describing and analyzing performance in terms of its conformance to ideal strategies.

The Incidence of Complete Adherence to Strategy Rules. To what degree, given a part or whole hypothesis, do subjects conform respectively to the rules of the scanning and focussing strategies—the strategies ideally suited for modifying such hypotheses? The bare findings can be stated quickly. Of the problems that were begun with a whole hypothesis, 47% were followed up on all subsequent contingencies with complete adherence to the rules of focussing. Of problems begun with a part hypothesis, 38% were followed through with complete adherence to the rules of scanning.

This incidence of complete and correct adherence is strikingly high. It is even more so when we inquire how they compare with what one would expect by chance. What is the chance expectancy for strict adherence?

There are various chance models that one can employ here: robots endowed, if you will, with differing amounts of inference and memory ability. A completely stupid robot, one who is as random as we can make him, would emit an hypothesis after each instance with no bias. For example, he would not even pay attention to the card being presented to him. This means that for a four-attribute array, he would choose indifferently among the 256 possible hypotheses in terms of which the array of instances may be subdivided into categories. If five instances are presented, and he must do something about his hypothesis each time an instance is encountered even if only maintain it, then the chances of obtaining any particular set of five hypotheses over the five instances would be one in 256^5 and this is a very small fraction indeed. And this, of course, is the probability that hypotheses would be changed consistently according to rule over five instances.

But surely this is too stupid a chance model to be anything but trivial. Let us construct a robot whose only rational property is that he emits an hypothesis upon the presentation of an instance that is consistent with that instance. On the first instance and indeed on every instance, his chances of choosing a particular hypothesis would be a function of the number of consistent hypotheses possible given any one instance. For three-attribute arrays, there are 8 such; for four-attribute arrays, 15; and for five- and six-attribute arrays, 31 and 63 respectively. Thus the chance of a particular hypothesis after any given instance would be $\frac{1}{8}$, $\frac{1}{15}$, $\frac{1}{31}$, and $\frac{1}{63}$ respectively. The chance expectancy that a focusser will follow all the rules consistently on a four-attribute problem containing 5 instances would be $(\frac{1}{15})^5$ or once in 15^5 problems. This is still astronomical, and is considerably greater when one goes to problems based on arrays with still more attributes and still larger numbers of instances. The modest example just taken gives us a prediction that only once in 759,375 problems should we expect to find the rules adhered to strictly throughout a problem. This is for a robot who has good enough sense to emit only hypotheses that are consistent with each instance placed before him.

One could go beyond the last model proposed and construct robots with better inference capacities and with the ability to store information from past instances. But this can only end in the construction of a model that shows the same rate of adherence as our subjects. While this might be a useful exercise in model construction, it is not within the range of our task. Our effort has been to show, simply, that the rate of adherence to the rules of strategy was greatly in excess of what one would obtain from people behaving in a random fashion.

RECEPTION STRATEGIES IN PERSPECTIVE

We began with the contrast between two great figures in the history of brain anatomy, Broca and Flourens; the one starting with the assumption that specific areas of the cortex provide one with the proper stuff for hypotheses about brain functioning, the other with the conviction that one must begin with the concept of the whole brain. The burden of the studies reported in the chapter is that one can proceed rationally from either initial position to the discovery of what features of the brain are indeed relevant to what kinds of mental functioning. But whichever way one starts, there are certain consequences that follow, for with each initial preference there goes a distinctive and appropriate strategy.

The task one faces in dealing with an arbitrary sequence of instances is one in which the major freedom of the problem-solver is in formulating or altering his hypotheses about what is common to an array of instances. Here is a patient with lung cancer: he smokes, lives in a city, has immediate kin with a history of cancer, and has had chest colds frequently during the last ten years. *All* or *some* of these must be taken initially as a relevant hypothesis about the "cause" of cancer of the lung. From then on, "freedom" consists in the handling of four contingencies: a problem-solver will encounter exemplars and nonexemplars of the category for whose definition he is searching, and each of these will perforce confirm or infirm the hypothesis he is entertaining at the time of encounter. What the problem-solver must learn is how to modify his initial hypothesis upon encountering each kind of contingency. And this task, we have seen, is bound by the nature of his initial hypothesis. In the main, the focussing strategy appropriate to an initial whole hypothesis is less demanding both on inference and memory than the scanning strategy required to make good an initial part hypothesis.

It appears that far more people prefer to start with a whole hypothesis than with any other form of hypothesis. Moreover, people are consistent from problem to problem in their initial approach. It further appears that, whether one prefers a whole hypothesis or a part one, one is likely thereafter to conform to the rules of the appropriate strategy overwhelmingly in excess of chance.

Because the appropriate scanning follow-up to a part hypothesis is more mnemonically and inferentially demanding than the focussing follow-up to an initial whole hypothesis, the former strategy may be considered more vulnerable to all those conditions that would make record-keeping difficult. An experiment illustrating one such condition has been reported. The condition is the effect of time pressure: reducing the time available for the subject to weigh, consider, or generally reflect on the nature of instances encountered. When such time pressures are applied, we find that the damage done to the user of the memory-bound part hypothesis is more severe than the damage to the wholist. The former cannot apply the rules of his strategy as effectively and one finds a sharp decrement in the proportion of problems that are successfully solved.

We have examined in these pages the manner in which a human being deals with the task of sorting out events that come to him in a haphazard sequence, finding out which of the events are significant and which are not. The experiment has utilized highly stylized materials—slips of cardboard with designs varying in certain properties printed on them—but the task is not so different from the task of the traveler learning what type of inn can be trusted by its externals and without the pain of sampling the service, or of any person who must learn what something is by means short of trying it out directly.

There are certain interesting ways in which our experiments differ from comparable problem-solving in everyday life. One of these is in the sheer concentratedness of the task. We are rarely flooded at such a rate with new instances to absorb. On the other hand, our subjects are required to retain only one concept at a time and are shielded from other distractions. Our subjects must also perform without the aid of such enormously important cultural tools as pencils and paper with all that these can do for us in extending the highly limited range of memory and attention. Interestingly enough, however, we find that allowing the use of pencil and paper and easy access to a record of past instances does not necessarily give an advantage in performance. (Cf. Goodnow, Bruner, Matter, and Potter, 1955.) Another difference between our procedures and what happens outside the laboratory we know from the preceding chapter. The materials with which our subjects deal do not lend themselves to thematizing, to encoding in the form of little plots or themas. This abstractness of the materials is, we know, a mixed blessing. On the one hand, it saves the problem-solver from his preconceptions as to what is relevant. But on the other hand, it prevents him from using the wonderfully diverse methods of conserving information through assimilation to familiar themes, the methods whose strengths and weaknesses are so vividly told in Bartlett's classic *Remembering* (1932) and more rigorously recounted in the studies of Miller and Selfridge (1950) and others who have applied information theory to memory phenomena.

Finally, the point will undoubtedly occur to the reader that the motivation of our subjects was either different from or "less than" what one might expect to find in ordinary life where the consequences or payoff attendant on attaining a concept may be greater. Certainly motivation is "different." Intuitively, having watched our subjects struggle and strain, we think it unlikely that it is any "less"— whatever "more or less" can be taken to mean. The sense in which the motivation of our subjects is "different" from what one would be likely to find in a "real-life" situation is worth a word in passing.

Our subjects were quite clearly "trying to succeed" and the task obviously aroused achievement needs and other extrinsic motives. But what is more important, they were trying to get information, to attain a concept. That this is a powerful motive, nobody will deny. We need not go into the question of the primary or secondary status of such a need. All we need know is that our subjects were impelled by it. As we remarked in Chapter 3, the "reinforcement" or satisfaction of such a need is the act of acquiring the information sought.

This keeps our subjects going. In so far as other motives are also aroused in the situation, the "act of getting information" takes on broader significance. It may mean to the subject "I am a bright fellow" or "I'll show this psychologist!" Such extrinsic consequences of information-getting may, of course, alter the patterning of the behavior observed in our subjects. It is conceivable that had we exposed our subjects to the kind of status stress employed by Postman and Bruner (1948) in their study of perceptual recognition, there would have been less incidence of adherence to strategy. We do not know. Obviously, our experiments are neither a proper sampling of real-life situations nor of the kinds of stress that can be applied to subjects. Such research remains to be done. The paradigm we have used will serve, we hope, to make that later research more technically feasible.

One other feature of motivation distinguishes our subjects from, say, the average scientist working on a comparable scientific problem. Our subjects had no passion to prove that a particular attribute was *the* correct attribute in the sense that Broca was impelled to prove that a particular brain center was responsible for human speech. This is a matter of importance, and it seems not unreasonable to extrapolate from experiments in the preceding chapter, that had there been such an investment in a particular attribute there would have been far more part-scanning. The preference for wholist focussing probably reflects a certain dispassionateness among our subjects with respect to the attributes that were used in the experiment.

Finally, one general point needs to be made. In dealing with the task of conceptualizing arbitrary sequences, human beings behave in a highly patterned, highly "rational" manner. The concept of strategy has made it possible to describe this sequential patterning. It is only when one departs from the analysis of individual acts-at-a-moment that the sequentially coherent nature of problem-solving becomes clear.

CHAPTER 6

On disjunctive concepts
and their attainment

Consider now the nature of a disjunctive concept. We begin with a class of objects that are uniform in terms of some ultimate criterion. All members, let us say, have the property of being edible or of being useful for building bridges or of producing a rash when touched. This much, an ultimate criterion, is a feature of an array of things which we call a class or category, disjunctive or otherwise. What makes a class disjunctive is the *manner* in which one can use the defining attributes of objects to determine whether or not they are indeed members of the class—whether they are edible, good for bridge building, or allergy-producing. Members of a disjunctive class exhibit defining attributes such that one *or* another of these attributes can be used in identifying or categorizing them. Thus, the class of substances capable of producing an identical allergic reaction in an individual may include *either* cat hair *or* chalk dust *or* sepia ink. A substance containing *any one or any combination* of these defining attributes is necessary and sufficient for producing the class-defining effect.*

When a person knows that he can use defining attributes in this disjunctive way or does indeed use them in this way for inferring that objects belong in a certain category, we say that he has learned the category. In our terms, learning a category is identical with "attaining a concept."

What is peculiarly difficult about attaining a disjunctive category is that two of its members, each uniform in terms of an ultimate

---

* In the precise but bizarre language of mathematical logic, the matter of disjunction is stated thus: "We may take next disjunction, 'p or q.' This is a function whose truth-value is truth when p is true and also when q is true, but is falsehood when both p and q are false." Bertrand Russell, 1919, p. 147.

156

criterion, may have no defining attributes in common. Two positive instances of the class, "allergy producers," may be as different as chalk dust from cat fur, sharing nothing save their like effect on an organism. The problem-solver faced with the task of discovering the defining attributes of such a class must, if he is to succeed, abandon the conventional strategies of attempting to isolate those features that are *common to all* members of the class. For in a disjunctive class, there are no such universal common features.

As an example of disjunctive concept attainment, take the brain anatomy problem discussed earlier. A neuroanatomist is trying to find out which of six cytoarchitectural areas of the cortex are necessary in order for an organism to show pattern vision. The class or concept being sought is "brains adequate to mediate pattern vision." Six cortical areas provide the attributes to be explored for their defining value, and each of these "attributes" has two values: it may either be intact or destroyed. All that our neuroanatomical problem-solver knows is that brains with *all* six areas intact exhibit the capacity for pattern vision; brains with none of the areas intact are incapable of mediating pattern vision.

If the class, "brain capable of mediating pattern vision," were disjunctive, experiments would in the end show—to give one example— that so long as *either or both of two specific areas are intact* pattern vision can be mediated. In this case, two of the areas, call them I and II, are defining attributes; four of them are "noisy" or nondefining. The defining properties of a brain capable of pattern vision, then, would be "instances of areas I and/or II." We say that "experiments would in the end" show this. But the fact of the matter is that in arriving at this end there would be interminable ground for controversy, unless at the outset the essential disjunctiveness of the concept had been recognized. If the assumption of conjunctiveness prevailed, one scientist, having found that destruction of Area I disrupted pattern vision, would publish an "Area I theory." Another, finding that Area II produced pattern agnosia, would publish a contradicting paper. A third, finding that destruction of both areas did the damage, would then claim that very likely the first two scientists had inadvertently destroyed both areas through secondary degeneration and that was why they had obtained the effects. What is crucial for utilization of the information obtained by these experiments is the adoption of a strategy for dealing with instances of a disjunctive class. And it is with this that much of the chapter will be concerned.

Disjunctive concepts have a rather special informational characteristic. It is the asymmetry of inference from defining attributes to class membership and from class membership to defining attributes: the asymmetry of inference from cue to label and from label to cue. Take the very first example given at the beginning of the book: to be a member of the class admissible to the Altavista civic association, one must *either* reside legally in Altavista, *or* own property there, *or* be engaged in business within the town's limits. Any one or any combination of these suffices for eligibility. One can predict from defining attributes to class membership with certainty. If one knows that Mr. Smith has a legal residence in Altavista, then one knows with certainty that he is a member of that class of human beings eligible for membership in the local civic association. But if, on the other hand, one knows only that Mr. Smith is so eligible, one can make no inference with certainty as to the nature of his defining characteristics. You will not know whether Mr. Smith lives in the town, runs a business there, owns property there, or is marked by all or some pair of these characteristics. Thus, knowing that a particular instance exemplifies a disjunctive class does not have the same predictive value as knowing that it belongs to a conjunctive class. A positive instance cannot help one as much in the task of locating defining attributes. This is the first difficulty and it leads immediately to a second difficulty.

We have often mentioned the preference for direct test shown by subjects. In attempting to gain information about the defining properties of a concept, subjects seek to test directly whether a given attribute value is or is not relevant. Our neuroanatomist will want to investigate each area directly: seeing how it operates when intact, what happens when it is ablated. In the case of disjunctive concepts, the usual methods of testing directly the relevance of various attributes prove to be inadequate. The usual conjunctive method is very simple. One takes an instance that is known to exemplify a concept. What features or attributes are responsible for its being an exemplar? To find out, we change one or several of its attribute values. If the resulting instance is positive, then the changed attribute or attributes can have nothing to do with the concept. If it is negative, then the value of the attribute before it was changed must have been part of the definition of the concept. This is indeed direct and it is very much part of the usual mode of operating in conjunctive problem-solving. See how inappropriate it is in the case of disjunctive concepts.

Let us work with the example of people who are eligible for the local civic association. Consider an imaginary experiment in the town of Altavista. Our investigator has the task of finding out what makes people eligible for the civic association. Let us say he already knows that the only attributes worth considering are whether or not a person has legal residence in Altavista, is in business there, or owns property there. We give him as instances to test a list of 100 people who represent all the variations of the three attributes, each with its two values. He chooses as a first instance to test somebody who lives in the town, owns property there, and runs one of the town's shops. He is informed that the man is eligible. He then chooses another person, one who has in common all but one characteristic: this man does not work in Altavista. He is told that this man too is eligible. But it will be the investigator's undoing if he assumes that the attribute he has changed is irrelevant to the concept because the change did not result in a negative instance. In sum, no direct test premised on the progressive change of a positive instance is possible.

What this means, of course, is that the investigator will have to devise a solution for approaching the concept "from the outside in." That is to say, if he is to use direct testing at all, he will have to start from the base of negative information. In terms of our example, one must start one's search for the definition of an eligible member by first finding someone who is ineligible. Then, keeping firmly in mind the characteristics of this negative case, one must find somebody who differs from him in one characteristic. If the new characteristic makes the difference of rendering a person eligible, then obviously it is a relevant attribute, and the value of the attribute that is defining is the one that characterizes the exemplar. In point of fact, it is difficult for subjects to proceed in this way, for most of our testing of the environment seems to be geared to working with positive instances and with variations on these.

Here, then, we have a type of category that at best seems clumsy. All members do not share the same defining attributes. In consequence, one cannot infer much about the defining attributes of a member simply by virtue of knowing its category membership. The possibility of using the "common features" of a collection of positive exemplars is ruled out. Such concepts have the property, finally, that to locate or learn their defining properties one must begin "backwards"—by taking as a focus an instance of what the category is *not*.

Before turning to the analysis of the behavior of subjects working with disjunctive concepts, we should do well to look more closely at the status of these concepts in everyday life.

DISJUNCTIVE CONCEPTS IN EVERYDAY LIFE

When one examines culturally defined forms of the disjunctive concept—social groups, for example, of elites or of the professions— one finds that there is a tendency for disjunctive definitions to be modified over time into more easily grasped conjunctive forms. The professions provide particularly striking examples of this. The category or concept, "clinical psychologist," is a nice contemporary example. In terms of ultimate criterion, the clinical psychologist is one who practices the arts of mental healing without a medical degree. Now in such groupings, the defining attributes of the class are a matter of grave concern for they constitute what is called the "qualifications" of a practitioner. Since the ultimate criterion of "practicing mental healing" has consequences for the public weal, it is necessary to control socially the appropriate defining attributes of practitioners. At the outset, before stringent control is imposed, the defining attributes of the class, "clinical psychologist," tend to be disjunctive. That is to say, a person who has had graduate training in psychology may be eligible in the sense of actually practicing; so too those individuals who, without benefit of academic training, have had experience in dealing with disturbed people in a hospital setting, in a pastoral role, or in some other way. Thus, the qualifications become an "either-or" affair. What is typical when social control is sought is that eventually regulations are passed serving to "regularize" the defining qualifications of the class. Almost invariably, such regularization takes the form of rendering the definition of the class conjunctive. In the case of clinical psychologists, a Board of Examiners is created and examinations are set. Passing the examination, then, constitutes the defining qualification for practice of the profession. When the cycle is complete, the class, "clinical psychologist," has been rendered conjunctive. One must have passed the examination, be of a certain age, have achieved a certain level of schooling, perhaps be a citizen of the nation or state where one will practice, and all the qualifications must be present simultaneously in each member of the class or profession. It is not surprising, then, to find a widespread movement to "conjunctivize" and professionalize many semiprofessional fields such as chiropractic, podiatry, accounting, dietetics, etc.

To be sure, the examples we have considered are not explicable in terms of a general "abhorrence of disjunctiveness," for it is apparent that other powerful, noncognitive motives are involved. Yet one can find examples of social categories less subject to immediate social pressures where such an abhorrence seems to be present. Consider any instance where inclusion or noninclusion in a given class or grouping is of consequence to the individuals involved, but where "professionalizing" pressures are not operative. Take as an example the concept of the *elite* in a culture. It may include a person of wealth, or a member of a distinguished family, or a distinguished practitioner of a certain profession (not necessarily highly remunerative), or any combination thereof. To simplify or render conjunctive such disjunctive definitions of "elite," we create institutions which put an official "brand" on individuals so that the brand may serve in place of the disjunctive attributes. *Who's Who*, the Royal Society, the French Academy, and the system of starring in *American Men of Science* are a few cases in point.

Finally, the realm of science provides a wide variety of examples of "justifiable" suspicion of disjunctively defined concepts. In physiology and physiological psychology, disjunctive concepts have often later been converted into conjunctive or relational terms. The sensory physiology of the skin was for a time bedevilled by the phenomena of paradoxical cold and paradoxical warm sensations. It had been observed by von Frey, by Alrutz, and by Thunberg (cf. Boring, 1942) around the turn of the present century that a sufficiently cold stimulus applied to a certain area gave a sensation of warmth but stimuli of *higher* temperature applied to the same area would under other conditions give a cold sensation. Similarly, it was found that a stimulus of sufficiently high temperature gave a sensation of cold when applied to a certain spot, yet cooler stimuli than this applied to the same area would give a sensation of warmth. In essence, then, the definition of a "stimulus adequate for producing a cold sensation" became disjunctive: sufficiently cool or sufficiently warm stimulation to an area of the skin could produce "coldness," the criterion attribute of the class. A similar disjunctivity characterized the class of "warmth-producing stimuli." In good season, the explanation turned out to be relational: depending upon the adaptation level of the receptors of the skin, an area stimulus would produce warmth or cold as a function of its relation to the adaptation level of the skin receptors. Below the level, it produced cold; above it, warmth. Disjunctiveness was merely an artifact of incomplete experimental technique.

A parallel case can be found in the disjunctive definition of therapeutic agents capable of relieving swelling of a bruised joint: ice pack *or* hot compress. Closer examination of the case shows that both can be defined in terms of their relational position to temperature at the site of injury: marked deviation from body temperature in either direction is what produces the increase in circulatory flow. The organism is reacting homeostatically to any stimulus outside the normal range of temperature.

So frequent have been these instances of eventual obsolescence of disjunctive definitions of classes of events that the very discovery of one such seems to act as a challenge to future research rather than as an occasion for celebrating a "finding." If one finds, for example, that insulin subcoma, electroshock therapy, and narcosynthesis all produce an increased rate of remission in schizophrenic psychotics, one is immediately tempted to inquire what these three forms of treatment have "in common"—the assumption being that some relational or conjunctive way of defining "adequate treatments for schizophrenia" must be forthcoming. And, indeed, they usually are. One eventually begins to wonder whether Nature herself does not abhor disjunctive groupings!

AN EXPLORATORY EXPERIMENT*

The exploratory experiment with which the remainder of the chapter is concerned was designed to examine the manner in which intelligent adults go about the attainment of disjunctive concepts. The subjects, again students in Harvard College, were 50 in number and were divided into five groups in a manner presently to be described. As in all of our experimental procedures, they were told openly what their task was: to find out which cards on a board before them were the positive cards and which were negative in the sense of exemplifying or not exemplifying a concept that the experimenter had in mind. They were told, moreover, that the concepts which they had to discover were of the disjunctive type and a full explanation of these was given. The explanation was readily grasped since it was illustrated by reference to the stimuli present before the subject. The subjects, always tested individually, could choose one card at a time in any order they wished and after each choice the experimenter would tell them whether the card was positive or negative. After each choice the subjects could offer an hypothesis as to the concept and these the experimenter honored by indicating whether they were right or wrong. If the former, the problem was considered finished. While the subjects were not told that they must

---

*The experiment reported here was designed, executed, and analyzed in collaboration with Lotte Lazarsfeld Bailyn and the present section of the chapter was written with her collaboration. Many of the techniques of analyzing disjunctive concept attainment reported here were developed by her.

limit themselves to one hypothesis after each choice, they rarely offered more than one and often offered none.

The stimulus array was always in view of the subject. It was composed of the combination of four attributes, each with two values, totalling 16 instances. Each instance contained two figures: a small one and a large one. The small figure varied in color (black or yellow, b or y) and in shape (rectangle or triangle, r or t); the large figure varied in the same way: yellow or black in color, (B or Y), rectangular or triangular in shape (R or T). Thus, a given instance might be a small black rectangular figure and a large yellow triangular figure or any of the 16 combinations possible in such an array. The cards were set out in a random array on the board.

Each subject had three concepts to attain, and all of the concepts used were defined by only two attributes. The subject was told this in advance and thus always knew that his task was to find *which two attributes* and their values were relevant for defining the concept. Thus, a concept might be a "small triangle or a large rectangle or both," and any instance that had either a small rectangle, or a large triangle, or both would be positive. Now, in this array, four instances would contain one half of the concept and thus be positive, four others would be positive because they exhibited the other half of the concept, and still four others would be positive and contain both features of the disjunctive concept. In all, then, 12 of the 16 cards would always be positive, the remainder negative in the sense of not exemplifying the concept.

There are in such an array as ours 24 different ways of grouping the instances into two-attribute disjunctive concepts or categories. The 24 possible concepts can be summarized as follows:

yY	rY	YR
yB	rB	YT
yR	rR	BR
yT	rT	BT
bY	tY	yr
bB	tB	yt
bR	tR	br
bT	rT	bt

We come now to the design of the experiment. Each subject, as we have said, had three problems to solve. On each of the three problems, as we have noted, the subject was first shown a card, in some cases a positive instance and in others a negative, depending upon the experimental group he was in. Following the presentation of this first card, he could choose whatever cards he wanted to and was permitted to offer hypotheses after each choice. When the subject offered the correct concept as his hypothesis, the problem was considered solved and no further choices were made.

The 50 subjects were given various "treatments." Some were given a positive instance to begin with, some a negative instance as a first illustrative card. When a positive card was shown initially, it sometimes contained half the defining attributes of the concept, sometimes all of them. The objective of these variations was, of course, to sample conditions that might affect the manner in which subjects would go about attaining a disjunctive concept. And indeed, as we shall see, one of the "treatments" turned out to be of major importance —whether one starts the task with a positive or a negative instance. Fifty problems were begun with a negative instance, the remainder with a positive instance.

INFORMATIONAL ANALYSIS OF INSTANCES

Before examining the problem-solving behavior of our 50 subjects, we must first look more searchingly at the informativeness of the different kinds of choices that can be made following the presentation of a first illustrative card. Imagine a person with complete memory and complete inference capacity. He begins the task with the knowledge that there are 24 possible concepts and is able to keep all of them in mind simultaneously. Now, the number of possible concepts eliminated by the first card presented depends upon whether it is positive or negative. A first illustrative card that is positive eliminates 6 of the 24 possible concepts. A first negative card is more useful informationally: it permits one to eliminate 18 possible concepts, leaving 6 including the correct one.

The information potentially available from a first card chosen by the subject after seeing an illustrative instance will depend upon whether it is positive or negative and in how many respects it differs from the illustrative card previously presented. The minimum difference between two cards will be in a single attribute value: the difference, say, between a small yellow rectangle with large yellow triangle (yrYT) on the one hand and a small yellow rectangle with large yellow rectangle (yrYR) on the other. And the maximum is between two instances different in *all four* of the attribute values (yrYT and btBR). The number of possible concepts logically eliminated by various initial choices, differing from the illustrative card in different numbers of attribute values and turning out to be positive or negative, is presented in Table 7.

TABLE 7

Number of Possible Concepts Logically Eliminated After a First Choice
That Follows the Presentation of an Illustrative Card to the Subject

Illustrative Card

Diff. Between Illust. Card and Choice	Positive (18 Possible Concepts Remain)		Negative (6 Possible Concepts Remain)	
	Positive Choice	Negative Choice	Positive Choice	Negative Choice
1	3	15	3	3
2	5	13	1	5
3	6	12	0	—
4	6	12	0	—

Several things about Table 7 should be noted. The first is that, after a positive illustrative card, a choice that turns out to be negative eliminates far more alternative hypotheses than does a positive choice. This is so no matter how many attribute values differentiate the illustrative card from the first choice. In the case of choices after a negative illustrative card, it should be said right off that there does not exist a negative instance that differs in more than two attribute values from the illustrative card, since the correct concept is defined by two of the four attributes. But if the subject should choose a card that differs in two attribute values from the negative illustrative instance, and if it should turn out to be negative, then he eliminates five of the six remaining hypotheses and, of course, can solve the problem. The choice of a positive instance after a negative illustrative card can yield relatively little information and indeed will be redundant if the choice represents a change in more than two attribute values of the illustrative card.

It is possible to construct a table to indicate the informational status of second choices, but little would be served by going through the exercise. The same general rule can be stated that negative instances will, on the whole, tend to be more valuable informationally than positive instances.

What we have described thus far is the formal informational or logical value of instances encountered in sequence. From this type of analysis we know what is the maximum information that can be obtained from any instance. This is, let it be said, a far cry from the information that is *in fact* assimilated by a problem-solver seeking to find the defining attributes of a disjunctive concept. For assimilability depends upon the nature of the strategy one employs in choosing and using instances. If a thoroughly inappropriate strategy is used, then no information will be assimilated and in spite of exposure to instances no progress toward the discovery of attributes will be made. It is only with an appropriate strategy that one can obtain the maximum information contained in encountered instances and achieve solution with a minimum number of choices.

SOME DISJUNCTIVE STRATEGIES

All appropriate strategies depend upon the use of one or more negative instances. In the most efficient strategy, one finds a negative instance and chooses instances that differ from it in a single value. If the change results in another negative instance (given two-value attributes), the attribute in question is irrelevant. If the change yields a positive instance, the new value is one of those that define the concept. After one value has been thus located, one *starts again from a negative instance*, changing the values of other attributes until, in this way, one has located all the disjunctive defining attributes. This procedure we shall call *negative focussing* and it makes complete use of all the information formally contained in a sequence of instances.

The following is a typical protocol of negative focussing. The correct concept is bR (small black figure and/or large rectangle).

Illustrative card ytYT (−)* eliminates 18 possibilities, 6 remain.
First choice　　　btYT (+) eliminates 3 possibilities, 3 remain (b is relevant).
Second choice　ytBT (−) eliminates 1 possibility, 2 remain (B is irrelevant).
Third choice　　ytYR (+) eliminates 1 possibility, 1 remains (R is relevant).
Hypothesis: bR (correct).

The subject uses the first negative instance (the illustrative card) as a focus, changing its attributes one at a time until he has explored enough to find the two disjunctive defining attribute values. When he changes y to b, the new instance becomes positive: therefore b is a part of the concept. When he changes Y to B, the new instance remains negative: therefore B is *not* part of the concept. When T gets changed to R, the new instance becomes positive: so R is a part of the concept. Therefore the concept is bR. It is not necessary in this experiment to check the remaining attribute by changing t to r, for subjects already know that the concept is defined by only two attribute values and both have been found.

A second procedure, also an appropriate strategy, makes less efficient

---

* (−)denotes a negative instance; (+) a positive instance.

use of instances. It consists of choosing cards until the subject has obtained *two or more negative instances*. Since there is a very high probability that positive instances will also be obtained in this pursuit, he will usually have encountered and identified two negative instances and one or more positive ones. The strategy consists of taking those values that are common to the negative instances at the subject's disposal and using their opposites as the features of the correct concept. It is a complex and rather inefficient procedure, which we call the *multiple negative strategy*.

A few examples of how one may go right and go wrong with the multiple negative strategy will provide a picture of its strengths and weaknesses. Suppose the correct concept is a small yellow figure and a large rectangle (yR). The most auspicious circumstances for correct solution is two negative instances that share two common values and differ in two others:

Illustrative card	brBT (−)	eliminates 18 possibilities, 6 remain.
First choice	btYT (−)	eliminates 5 possibilities, 1 remains.

The two instances share the values bT. The opposites of these two values, yR, are taken properly as the correct concept. The correct concept is completely determined by the two instances. The worst case can be described as one in which the strategy is followed to the letter—and a wrong answer obtained. An example is the following, the correct concept again being yR.

Illustrative card	ytBT (+)	eliminates 6 possibilities, 18 remain.
First choice	yrYT (+)	eliminates 5 possibilities, 13 remain.
Second choice	brBT (−)	eliminates 3 possibilities, 10 remain.
Third choice	yrBT (+)	eliminates 2 possibilities, 8 remain.
Fourth choice	btBT (−)	eliminates 1 possibility, 7 remain.

Following this sequence, the subject finds three values common to the two negative instances encountered: b, B, and T. He examines the positive instances to find the opposite values and finds the opposites of b and B. He then concludes that the correct concept is y and/or Y—an incorrect deduction. At best, the strategy is excellent, at worst it is misleading. More often than not, it is adequate. Always it depends upon indirect test in the sense that the subject must use the *opposite values* of what is common to negative instances as his hypothesis.

Both the appropriate strategies, negative focussing and multiple negative, it can readily be seen, lean heavily upon the use of instances that are negative: illustrations of what the concept is not. In this sense, one can see that negative instances have a special psychological value as a "starting point" for appropriately handling a disjunctive concept.

Consider now the actual behavior of subjects attempting to locate the defining attributes of a disjunctive concept.

CONJUNCTIVE TENDENCIES IN ATTEMPTED SOLUTIONS

The most general statement that can be made about attempts to attain disjunctive concepts is that they seem on the whole to be designed to attain conjunctive concepts. In spite of the fact that the disjunctive concepts and their properties had been carefully explained, subjects showed regularly what can only be called "conjunctive tendencies": making choices and using information in a manner specifically suited to the solution of conjunctive concepts and unsuited to the solution of disjunctive ones.

The first of these was a tendency on the part of subjects to *utilize only positive instances as a basis for forming hypotheses.* This approach is designed to provide an answer to the question: what is common to an array of positive instances? This question, as we have seen, is inappropriate to the disjunctive case. One indication of this differential use of positive and negative instances can be found in the inconsistent hypotheses offered by subjects. An inconsistent hypothesis is one that has already been eliminated by an instance previously encountered. If we consider, for simplicity's sake, only the first hypotheses offered by subjects, we find that 37 are inconsistent with a prior instance encountered. Of these, 28 are inconsistent with a prior *negative* instance, 6 with both positive and negative instances, and only 3 with positive instances alone. Subjects seemed not as willing or able to absorb the information of negative instances.

In its most striking form, this tendency to use positive instances only may be called the *common-element fallacy.* As the name suggests, it consists in collating all the features common to the positive instances one has encountered and proposing these common features as an hypothesis about the correct concept. If all the positive instances thus far encountered contained a large rectangle and a small yellow figure, a person committing the common-element fallacy would then propose "small yellow figure and/or large rectangle" (y and/or R) as his hypothesis. Such hypotheses can, of course, be correct by chance, but not very often. For the common elements may very well be those attribute values that are irrelevant to the concept. After all, two positive instances may have no attribute values in common at all: one of them may be positive because it contains one half of the defining attributes, the other because it contains the other half of the two attribute values defining the concept.

There is a rather roughshod form of the common-element fallacy worth remarking. This we have called the *majority fallacy*. Rather than use the common element of an array of positive instances as the basis of formulating an hypothesis, the subject will use those attribute values that occur in a *majority* of the positive instances he has encountered. The origin of the fallacy is readily understandable. The subject attempts to use the common-element strategy, but he is faced with the fact that there is no element or elements common to *all* the positive instances encountered. In formulating his hypothesis, then, he will choose those attribute values of the array of positive instances encountered which come closest to being common elements.

The next form of inappropriate strategy is not so "bad," perhaps, as those already discussed. Its difficulty rests on the failure of the subject to bear in mind what can make a positive instance positive when dealing with disjunctive concepts. In simple form it consists of the error of assuming that a positive instance is positive because it contains *both* values defining the concept. In this erring strategy, which we call *positive anchoring*, the subject derives his hypotheses by comparing a negative card encountered with a positive illustrative instance he has been shown and adopting those *two* values of the positive illustrative card that distinguish it from the negative card. It is very tempting and can be readily verbalized as "choosing the two things that the positive card has and the negative one doesn't." While it is an ideal conjunctive strategy, it leads to grief when applied in the present case. The subject has been told that the concept is defined by two "either-or" attributes. He has before him a positive illustration of the concept and a negative instance, differing in two values. Now, *if* the positive illustrative card contained *both* values defining the concept, the subject's hypothesis would be completely correct—although, paradoxically enough, the two instances before him would not contain sufficient formal information to make the hypothesis certain. Indeed, the strategy is a "gambling" type of negative focussing. But if, as in 70 problems worked by subjects, the initial positive illustration is positive because it has only one of the defining values, then the subject cannot be correct.

Two examples serve to illustrate the "lucky" use of the strategy—the occasions when it works because the positive illustrative card has both defining values present—and the "ill-fated" use of the strategy. Let us say that the concept is a small yellow figure and a large triangle (y and/or T).

Illustrative instance   yrBT (+) eliminates 6 possibilities, 18 remain.
First choice   brBR (−) eliminates 5 possibilities, 13 remain.
Hypothesis: yT.

By following this strategy, the subject is correct fortuitously, although there remain 13 possible but untested hypotheses. It is a lucky stroke. When it occurred, we scored it as an appropriate strategy, for subjects were free to offer hypotheses after each choice, and it is a reasonable one to offer. Consider, however, an unfortunate use of the strategy. Again the correct concept is yT, but the positive illustrative instance contains only one of the defining values of the concept.

Illustrative instance   yrBR (+) eliminates 6 possibilities, 18 remain.
First choice   btBR (−) eliminates 5 possibilities, 13 remain.
Hypothesis: yr.

To be sure, y and r are the two characteristics of the positive illustration that distinguish it from the negative instance encountered. But they do not define the concept. Under these circumstances, the subject can at best choose one of the two defining values of the correct concept.

It is interesting both with respect to the lucky and the unlucky forms of positive anchoring that subjects frequently used this device of comparing a positive illustrative card and a negative instance even though there had been a series of positive instances intervening between the two. The positive illustrative card undoubtedly had a special status in the eyes of our subject: it was the first card shown them at the outset of the problem and derived distinction by this fact.

A similar use of a negative instance occurs in conjunction with the so-called majority effect described earlier. We call it *majority anchoring*. Recall that the majority effect in its simplest form consists of basing one's hypothesis about the correct concept on those attribute values shared by the largest proportion of the positive instances one has encountered. It is rather a magical gambit and reminiscent of probabilistic concept attainment of the kind to be described in Chapter 7. In the variant of this stratagem we discuss now, the majority effect is used in connection with a negative instance. That is to say, a subject is given a positive illustrative instance and then chooses a series of instances that all turn out to be positive but have no attribute values common to all of them. Then the subject encounters a negative instance. In formulating his hypothesis, he chooses a concept that is consistent with the negative instance in the sense that its values do not appear on the negative card. But at the same time, he makes his concept consistent with the majority effect. He chooses those attributes that occur in the majority of the positive instances encountered and that are also consistent with the negative card encountered. A nice example of this maneuver is provided by one of our subjects.

Concept: yr
Illustrative instance	brYR	(+)	eliminates	6	possibilities,	18 remain.
First choice	brBR	(+)	eliminates	3	possibilities,	15 remain.
Second choice	ytBT	(+)	eliminates	6	possibilities,	9 remain.
Third choice	brBT	(+)	eliminates	2	possibilities,	7 remain.
Fourth choice	btYR	(−)	eliminates	4	possibilities,	3 remain.
Fifth choice	yrBT	(+)	eliminates	0	possibilities,	0 remain.

Hypothesis: rB

As before, the hypothesis is consistent with the negative instance. The elements of the hypothesis are chosen from those attribute values that occur in the majority of the positive instances encountered. The final choice made, after encountering a negative instance, is in the nature of a check.

Both of the stratagems just described, *positive anchoring* and *majority anchoring*, are not bad compromise strategies. It can readily be demonstrated that when an hypothesis is formulated with the sole property that it is not ruled out by a negative instance encountered, there is one chance in six of hitting the correct concept. This follows from the fact that, first, a single negative instance encountered in the present experiment eliminates 18 of the possible 24 disjunctive concepts that can be constructed from two attribute values. Second, if the subject will only avoid stating an hypothesis that has something in common with this instance, he has done what is tantamount to utilizing the information it contains. In essence he treats the negative instance as if it were the first instance encountered. So long as he avoids any overlap between his hypothesis and a negative instance, he limits himself to six hypotheses, and one of these must be correct. The irony of the two stratagems just described is that the subject gains nothing whatever either from anchoring one of these six hypotheses to a "half-right" positive illustrative instance or from choosing the "majority" attribute values of a set of positive instances as a basis for selecting among the six. In each case, his chances of hitting the correct concept upon formulating an hypothesis remain precisely one in six.

We may finally summarize the various strategies and fallacies before considering the conditions that predispose subjects to use them.

Appropriate Strategies. Here we include negative focussing as well as the less efficient multiple negative strategy. These contrast with the following inappropriate strategies.

Common-Element Strategies. These include simple common-element strategies based solely on the common element of an array of positive instances as well as the more subtle common-element strategy where the subject's hypothesis is made to be consistent with a negative instance as well.

Majority Effects. Here the subject builds his hypotheses out of those attribute values that appear in the majority of the positive instances encountered. The more subtle form of the majority effect is also marked by an hypothesis consistent with a negative instance encountered.

Positive Anchoring. This includes only those cases that begin a problem with a positive illustrative card containing but one defining attribute value. The strategy consists of choosing the two values that distinguish a negative instance from a positive illustrative card as one's hypothesis. If the positive illustration contains both defining values the hypothesis is automatically correct. Such cases were scored as appropriate strategies, for they are good examples of negative focussing.

ON USING APPROPRIATE AND INAPPROPRIATE STRATEGIES

For a person inexperienced in attaining disjunctive concepts—and we came to the conclusion that most people are told about them rather than having to attain them—there seem to be three things that determine whether they will use an appropriate strategy in the task we set them. The first of these we can do no better than to call "insight." Some few of our subjects "see through" the problem, "understand" it after some pondering, and it is characteristic that their discovery gives them a certain delight. We do not pretend to know what is involved in such insight and since it has the character of most "aha experiences," it is almost too all-or-none to analyze. But the two other factors associated with the adoption of an appropriate strategy shed some light on what is necessary for such understanding. The first of these is whether or not the problem-solver has the good fortune of beginning his task with a negative instance, a nonexemplar of the class he is seeking. The second factor involved is whether or not the instance encountered immediately after encountering an initial nonexemplar makes it easy for the person to adopt this nonexemplar as a focus or a base for further exploration. It is principally with these two conditions that we are concerned in this section.

Consider first the frequency with which problems were attacked appropriately and inappropriately, bearing in mind while doing so that any figures we present inevitably reflect the procedures we have employed and very likely too the high intellectual quality of the subjects participating. The following provides a brief summary:

> 28% of the problems were attacked by an *appropriate strategy*.
> 38% by the use of the *common-element strategy*.
> 17% by the use of the *majority-effect strategy*.
> 10% by the use of *positive anchoring*.
> 7% in a manner that was *unclassifiable*.

In fine, even with a relatively gifted group of subjects, it is the exception for problems to be attacked by the use of informationally efficient strategies. Nor did there appear to be much learning over the course of the three problems. Close to half of the subjects attacked all of the problems by inappropriate strategies and a few did all of them appropriately. As for the remaining half of the subjects, they showed no consistent learning trend, approaching one problem appropriately and then going about the next in a highly wasteful way. But such erratic performance must be understood in the light of our procedure. For it was the case that a subject might go about his task in an exemplary manner on one problem that began with a negative instance, and then boot completely the next problem that began with the presentation of a positive instance. In any case, it is not surprising that three problems do not provide a sufficient occasion for learning, for we know strong "antidisjunctive" tendencies exist in intelligent adults that probably require prolonged buffeting before they are abandoned.

What leads a subject to attack a disjunctive problem appropriately? We had better first understand what is meant by "attack." A subject is presented an initial card: an exemplar or a nonexemplar of the disjunctive concept whose defining properties he is to discover. He chooses instances to test. In time, he offers an hypothesis about the two attribute values that he believes define the concept.* It is with this first hypothesis that we are concerned, and it is offered on the average after the subject has made 4.4 choices. It is the behavior leading up to this first hypothesis that concerns us and that we speak of as a subject's "attack on the problem." There are several reasons why we choose to concentrate on this feature of behavior. The principal among them, as we shall see later, is that the most general conclusion we are able to reach about disjunctive concept attainment is that "well begun is half done." There was also a pragmatic reason for concentrating on first hypotheses. Subjects, the reader will recall, were allowed to go on choosing instances and offering hypotheses as long as their patience held out or until they finally hit upon the correct

---

* Hypotheses about single attributes were not responded to by the experimenter.

answer. It is extremely difficult to discern just what it is that guides a subject's choice after he has offered his first hypothesis and is told that it is wrong. Nor did the highly contorted verbalizations of subjects help us much in determining what was going on. But one can readily analyze the pattern of choices that leads to the first attempt at a solution. Indeed, the procedure utilized for analyzing the first hypothesis was to determine which of the several strategies was the one and only strategy that could describe the set of choices preceding a correct hypothesis—and the reader will recall that only 7% of the problems were unclassifiable by the use of this method. Later, in considering success and failure, we will examine in more detail what kind of behavior one finds after a first hypothesis has proved wanting. For the time being, then, our interest is in the initial attack employed.

As we have said, the good luck of beginning one's search with a negative instance is a critical determinant of whether or not our subjects adopt an appropriate strategy. The facts are quickly told:

15% of problems begun with a *positive instance* were attacked appropriately.

48% of problems begun with a *negative instance* were attacked appropriately.

But in a sense, the "facts" are somewhat misleading, for the critical matter is not so much whether one starts with a negative instance as whether, having so started, one chooses a first instance to test that is only a "small change" from the initial negative illustration. Recall that each instance contains values of four different attributes. One has, let us say, been shown a nonexemplar for illustration. If the instance one then chooses for testing differs in two or fewer values from his first illustrative instance, it is almost in the nature of the materials encountered that one will hit on an appropriate strategy. If this first chosen card differs in only one attribute from the illustrative instance, one automatically knows whether the changed attribute value is or is not relevant to the concept. One readily falls into a focussing procedure whether the first chosen card is positive or negative. And if two attributes are changed in making the first choice—and the reader must recall now that the correct concept was always defined by two attributes—then again the results are favorable. If the chosen instance is negative, then one eliminates the two changed attributes and has attained the concept. If positive, then one can adopt the risky option of assuming that both of the changed attribute values are defining of the concept, and sometimes this is right. If, on the other hand, one makes a big change in choosing a first instance, one is very likely to come to grief. It is in the nature of the array of instances that such a choice will turn out to be positive. In which event, one is in the position of having to guess which of the three or more changed attribute values of the chosen instance are relevant—and here one does no better than chance in guessing. Such a first choice is not conducive to continuing with an appropriate strategy. In consequence, it matters greatly, given a first negative instance, whether a subject's first choice is a big change or a small change. The first hypothesis was determined by an appropriate strategy in

61% of the problems begun with a negative instance where the first choice was a small change, and in
15% of such problems where the first choice was a big change.

Where the initial instance presented was positive, the nature of the subject's first choice made no difference as far as leading to the adoption of an appropriate strategy. But it did make a difference, as we shall see now, in terms of whether he was lured into a common-element strategy.

The common-element strategy—the use of those values common to positive instances encountered as a basis of one's hypothesis—is the most frequently employed by our subjects: nearly four in ten of the problems were attacked in this way. Again, the utilization of such a strategy seems to depend heavily upon the fortunes of one's first encounter and upon the nature of one's first choice. Here we can paraphrase the proverb by saying that "Badly begun is to be undone." If one begins with a positive illustration and follows it with a small-change choice, there is a very high likelihood that one will encounter a positive instance and so too that one will fall into a common-element strategy. But if one makes a big change, the likelihood decreases markedly. The opposite holds for problems begun with a negative illustration: a small change minimizes the likelihood of falling into a common-element attack; a big change makes it very likely. The data are as follows:

54% of the problems begun with a *positive illustration* and followed by a *small-change* choice are attacked by a common-element strategy.
25% of the problems begun with a *positive illustration* and followed by a *big-change* choice are attacked by a common-element strategy.
14% of the problems begun with a *negative illustration* and followed by a *small-change* choice are attacked by a common-element strategy.
57% of the problems begun with a *negative illustration* and followed by a *big-change* choice are attacked by a common-element strategy.

It is very likely that the common-element strategy is a response to perceived similarity of an illustrative instance and a chosen instance. A subject is shown a card bearing four values and informed that it illustrates a concept. Now he chooses an instance. It may resemble the illustrative instances in either of two respects: in the values that constitute it and/or in its positive or negative status. If the chosen card is similar to the illustration both in half or more of its values *and* in its positive illustration of the concept, then it is highly tempting to proceed by considering what is common to the two instances and to all instances chosen thereafter. Now it happens that in the array used in this experiment (the 16 combinations of four attributes, each with two values), there is a very high probability of encountering another positive instance if the subject chooses a card differing from a positive illustrative card in only one or two values. Indeed, the probability when choosing "small-change" instances is 0.73. This means that many subjects are hitting a first choice that resembles the positive illustrative card in at least half its values and in its status. It is not surprising, then, that many of such subjects fall into the common-element fallacy.

Now "big changers" who start with a positive illustration also have a high probability of choosing a positive card: 0.71. But here the values of the illustrative card and of the first choice *differ* markedly. Only one or no values are common to the two. There is much less temptation to search for common elements. The per cent of problems handled in this way drops to 25.

The low proportion of common-element usage among "small changers" who begin with a negative illustration can be explained, we think, by the relative ease of adopting negative focussing as a means of handling the first two instances. Given a negative illustration and a choice differing in only one or two values, there is a probability of 0.70 that a person will choose a positive card. A positive choice differing only slightly from a negative illustration readily suggests negative focussing. It is not surprising, then, that only 14% of cases of this sort adopt the common-element approach.

Finally, how account for the predisposition of "big changers" to fall into common-element reasoning when they begin with a negative illustration? First, the probability of choosing a positive when making a "big change" is 1.0; there is no other possibility. The subject then has a negative illustrative instance and a positive choice differing radically from it. There is a very high probability, whatever he does next, that his following choice will be positive. It is then that he falls into the common-element procedure.

We have examined the matter of the common-element strategy partly because of its intrinsic interest, and partly as an exercise in analyzing the temptation to error. Error is not random. It is a response to certain systematic characteristics of the members of a universe of instances that one has sampled in search of a concept. Given a preference for conjunctive concepts and given an encounter with a set of instances that have much in common, the temptation to use common elements as a basis for forming a concept becomes very strong indeed.

To sum up, the following general points seem to be in order. For a person inexperienced in dealing with disjunctive concepts, two factors seem to account for whether or not he will adopt an appropriate strategy. The first of these is whether he has been fortunate enough to begin with an illustration of what the concept is not: a negative illustration. The second is whether he makes a first choice of an instance that stays close enough to the first negative illustration to permit the use of a negative-focussing procedure. The latter step, "staying close to the negative illustration," may be intentional on the part of the subject and may reflect the choice of a strategy, or it may be accidental, in which case the accident is a happy one for it permits the person to recognize that a negative-focussing strategy is possible. In any case, what is necessary for an efficient solution of a disjunctive problem is that the person begin his solution from "outside the category" and proceed into it. A negative illustrative instance helps. Two or more negative instances the mirror-image of whose common values can be used for formulating an hypothesis also help. A positive illustration hinders. So does anything that tempts the subject to consider the similarity of a set of positive cards, as in the common-element strategy. In the end what helps most of all is the good luck of negative instances—both informationally and psychologically— and what hinders most of all is a series of similar positive instances.

SUCCESS AND FAILURE

Thus far our concern has been exclusively with the *process* of attainment and we have, we think, properly avoided the question of whether or not subjects "solve" the problems given them. For solution or nonsolution is basically an end product of the appropriateness of one's strategy of attempted solution.

Take first the criterion of whether a subject is efficient in choosing an array of instances informationally adequate for deducing the concept. If he goes on choosing instances interminably, then obviously he will eventually collect instances enough for such a deduction.

This solution does not require an intelligent subject, nor indeed does it require an organism: a random number table could do it as well. What we wish to know is whether a subject is able to arrange his choices in such a way that he achieves the requisite information in a reasonable minimum of choices. In the present case, the "reasonable minimum" will depend upon whether the subject begins a problem with a positive or a negative illustrative instance. For recall that a negative instance eliminates 18 and leaves 6 hypothetical concepts possible, while a positive instance eliminates 6 and leaves 18. An efficient method of choice following exposure to a negative illustrative card should require only three instances to eliminate all but one, the correct concept. Following a positive illustration, five choices should suffice. These are the requirements for the maximally efficient strategies possible.

On 30% of the problems undertaken, subjects managed to obtain requisite information in the "reasonable minimum" of choices. In the other 70%, choices were of such a kind that they were either redundant or contained so little information that when summed they failed to meet the criterion set.

The critical factor is whether the subject started out with an appropriate procedure in formulating his first hypothesis. If he did, then with very notable regularity he gets requisite information in the minimum number of choices. If not, he fails to. Take first the problems initiated with a positive illustration. There were 86 of them altogether.

Of the 13 begun with an appropriate strategy:

10 *were* informationally determined in the minimum number of choices.
 3 *were not* informationally determined in the minimum number of choices.

Of the 73 begun with an inappropriate strategy:

15 *were* informationally determined in the minimum number of choices.
58 *were not* informationally determined in the minimum number.

Precisely the same pattern holds in the case of problems begun with a negative illustration. There were 50 such problems.

Of the 24 begun with an appropriate strategy:

14 *were* informationally determined in the minimum number of choices.
10 *were not* informationally determined in the minimum number.

Of the 26 begun with an inappropriate strategy:

2 *were* informationally determined in the minimum number of choices.

24 *were not* informationally determined in the minimum number.

It should be no surprise that the use of an appropriate strategy does not guarantee determination in the minimum number of choices, for even appropriate strategies (particularly where "big-change" choices are made) can lead to the choice of redundant instances.

Now consider success in the more conventional meaning of the term: attaining the concept correctly. Recall that when a subject stated the correct concept, he was told that his answer was correct and the problem was terminated. Two kinds of success may be distinguished here: correct statement of the concept after the subject has chosen instances that, formally speaking, contained enough information to permit full determination of the correct answer, and correct statement of the concept prior to achieving enough information. Call the first "full determination," the second "good guessing." Sixty per cent of the problems were solved with full determination, nearly all the remainder with good guessing. Given the fact that the subject could take the whole day on a problem if he had the time, it is not surprising that only a small handful of problems went unsolved.

With respect to the frequency of solution with full determination, it makes no difference what kind of strategy one employs given the fact that we let our subjects go on choosing instances. All that we can do is compare the efficiency of the performance en route to solution, and as always the best measure of efficiency is the number of redundant instances a subject chooses over and beyond those instances that provide full determination of the concept. If we take as a bench mark against which to compare efficiency the choosing of more than three redundant instances prior to determined solution, we find somewhat more than half of the subjects who began inappropriately exceeding this figure, but only a fifth of those who employ appropriate strategies in their initial attack on the problem.

Indeed, whatever measure one uses in comparing those who begin with appropriate and those who begin with inappropriate strategies, the former group turn in a better performance. Their hypotheses are more often consistent with past information, they offer their correct hypotheses much sooner after having achieved full determination in the instances they have selected, and in general show a more economical performance.

Or take good guessing. Thirty-three per cent of the problems begun inappropriately were solved in this way, 16% of those begun appropriately. A better measure is provided by the "wildness" of the guess that succeeded. This can be stated as the number of hypotheses still formally possible when the good guess is made. For problems begun appropriately, a mean of 2.3 alternatives were still possible; for those begun inappropriately, 3.7 remained.

We end this section where we began it. Starting a problem with an appropriate strategy, while not a guarantee of success, is far more prognostic of success than starting it inappropriately. Again, well begun is half done.

CONCLUSION

In the end, we may ask again why it is that disjunctive concepts seem so clumsy and inelegant and why, indeed, they are so badly handled. The *a priori* reasons we have already considered: that one can predict only faultily or probabilistically from class membership to the properties of members, that two positive exemplars of a class may share no common characteristic, that practice shows we can usually replace a disjunctive definition of a class by one that is comprehensibly relational or comfortably conjunctive, and that oftentimes social pressure militates against the disjunctive concepts for reasons quite noncognitive.

To this list of liabilities we may now add another. To determine a disjunctive concept one must lean heavily upon information derivable only from negative instances. In sum, to know what the class is like one must begin one's exploration by asking what the class is *not* like. We are placed in the position of the allergist seeking to find what foods produce an allergic reaction in his patient. Before he can even start his inquiry, he must first find a diet on which it is possible for his patient to live without any allergic reaction at all. If need be, the patient is put on rice. Then and only then, after he has found what is *not* responsible for the patient's malaise, can he begin the task of "choosing instances." He adds to the diet until the allergic reaction occurs. Whatever added matter brings on the reaction is a responsible agent, a defining attribute of the disjunctive class, allergy producers. Ideally, the allergist will upon finding a first agent revert again to the rice and begin adding new foods once more, until finally he has discovered all the defining attributes to be found. But always he must act from the outside in, never from the inside of the class out.

We know from the careful studies of Hovland and Weiss (1953) and from our own investigations of conjunctive categorizing that subjects seem not as willing or able to use negative information—instances telling what the concept is not—in the process of attaining a concept. The reluctance, it would seem, carries over to disjunctive categorizing. Negative information is not preferred, perhaps simply because it gives indirect information, perhaps for other reasons. In any case, when it is possible to use positive information and when such information is available, subjects will use it. It is not by accident that the strategy most frequently employed by our subjects in attaining a first hypothesis was one based entirely on positive information: the common-element fallacy wherein one uses as an hypothesis the common values of a set of positive instances. It reflects, we think, the general tendency to avoid using the knowledge contained in examples that tell us "what something is not."

The objective of this chapter has been to explore the manner in which human cognitive behavior diverges from ideal rational strategy in a particular problem setting. If the present chapter has contributed' anything to our understanding of this divergence, it has been to underline the fact that two differences do exist. The first is in the dislike of and clumsiness with disjunctive concepts shown by human subjects. The study reported has been primarily an account of systematic errors that lead people to treat a disjunctive concept as if it were something else. The second divergence is in the inability or reluctance of human subjects to use the information contained in an instance that illustrates the negative case.

Perhaps in closing it would be well to mention one feature of Western culture that may have some historical relevance to our concern. It is a characteristic of much scientific thinking to assume at the outset that whatever behaves in a common way does so for a common cause. Common effects have common causes. The disjunctive category is a violation of this classical conception. Events that have the same ultimate criterion do not have the same sign. Things that cause allergies, cause cards to be correct, lead substances to be edible, make for eligibility in a society: these things should be that way for the same reason. This is a highly persistent conception of cause and effect and there is little question that we teach it to our children and to our students. When cards can be "right" for several reasons, or rashes can be caused by different and apparently unrelated agents, we are face to face with a violation of our primitive notion that common effects have common causes. Perhaps it is that we have learned such rules too well and here lies the origin of our clumsiness with disjunctive concepts.

CHAPTER 7

On categorizing
with probabilistic cues

$\bigcup$p to this point, we have dealt with experiments and observations in which a person could eventually infer *with certainty* that objects exhibiting certain defining properties belonged in a particular class.   That is to say, these studies were about a state of nature in which class membership could always be foretold from a knowledge of certain attributes exhibited by an object.   This was the case in principle if the person could but learn to distinguish those attributes of objects that were relevant to class membership from those that were not.   "Class membership" in this context refers, of course, to some shared ultimate property of an array of objects, an ultimate propery such as edibility, or rewardingness, or "correctness," or what have you.   Eventually a subject in such experiments may emerge into the light of certainty and learn an infallible rule such as "all red mushrooms are poisonous."

Now we must deal with the perhaps more usual state of nature in which *certainty of inference from defining attributes to categorial identity cannot be achieved.*   Here the environment is so ordered that probabilistic rather than certain relationships hold between the attributes of objects and their categorial identity.   What are the marks of an original painting as against a copy?   To what extent is a direct rather than a shifty gaze the mark of an honest man?   What are the defining attributes of a successful parolee?

What is the nature of the decision involved in placing instances in a category on the basis of probable defining attributes?   Here we must make a distinction between *decisions about a particular instance and decisions about a series of instances.*   We are often in a position where our interest is centered upon the categorizations of particular instances or events.   The parole board must decide whether *this*

182

prisoner is a good risk. The physician must decide whether *this* patient is in the class of patients who will be helped by prefrontal lobotomy. The art dealer must decide whether *this* canvas is by Hieronymus Bosch or by a skillful apprentice in his atelier.

It seldom happens, however, that we can consider the categorization of single instances without reference to the way a person has categorized other instances which are identical or similar. We need to look at a series of instances in order to know what the properties are upon which the person is basing a categorization and what over-all procedures he is following. Suppose, for example, it is established that about 70% of the patients in a given diagnostic group are helped by prefrontal lobotomy but it is not known with certainty what the characteristics are which mark off this 70% from the 30% who will not be helped. We may find three physicians independently deciding that a given patient will be helped by lobotomy. These three decisions about a particular patient acquire different meanings when we note that one physician has a record of recommending lobotomy for all or almost all of the patients in that clinical group while the other two, recommending it for 70% or so of the patients in the group, do not recommend the same patients in their 70%.

There are also differences in the kind of information one searches for in order to make a particular as against a "series" decision. To quote the economist Shackle (1949): "If I am faced with the need to choose a career, . . . does it help me much to know that the proportion of successes in this or that line is such and such?" (p. 110). Shackle, as well as other economists such as Knight (1921) and Fellner (1943), emphasizes the need to know not simply the over-all probabilities but also the relevant differences between individual events. In a choice of career, one must know what the characteristics are which mark the successes and the failures and the extent to which one possesses these characteristics oneself. And even this is insufficient if these characteristics do not predict perfectly. For particular decisions, then, the search for criterial attributes or cues is the predominant feature even if it is insufficient.

The other respect, and a most important one, in which single and series decisions differ is in their consequences. If the individual expects to have later chances at categorizing similar instances or making similar decisions, one of the things that he will aim for on any particular occasion is information which will be useful for later attempts. In fact, an individual may make decisions or categorizations which carry little chance of immediate success but promise to yield considerable subsequently relevant information. This expectation of recouping, of being able to nullify past errors or losses, is one of the most comforting and significant features of series decisions.

The way in which people categorize individual instances and the way they categorize a series of instances are then inextricably related. We shall best proceed by studying a series of individual categorizations given the presence of various kinds of attributes in the instances about which decisions must be made and given situations where these attributes can be used with different degrees of validity to determine membership in a category. We shall always be asking: *a.* What general procedures does the person follow in the over-all frequency with which he places instances in one category rather than another? *b.* What specific procedures—what properties or attributes—does the person use in placing a particular instance in one category rather than another? We turn first to some general points which run through the variety of probabilistic situations we shall be analyzing.

SOME PRIMARY CONSIDERATIONS

A particular emplacement on a battlefield has been undergoing prolonged artillery bombardment. High-explosive shells are landing in its vicinity, each heralded by a familiar whine of a duration sufficient for the men to take cover if they so choose. Some of the shells are live; some are "duds" which fail to explode upon landing. We concentrate on a particular soldier. What will determine: *a.* whether he takes cover or stays exposed on any particular approach, and *b.* the frequency with which he adopts each course of action over a series of shell approaches?

Estimated Probability of Live and Dud Shells. Let us take a situation where 70% of the shells are live and 30% are dud. How accurate is the soldier likely to become in his estimate of the probability of live and dud shells? He may come to believe that there are more live shells than there actually are, or more dud shells than there actually are, or that the ratio is close to the 70:30 ratio which actually exists.

Let us suppose for the purposes of argument that our soldier's estimate is 70:30. How does this estimate affect the frequency with which he makes the response of taking cover *versus* remaining exposed?* He may respond as if all the shells were going to be live and

---

* For the sake of convenience, we are assuming that an estimate precedes a response and that an estimate is obtainable. In practice, it is not unusual for response frequencies to be stably established long before a verbal estimate can

take cover every time. This is what we call an *100:0 or an all-and-none response distribution.* For reasons which are not immediately obvious, the soldier may on the other hand adopt what we call an *event-matching response distribution.* In the present example, this means taking cover on 70% of the approaches and remaining exposed on 30% of them. Most of the points we have to discuss are about conditions important in determining whether response distributions tend towards the event-matching or the all-and-none type.

Presence of Potentially Criterial Cues. There are some situations in which individuals can be guided only by the relative frequency with which instances turn out to belong to one category or another—situations, for instance, where there is such a poverty of discriminable attributes that it is hard to know where to start. In situations such as these, we shall see that one of the most interesting features of the individual's behavior is a kind of *"cue searching,"* an attempt to find attributes he can use as a basis for deciding whether a particular object should be placed in one category or another.

Equally often, however, the environment or one's previous experience provides some guidance as to the attribute cues which should be used, but these are cues with less than complete validity. Aerial perspective, binocular parallax, superposition: all these are cues to the judgment of distance. They are, however, as Brunswik (1943, 1952) has so clearly remarked, only partially valid cues. From no one of them can we infer with complete certainty that an object is near or far.

In such situations, the feature of behavior that is of most interest is the *correspondence between cue criteriality and cue validity,* between the extent to which a cue is used and the extent to which it is in fact predictive. Is the validity of a cue accurately reflected in the individual's placements? Or does he regard some cues as more valid than they actually are and others as less valid than they are? If so, is there anything about the quality of the cue which will help to clarify why, say, a particular cue comes to be regarded as more valid than it actually is? We shall see that one quality which is of importance is the *Eindringlichkeit* of a cue—its impressiveness or salience.

Payoff Matrix Governing Categorizing Decision. What are the possible consequences of making each decision? Let us assume that in the soldier's opinion only two kinds of outcome can follow being

---

be made, or for the response frequencies to reflect accurately the environmental probabilities while the verbal estimates do not.

exposed to a shell: life and death. We may represent the operative payoff matrix in this way:

	Anticipated Events and Outcomes	
Decision Alternatives	Live Shell	Dud Shell
Take cover	Life	Life
Stay exposed	Death	Life
Estimated probability of event	0.70	0.30

This matrix is a simple one, and it is the kind of matrix where, if life is wanted and death not wanted at all, we would expect the soldier to take cover every time. The situation becomes more complex if the outcomes are less simple than they are here; if, for example, taking cover means staying alive this time but being in no better position for the future whereas staying exposed means death if the shell is live, but, if the shell is dud, moving forward to a better position for meeting the future. Here there are three possible outcomes: death, life but no further ahead, and life plus being further ahead. Now it is clear that both the extent to which the individual likes each of these outcomes and the probability estimates he makes of each of these occurring will affect the decision he makes. As we mentioned in Chapter 3, it is very much a moot point as to how various considerations are balanced in establishing a preference, how preferences can be ordered, and how probability estimates and outcome values combine to determine how a particular decision or a series of decisions is made. We shall be concerned mainly with determining the psychological variables which are involved.

Conception of the Task and of Its Final Resolution. How does the individual view his task? If he sees it as one in which a final and unique solution is possible—in our example, if the soldier believes that eventually he will be able to find the cues that will tell him with complete validity whether a shell is live or not—then his categorizing procedure may well be different from that of the soldier who sees the situation as always and forever one into which uncertainty will enter.

One difference which the conception of the task makes is in the attitude towards taking a chance and making an error. The individual who aspires to eventual certainty and who expects to be able to continue categorizing and exploring will often risk errors more readily on the assumption that a successful final solution will negate the errors incurred along the way. Furthermore he will be tempted to take steps which offer little chance of immediate success but whose outcome will provide information especially useful for future decisions. This search for information then, arising from the person's conception of the categorizing task, may in itself be expected to affect the manner in which probabilistic categorizing proceeds.

Opportunity for Validation. We have proceeded so far with the amiable fiction that our soldier could always check whether a shell was really live or not. Every prediction he made could be tested against an external standard. But we are seldom in so excellent a testing situation. We can imagine very easily, for example, a situation where the opportunity for validation is removed. Suppose a man learns to identify the sounds of live and dud shells under the best of training conditions, where all relevant information is immediately available.

Now what would be the effect on a trainee's performance if, say, the instructor no longer announced what the shell was and the trainee no longer had an external standard against which to check his predictions? He would continue to be exposed to the shell's whine but with no further opportunity for testing his judgments.

Or imagine situations where validation is one-sided. The soldier will know, for example, that if the shell explodes on contact it is live. But if it does not explode, it may be either a dud or a delayed-action live shell. As we shall see later, the presence of such incomplete opportunity for validation affects considerably the occurrence of all-and-none behavior.

Here then are five factors that may affect the manner in which individuals will categorize instances in a probabilistic situation: 1. the estimated probability that the events will belong to one or another class; 2. the presence of potentially criterial cues and their validity; 3. the payoff matrix governing the categorizing situation; 4. the person's conception of the task; and 5. the opportunity for validation. Each of these, we shall find, affects both the way in which the individual categorizes particular events and the extent to which he categorizes a series of events in an event-matching or an all-and-none manner.

CATEGORIZING WITH EVENT FREQUENCY AS THE ONLY CUE

For purposes of exposition, we should like to begin our discussion of how people proceed in probabilistic categorization with the extreme situation in which the attributes offer a minimum of possible cues in distinguishing categorially between one event and another and in which the consequences of correct and incorrect categorizations are slight and relatively equal. This is as "stripped down" a decision-making situation as one may find. It serves as a good bench mark from which to build an account of probabilistic categorizing.

Our soldier, let us say, has now ensconced himself in a deep bunker where, save for the contingency of a direct hit, he is safe. It makes no difference whether he calls the approaching shell live or dud in terms of any action he can take, but he is interested nonetheless in learning to predict as accurately as possible. He is, however, unable to find any feature in the sounds of approaching shells that can be used for predicting purposes. He can tell, after a shell has fallen, whether it was live or defective. Whatever his motive, he is in the habit of predicting, each time he hears an approaching shell, whether it is live or not.

What can we expect about a subject's general procedure in such a situation? One prediction we can make, based on studies by Humphreys (1939) and others, is that his categorizations of live and defective shells will conform to the actual proportions of live and defective shells falling. If the ratio of live shells to duds is 70:30, the calls of "live" and "dud" will be distributed in roughly the same proportion.

Humphreys (1939) arranged his study in much the same manner as our soldier's task is arranged. When a light came on, his subject had the task of predicting whether or not a second light would appear. This first light was always identical. In Humphrey's experiment, the probability with which a second light would follow was 0.5. Later experimenters, using the same situation, varied the probability with which a second light would follow: 0.25, 0.50, or 0.75 (Grant, Hake and Hornseth, 1951). In this second experiment, subjects again matched the frequency of their predictions of a second light to the actual probability of its occurrence.

How do these subjects decide upon the answer they will give on a particular trial? What cues or discriminable attributes, if any, have they found to guide their categorizing of particular instances? Certainly subjects are using the over-all relative frequency of the two events as a general guide. If we analyze the sequence of subjects' answers, however, we find that they are also using as a more specific guide the position of an event in a series. Let us look at the way in which subjects responded to a run of six events in an experiment by Jarvik (1951), where subjects predicted whether the experimenter would call "check" or "plus." After the first call of "check," a second was predicted by 95% of the subjects. After two calls of "check," about 87% predicted that the next call would be "check" again. After three, the figure dropped to 68% and after four it was down to 33%. After five successive occurrences of "check" it reached 18%.*

Why do subjects use sequence cues? First of all, in such a homogeneous array the only difference between one instance and the next is temporal position. Further, the subject is treating the task as a problem to be solved, a point which may appear banal but which is of the utmost importance. The subject has been instructed to try and predict as accurately as possible and he usually attempts to do this by looking for some "pattern" or "system" that will enable him eventually to be correct on every prediction or at least to improve his performance. The particular kind of pattern he searches for is one based on the order of events, and behind his search lies a widespread assumption about relationships between events that are closely associated in time. It is a very general human tendency to deny the independence of temporally related events, to assume that if a series of events has gone in one direction over a period of time, "it is ripe for a change." The gambler's fallacy (Jarvik, 1951)—the notion that since black has paid off for a long succession of times, red is due to come up—can be observed at virtually any gaming table or slot machine in the world. An amusing example is given by Laplace (1825): "I have seen men, ardently desirous of having a son, who could learn only with anxiety of the birth of boys in the month when they expected to become fathers. Imagining that the ratio of these births to those of girls ought to be the same at the end of the month, they judged that the boys already born would render more probable the births next of girls" (p. 164). Combined with such an assumption of event-interdependence is usually the further tendency to operate on the basis of shorter runs of events than occur on a chance basis, regarding long runs of the same event as extremely unlikely (cf. Smith, 1949; Whitfield, 1950; Cohen, 1954).

---

* In Jarvik's experiment, the concern was entirely with the sequences of events, regardless of how the subject was categorizing these events. But the subject's behavior vis-à-vis these past events was also determinative of his future behavior.

In a study by J. J. Goodnow (1955b) where a 70:30 probability was involved, we can look at the effects of correct and incorrect calls where the actual events were the same. When the event was the equivalent of a dud and duds occurred 30% of the time, a correct call of "dud" by the subject led with a probability of 0.48 to a second call of dud. Where the event was a dud but the subject incorrectly called it "live," the probability of the next call being dud was down to 0.31. The effect of past calls and their relation to future calls has also been discussed by Hake and Hyman (1953) who similarly remark that previous calls as well as previous events must be taken into account. For the present discussion, we shall refer only to sequences of previous events, without regard to previous calls and their correctness.

How reasonable, objectively speaking, is a subject's use of sequences in such "cueless" situations? If the series of events to be categorized is truly random, then position in a series is not a valid attribute for categorizing individual instances. We could legitimately say that the subject, in his attempt at event matching, latches on to the only discriminable difference there is between instances and gives it a value in making decisions which has no basis in fact. We could almost say that subjects' behavior, when it comes to categorizing particular instances, is completely superstitious.

Although in many respects the subjects' behavior is superstitious, we must say—in all fairness to them—that the use of probable short runs of events as a basis for making decisions is not entirely without foundation in most of the experimental situations studied. Where, for instance, a series of 100, 150, or 180 trials is to be given, it is customary experimental procedure to randomize events within blocks of 10, 20, or 30 trials so that learning effects can be observed. Also it often happens that an experimenter will place an upper limit on the number of times in a row that a particular event can occur. Under such circumstances, subjects show a certain reasonableness in attempting to estimate the probable length of a run and in regarding runs as being shorter than they would be in a completely random arrangement over a long series of trials. The attribute of position in the series has then some slight predictive value. It is, however, slight in fact and tremendously exaggerated by subjects. What the subjects do is to take this merest hint of a predictive property and elevate it to the status of a highly valid cue.

We have considered this form of behavior at some length because it illustrates a point that will be of relevance on several later occasions: the tendency to search out attributes as guides to categorizing. Indeed if one can speak generally of "effort after meaning," as Bartlett (1932) has, one species of the tendency may be described as a "search for signalling attributes."

Let us summarize matters briefly before moving on to the study of categorization situations that are more complex and perhaps a little closer to life. When there are no valid attributes to use in categorizing individual instances but the subject can observe the frequency with which exemplars of two categories occur, a subject matches his categorizing probabilities to the actual probabilities with which exemplars of various categories occur in the environment. To categorize individual instances, he uses the temporal order of events in a sequence as his guide. Finally, and this is a point too readily overlooked, such a matching of categorizing probability to event probability occurs under a problem-solving set and under the condition of slight and relatively equal consequences to success and failure.

Let us now change the Humphreys-type "cueless" situation in only one respect. This time, rather than starving our subjects for attributes to work with, we flood them with attributes that, for identification purposes, are worthless. By providing this rich array of seemingly utilizable attributes, the situation *appears* at the outset as a complex problem-solving situation. In essence, however, it is basically a task like the one used by Humphreys save that when the "first light" appears, it may appear in many discriminably different guises.

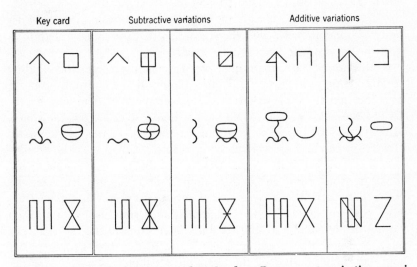

Figure 5. Geometrical designs used in Goodnow-Postman categorization experiment.

The experimental observations illustrating this change, reported by J. J. Goodnow and Postman (1955) can be briefly described. The subject is presented on each trial with three cards: a "key card" containing two geometric designs, and two "variation cards" each of which contains a slight rearrangement of the figures on the key cards. One of the variation cards represents an addition of a line, the other a subtraction of a line from the left figure of the key card. The subject's task is to couple one variation card with the key cards—either the subtractive or the additive variation. All told, there are ten key cards, each with a different design, and for each key card there are two additive and two subtractive variations, all of them sufficiently alike to make the memory task difficult. Figure 5 shows three of the ten sets of designs. In essence, the subject must say each time, "Is this a time when I couple the key with an additive or a subtractive variation?" and he may make up his mind by inspecting numerous properties of each trio of cards set before him. There is in fact no general rule whereby a particular kind of stimulus property can lead one to choose the correct variation although the subject is led to believe that such a general rule can be found. Indeed, the only general rule that prevails, although the subject is not aware of this, is that on a certain proportion of trials the additive variation is correct and on a certain proportion the subtractive. For different groups, the proportion of times that additive and subtractive are correct is 50:50, 60:40, 70:30, 80:20, and 90:10. Whether a given choice by a subject is called correct or incorrect by the experimenter is decided by random order with the restriction that the same probabilities apply as far as possible to each key card.

In all but one case, the frequency with which subjects called adding or subtracting correct matched fairly closely the actual proportion of the time that these variations were in fact correct. The only exception to the rule was the 60:40 case, where subjects responded on a 50:50 basis. In terms of performance over the series of decisions, there is no difference between the results obtained in the "multi-attribute" and the "cueless" situations. In both, event-matching behavior prevails. But there is an important difference between the two situations in the way in which subjects proceed in categorizing individual instances. In the "multiattribute" situation, with its rich variety of potential cues, the attribute of position in the series is very seldom employed (Goodnow, 1955b). Instead, subjects report using now one, now another of the available attributes as a basis for decision. Some subjects, for example, come to the hypothesis that the presence of curved lines is the attribute to use, others choose straight lines or the presence of a wriggly line on top, while still others use as a criterion the gracefulness of the figures. The interesting thing to note is that though subjects respond so variably on a verbal level, their categorizations over the series correspond quite closely to event probabilities. And this event-matching performance, once established, holds steady throughout the learning series even though the subject may be changing his mind about the attribute or attributes on which to base his individual categorizations.

How do subjects come to use stimulus attributes in this seemingly mysterious way? The most general answer we can give is to say that the subjects' hypotheses are based on coincidence and on an attempt to remember the way in which previous similar instances were categorized. The role of coincidence is most marked when two or three consecutive cards all exhibit a common feature and the answers happen to have been the same for all. In such cases, the subject feels sure that this common feature is the one on which all further categorizations should be made. He is then likely to continue to use this cue for a time before giving it up. As is the nature of judgments based on coincidence, the occasions which run counter to the individual's hypothesis are far less impressive than the occasions which agree with it. Given a great deal of leeway in the kind of coincidence which may be encountered, and a readiness to be impressed by coincidence, it is not surprising that individuals vary so much among themselves in their selection of relevant attributes and at the same time express such confidence in the attribute they have selected. Their reliance upon such cues adds up to a level of performance that approximates event-matching.

Now we wish to raise the question: Why is it that in both "multiattribute" and "cueless" situations we find event matching or an approximation to it over the series of decisions? There appear to be several conditions underlying event matching. We must examine these now if we are to understand the behavior of subjects in later situations where attributes are more valid but are still not completely certain bases for categorization.*

Hope of a Unique Solution. If a subject feels that he should aim for a perfect or unique solution of the problem before him, such that he will be able to predict every event correctly, then he will venture away from the strategy of predicting all the time the alternative that is occurring more frequently. In the words of one subject: "If I want to be correct every time, then I'll have to choose each type just as often as it's going to be correct, no oftener and no less." In other words, he will have to respond in a 50:50 fashion in a 50:50 situation, in a 70:30 fashion in a 70:30 situation, etc. If, however, the subject feels that he does not have to aim for correct prediction on every trial, then all-and-none behavior becomes feasible. In a 70:30 situation, all-and-none behavior (choosing every time the 70% alternative) will result in being correct 70% of the time. Such a level of success may be more than acceptable to a subject in a gambling situation. But it is equivalent to giving up hope as far as problem-solving is concerned.

---

* These conditions are drawn from a comparison of performance and response to inquiry in two matched tasks: one the "multiattribute" task already described and the other a gambling task (Goodnow, 1955a). A discussion of the former experiment is given on pages 191–192.

Need for Direct Test of Hypothesis. Frequently, when a subject was asked why he had chosen the less probable alternative, he would reply, "Well I had an idea about that card and wanted to check it." Actually, the subject can check hypotheses about the infrequent alternative by continuing to choose the more frequent alternative, since in the situation we are describing he is told explicitly that when one alternative proves wrong the other will be correct, and vice versa. Almost universally subjects report a certain dissatisfaction with checking an hypothesis about a *less* likely alternative in such a way, i.e., by choosing the *more* likely alternative and seeing whether it turned out to be wrong. This procedure they found "too indirect:" "The only real way to check an hypothesis about a card is to choose it and see what happens." It is our impression that this tendency to "direct test" is more often encountered in the "multiattribute" situation where more stimulus attributes are available for testing as possible cues than in the stripped-down "cueless" situation. Indeed, it seems possible that the richer the array of attributes and therefore the larger the number of possible hypotheses to be entertained, the greater will be the tendency to direct test. Note that this is not the same as preference for positive instances observed earlier in conjunctive concept attainment. Subjects do not mind negative instances—in the sense of "errors"—provided the errors give them a direct test of an hypothesis with the possibility of being able to reject it. It is when an instance yields information that has to be transformed to throw light upon its alternative that subjects seem to develop a cognitive malaise.

Interest in the Less Frequent Alternative. There is a strong tendency for subjects to regard prediction of the infrequent event as a greater test of skill than prediction of the more frequent event. In the words of one subject: "If I knew when to pick the [less frequent] subtractive cards, I'd have the whole answer to the problem." To a large extent, subjects use the placing of instances in the less frequent category as a test case to verify hypotheses. A hypothesis is regarded as more strongly confirmed if it leads to a correct placing in the less frequent category; conversely, a hypothesis by which one "can't even pick the [more frequent] additives" is regarded by many subjects as really useless.

These three conditions—hope of a unique solution, need for direct test, and interest in the less frequent alternative—all underlie the occurrence of event-matching rather than all-and-none behavior. There are certainly other relevant conditions, such as the consequences of a categorization, but these three are the ones to which we will make most reference throughout the remainder of the chapter.

In conclusion we can note that the categorization of particular instances is marked by a search for attributes to be used as cues, to the extent of leading individuals to latch on to irrelevant attributes or to exaggerate minimally valid ones. The categorization of the series of instances is marked by event matching.

CATEGORIZING WITH PARTIALLY VALID ATTRIBUTES

Thus far we have considered the rather special case of categorizing in the absence of valid or even partially valid attribute-cues on which to base decisions about particular events. We turn now to the more usual case where moderately good although not completely valid attribute-cues are available.

Let us revert again to a military situation for purposes of illustration. The task, say, is one of identifying approaching fighter aircraft as "enemy" or "friend" where few if any features of the planes provide a completely valid cue. Friendly planes usually have a certain type of wing, tail, and scoop—but only usually, not always. So too enemy planes. Moreover, friend and enemy alike may sometimes have common features. Finally, it may not be possible because of the approach angle of any particular plane to see all of the helpful, if only partially valid, defining attributes. A plane coming straight on, for example, betrays only a knife-edge silhouette of wings and tail. In such a case, these cues, though they may be relevant, cannot be used.

This is the type of situation with which we shall be dealing now. Strictly speaking it has two notable features:

a. There are partially valid but not sure cues present for guiding decision as to the categorial identity of instances.
b. Vis-à-vis any particular instance that must be categorized, the decision-maker may not have all of the relevant cues available to him.

It is immediately evident that we are dealing here with a most conventional and common type of categorizing situation. In many ways it is the position in which we find ourselves in the early stages of learning. We often may know what to look for as a basis of categorizing, thanks to some prior guidance and learning, but we do not yet know how much reliance to place in what we see. As we mentioned earlier, Egon Brunswik (1943, 1952) has suggested that much of the cognitive activity of everyday life is of a probabilistic order. Most of our judgments as to whether objects are near or far, for example, rely upon combinations of partially valid cues. These are cues which are not only partially valid but which may also be absent or indeterminate on any given occasion when a categorization must be made. Indeed, as we remarked in an earlier chapter when discussing partially valid attributes, much if not most of the socially relevant categorizations one must make—particularly in "placing" people—are of this order. Is a man intelligent or not, liberal in his political views or not, sympathetic or not? The cues are only partially valid and often only partially present.

The military illustration with which we began also serves as an experimental paradigm. Such material was used by Robert E. Goodnow (1954) in one of his experiments on probabilistic categorizing and upon these experiments we shall rely heavily in this section. His objective was to ascertain the manner in which subjects learned to utilize probabilistic cues and to assess the extent to which their use of cues corresponded to the cues' ecological validity. Briefly, the first of his experiments was as follows. The subject is shown an example of a type X plane and one that is not of this type—"not-X" is the term used. The task the subject faces is to identify a series of aircraft silhouettes projected singly on a screen. He must place them in one of these two categories. It is made clear to the subject that the two types, of planes are experimental models and that all of them will not be alike. After the subject has given his response to each aircraft silhouette, he is told what type of plane it was. Care is taken to indicate to the subject that the relevant features to be watched for are *wing, air scoop,* and *tail.* Two values of each attribute are demonstrated: wings may be swept back or delta shape; tails may be either of the rounded or straight type; air scoops may be single and under the fuselage, or double and at the sides of the fuselage. The variations of each attribute are shown in Figure 6.

In Goodnow's experiment the subject is not faced with complete lack of certainty. One of the attributes provides an 100:0 or completely valid cue, but the other two attributes provide only partially valid cues. A different attribute is used as the 100:0 cue for different subgroups. In the group where the wing is the 100:0 or the completely valid cue, a delta wing always turns out to be a type X, and a swept-wing model is always a not-X. The other two attributes, type of tail and position of air scoops, are what we shall call 67:33 attributes. That is to say, a straight tail turns out to indicate a type X 67% of the time, a not-X 33% of the time; and conversely, a round tail is a not-X 67% of the time and a type X 33% of the time. So too with air scoops; they also are 67:33.

When the aircraft silhouettes are presented, the subject is able to see either a single cue or two cues, but never three cues together: wing and tail, tail and scoop, scoop and wing, or any one of these.*

Note carefully one feature of the experiments; type X and not-X occur with equal frequency. There is no reason for a subject to believe that one is more frequent than the other. It is the relationship between type of plane and the possession of certain attributes that differ from randomness.

This experiment makes it possible to study several important features of probabilistic categorizing. When, for example, only a single cue is present to the observer, will the subject show the kind of event

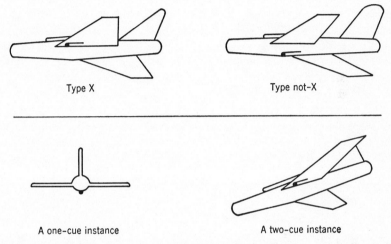

Type X   Type not-X

A one-cue instance   A two-cue instance

Figure 6. Examples of instances used in aircraft identification task (after R. E. Goodnow).

matching discussed in the preceding section? That is to say, when presented with instances in which the cue indicates type X with a 67:33 frequency, will the observer name these planes type X 67% of the time? If he does, then his behavior is in some ways akin to the performance of subjects in experiments where no valid attributes are available. This then is the first question: Will subjects use a single cue with a frequency that matches its objective validity?

The second question we may ask is about the handling of several cues appearing in a single instance. Does the simultaneous presence of a 100:0 cue and 67:33 cue, both pointing to type X, increase the certainty of the subject? What of two cues pointing to type X, each

---

* All three cues are shown together only in the initial examples given subjects of a type X and a type not-X.

with a validity of 67:33? These are questions of cue compounding. What finally does the subject do in the face of cue conflict, where, for example, one cue points to type X with a validity of 67:33 and the other cue points to type not-X with equal probability?

The Handling of Single Cues. The design of Goodnow's experiment was such that some subjects had the wing, some the scoops, and some the tail as the 100:0 cue, the other attributes being 67:33. For the moment, let us treat all the cues indifferently, speaking of a

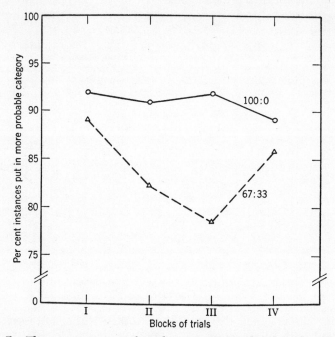

Figure 7. The mean per cent of single-cue instances placed in the more probable category when the cue pointed to this category with 67:33 or 100:00 validity. In all, 120 trials were given and the task was aircraft identification.

100:0 or a 67:33 cue without regard to whether it was wing, tail, or scoop. How do subjects handle single-cue instances?

Figures 7 and 8 present the data necessary for answering this question. In Figure 7 the 120 trials* are broken down for convenience into four periods of 30 trials each, and the extent of choice of the more probable category is shown for each of the four periods. Figure 8 shows the distribution of subjects' choices of the more probable category over the entire series of decisions.

---

* In all, there are 60 one-cue instances and 60 two-cue instances.

What is immediately relevant is that in categorizing with partially valid cues subjects do not completely show the kind of event matching with which we became familiar in the preceding section. First, a number of subjects treat the 100:0 cue as if it were less than certain, using it to place planes in the appropriate categories only about 90% or less of the time. And with respect to a single 67:33 cue, the

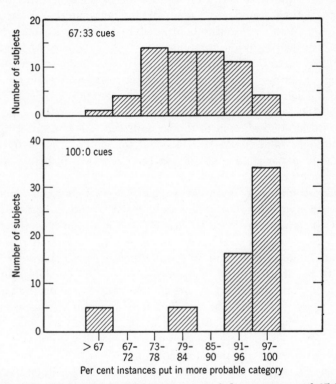

Figure 8. The distribution of subjects in terms of the percentage of 67:33 and 100:0 single-cue instances placed by them in the more probable category.

picture is reversed. A cue with an objective association of 67:33 with type X is not used to predict type X 67% of the time but closer to 80% of the time. The certain cue is underplayed; the partially valid one exaggerated.

In two other categorizing situations identical in design—one involving the categorization of faces on the basis of three features, and the other involving the identification of light patterns on an instrument panel—R. E. Goodnow obtains comparable results. In all three experiments, moreover, the subject was asked at the end of the experiment to estimate the percentage of times that different features of the plane (or its equivalent) were associated with type X and not-X. Here again one notes that many subjects underestimate the 100:0 cue and overestimate the 67:33 cues.

Why are 100:0 cues not regarded and adopted by all subjects as certain guides to categorization? R. E. Goodnow explains the phenomenon partly in terms of "the spread of doubt." A number of subjects, having found that *some* of the attributes are uncertain, develop a generalized doubt about attribute validity. As one of them put it, "You can't rely on anything too much." In essence then, in a probabilistic *situation,* a subject is sometimes reluctant to treat categorizing in terms of the kind of certainty observed earlier in conventional conjunctive and disjunctive categorizing.

While the "spread of doubt" is applicable to the first finding, it is in a sense in contradiction to the second: the *exaggerated* utilization of middlingly valid cues. How account for the fact that a 67:33 cue pointing to a particular category is used to place instances in that category approximately 80% of the time?

Goodnow points to several interesting factors that may lead the subject to overvalue the moderately reliable cue. He notes that subjects have a tendency to treat *one* 67:33 cue as if it were certain, using it for a stretch to make the more likely categorization 100% of the time, while at the same time experimenting with the *other* 67:33 cue. To put it in terms of an example, the subject would go through a series of trials predicting a type X 100% of the time on the basis of a 67:33 delta wing, while at the same time apportioning his calls very carefully on the basis of a 67:33 air scoop type between type X and not-X. Then would come the turn of air scoop to be responded to in a 100:0 manner while the subject experimented with wing shape. To some extent, this pro tempore acceptance of a 67:33 cue as completely valid—a stratagem intended to free the subject for work elsewhere—could account for the overutilization by subjects of such cues over an extended series of trials. Similar tendencies to test one cue at a time are often observed in problem-solving experiments and have been especially noted in Smedslund's (1955) experiment on probability learning with multiple cues.

This predilection for working on one cue at a time is worth especial note. "Holding one attribute constant while checking another" is, after all, the essence of both the successive scanning and focussing strategies in conjunctive categorizing and is also at the root of the negative focussing discussed in connection with disjunctive categories. There is, of course, a considerable lessening of cognitive strain gained by coping with one attribute at a time, dealing with it in such a way, moreover, that one may have a *direct* test of one's hypotheses.

R. E. Goodnow proposes one additional hypothesis to account for the undervaluation of certain cues and the overvaluation of partly valid cues in probabilistic categorizing. This he refers to as the "collapsing of the range of probabilities" with which a person must deal. Such "collapsing of a range" is not too outlandish a conception if one likens it to forms of scale contraction known in psychophysics.* If one puts the matter in terms of central tendency or adaptation level effects operating on cue probabilities much as they are known to operate for weights or brightnesses, a number of interesting possibilities emerge. We would expect to find that both the 100:0 and the 67:33 cases would show regression on some "probability adaptation level." How one would compute the value of such an adaptation level for a collection of three probabilities (100:0, 67:33, and 67:33) is, to be sure, problematical. But if such an explanation as this were reasonable, then we would expect that subjects would be regressing in their responses to their *conception* of the "average" reliability of cues present in the situation. Indeed, the fact that *after the experiment* subjects actually did overestimate the reliability of 67:33 cues and often underestimate the reliability of those with 100:0 value lends a certain credence to the adaptation level argument. Acceptance of an adaptation level effect does not, however, rule out the possibility of other effects also being present. The spread of doubt, direct test of hypotheses, and the predilection for working with one cue at a time are still relevant explanations, within the framework of a general adaptation effect. The understanding of such tendencies is especially needed if we are to go beyond a statement of general results and concern ourselves with how individual instances are categorized.

The reader was duly warned on an earlier page that we were treating single cues as if, so to speak, any cue operated in much the same way as any other. This fiction has now outlived its usefulness. Even in the present experiment using cues as seemingly equivalent in immediacy or vividness as wings, tails, and scoops, it turns out that there are some striking differences that cannot be accounted for simply in terms of the relative validity of cues. We are, in short,

---

* Several experimenters have observed the tendency for subjects in gambling and prediction situations to underestimate the higher probabilities while overestimating lower ones and have raised the question as to whether central tendency scaling effects were not at work, e.g., Preston and Baratta (1946), Attneave (1953).

face to face with the problem of *Eindringlichkeit*—the impressiveness or preferential value of different attributes—and its effect upon the utilization of cues.

In this task it turns out that the two cues most affected by *Eindringlichkeit* are wings and tails: the former being overvalued, the latter undervalued. When *wing* is a 100:0 cue, for example, it is used as

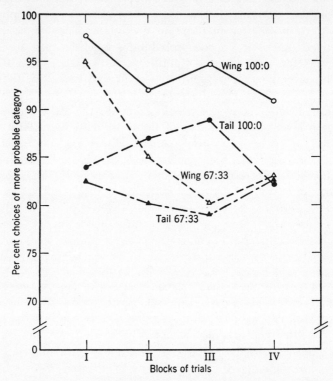

Figure 9. Effects of *Eindringlichkeit* in aircraft identification. The mean per cent of single-cue instances placed in the more probable category when the cue pointed to this category with 67:33 or 100:0 validity. The cue was either shape of wing or shape of tail.

a basis of appropriate inference over the range of 120 trials with a frequency of about 95%. When tail has the status of a 100:0 cue, it is used as if it were 85% valid. Indeed, in the last block of 20 presentations of aircraft silhouettes, we find subjects utilizing a 67:33 wing cue in the same way as they do a 100:0 tail cue. This differential utilization of individual cues is shown graphically in Figure 9.

The reader may properly argue with Goodnow's interpretation of the difference between wing and tail as due to "impressiveness" or "cue preference." For the interpretation is *post hoc* and the experimenter had no independent definition of impressiveness or preference before the fact. To pin the matter down, Goodnow adapted the well-known schematic faces used by Brunswik and Reiter (1938) in their ingenious study of cue utilization in judgments of intelligence. Goodnow's versions of these faces, varying in height of brow, length of nose, and size of chin, are reproduced in Figure 10. Brunswik

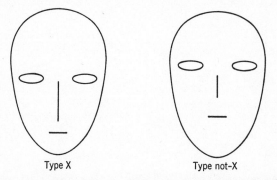

Type X   Type not-X

Figure 10.   Examples of faces used in task of categorizing facial types.

and Reiter had found in their study that the feature most determinative of whether a schematized face would be judged intelligent was, as one might expect, height of brow. With this as a prior definition of impressiveness or cue preference, Goodnow then set out to replicate exactly the aircraft experiment, substituting brow, nose, and chin for the aircraft features of wing, tail, and scoop. Subjects were not asked, however, to judge intelligence but rather to categorize instances into two types, again type X and type not-X. For one and two cue instances, different features are simply blacked out.

Under these conditions, Goodnow finds the effects of cue preference overwhelming. Brow-height cues are eventually treated as if they were virtually certain cues whether their validity is 100:0 or 67:33. Length of nose, even when it has 100:0 value, is finally used as a basis for making the objectively proper inference only 80% of the time, somewhat less still when it is a 67:33 cue. The differences in handling these cues over the four blocks of trials are depicted in Figure 11.

It is apparent from these results that preference or impressiveness serves drastically to alter the effects produced by the objective validity of cues. We would venture to propose that the more one moves toward "real-life" categorizations involving forms of grouping that touch upon everyday adjustment, the more will such "nonrational"

effects operate. Such effects are, indeed, the stuff of which stereo-
types are made: conceptions of relationship and identity that take
insufficiently into account the actual state of nature. The kind of
"prejudiced categorizing" to which Allport (1954) refers in his book
on prejudice is in large measure an example of overdependence upon

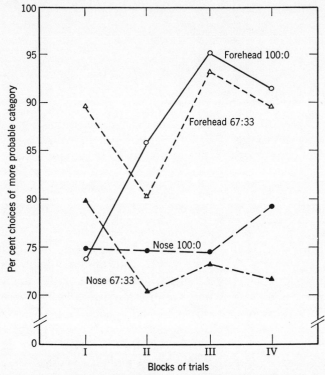

Figure 11. Effects of *Eindringlichkeit* in identification of facial types. The
mean per cent of single-cue instances placed in the more probable category
when the cue pointed to this category with 67:33 or 100:0 validity. The cue
was either height of forehead or length of nose.

preferred but highly unreliable cues for the achievement of over-
determined ends.*

In support of the view that more "meaningful" or "social" categories
are affected by reliance on preferential attributes, one can go for a
test in a direction opposite from the comparison of the Brunswik-
Reiter faces and the aircraft. One could, for example, take a situation

---

* The reader is referred back to Chapter 4 for a discussion of the role of cue
preference in conjunctive categorizing with thematic material.

even more "laboratorylike" or "meaningless." R. E. Goodnow has done just this. He paralleled exactly the aircraft recognition procedure with an experiment in which the subject had the task of categorizing patterns of lights on the basis of quite indifferent and nonpreferential cues. In this setting, no impressiveness or preferential factors could be noted.

Handling Cue Compounds and Cue Conflicts. All of the previous observations are based on instances in which the subject has before him only a single cue, the other two cues in the situation being obscured. What of the handling of two cues at a time? Much has been said in the classical literature—notably as a result of Helmholtz's conceptions—about the "weighing" of cues, unconsciously or otherwise. Among contemporary theorists, it is perhaps Ames (1955), Cantril (1950), M. Lawrence (1949), and in general the transactionalists who have most emphasized the importance of cue weighing.

Consider two examples of cue combinations: two-cue compounds where both a 100:0 cue and a 67:33 cue point to the same identity, and two-cue conflicts where a 100:0 cue and a 67:33 cue point to opposite identities. In these instances, identity is always objectively determined by the 100:0 cue.

There is, as we might expect, little discernible difference between categorizing with the 100:0 cue alone and categorizing with the compounding 100:0 and 67:33 cues. With the 100:0 cue alone, we are so close to the ceiling that there can be little increase in choice of the more probable alternative. In contrast, there is a striking difference between treatment of the 100:0 cue alone and treatment of the 100:0 cue combined with a conflicting 67:33 cue. Subjects are following the lead of the 100:0 cue far less often. The data are presented in Table 8.

TABLE 8

Categorization of Some Cue Compounds and Cue Conflicts,
Compared With Categorization of a 100:0 Cue Alone

Per-Cent Choices of More Probable Alternative	Number of Subjects		
	100:0 Cue Alone	100:0 Cue With 67:33 Compounding	100:0 Cue With 67:33 Conflicting
92–100	50	46	25
83–91	—	5	12
75–82	5	5	7
66–74	—	1	—
58–65	—	3	1
49–57	3	—	3
7–48	2	—	12

If we analyze the categorizations of such two-cue conflicting instances block by block, we find an interesting growth of reliance on the 100:0 cue and, concomitantly, a decreased concern with the 67:33 conflicting cue. The mean per cent of categorizations following the lead of the 100:0 cue for the 120 trials given the subjects is as follows:

Trials	100:0 Cue Alone, Per Cent	100:0 Combined With Conflicting 67:33 Cue, Per Cent
1–30	91	77
31–60	92	80
61–90	93	83
91–120	89	87

The conflicting cue is quite clearly affecting reliance on the 100:0 certainty cue. The effect, however, is one that appears to wear off with more and more opportunity for testing. Perhaps it should be made clear again that whenever the 100:0 cue is combined with one of 67:33, the 100:0 cue always prevails in fact, i.e., the experimenter's call always follows the 100:0 cue. The subject learns over a time that he can trust the 100:0 cue even when it is coupled with one which, when alone, points in an opposite direction 67% of the time.

There is a nice point to be made here about the psychology of contradiction. Contradiction of a certainty—particularly in the setting of a probabilistic situation where the subject often has in any case somewhat shaky confidence in certainty—has the effect of lessening confidence still further. It is striking to us, moreover, that a large number of trials is needed before the subject will fully utilize the 100:0 cue in the face of conflict. In the first three blocks of 30 trials each, the period before the subjects attain full confidence in the goodness of the 100:0 cue, there are 30 opportunities for them to see that whenever a 100:0 cue is present it prevails. Contradiction, apparently, is resolved only slowly.

What of the cue compounds and conflicts where both cues have 67:33 validity? In a two-cue instance where both 67:33 cues point to the same identity, what is to be the ecological validity of the cue combination? It can be the case that in fact the cue combination is more valid than either cue taken singly, or that it has the same predictive value as either of the two cues, or that it is equivalent to a 100:0 cue. What ecological validity is to be assigned?

Goodnow presents two treatments of this problem. One is to assign an ecological validity of 80:20 to the cue compounds (i.e., giving the more probable category as correct 80% of the time), and an ecological validity of 50:50 to the cue conflicts (i.e., giving one category as correct half the time, and the other as correct the remainder of the time). The other treatment avoids the problem of ecological validity by not providing knowledge of the identity of the planes whenever cue compounds and cue conflicts with two 67:33 cues are presented. The first of these treatments we turn to immediately, the second in a later place.

Take for the moment the case where the compounds have 80:20 validity and the conflicts 50:50 validity. The most frequent form of response to the compounds is to place them 90% of the time in the more probable category. As for the cue conflicts, they are placed by subjects half the time in one category and half the time in the other. There are, however, some special features of the handling of cue conflict that warrant attention.

One notable characteristic of cue conflicts is their effect on the subjects' surety. When an instance exemplifies such a conflict, Goodnow's subjects report that there is something "funny" or "odd" about it and they seem to be uncertain as to what to do. This is the case even though they may not be able to verbalize that the cues before them are "in conflict" or "point in opposite directions." Unfortunately, the time required by subjects to decide into which category such instances should be put was not recorded. Goodnow reports, however, that there appeared to be a slowing down of decision time, a usual concomitant of lack of confidence. The observation of "oddness" along with the weakening of confidence seems to be paralleled in other studies where conflicting cues are characteristic of the person's environment. Lawrence (1949), for example, in commenting on the reaction of people to the Ames distorted room, notes that there is a "lack of surety." Bruner and Postman (1949) and again Postman, Bruner, and Walk (1951) have also commented upon this effect in connection with the recognition of environmental incongruities such as a red four of clubs.

In cue conflicts, *Eindringlichkeit* or cue preference is also a factor. For it is critical in determining the resolution of conflicts. The role of preference in cue-conflict resolution is best studied in the task of categorizing faces. Three kinds of conflict are possible: brow *versus* nose, brow *versus* chin, and nose *versus* chin. By chance, one would expect that if each were equally criterial the chin should win out a third of the time, the nose a third of the time, and the brow a third of the time—win out in the sense of the conflict of cues being resolved in favor of a particular cue. To sum the matter up, the conflict is resolved in favor of brow cues 52% of the time, in favor of nose cues 28% of the time, and in favor of chin cues in only 20% of the conflicts.

In short, the preferred cue is chosen as the basis of decision in the face of a conflict with other cues of equal objective validity. This result is nicely in agreement with what we have already observed about the effect of *Eindringlichkeit* or preference, namely that it leads to overevaluation of the validity of a cue.

Now finding that subjects respond on a 90:10 basis to two compounding 67:33 cues and on a 50:50 basis to two conflicting 67:33 cues carries with it a problem of interpretation. Does it mean that subjects are "weighing" the evidence of the two cues or does it mean that subjects are simply responding to the way the experimenter has "weighed" the cues for them and distributed his calls? Suppose we look at the treatment of conflicting cues. If it were not for the experimenter's following half the time the lead of one cue and half the time the lead of the other in naming the identities of the planes, would subjects categorize in a 50:50 fashion? Or would they find some other way of resolving conflict, such as selecting one of the two cues and always following its lead?

The only way to answer this is to see what individuals will do when the experimenter provides no validating identification of a plane. Train a subject to the point where he knows the validity of each 67:33 cue singly. Then face him for the first time with compounds and conflicts combining the same cues. Each time he meets such a compound or conflict, the identity of the plane is withheld from him. How will he handle them under such circumstances?

This is the problem of the section that follows.

ON REDUCED OPPORTUNITY FOR VALIDATION

In considering the problem before us now, we must remind ourselves of what is involved in categorizing. Categorizing consists of anticipating ultimate consequences on the basis of signal attributes available to us in advance of the consequences. Thus, the whine of a shell serves as a means of predicting whether it will be live or dud; the wings, tail, and air scoops of aircraft serve to predict whether the plane will be friend or foe; the height of a brow whether a man will be intelligent. When there is steady opportunity to check the predictiveness of a cue, we may speak of the categorizer having a full opportunity for validating his categorizing decisions.

It is often the case that such steady opportunity for validation does not exist. Medicine provides a neat example in this age of antibiotics and "wonder drugs." It is often difficult to validate diagnostic cues that point to a certain disease entity if one prescribes such a general medication as penicillin, for the medication has the effect of preventing the occurrence of the validating consequences by which to check one's diagnosis.

An even more striking example of reduced or impaired opportunity for validation can be found in daily social life. We are constantly classifying people in terms of their "type," into those who are "our kind" and "not our kind," into the class of those who are "reliable" and those who are not. The work of Tagiuri (1952) and others indicates, for instance, that people have little trouble in sorting fellow group members into "those who like me" and "those who don't." Our opportunities to validate such categorizations and the bases we use in making judgments are relatively few and far between. We accept this intermittence of validation as a feature of social life and early come to terms with the poverty of guidance our world provides.

There are indeed circumstances in daily life where it becomes impossible in principle to validate our categorizations. This is particularly the case where the use of an ultimate defining standard must be prevented as a matter of social necessity. New York State has upon its statute books the so-called Baumes Law which categorizes any criminal as incorrigible who has been convicted four times of an armed crime. For all criminals who exhibit this defining attribute, the sentence is life imprisonment. Under these circumstances, it becomes impossible to continue to test the adequacy of the defining attribute used: all exemplars of the category are in jail where it is no longer possible to determine whether they will repeat criminal acts. The McCarran-Walter Immigration Act is a more serious case in point. An "undesirable alien" is elaborately defined in terms of certain forms of past association, political affiliations, and other attributes. There is no way of continuing to test the adequacy of categorization in terms of such attributes, for such applicants for immigration visas are automatically denied admission to the United States. This is not the place to examine the social consequences of drastically reduced opportunity for validation, yet it is not amiss to remark that such conditions are usually first steps toward the creation of cultural lags: categorizing is fixed on the basis of attributes found predictive in the past with no opportunity for checking them in the future.

What functions are served by validation as far as categorizing is concerned? The answer, we think, is fourfold.

Having an opportunity to check one's categorization against an ultimate criterion—to see whether a high forehead *does* indicate intelligence or whether a shell with a low whistle *will* fail to explode—may have the effect of making one less casual towards error. Put more directly, this amounts simply to the fact that where validation is possible, so too is error. If and only if error has consequences for the person will this matter. The point is obvious, but it is not trivial. For concern about error, we contend, is a necessary condition for *evoking problem-solving behavior.*

It hardly needs saying that a second function of validation is the chance it affords to check one's hypotheses. In this sense, it provides *the means whereby problem-solving proceeds.*

Validation, thirdly, provides a means of score-keeping: the means whereby the present categorization of an event can be guided by the outcome of past decisions about similar events. This again is an obvious point, yet it needs explicit statement for score-keeping provides the basis for *the regulation of problem-solving behavior.*

Finally, repeated validation—the accumulation of scores or norms— provides the individual with a basis for assessing how well he is doing. In this sense, it is a *regulator of one's level of aspiration,* it determines how much risk one is willing to take, and in a major way sets limits on the kinds of strategies one is ready to pursue in approaching problems of categorizing.

What may be said about probabilistic categorization on the basis of the four points just made? Reduction of opportunity to validate serves, we predict, to diminish problem-solving activity. We are using the term "problem-solving activity" in the sense of an attempt to eliminate error, or at least to decrease the percentage of error in one's predictions. We would further predict that such reduction in problem-solving activity would lead the person to adopt all-and-none behavior, to make his choice always one of the more probable alternatives. If one is enabled by reduced opportunity to become more casual toward error, then all-and-none categorizing should become more attractive and a certain margin of error will come to be accepted as inevitable. If one cannot keep score of the outcomes of past events and if one is also unable to test one's hypotheses, then problem-solving efforts should likewise decrease. Moreover, the inability to keep score may lead the person to adopt a form of behavior which has at least the advantage of keeping error within predictable limits. The adoption of all-and-none behavior performs this service uniquely. On all these grounds, we would predict that when the opportunity for validation is reduced behavior will approximate all-and-none categorization.

What other possibility of action is there under conditions of no external validation? The only other possibility we can suggest is that people will be able to find a new basis of decision that will sustain their problem-solving efforts. This new basis for decision could be a *knowledge of the general frequency* with which events will fall into one or the other category; knowing, for example, that 75% of the events fall into one category and 25% into the other. Individuals could then decide that over a series of trials they would *apportion their responses* between the categories in the 75:25 ratio expected in event-occurrence. Such behavior would constitute event matching rather than all-and-none behavior.

What bases of decision could subjects then use in categorizing individual instances? It could be a knowledge, not of past stimulus events and choice outcomes, but of their own previous responses. They could place instances in the more likely category trial after trial until they felt that it was about time to shift, a point occurring when their apportionment of past responses began to feel out of line with the general ratio they had decided to follow.

Such a tendency to make identical categorizations and then to shift has been noted by Senders and Sowards (1952) and Senders (1953) in an experiment where the subject has no knowledge of the outcome of his categorizations. The subjects in their study were given the task of judging whether a light and a sound had occurred simultaneously or successively. The onset of the two stimuli was so close in time that the subject was unable to judge. One group of subjects was told that the simultaneous pairs would comprise 75% of the presentations, the remainder being successive; another group was given opposite instructions that the ratio of simultaneous to successive was to be 25:75. Here subjects exhibited event-matching behavior over the series; in making individual decisions, they showed a tendency to respond to the history of their own responses.

We have then two possibilities as to what will happen when opportunity for validation is reduced. Our general prediction is that behavior will move away from a problem-solving pattern toward all-and-none behavior. The work of Senders and Sowards (1952) suggests that, if an indirect basis for decision is found, this tendency will be forestalled. We consider now some experiments where opportunity for validation is not fully available.

An experiment by R. E. Goodnow (1954) provides one test of the way categorizing proceeds when the opportunity for validation is removed after the person has become accustomed to its presence. Again Goodnow uses the aircraft silhouettes to be categorized into type X and not-X. All of his 60 subjects were given 84 initial categorizing trials with the experimenter serving as the source of validation. After each trial he would announce what the correct categorization was. All instances in which two 67:33 cues were combined, either in a compounding or a conflicting manner, were omitted from this training series.

After the training trials, half the subjects were moved on without any interruption to 36 additional trials in which cue compounds and cue conflicts involving two 67:33 cues were presented. Validation was provided as before, on an 80:20 basis for the cue compounds, and on a 50:50 basis for the cue conflicts.

The other half of the subjects were given presentations of aircraft in all respects identical to the group just described, the only and major difference being that after the original training trials they were provided with no further opportunity for validation. At the end of the training trials, the experimenter informed them that they "seemed to be doing pretty well" and that he would no longer announce the correct answer after each presentation.

Consider first the manner in which the two groups handled the *cue compounds*. We would expect the subjects who had no further opportunity for validation to treat a compound more in the manner of a certainty: choosing the more likely category closer to 100% of the time. The group with continued validation should on the other hand show a more marked tendency to distribute their categorizations in a manner akin to event matching.

The results are instructive. Of the subjects who operated without benefit of validation:

57% categorized the compounds in an absolutely all-and-none manner, and another
20% categorized the compounds in the more likely category between 95% and 100% of the time.

Of the subjects who continued to receive validation:

30% categorized the compounds in an all-and-none manner, while
20% categorized the compounds in the more likely category between 95% and 100% of the time.

Thus, in the no-validation condition, 77% of the subjects approached all-and-none behavior, as against 50% in the validation procedure.

It is interesting to note that this approximation to all-and-none behavior under conditions of no validation lasts over a long series of trials. In an extension of Goodnow's experiment, we have given subjects 72 rather than 36 trials with no validation.* Over four blocks of trials, each containing 10 two-cue compounding instances, the mean percentage of choices of the more probable category was 90%, 90%, 92%, and 97.5%—a steady maintenance of almost complete preference for the

* Mr. Donald D. O'Dowd assisted in the execution of this experiment.

more probable alternative with, if anything, a slight increase in preference as the series is extended.

Consider now the manner in which *cue conflicts* are handled by the validation and no-validation groups. Where two cues conflict, what form can all-and-none behavior take? There is no question of choosing the more probable category, for both are equally probable. Will a subject select one of the two conflicting cues and always follow its lead? Or what? All told, there are three ways in which subjects seem to proceed in dealing with cue conflicts.

50:50 Response. Here the subject follows the lead of one cue half the time, the other half the time. What results is an equal division of placements in the two categories. In essence, the subject is not making up his mind, switching from one cue to the other impartially.

Mixed Response. This is as if the subject were to say: "Whenever the plane has a delta wing, it is always an X; but when it has a swept-back wing, it is sometimes X and sometimes not-X." The subject is breaking up the two values of the attribute and responding to them independently and differently: one value on a 100:0 basis, the other on a 50:50 basis. What results is a placement of cue conflicts somewhere between 50:50 and 100:0, usually around 75% of the time into the more favored category.

All-and-None Response. Here the subject follows the lead of one of the two cues and disregards the evidence of the other. Delta-winged planes, for example, are always placed in category X; planes with swept-back wings always in not-X. The nature of the other conflicting cue is ignored.*

We find a sharp contrast in the forms of response with and without validation. With it, the 50:50 response prevails and the all-and-none response is almost completely absent. Without it, the dominant response is all-and-none and the 50:50 response occurs relatively seldom. The results are presented graphically in Figure 12.

In this experiment of Goodnow's, validation is first available and then removed. There is another way in which opportunity for validation can be reduced. It is a reduction of validation that is, if you will, built into a categorizing situation. Imagine a situation where identification of an instance as belonging in one category does not preclude the possibility that it may also belong in another category. Take the categorization of faces on the basis of brow height, length of nose, and length of chin. The task is to place these faces into two categories, X

---

* In coding responses, we include 50:50 and 60:40 frequency within the 50:50 response. The all-and-none response includes response frequencies between 90:10 and 100:0.

and Y. Up to now we have considered only what can be termed a binary case. If one called a face X, and was correct, one could infer that the face could *not* be an exemplar of the category Y. Similarly, if it were called X, and this was incorrect, one could infer that the face *must* be an exemplar of the category Y. Under these conditions, the subject can use both direct and indirect information from his placements and their correctness or incorrectness.

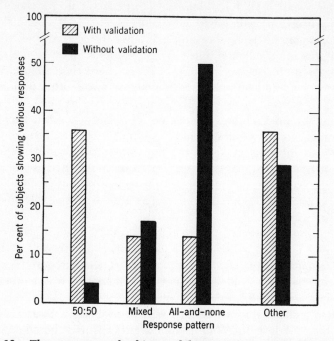

Figure 12. **The percentage of subjects exhibiting various types of response patterns when faced with two-cue instances with the cues in conflict. Percentages are computed separately for subjects who received validation of their categorizations and those who did not.**

But consider now a less favorable situation, one in which such indirect information is not possible. A face is presented. The subject calls it an X. He is told that he is wrong. But now he cannot infer that the face is an exemplar of Y; in fact, it may be neither an X nor a Y. Moreover, one can call a face an X and be correct, but there is no assurance that the face could not also be in the Y category.

There are a number of experiments that deal with choice behavior under just such slippery conditions. We need not consider them in detail, since they have recently been reviewed by Bush and Mosteller (1955). The findings of these studies where alternatives are not mutually exclusive is clear. Behavior moves closer to the all-and-none pattern, and away from event matching. It seems more than reasonable that the conditions of reduced information and reduced validation lead individuals to abandon a problem-solving approach with its hope of eventual elimination of error and to adopt instead the policy of keeping error within as predictable bounds as possible.

In sum, if we go back to our original question, "How do individuals categorize when there is reduced opportunity for validation?" the answer seems to be this. They abandon efforts to reduce or completely eliminate error and attempt instead to keep it within tolerable limits.

We are still left, however, with some questions. Why do not all subjects respond to the lack of validation with all-and-none categorizing? And, moreover, why is it that we so often find an approximation to all-and-none behavior rather than an exact form of it?

We suggest that there may be two responsible factors here. One is an abhorrence of monotony: to make the same response again and again when this is one's only activity is for many people simply boring. It becomes bearable only when the individual is able to vary his behavior by some means other than the making of categorization responses. Suppose a person has the task of choosing one of two keys with the objective of predicting which one will pay off—essentially a "cueless" categorizing task. He learns in time that one key pays off far more often than the other. If he is to perform in an all-and-none manner, he will have to press the same key time and again. For some subjects, this seems to be possible only when they can invent some other "game" with which to keep themselves "interested" (to use a term often reported by them). One of J. J. Goodnow's (1955a) subjects, for example, varied the pressure with which he struck the key, another varied the hand he used. Both subjects insisted that they knew their variations were making no difference in payoff, but that without the diversion of such "games" they would not have been able to resist risking a bet on the key with the lesser frequency of payoff and the greater challenge.

The second responsible factor is the individual's continuing concern with improving his performance. It is relatively easy to *say* that one will categorize in an all-and-none manner, and accept as inevitable a certain margin of error. But the temptation is always there to believe that one *can* do better, that it would be worth while to risk the chance of making a few more mistakes for the sake of possibly doing a little better. Every error one experiences tends to reactivate this belief. The reactivation is particularly strong when error is made especially vivid by a restriction of one's activity to this one categorizing task or by the feeling that one is expected to try to do "one's best."

In conclusion, we must remain with our admittedly simplified generalization: reduced opportunity for validation leads towards that departure from problem-solving that we call the all-and-none response. The conclusion must remain in this simple form, for research on behavior with reduced opportunity for validation has barely begun. There are, for example, no studies on the effect of intermittent validation or of ambiguous validation. All that can be said, finally, is that the problem is a critical one in understanding the handling of probabilistic cues.

ON EXPECTED OUTCOMES

Each categorizing decision has consequences for the individual. Moreover, one learns to expect certain consequences in categorizing, and behavior is adjusted to fit these expectations. In the pages that follow, we shall be concerned with the nature and effect of expected outcomes when an individual must establish identity on the basis of probable cues and consequences have to be estimated.

Consider first the "accuracy" and "sentry" matrices discussed in Chapter 3. In the accuracy matrix, the values of making successful and unsuccessful placements in either of two categories are the same, whatever the category chosen. Correct placement in one category is as good as correct placement in the other. Incorrect placement in one category is as negative in value as incorrect placement in the other. This is a standard matrix in psychophysical experiments. When it governs categorizing decisions, we expect that placement in one category or another will correspond to the individual's estimate of the likelihood of the instance belonging to a particular category.

In our everyday categorizations, however, it frequently happens that the values of correct and incorrect categorizations are different depending upon the alternative chosen. This is the case, for example, when the individual categorizes under the conditions of the sentry matrix. The sentry is faced with the task of identifying an oncoming figure as friend or foe. If he calls it friend and is wrong, his death may result. If he calls it foe and is wrong, at least his life has not been endangered. The two errors have different negative values. So too the two ways of being correct: identifying an oncoming foe correctly has more crucial consequences than identifying a friend correctly. All in all, the cards are stacked toward identifying an oncoming figure as a foe.

An unpublished study by Bruner, Potter, and Bartholomew serves to compare categorizing under accuracy and sentry payoffs. Subjects were set the task of judging whether a rapidly projected field of dots contained or did not contain a certain number of dots. The dots were arranged at random on the field and any given field contained a number from 20 to 30 dots. Equal numbers of each kind of field were presented to the subject in a prearranged random order. The field was exposed for 0.10 second. Sixty undergraduate men served as subjects. A third of them had the task of discriminating the dot fields containing "20 dots" from all others; another third discriminated "25 dots" from all others; and the remainder had the job of discriminating the "30's" from the "non-30's." Half the subjects in each condition operated under an accuracy matrix, the other half under a sentry matrix. Because instructions are so important in this type of experiment, it is worth reproducing the instructions given at the outset to each of the groups which were set to discriminate "25's" from "non-25's."

To the accuracy group, the following account was given of the rationale of the experiment.

> This is an experiment on radar observation that we are doing for the Office of Naval Research. We are going to flash sets of dots on the screen before you for a brief period. Your task is that of a radar observer. Your job is to spot whether the flashes contain 25 dots or do not contain 25 dots. Let me tell you more about your job. It is extremely important to spot the 25's from the non-25's. The 25's are enemy observation planes and the non-25's are your own planes. It would be good to spot a 25 but it would be poor business to mistake a non-25 for it and shoot down one of your own planes. You want to keep the observation planes from getting through, but you don't want to knock down your own people. So be sure to distinguish between the two. Remember your job is to distinguish the 25's from the non-25's.

The subjects who had to work under the sentry payoff matrix were given the following instructions.

> This is an experiment on radar observation that we are doing for the Office of Naval Research. We are going to flash sets of dots on the screen before you for a brief period. Your task is that of a radar observer. Your job is to spot the flashes containing 25 dots. Let me tell you more about your job. It is extremely important not to let a 25 get by. You are in the position of a sentry. 25's on the screen indicate the approach of an enemy aircraft. If you fail to spot a 25 it means that an enemy bomber gets through for a bombing run. So be sure not to miss the 25's but spot them at all costs. Remember, you're a sentry and your job is to spot the 25's.

The subjects were then shown a slide with 20 dots on it. This was described as the minimum number they would encounter, though they were not told the actual number of dots contained. Subjects were next shown a slide containing the maximum number (30), and one containing the midmost number (25). These three points served as anchors for them in their judgments. The subjects had the task of marking a plus on a score sheet when they thought the appropriate number (20, 25, or 30 dependent upon instruction) had appeared and a minus when they thought the number of dots was not appropriate.

What we are concerned with is the nature of categorizing under these two sets of instructions which create such different payoff expectancies in our subjects. The first and simplest question we may ask is about the number of objects that are included within the target category, be it 20, 25, or 30 dots. We compare the number of stimuli, regardless of their characteristics, that subjects were willing to include in their target or "enemy" category. Each subject received 220 stimulus presentations. The percentage of these placed in the "enemy" category by the six groups of subjects is as follows:

Per Cent   "Enemy" Categorizations

	20	Target 25	30
Accuracy payoff	29%	32%	21%
Sentry payoff	37%	37%	32%

Clearly, then, the sentry matrix increases the frequency of "enemy" decisions. Furthermore, the closer in similarity a stimulus is to the target that is to be identified, the greater the differential effect of the two matrices. This is clearly shown in Figure 13, where the results for calls of "20" and "30" are presented.

Now what is left unanswered by the experiment on "radar observation" is the question of probability estimates. The subjects in this experiment were operating with the rough assumption that different stimuli would occur with equal frequency, or at least that there would be an equal number of "maximum," "middling," and "minimum" dot patterns. The consequences essentially bring about a different utilization of these estimates in actual performance. It might be the better part of wisdom, however, to look at these estimates more closely. In particular, one must ask: Are probability estimates indeed independent of the desirability of outcomes?

Rose Marks (1951) has performed an intriguing experiment that relates to this problem. Her subjects were children in fifth and sixth grades of primary school. The children were shown the cards contained in a deck, some of them blank, some of them with pictures.

Their task was to predict when a picture card would occur. The decks were set up in such a way that, for different groups, different percentages of picture cards were present in a deck: 10, 30, 50, 70, and 90% respectively. For some of the children, the appearance of a picture card meant "winning a point," for others it meant "losing a point." Predicting or not predicting a picture card correctly did not

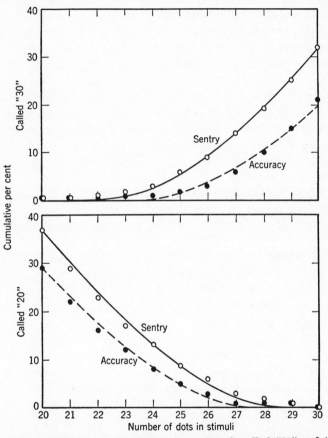

Figure 13. Cumulative per cent of dot-pattern stimuli called "20" and "30" by subjects operating under sentry and accuracy payoff matrices.

affect this fact: one lost or gained, depending upon the card which was turned up, regardless of the correctness of prediction. In sum, a picture outcome represented something desirable for one group, undesirable for the other.

The results of the experiment were quite clear and consistent. Children for whom picture cards were undesirable predicted them less often than these actually occurred. Thus, when picture cards had an objective probability of occurrence of 0.9, children predicted their occurrence only half the time; for the probability of 0.7, the proportion of picture predictions amounted to a third of their calls, etc. Among the children for whom picture cards meant winning a point, the results were quite the reverse. The proportion of their picture predictions always exceeded the probability of the occurrence of a picture. Similar results were obtained by Irwin (1953) in a replication of Marks' experiment with college students.

In short, the estimates of probability that a subject develops in a categorizing task may well depend to some degree on the nature of the outcomes foreseen. They may also, of course, vary with our need to justify the action we take on the basis of an estimate, as when we take extreme action to guard against a relatively unlikely disaster and then convince ourselves that the disaster is not so unlikely after all. Nonetheless, we consider it of prime importance to investigate within the limits of such confounding the manner in which probability estimates interact with the nature of a payoff matrix in determining a categorizing response.

In line with this decision we now ask: does the nature of the payoff matrix affect not only the extent to which the individual places events in one category or another but also the manner in which he arrives at his final level of performance? Consider a situation where errors count as compared with one in which errors do not. The latter is akin to a progressive nursery school where one is permissive toward error. The former is familiar enough. In a permissive situation, we would expect individuals to adopt and persist in an exploratory approach, trying out any cue that might appear relevant. Where error has consequence, one would expect not only less of such exploratory behavior but also an earlier abandonment of it where it does appear.

An illustration is provided by an experiment of Mosteller, Bush, and J. J. Goodnow (reported in Bush and Mosteller, 1955). The subjects have to decide whether to bet on the right or the left key of a gambling device. Half the subjects operate under a "pay-to-play" arrangement: if they choose the correct key, they win a sum; if not, they lose the sum they have bet. The other half operate under a more benign "play-free" arrangement: choice of the correct key leads to winning a sum; choice of the wrong key means simply not winning. Very rapidly, the "pay-to-play" subjects move toward exclusive choice of the key with the higher frequency of payoff. Exploration of the payoff possibilities of the less favorable key dies out both more quickly and more completely than among those subjects to whom loss is of lesser consequence.

Determining Outcome Value. Having considered some specific examples of how outcome values and likelihood estimates affect categorizing with partially valid cues, we may now turn to the more general problem. What is meant by the "value of an outcome"? How can value be stated? What are the criteria which individuals use in assigning some degree of value to a particular outcome?

Let us start with this last question: the criteria which lie behind the assignment of value. We are by no means alone in facing this problem. It is a crucial one in economic theories of choice under risk or uncertainty conditions, and we can profit from a brief look at the way in which economists have tackled the problem. The early assumption that "value" means "money profits" has often been assailed, as has been the tendency to postulate "nonpecuniary profits" or "net satisfactions" or "tastes of consumers" to account for the fact that frequently people do not act as they would if their sole concern were with profit-maximization (cf. Walker, 1946; Stigler, 1950; Katona, 1953). On the one hand there is the argument that economists should consider a variety of forms of value. On the other hand there is the vital consideration stressed by Walker (1946), namely that "the maximum principle . . . is . . . not susceptible of measurement unless it is cast in a form which specifies what is maximized" (p. 73).

As a way out of this problem, it has been suggested that different specified criteria for determining value can be considered as operating at different specified times. For example, Hayes (1950) has suggested some differences in the criteria that are used for determining "value" in boom times and times of depression; Katona has suggested ordering different "motivational patterns," with "striving for high immediate profits . . . at one extreme of the scale [and] . . . at the other extreme . . . the striving for prestige or power" (1953, p. 114). Questions about value can then be asked in these terms: "Under what kinds of business conditions will motivational patterns tend to conform with one or the other end of the scale?" (*ibid.*). Katona states that "preliminary studies indicate that the worse the business situation is, the more frequent the striving for high immediate profits; and the better the business situation is, the more frequent is striving for non-pecuniary goals" (*ibid.*).

While we agree that the general idea of relating different specific forms of value or consequence to particular kinds of situations is a promising one, we would like to stress that any knowledge so achieved is likely to be rather discrete if one limits oneself to parametric studies and to a listing of different business conditions or judgment situations. The advantage of more formal theory is that it focusses upon the common and essential features of certain kinds of situations, suggesting those underlying features which enable us to explain why the same judgment tendencies appear in situations which seem on the face of things different from one another.

One such general feature is the relation between the outcome of a *single* choice and the nature of the *final* outcome. In Chapter 3, much was made of the fact that categorizing behavior can be considered as a series of sequentially related decisions designed to obtain information and to reach other objectives where feasible. In such a series of related decisions each step in performance, or each tentative placement in a category, has a consequence and the series of steps or categorizations also has a consequence. We regard it as essential to analyze the relation between the outcome of an individual decision and the final outcome that constitutes success as a whole if one is to talk reasonably about the effect of outcome values on categorizing or indeed about the value of an outcome.

Von Neumann and Morgenstern (1944) have stressed most explicitly that the effect of a single loss risked or sustained must be considered as relative to the total outcome, and that strategies will vary to take account of differences in the relationships between single outcomes and final outcomes. On a more day-to-day level, we are all familiar with the well-worn phrase of military commentators to the effect that one can lose many battles and still win a war. We are equally familiar with the difference between hunters who can hunt deer several times during a season and those who have one and only one opportunity to hunt.

There are at least three basic questions to be asked about the relation between final and proximal consequences.

1. *What* is the desired final outcome? Is it 100% success (correct categorization on every trial) or something less than 100% success? If it is less than 100% success, is the aim still one of doing better than one would by chance or by making no effort at all? A prison warden, for instance, may regard himself as successful if he can predict on the basis of whatever prognostic cues are available that one out of four parolees selected will make a successful adjustment "outside," considering that without some effort in selecting cases his score might well be zero out of four.

2. *How* is the final outcome computed? Are errors counted in the final tally? Is it possible for an occasional "big win," especially towards the end of the game, to erase the significance of previous errors? This is possible in gambling, where one can recoup. It is

also characteristic of problem-solving. For example, final discovery of the etiology of cancer may well make insignificant one's previously negative results.

3. *When* is the final outcome computed? Is the game or task over when, for instance, one has made five errors in a row and has exhausted either one's resources or the goodwill of some sponsoring Foundation? Or is one promised a definite number of tries, with the outcome to be computed only when the series is completely over? In the academic world, for example, there is a world of difference between an outright 5-year research grant and a 1-year grant with the possibility of renewal.

Now psychologists may feel that such notions are of little relevance to the kind of judgment situations with which they usually deal. In fact, however, the distinctions between single outcomes and final outcomes can increase considerably our understanding of the familiar "problem-solving situation." As we remarked earlier, one's expectation about the nature of the task is a critical determinant of problem-solving behavior. Does the person see the task as one in which a unique solution is possible, as a "real" problem? Or is the task seen as one in which, no matter how hard one tries, one is still subject to the vagaries of chance? J. J. Goodnow (1955a) has investigated the differences in behavior in two matched tasks: one a gambling task and the other a multiattribute categorizing task presented as an exercise in problem-solving. Her analysis is apropos here.

A problem-solving task seems to have the following features:

"A. *The desired final outcome is 100% success*, i.e., eventually solving the problem so that one can predict correctly on every trial. Anything less than this is not really success.

B. *The final outcome is not determined by a count of wins and losses.* On the contrary, finding the solution at the end makes unimportant all previous errors. In this sense, S can afford errors while searching for the correct principle.

C. *Under such conditions, 100:0 choice-distributions should not occur.* In a 70:30 situation, for example, 100:0 choice-distributions allow one to be correct only 70% of the time and this cannot be considered as solving a problem. Logically, the only kind of choice-distribution which allows one to be correct on every trial is one which matches the event probabilities—a 70:30 choice-distribution in a 70:30 case, a 90:10 choice-distribution in a 90:10 case, and so on" (p. 107).

In contrast, the gambling task has these features:

"A. *The desired final outcome is not necessarily 100% success.* One can be successful without having to know how to win on every trial.

B. *The final outcome is determined by a count of single wins and losses.* The task can easily be set up so that a win at the end cannot

wipe out previous losses. All that this involves is the restriction of
having the same amount of money involved in each bet and each
payoff. In this sense, there are limits placed on the extent to which
S can afford losses.

C. *Under such conditions, choice-distributions should tend to be of
the 100:0 type.* In a 70:30 case, for example, a 100:0 choice-distribution will allow one to win on 70% of one's bets and this can easily
be regarded as 'success' " (pp. 107–8).

In practice, Goodnow finds that behavior does indeed conform to
these predictions when subjects operate with gambling and problem-
solving orientations. Where they appear to be diverging from these
expected patterns, what usually has happened is that the subject
interprets what has been *presented* as a gambling task to be "really"
a problem task, or *vice versa*.

Scaling Probability Estimates and Outcome Values. Throughout
the preceding discussion we have deliberately skirted the problem of
whether and how subjective values and probability estimates can be
stated in numerical terms. In general, there is agreement among
both economists and psychologists that the construction of formal
theory and the making of precise predictions about decisions in
uncertainty situations rest upon the development of satisfactory
scales for both subjective values and probability estimates. The
source for such scales is commonly the pattern of preferences and
indifferences shown by an individual in choosing between alternatives.
Methods for constructing utility curves, or scales for the subjective
value of money, have been discussed by Von Neumann and Morgenstern (1944) and have also been used experimentally (cf. Mosteller
and Nogee, 1951). Methods for deriving and scaling an individual's
probability estimates have been discussed by Ramsey (1926) and
more recently by Savage (1954).

As is to be expected, the construction of such scales is by no means
an easy matter (cf. Edwards, 1954), and raises some very interesting
psychological problems. One of these has already been discussed,
namely the form in which value is to be stated, whether money or
prestige or some combination or ordering of specified objectives.
Another is the way in which individuals combine several criteria in
assessing the value of a set of outcomes. If we assign a scalar value
to a set or bundle of outcomes such as "alive, regretful at having
shot a friend but consoled by the thought of duty fulfilled," we
immediately become interested in knowing how these various criteria
are weighted and combined by an individual. A third problem,
and a thorny one, is the question of what happens when there is a
large number of possible outcomes to each of a number of alternative

actions. We have, for example, simplified our sentry's situation by assuming that he regards himself as a perfect marksman and that he expects any man he shoots at to be a "dead duck." What if the outcomes were more complicated than this? The sentry might have to entertain a whole array of possible consequences, combinations of firing or not firing, missing or not missing, wounding or killing, being found out by Captain X rather than Captain Y, being able or unable to fire a second shot in time if he waits or if the first shot misses. For situations such as these, Shackle (1949) provides an interesting argument. "In order to assess the merits of any given course of action, a man must find some way of reducing the great array of hypotheses about the relevant consequences of this course . . . to some compact and vivid statement" (p. 14). This reduction, he argues, is based partly on a desire for stability and also on the fact that the keenness of anticipation becomes dissipated when spread over too many alternatives. These considerations lead Shackle to the construction of "focus-outcomes," focus points which represent to the individual what he "stands to lose" and "what he stands to win" given a certain course of action.

We have limited ourselves severely in this description of some economic models for the making of choices, particularly in respect to the more formal properties of such models. For our purposes, we have preferred to concentrate on psychological considerations. We do not wish thereby to decry the value of formal models. They are immensely stimulating to research. They offer a guide to experimentation. And they sharpen the search for variables that must be taken into account if a model is to fit more closely the ways in which individuals in fact make decisions and allocate choices. Our "ideal strategies" are offered in much the same spirit.

TWO NEGLECTED VARIABLES

Thus far, the large problems that have concerned us in this chapter are four: the nature and availability of cues for probabilistic categorizing, the individual's conception of the task, the opportunity to validate one's use of cues, and the way in which the consequences of categorization affect cue usage. These are massive topics, and we have made only a beginning in treating them. At least two problems of equal magnitude remain undiscussed. The first has to do with the role and nature of *confidence* in one's use of cues and how this admittedly "subjective" factor affects categorizing behavior. The second relates to the conditions under which an individual abstains from categorizing. We consider each briefly in turn.

"Confidence" is essentially the degree of sureness a person feels in making a categorization. It comprises two elements. The first is the confidence an individual reports in making a *specific* identification of something as being a member of a certain class, that a particular man, for example, is honest. There is also a more extended meaning of confidence. It is the degree of confidence one has in one's estimate of the general validity of a cue. How much confidence can one place in the estimate that a "straightforward regard" is a cue of better-than-chance validity in judging honesty, or that "shifty eyes" have only chance validity in judging dishonesty?

The first of these phenomena—confidence in a specific judgment—is not our principal concern here. There is a considerable body of research on judgmental confidence under psychophysical conditions. Its relationship to the validity of cues, its effect on time spent in making decisions, its alteration following success or failure; these and other topics have been fairly well studied, e.g., Cartwright (1941a, 1941b), Festinger (1943a, 1943b), and Cartwright and Festinger (1943).

What are the determinants of general confidence in a cue? Some of the determinants of general confidence are intuitively evident. Is the estimate of cue validity based on experience that one feels to be limited? Does one's information about the past validity of a cue come from an impeccable source? How many sources of variability does one think are operative and how sure is one that it is possible to balance these against one another? How successful has one been in using a particular cue? Certainly we know from studies of aspiration level that degree of confidence is based on a general summary of success and failure in situations seen as comparable to the present one being faced, and, more immediately, upon the success or failure of recent performance. Indeed, then, confidence can be increased by a tendency to emphasize or remember selectively one's successes and also by the tendency to see a present task as similar to past tasks on which one has used a cue successfully. There seems to be evidence, moreover, that past success has the effect of increasing confidence more than past failure reduces it (e.g., Winder and Wurtz's study, 1954).

The preceding paragraph is arbitrary in the sense that one could have chosen other possible determinants—so wide open is the area of "confidence determinants." It suffices, however, to point to the rich variety of problems that exist in this interesting branch of inquiry.

How does general confidence in cues affect one's categorizing behavior? Studies in problem solving are revealing. A lack of confidence seems to give rise to a lack of persistence in problem solving or predisposes one to think a problem is insoluble (e.g., Keister, 1943; Bloom and Broder, 1950). One would expect on the basis of such findings that in probabilistic categorizing or in concept attainment of the certainty type discussed in previous chapters, a lack of confidence might have the effect of leading to inefficient strategies or, in the probabilistic case, to all-and-none categorizing behavior in the face of objectively less than certain cues.

In terms of effect on individual decisions, it is possible to propose some reasonable hypotheses based on the general theorem that, given two cues which the subject estimates to be equally valid, that cue will be preferred in which the person feels greater confidence. If, for example, one utilizes the kind of judging situation employed by R. E. Goodnow and gives the subject two cues to work with, one pointing 70:30 to type X, the other 70:30 to type Y aircraft, a conflict between the two may be resolved on the basis of the amount of validated experience the person has had with each cue. A subject in such an experiment would have enough experience with both to know that each cue is about 70:30 valid in its own right, but one of the two cues would have been based on a longer learning experience. In a sense, one cue would have been "overlearned."

It is conceivable, finally, that where the outcome of categorizing is governed by a payoff matrix of a drastic nature—where losses to be incurred and gains to be won are great in magnitude—decisions in favor of the "high-confidence" cue will be more marked. Such a prediction is based on the general assumption that under these conditions the individual cannot afford the luxury of exploring and trying out the "lesser confidence" cue.

We now come to the question of making or withholding a categorizing decision. Shall one make a definite choice of alternatives on the basis of available cues or postpone decision? Consider a concrete example. A doctor is faced with a task of differential diagnosis: whether a patient under observation, showing certain symptoms, should be placed in one or another diagnostic category and treated accordingly. How much observation can and will the physician allow before making his diagnosis?

What are some of the factors that determine when one passes from deliberation to decision? One way of approaching the problem is to ask what kinds of psychological factors tend to increase deliberation and what kinds to precipitate decision, recognizing, of course, that such a dichotomy is only heuristic. Two economists, Knight (1921) and Shackle (1949), have each proposed conditions that lead to continued deliberation. Both of these writers speak of the enjoyment of being in a position of choice, uncommitted. The latter remarks on the "pleasure of imagining possibilities" when in such position. Intuitively, their point seems reasonable, particularly where postponement of decision is without much cost to the individual and where choice is between two alternative means to a goal, both of them highly promising, rather than between two incompatible goals, both of which one wants to reach. Yet various psychological writers have suggested that there is an intrinsic cost often involved in delaying identification or categorization. Bartlett (1932), for example, has made much of the "effort after meaning" and the abhorrence of ambiguity, marshalling much compelling evidence on the tendency to structure and to give meaning to ambiguous features of the environment. More recently, Tolman (1951) has proposed that it may be necessary to add to the list of human needs a "placing need" conceived of as an urge to give objects and events definite identity, and the studies of the California group on the prejudiced personality (Adorno, *et al.*, 1950) suggest the strong role of "intolerance of ambiguity" in cognitive functioning.

Generalization about the "enjoyment of choice" on the one hand and the "resolution need" on the other inevitably leads to conflict in prediction. It is quite evident that it is only when one inquires in more detail about the consequences of delay *versus* action that contradiction is avoided. The consequences may be sheerly informational in nature. By delaying one may have the objective of gaining fresh information or of organizing more efficiently the information one already has. But if delay leads to present information becoming obsolescent faster than one can replace it with fresh information, then delay is obviously not so desirable informationally. Shackle (1949) has stimulating things to say about "the possibility of impending fresh information," and the reader is referred to his work for further discussion of this problem. The cost of further information to be obtained during delay is another consideration, one treated in the theory of statistical decision: how shall one balance the value of a decision taken now against the cost of obtaining more information still and the possible value of new information? In sum, the pleasure or displeasure of suspense can be concretely stated in terms of the values and costs, the positive and negative outcomes expected with delay and action.

There are data in the field of psychology which, though not collected for the purpose, do shed light on the relation of consequence to delay. Studies of vicarious trial-and-error behavior (VTE) at choice points in learning situations provide such data. How long will a motivated organism delay its choice of discriminable, alternative pathways to a desired goal, one pathway being a good one, the other being blocked? One illustrative finding, reported by Bruner, Matter, and Papanek (1955), is that more highly motivated rats show fewer VTE responses at choice points in a maze than do moderately motivated rats—the motive being hunger and the reward food. The only "cost" for such VTE deliberation is delaying slightly the consumption of food at the end of the maze. The "gain" from further "looking at the cues" is in reducing subsequent error. It would appear from this study that when a rat is deprived of food for 36 hours the error-reduction gain to be achieved from VTE behavior is less than the loss to be incurred from the delay of obtaining food that such behavior imposes. With the animals deprived for 12 hours, the balance seems to be more in the direction of error reduction and VTE, with time delay becoming secondary. Such an account is, to be sure, grossly simplified, but it suggests the importance of analyzing the payoffs to be achieved by deliberation and decision as factors in choice behavior.

The difference between "spectator" behavior and "participant" behavior noted by Heidbreder (1924) in her early study of thinking also raises interesting questions about deliberation. What leads a subject to "stop and think" when an instance is presented in a concept-formation task, rather than rush into a hasty decision? Heidbreder notes that such a delay in response is rare. "With a situation before them, the subjects seemed impelled to act promptly, though the experiment set no limit to the amount of time to be devoted" (*ibid.*). Frequently subjects would decide on the basis of a hypothesis they knew to be wrong rather than delay response. In our own studies on categorizing with probable cues, this tendency to almost impulsively rapid decision is especially striking.

It may be that we have here a strong desire "to do something" about a problem or a belief that inaction is a sign that not only does one not know what to do but also that one has been reduced to "running out of ideas" (an admission most of our subjects would be loath to make.* We can also speculate that there is something inherent in a psychological experiment that leads to such decisive behavior, for the psychological experiment is an occasion when the subject sees himself as being "tested by a psychologist" for his actions—and "watch-

---

* Oddly enough, waiting for the data to reveal a trend rather than trying to anticipate the trend before the data are complete is regarded by many subjects as a form of failure. Special training is usually required to overcome this attitude (cf. Goodnow and Pettigrew, 1955).

ing and waiting" is not "action." Perhaps we tend too readily to think of our experimental procedures as neutral. It is doubtful that they appear so to the naive subject. All in all, however, our best guess is that the reluctance to delay a categorizing decision and to delay the testing of hypotheses are further aspects of the search for direct information.

Cultural differences and individual differences in venturesomeness with respect to the use of cues doubtless exist. The speed with which one person will pigeonhole another on the basis of slender external cues—this is one of the most characteristic aspects of man's general cognitive style: willingness to sustain indecision, whether it be equated to "tolerance for ambiguity" or not—gives the appearance of being a relatively consistent trait. It may be a function of how much information a person requires before making a decision, or, indeed, a function of how much risk he is willing to take. The economist Marschak (1941) suggests that there may be important individual differences in "venturesomeness," in the odds people require in making a risky decision. Equally, there may be differences in the amount of information individuals require.

Our object in treating the two "neglected variables" of confidence and decision delay has been to raise rather than answer questions, for to do the latter would require far more data than are now available to the psychologist. Rather, we wish to point to the rich possibilities of research in this field and to underline the centrality of such problems for a full understanding of probabilistic categorizing.

CHAPTER 8

An overview

Much of our commerce with the environment involves dealing with classes of things rather than with unique events and objects. Indeed, the case can be made that all cognitive activity depends upon a prior placing of events in terms of their category membership. A category is, simply, a range of discriminably different events that are treated "as if" equivalent. In the preceding chapters, we have been concerned with the nature of psychological categories and with the strategies by which people come to discover what cues they can appropriately use for inferring the category membership of objects and events they may encounter.

It is quite apparent that a good many phenomena in psychology, often treated as quite diverse and put into different chapters of our textbooks, can be treated as instances of categorizing. Conventionally, the term is reserved for various forms of conceptual behavior. But any behavior involving the placement of objects or events on the basis of selected cues may be profitably conceived of as categorizing, whether perceptual or conceptual. The principal difference between identifying a visually presented object as an "apple" and a 19th century statesman as a "Tory" lies not in the process of placement or identification but·in the materials and cues utilized. Indeed, there are examples in which it is almost impossible to differentiate perceptual and conceptual categorizing, notably in language learning. For language learning involves learning to group those sounds that are functionally equivalent and to ignore those differences in sounds that "make no difference" as far as distinguishing words is concerned. We have proposed in earlier chapters that category learning is one of the principal means by which a growing member of a society is socialized, for the categories that one is taught and comes to use habitually reflect the demands of the culture in which they arise. To get on in his culture, the Navaho had best learn to make distinction between events that occur naturally and those traceable to witch-craft, and the Englishman becomes adept indeed in placing a man by the stripes on his tie.

While there are differences, to be sure, in the various phenomena we group as categorizing, it has been our conviction that a closer ex-amination of the general nature of categories and of categorizing would not only elucidate these diverse activities but would show the degree and manner in which they are similar in nature. The research we have reported has mainly been drawn from the field of "concept formation" so-called, but we would propose that our conclusions are applicable to any phenomenon where an organism is faced with the task of identifying and placing events into classes on the basis of using certain criterial cues and ignoring others.

The categories in terms of which we group the events of the world around us are constructions or inventions. The class of prime num-bers, animal species, the huge range of colors dumped into the cate-gory "blue," squares and circles: all of these are inventions and not "discoveries." They do not "exist" in the environment. The objects of the environment provide the cues or features on which our group-ings may be based, but they provide cues that could serve for many groupings other than the ones we make. We select and utilize cer-tain cues rather than others. In the first three chapters of this book, we have been much concerned with the selective utilization of dif-ferent forms of grouping; why some cues are used rather than others, how they come to be combined in certain ways, how one goes from the recognition of defining properties to the placement of the object in a particular category. In the four following chapters this more general discussion has been elaborated by the presentation of an ex-tensive series of experiments.

Both the general discussion of categorizing and its experimental in-vestigation have been based upon a conception of the components of categorizing activity, and to these we must turn now.

There is, first of all, the act of concept or category formation—the inventive act by which classes are constructed. Of this process, we have had relatively little to say here. Categories are developed in response to events, as when a generalization continuum emerges in response to a specific stimulus. They may also be constructed by combinatorial activity as when one proposes the class of "female presidents of the United States" or the class of creatures called centaurs. Or finally, they may approximate pure inventions as when one proposes a concept like the ether or phlogiston. There is a second component of categorizing activity, one that we have been principally concerned with in these pages. This component, which we have called "concept attainment" in contrast to "concept formation," is the search for and testing of attributes that can be used to distinguish exemplars from nonexemplars of various categories, the search for good and valid anticipatory cues. Since our concern has been with concept attainment, we have scrutinized it with more care than we have given to the process of concept formation, not that we think one is more important than the other, but simply that one must place some limit on inquiry.

Let us take as an example of concept attainment the work of a physicist who wishes to distinguish between substances that undergo fission under certain forms of neutron bombardment from substances that do not. Note that our physicist does not have to form the concepts "fissile" and "nonfissile." The essence of his problem is to determine what qualities are associated with fissile and nonfissile substances and eventually to determine which substances will be fissile and which ones nonfissile by means short of neutron bombardment. This kind of problem is hardly unique. The child seeks to distinguish cats and dogs by means other than a parent's say-so; the Army psychiatrist seeks out traits that will predict ultimate adjustment to and performance in the Army. All such tasks can be stripped down to the following elements:

1. There is an array of *instances* to be tested, and from this testing is to come the attainment of the concept. The instances can be characterized in terms of their *attributes,* e.g., color, weight per volume, and in terms of attribute *values,* the particular color, the particular weight per volume, etc.

2. With each instance, or at least most of them once the task is underway, a person makes a tentative prediction or *decision* whether or not the sample before him is, say, fissile, and before he is through with his task there will be a series of such decisions to be made.

3. Any given decision will be found to be correct, incorrect, or varyingly indeterminate; i.e., whatever the decision, the instance will turn out to be fissile, nonfissile, or indeterminate. We refer to this as *validation* of a decision, the major source of information about the relevance of cues exhibited by an instance for its category membership.

4. Each decision-and-test may be regarded as providing potential *information* by limiting the number of attributes and attribute values that can be considered as predictive of the fissibility of substances.

5. The sequence of decisions made by the person en route to attaining the concept, i.e., en route to the discovery of more or less valid cues, may be regarded as a *strategy* embodying certain *objectives*. These objectives may be various in kind but in general one may distinguish three kinds of objectives: *a.* to maximize the information gained from each decision and test of an instance; *b.* to keep the cognitive strain involved in the task within manageable or appropriate limits and certainly within the limits imposed by one's cognitive capacity; and *c.* to regulate the risk of failing to attain the concept within a specifiable time or energy limit and to regulate any other forms of risk consequent to making a decision and testing it. A sequence of decisions or a strategy may be evaluated in the light of these objectives whether the subject "intends" these as his objectives consciously or not. Strategies are not here considered as conscious or deliberate behavior sequences. Whether or not the subject is conscious of the strategy he is employing and can tell you its objectives is an interesting but not a critical datum.

6. Any decision about the nature of an instance may be regarded as having consequences for the decision-maker. Whether the instance is called fissile or nonfissile and whether it turns out on test to be one, the other, or indeterminate, there are consequences to be considered—sometimes grave, sometimes not. A given wrong decision may mean one's job and one's contract, a right one (e.g., coding a fissile instance correctly) may mean a new grant, etc. The set of consequences following upon each decision and each outcome we refer to as the *payoff matrix* of a decision, and the relevant consequences reflect the objectives of the strategy and the over-all task.

Given this analysis of the nature of categorizing, the experimental task that one must undertake is self-evident. For if it can be shown, first, that concept-attainment strategies can be isolated and described, then it should follow, second, that such strategies will be systematically affected by changes in the informational, strain, and risk characteristics of the problems in which the strategies are used. If a strategy is designed to balance informational intake, cognitive strain, and failure risks, then it should be discernibly altered by any imposed conditions that alter the components of this balance. If, for example, cognitive strain is increased, one might expect a change in strategy that reduces informational intake and increases risk of failure—if these are in the interest of cutting down on cognitive strain. It is with the study of such maintenance of balance that most of our experimental investigations have been concerned.

With respect to the nature of the potential information provided, we have used concepts of different kinds (conjunctive, disjunctive, and probabilistic), and have varied the amount of information provided as well as its form (whether by positive instances, examples of what the category is, or by negative instances, examples of what the category is not). We have also on one occasion varied the opportunity for validating one's decisions about membership of instances in a category. To alter cognitive strain, a variety of techniques has been used: increasing the number of attributes and values to be searched in pursuit of correct cues, using abstract *versus* concrete materials, arranging the instances encountered in an orderly as against a random form, speeding up the pace, and other forms of harassment. Risk conditions, as embodied in the use of different payoff matrices, we have also varied by asking such questions as: "How does one categorize if one is a sentry as compared to a searcher after accuracy?" or "What is the effect of changing the probability of obtaining instances for test of a particularly useful kind?" We cannot claim to anything like exhaustive testing of all the possible and relevant conditions and parameters. Rather, we have aimed at selecting those that seemed both theoretically relevant and relevant too in everyday concept attainment. Several other variables, which for reasons of limited energy and resources were not studied, the reader will find referred to in the first three general chapters and scattered through the later chapters as well. If still others are suggested to the reader by omissions on our part or by our stopping short in our arguments, we shall have been well rewarded.

Our first principal finding is that it is possible to describe and to evaluate strategies in a relatively systematic way, both in terms of their objectives and in terms of the steps taken to achieve these. There are, for example, some strategies that under certain conditions are informationally moderately efficient, cognitively unstrenuous, and almost failure-proof. Conservative focussing, mentioned in Chapter 4, is a case in point. Each decision made about an instance encountered yields a guaranteed intake of information, and this intake can if one wishes be measured in terms of "bits" per decision. The strategy neither requires the carrying of a large quantity of information in memory nor the making of involved inferences. Further, given no imposition of limits on time or decisions permitted prior to attainment, the strategy involves no risk whatever, for success is assured. It is a strategy nicely adapted to leisurely conditions in which the subject nonetheless is seeking an efficient solution, and it is not surprising that under these conditions our intelligent subjects employ it (if such a voluntaristic word as "employ" is appropriate here). But should conditions become pressing, should there be a limitation imposed on the number of instances one can test before one discovers which kinds of substances are "fissile" or "edible" or what not, then the strategy becomes less appropriate in the sense that its use now risks the chance of complete failure. There is also a strategy which in Chapter 4 was called focus gambling and it has many of the same properties as the conservative focussing strategy, at least as far as cognitive strain is concerned. Its difference is that each decision made either leads to the assimilation of a considerable amount of information or none at all. Given a limitation on the number of decisions that a person may make prior to concept attainment, it has the property of increasing the chances of attainment over the poorer chances involved in conservative focussing. The greater the limitation imposed, the more striking is the difference between the two. We find, to use these two strategies as an example, that as one imposes upon subjects a restriction in the number of instances they can test on the way to attaining a concept, the greater the likelihood of their shifting away from conservative focussing in the direction of focus gambling. Each of the strategies is amenable to relatively rigorous description, and it is fairly simple to employ a quite precise measure for describing the shift from one strategy to the other. The reader will recall the discussion of these experiments in Chapter 4 and we need not labor the details again here. We bring up the matter only to underline the first general point we wish to make about our findings: that strategies can be located and described, and by the same token, a shift in strategy can also be described and related to changes in the requirement of the task set.

A second major finding implied in what was just said is that it is possible to demonstrate the effect of relevant conditions upon measurable aspects of categorizing strategies.. By so doing, we have been able to "get into" the *process* of concept attainment rather than being limited to evaluations simply in terms of whether a subject succeeded or failed in attaining a concept. We have been able to analyze, with a fair degree of definiteness and an occasional feeling of real understanding, the way to the attainment of a concept. This is not a "finding" in the formal sense, but it is for us one of the most satisfying resultants of our experimental studies.

A third general finding is less readily summarized. When one utilizes somewhat novel techniques of experimentation and analysis on rather old problems—and the problems of categorizing and concept attainment can all be found lucidly presented in Aristotle's *De Sensu* —one is likely to come upon certain general tendencies in information-getting and information-using behavior that are worth especial note. For many of these general tendencies, we suspect, can be found in a variety of cognitive activities that may not, on the surface, seem related to the tasks we set our subjects. One of these is the tendency of people to fall back on a criterion of verisimilitude in using and evaluating cues for categorization. That is to say, in attempting to differentiate exemplars from nonexemplars of a category, as one so frequently must in science, medicine, and indeed in daily life, the person will, in the absence of other information, tend to fall back on cues that in the past have seemed useful, whether these cues have been useful in an analogous situation or not. When the person is working with familiar cues but with unfamiliar categories this tendency will emerge and it accounts in part for the difference between behavior toward what we commonly call concrete materials (where such verisimilar cues are present) and toward abstract materials (where they are not). This "persistence-forecasting," evaluating cues on the basis of their apparent past relevance, while it obviously has value, can prove to be a chief obstacle to the adoption of informationally efficient strategies.

Another general tendency is the inability or unwillingness of subjects to use efficiently information which is based on negative instances or derives from indirect test of an hypothesis. Both of these require the transformation of information. An instance that illustrates the negative case, what a concept is *not*, requires that one use it to infer what the concept might be. So too knowledge from an indirect test, so-called. An indirect test of an hypothesis, the reader will recall, is illustrated by proving *through elimination* that one's hypothesis is correct rather than proving it directly. We have found that, in dealing with the task of sorting out relevant from irrelevant cues in the environment, subjects persist until they are able to make direct tests with positive instances, and we have been at pains in earlier chapters to evaluate the significance of this tendency for cognitive behavior. In general, it is as if information that results from "in-the-head" transformations is distrusted perhaps through an appreciation of the possibility of the errors one can make in such transformations.

Finally, we may note one additional tendency to the others noticed; it may be called the tendency to prefer common-element or conjunctive concepts and to use (often inappropriately) strategies of cue-searching that are relevant to such concepts. We have noted frequently enough the primitive assumption that a class or category of objects should be defined by a set of defining attribute values that are additive: to be an exemplar of a class, an object should have this characteristic *and* that characteristic *and* that other characteristic. Disjunctive concepts (and to a considerable degree, relational ones as well, although these have not been discussed at any length) require getting used to, and in searching for their defining properties subjects often slip back into their primitive assumptions about conjunctivity. Whether this is a universal characteristic of human thought or whether it is a reflection of the predominantly conjunctive logic and language of Western cultures we are not prepared to say.

As for other trends observed—the greater amount of information required for abandoning an hypothesis that fits one's general notions, the tendency to reduce the number of cues one considers in making categorial placements, the inclination to assume in problem-solving that "change means progress," the impulsion to make use of every source of information when the going gets rough even though such eclecticism overwhelms limited capacity—these and many others are suggested by specific findings and seem eminently to deserve further investigation.

In general, we are struck by the notable flexibility and intelligence of our subjects in adapting their strategies to the information, capacity, and risk requirements we have imposed on them. They have altered their strategies to take into account the increased difficulty of the problems being tackled, choosing methods of information gathering that were abstractly less than ideal but that lightened pressures imposed on them by the tasks set them. They have changed from safe-but-slow to risky-but-fast strategies in the light of the number of moves allowed them. They have shown themselves able to adapt to cues that were less than perfect in validity and have shown good judgment in dealing with various kinds of payoff matrices. They have shown an ability to combine partially valid cues and to resolve conflicting cues.

There are, to be sure, certain systematic errors that are observable. But these may be conceived of not so much as "errors" as systematic behavior related to the strategy being followed. One may distinguish several kinds of systematic "errors." One of them has to do with the extent to which people trust and use cues as bases for inferring exemplars of a category. Does the person accord a cue the same degree of trust as its validity merits—and is this a meaningful question? A second type of "error" has to do with failure to assimilate as much information as is potentially available from testing an instance. Finally, there is the type of error involved in misestimating the nature of the inference that one must make: seeking cues that permit certainty inferences where only probabilistic ones are available, or trying to deal with a disjunctive concept as though it were conjunctive.

About the reliance people place on cues, as judged by the readiness with which they will use them as a basis for inference, this will depend in large measure upon the nature of the decision to be made. If one must make a decision fast about the identity of instances, one will come to place great reliance on cues that are immediately available for use. It is all very well to say that the criteriality of a cue—the degree to which it will be used for making an inference—will reflect its validity or the degree to which *in fact* it provides a correct basis for such an inference. In general and under relaxed circumstances, this is the case. But to leave the matter at that and call all deviations from the rule "errors" is to miss most of what is interesting about the criteriality of cues. For cues will be used in a fashion commensurate with the objectives and payoff matrix governing a categorizing situation. If the objective is to reduce cognitive strain, a simpler and more easily ascertained cue will be used in preference to a more complex one of higher validity. If the risk of any form of wrong prediction from cue to identity is very grave, very likely the most valid one available will be used to the exclusion of all others, *ceteris paribus.* Indeed, one may think of the relation between cue validity and cue criteriality—the actual goodness of a cue and the degree to which it is relied upon in judgment—as being mediated by the payoff matrix governing the situation. One cannot call it an "error" if Selective Service doctors use an indication like bed-wetting as a criterial attribute for weeding out potentially unstable soldiers, even if there are better cues available. For the limit of time placed upon the examining military physician makes less immediately available cues worthless, even if they are more valid.

With respect to the failure of subjects to assimilate all the information that can be extracted from testing an instance, again it is doubtful whether such phenomena should be conceived of as "errors." If an individual adopts a strategy, say the "lazy" successive-scanning strategy, he is destined not to learn as much from each test encounter as a person who uses conservative focussing. It is not a question of error, but of the nature of the strategy being employed. If a strategy is built on direct test of cues, then negative information does not fit into the pattern he is employing. If he attempts to use negative instances, indeed, he may end up by confusing himself and departing from the nicety of the strategy he has been employing. Errors in this sense have the status of "useful inefficient statistics" that throw away data but which are still helpful in getting the test made so long as the distinctions to be drawn are not too subtle.

The last type of "error"—misjudging the type of inference to be made—is again not profitably viewed as error but should be viewed as a systematic response tendency related to strategy. We dislike disjunctive inferences, as mentioned earlier, perhaps because they are rare and not simply because they are ugly. So too probabilistic cues; we sometimes tend to make them more certain than they are, particularly if they seem "reasonable" or "impressive." It is a nice problem how these tendencies come about, whether, as we have suggested, the structure of our language and logic imposes them upon us. Little is added by calling them errors. They are dependent variables, these tendencies, whose determinants have yet to be discovered. We suspect that such misestimates derive from larger scale strategies of problem-solving: aspects of behavior that might almost be called "style" or, as the French put it, *"déformation professionelle."* One develops on the basis of past encounters with one's particular world an expectancy concerning the nature of classes of events. One may, by virtue of circumstances, develop a "gambling orientation" whereby cues tend to be treated as probabilistic. Or the mathematician may develop specialized deformations about the relational nature of classes. These deformations, though they may lead to inefficient behavior in particular problem-solving situations, may represent highly efficient strategies when viewed in the broader context of a person's normal life.

Perhaps the term "error" should be used for two specific forms of behavior not conventionally labelled in this way. The failure of an over-all strategy to meet the requirements imposed by a task, to the degree that it is maladaptive, is an "error." Note, however, that only a large segment of sequential behavior may be characterized in this way and not any particular response. For example, a few subjects of very superior intelligence and usually with mathematical training attempt to attain conjunctive concepts by the use of simultaneous scanning—keeping all possible hypotheses in mind at each step—and their efforts came to grief. Their strategies were in error, by which we mean that the strategies employed failed to meet the objectives of an adequate strategy. So we may speak of error in this sense as a strategy that proves to be dysfunctional in a given problem situation.

The other form of behavior that may be called an error is related to the first. It is deviation from a strategy that has the effect of disrupting behavior. We have observed cases of the use of focus gambling (which is premised on the utilization of positive instances only) where the subject, upon encountering a negative instance, feels impelled to use the information. This has the effect of making him ride two horses: simultaneous scanning and focus gambling. By so doing, he ends by confusing himself. But here again, error must be defined not with reference to the abstract success or failure of a given response, but by reference to the fittingness of a particular act in a sequence of acts.

The various detailed features of concept-attainment strategies need not be passed in review here. Their principal features are already plain enough. What psychological status shall we afford the construct of a strategy? The point has already been made that they are not necessarily deliberate or conscious forms of behavior decided upon in advance by subjects and then put into operation. Oftentimes subjects were unable to tell us in any coherent way how they had proceeded although the sequence of behavior showed systematic features of a highly regular and skilled order. The concept of strategy has, we would say, a kind of middling status. It is not a construct in the grand manner such as *libido* or *habit strength,* for it is in no sense proposed as an "explanation" of the behavior from which it is inferred. At the same time, it is more than a bare account of moves made by an organism. It is, rather, a description of extended sequences of behavior, a description that is also evaluative in the sense that it proposes to consider what the behavior sequence accomplishes for the organism in terms of information getting, conservation of capacity, and risk regulation.

As a step toward formalizing the description of the series of decisions that make up a strategy, we have introduced the concept of the *ideal strategy.* An ideal strategy is basically an analytic device used as a yardstick against which to compare the performance of human operators in the situations we set them. It is our conception of the "pure form" of the kind of behavior we have been observing: the way we would set a computer to do what the subject appears to be doing. It is, if you will, the opposite of the null hypothesis which states how a subject's sequence of responses should look if they were "guided by random numbers." We set a subject the task of categorizing a series of instances exhibiting one of two possible values of an attribute. One value indicates the instance is an exemplar of a category 70% of the time, the other signals exemplar status in 30% of the instances: a so-called 70:30 case. We will find that under certain conditions of payoff and risk subjects will call instances containing the more probable value an exemplar of the category 95% of the time on the average, the other only 5%. We postulate that the ideal strategy is an "all-and-none" approach: *always* calling the more probably valued instance an exemplar, *never* calling the less probably valued one such. Only a minority of our subjects may actually show a performance record of this ideal type, but we nonetheless speak of the subjects as tending toward this ideal strategy. So too in disjunctive concept attainment where we find behavior tending toward "ideal" negative focussing or "ideal" common-element strategies, although there will be few cases of the pure thing in actual behavior.

This is indeed a common form of middling "model construction," of the same order as proposing that in a tracking task subjects not only do not perform randomly (the null hypothesis) but that they perform in approximation to a servomechanism. Note, however, that while we have stated the formal or logical properties of various strategies, we have left completely open the issue of how they come about; whether by the operation of the laws of association, by the gradual growth of habit strength (although it is not evident what the reinforcements are), or by the subtle concatenation of phase sequences in the cortex. We have sought to describe large segments or long sequences of behavior in systematic terms and whoever deals in "less middling" or "more basic" theories will one day have to explain how these large segments come into being, how they are maintained and changed, and the rest. That has not been our job: the job could not exist before the behavior had been described and preliminary means of measurement devised. Developmental studies, studies of the effect of different experiential histories, investigations of cognitive and other pathologies—these will be the research tools required for the more basic job of investigating the origins of strategies.

There are three methodological conclusions to which we must turn now: the first has to do with techniques for the study of cognitive processes, the second concerns the working definition of what has been traditionally called "concepts," and the third deals with the relation between conceptualizing, inference, and other forms of cognitive activity.

With respect to the first of these—techniques for the study of cognitive processes, the processes whereby information about the environment is achieved, retained, and transformed so that it may be utilized in situations other than the one in which acquisition occurred —it seems to us that there are several desiderata. First of all, to understand the intelligent or adaptive nature of behavior, one must work with units larger than a single response, no matter how "molar" that response may be. One must, moreover, work with *sequences* of response if one is to appreciate the unfolding interplay between successive responses in reaction to prior consequences. Since the consequences of a previous act serve to guide subsequent responses and since the final objective being sought by the organism will determine the goodness or badness of a given consequence, it behooves the student of behavior to pay closer heed to the sequential patterning of the behavior he is studying. These are points that have been made much of in recent years and they are obvious. They deserve remaking here because they are peculiarly apposite to the study of cognitive activity.

If, in studying problem-solving and conceptualizing and other allied activities, we are to emphasize the analysis of behavior sequences, then it becomes necessary to *externalize* the component steps or decisions in order to get at them. The so-called "eureka" problems in which the subject is given all the elements out of which a solution must be fashioned are peculiarly unsuited to the requirements of getting behavior observably externalized, unless the problem is such that successive, attempted solutions can be observed. In the study of thinking, inference, conceptualizing, and other such diversely labelled activities, the great technical problem is precisely this one. If behavior is to be viewed as strategy, the task of analysis can only be accomplished by devising experiments that can get a lot of sequentially linked behavior out of the organism where it can be observed.

One other matter of technique also derives from our emphasis upon the analysis of strategies. It has to do with the use of indirect or "cover-story" methods of studying cognition, a matter that has bedevilled the field of concept attainment particularly. If one presents a concept-attainment task to subjects with the cover-story instruction that it is a task of rote memory (associating DAXes and CIVs with various curlecues), then the behavior of the subject will be geared to the objectives of the task as stated and his strategy will reflect the requirements set him. Let it be clear that the problem of setting the objectives in problem-solving and conceptualizing experiments is not a nuisance to be got rid of by "cute" instructions that conceal the purpose of the research. Objective-setting is a critical variable to be studied as a variable; it is neither a parameter one can hold constant with safety nor an embarrassment to be swept under the procedural rug.

The second procedural problem has to do with the working definition of what are conventionally called concepts. A certain confusion is contributed by the philosophical controversy over the nature of concepts as universals: whether a universal is something that resides in objects and may be directly known or whether it is in a Platonic realm of universals that can only be "prehended" in corrupted form or whether it is something that is imposed on regularities in nature by a conceptualizing mind. And the confusion comes partly from controversies within psychological theory. We fail to see that the philosophical controversy has any bearing on the *empirical* study of conceptualizing behavior. The principal psychological controversy has been between two views. There are those who urge that a concept, psychologically, is defined by the common elements shared by an array of objects and that arriving at a concept inductively is much like "arriving at" a composite photograph by superimposing instances on a common photographic plate until all that is idiosyncratic is washed out and all that is common emerges. A second school of thought holds that a concept is not the common elements in an array, but rather is a relational thing, a relationship between constituent part processes.

We submit that such a controversy is relatively fruitless. We have found it more meaningful to regard a concept as a network of sign-significate inferences by which one goes beyond a set of *observed* criterial properties exhibited by an object or event to the class identity of the object or event in question, and thence to additional inferences about other *unobserved* properties of the object or event. We see an object that is red, shiny, and roundish and infer that it is an apple; we are then enabled to infer further that "if it is an apple, it is also edible, juicy, will rot if left unrefrigerated, etc." The working definition of a concept is the network of inferences that are or may be set into play by an act of categorization.

As we have been at pains to point out, the criterial attribute values from which class identity is inferred and the inferences that are then made from class identity to other properties need *not* be of a common-element type *nor* need they be relationally connected. There are conjunctive, relational, and disjunctive concepts and each of these may be of a "certainty type" or probabilistic in nature, depending upon whether criterial attributes point with certainty to class membership or. not. A conjunctive class may be defined psychologically by the conjoint presence of several attribute values: when and only when all such values are present may an object be considered as an exemplar of the category. This is a conjunctive concept, and there are strategies appropriate to the attainment of such concepts (Chapters 4 and 5). A relational class is one in which the "rule" of inference requires that values of different attributes bear a specified relation to each other: the definition of the class of events known as "equations" requires a relationship between quantities on either side of an equal sign. A disjunctive concept is one in which one works with vicarious "attribute-class–other-attribute" inference patterns. An exemplar of a disjunctive class may be defined by the presence of property A_i or B_i or C_i or A_iB_i, A_iC_i, B_iC_i, or $A_iB_iC_i$. One may be a member of the University Combination Room at Cambridge if one is *a.* a member of the Regent House, or *b.* a member of the staff of the University, or *c.* elected by the Committee of Management, or any feasible combination of these. One may infer from any of these to "eligibility" with certainty, but one cannot infer from "eligibility" to any one or any combination of these properties. It is a class that is neither comfortably conjunctive nor elegantly relational. And it is one that people have great difficulty mastering both in everyday life and in experiments (cf. Chapter 6), for the vicarious functioning of cues in pointing to class membership seems to violate the expectation that to each effect there be but one cause.

It must be apparent to the reader, from our discussion of strategy and the analysis of "errors" just set forth, that our inquiry has started from a premise that may be called "functionalist." That is to say, we began our inquiry with the simple and inevitable question, "What does categorizing accomplish for the organism?" Such an opening question—and it is almost a universal opening question in the biological sciences, where one begins by asking, say, what does the circulation of blood accomplish for the organism—such a question tends quickly to recede into the background. Circulation, to be sure, may indeed serve the function of bringing nutriment, oxygen, etc., to the tissues of the body, but before long one is more occupied with the means by which this is accomplished. So too with categorizing. One begins by answering the first functional question by guessing that categorizing serves to cut down the diversity of objects and events that must be dealt with uniquely by an organism of limited capacities and that it makes possible the sorting of functionally significant groupings in the world. Eventually, one goes beyond this, as we have gone beyond to the conception of categorizing strategies. But the first step leaves its impress: what we have spoken of as the "objectives" of a strategy are, if you will, a more evolved representation of our first functional concern. Many psychologists, it would appear, deplore any admission of functionalism, feeling somehow that it is an invitation to the purposivist with his cheap solutions. But to describe a function is not to explain it; it is only a preliminary to asking further questions, and it has been our aim in these pages to ask further questions. If the reader feels that our approach to conceptualizing warrants the label of "functionalism," we shall be not at all offended. Perhaps it would be even more appropriate to call us "empiricists."

We have chosen to call this volume *A Study of Thinking*. A word in explanation of this title brings the enterprise to a close. Concept attainment is, to be sure, an aspect of what is conventionally called thinking, and in this sense the title justifies itself. But we have also urged a broader view: that virtually all cognitive activity involves and is dependent on the process of categorizing. More critical still, the act of categorizing derives from man's capacity to infer from sign to significate, and in so far as we have shed any light on categorizing as such it is our hope that we have also made clearer the nature of inference as a psychological phenomenon.

Finally, it has been our intention to investigate paradigms of behavior that represent in stripped-down form the kind of behavior called problem-solving or thinking in everyday life. Repeatedly we have sought parallels in the behavior of the scientist going about his business. Seeking to discover what areas of the cortex mediate speech or what substances evoke allergic reactions, the scientist is engaged in much the same kind of behavior as were our subjects. The scientist too is faced with the task of assimilating information, conserving cognitive strain, and regulating the risk of failure and folly. We have idealized the experimental situations employed in our investigations beyond what is normal in daily life, but that is the price one pays for experimenting at all. It is our hope that by reaching a fuller understanding of these more idealized forms of thinking *in vitro*, the complexities of thinking as we observe it around us will be more readily understood.

Language
and
categories

By Roger W. Brown

This discussion of the psychology of language is divided into three parts. The first deals with the speech system. The second discusses linguistic meaning. The third considers the relation between language and culture. The unit of analysis throughout is the cognitive category.

Several recent publications have described for psychologists the major findings of linguistic science. We know about the phoneme and form class but cannot yet be said to have assimilated them. They appear in our vocabulary as newly borrowed foreign terms, pronounced hesitatingly and integrated with difficulty into the local dialect. The linguist's knowledge of the microscopic detail and elaborate structure of his subject can correct our own impoverished models of the language process. The findings of descriptive linguistics translate very naturally into the language of categories—the language of this book—and in this form may be useful to the psychologist.

Ultimately, we are interested in speech only because it is meaningful, because the larger units of speech have reference to objects and events. Reference involves the co-ordination of speech categories with categories of the nonlinguistic world. Correct speech means more than correct pronunciation. It means the properly selective use of meaningful units. One cannot speak a language until one has formed the governing nonlinguistic concepts. First-language learning, then, is more than the acquisition of a motor skill. It is a process of cognitive socialization. In this process we shall see that the peculiar structure of speech has great importance and in the study of this process appears our justification for the preliminary study of descriptive linguistics.

Cognitive socialization means the taking on of culture. Because speech is so important in the process we are prepared to find some intimate relations between the structure of a language and the structure of nonlinguistic culture. From anthropology have come strong statements of Linguistic Relativity and Linguistic Determinism, statements founded on certain striking parallels between language and other cultural systems. We will examine these statements from the point of view of cognitive psychology to determine what kinds of relationship between language and culture are probable and what kinds are improbable.

So we begin with language cut back to its sounds. The good things of life, meaning and culture, are added at later stages. These are all systems of categories in interconnection.

THE CATEGORIES OF SPEECH

The movement to devise an international phonetic alphabet had, as its original impulse, the desire to provide a distinct sign for each distinguishable speech sound (phone) that might be heard anywhere in the world. The speech sounds were to be analyzed into a set of articulational attributes, so that each sound would be a unique conjunction of positions and movements of the speech apparatus. There are now many phonetic alphabets but none of them accomplishes this original purpose. The goal is unattainable for the reason that speech sounds are infinitely varied. The wonder is that alphabets of about 50 symbols and a dozen diacritics could ever have been thought equal to the task. A further wonder is the amount of agreement between authors of different alphabets. How did they happen to recognize the same microscopic fraction of the infinitely large number of attributes differentiating speech sounds? Both wonders were possible because the phoneticians, like other human beings, categorized the speech they heard and the symbols of their phonetic alphabets stand for sound categories rather than unique sounds. The articulational attributes defining these categories seem to have been selected because of their significance in one or another of the languages then known. This is not to say that the alphabet was intended to be limited in this way but rather that the language background of the phoneticians caused them to hear some speech differences and to overlook others. The naive member of a language community categorizes the speech he hears. He has a *Sprachgefühl* that will actively affect his perception of unfamiliar speech. In an international phonetic alphabet that aspires to provide unique symbols for all distinct sounds any such *Sprachgefühl* is out of place. A phonemic alphabet, on the other hand, is intended to represent the categories of the naive speakers of a particular language.

The Phoneme as a Category. The phoneme is often called the smallest unit of speech that "makes a difference" to a listener or speaker. Linguistic scientists have developed intricate but generally reliable techniques for discovering these units in any speech corpus. There is some disagreement about minor points of procedure and a good deal of disagreement concerning the psychological status of the phoneme. The following treatment does not detail all of these differences of opinion. It draws most heavily on Z. S. Harris' admirably precise *Methods in Structural Linguistics* (1951) but is not a presentation of Harris since it is written with an eye to the problems of psychology rather than linguistics.

Our definition begins with the parable of the coins which is an exact analogue of the first stage in phoneme identification. Individual coins, though never identical as stimulus objects, are said to be of the same denomination when they have a functional equivalence for economic exchange. Individual phones also fall into functional equivalence classes. Phones belonging to the same functional class can be substituted for one another in a given utterance without changing the meaning of the utterance. Thus one can make slight changes in the duration, quality, and pitch of the [p] in "pill" without changing "pill" into another word. Mutually substitutable phones are said to be in free variation and the discovery of classes of free variants is the first stage in phoneme identification. However, the class of freely varying phones is not yet a phoneme. There is a second step in phoneme identification and this step is described after the procedure for discovering classes of free variants.

Suppose that we have undertaken to classify the metal currency of a country. We have available a sample of eight coins like those pictured in Figure 14. If these specimens are closely examined it is clear that no two are identical. It may be our first impulse to divide them into two groups: the large and the small. The size attribute is highly criterial for identifying American coins. It is predictive of the ultimate criterion—the exchange value of the coin. However, if we observed the buying and selling of the people who use this currency we might discover that they treat coins A, C, E, and G as equivalent but distinct from a second group, coins B, D, F, and H. They might pay no attention to size but concentrate on the nature of the coin edge, whether it is rough or smooth. Size would then be a noisy attribute in their categorizing of these coins. As another alternative they might use the darkness or brightness of the surface as a criterial attribute.

This seems an unlikely choice, however, since the coins would change brightness value as they passed from hand to hand and an unstable currency is something to avoid. The degree of soiling and tarnish is a noisy attribute in American currency. This dimension is criterial in so many areas of our life, such as utensils and clothing, that it is not surprising if we vaguely feel it an unfair exchange to give up a new half dollar for an old dingy one.

The linguistic scientist who studies the speech of an unfamiliar preliterate people is in a position resembling that of the coin classifier. He too collects a group of specimens (a speech corpus) and tries to

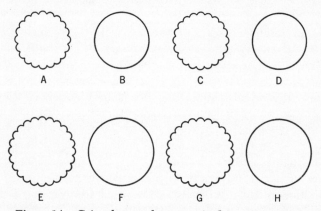

Figure 14.　Coins that can be categorized in various ways.

discover the local categorization of the sounds recorded. He, too, must beware of his own categorial predispositions which might falsify the local system. The local speech system like the currency system is revealed in a process of social interchanges.

The first step is a phonetic transcription of the corpus of speech. This transcription should be as narrow as one can manage. Since the transcription will not be ultimately narrow (a symbol for each unique sound), there are sure to be some recurrent phonetic sequences. Distinguishable sounds will sometimes be found imbedded in identical phonetic contexts. These sounds are the focus of the first stage of phonetic study.

Are two discriminable phones, A and A', that occurs in identical phonetic contexts, categorized together or separately categorized by a native speaker? Notice that, if the object language were English, A and A' might correspond to [p] and [b] in "pan" and "ban" with the prime mark indicating the voice that is added to the bilabial plosive [p] to make [b]. Alternatively A and A′ might correspond to [pʰ] and [p¹] in which the second phone is unreleased as it sometimes is in "nip." The same word is, however, sometimes pronounced with a released aspirated [pʰ] of the kind heard in "pin." Either form of [p] is possible in final position. Our *Sprachgefühl* classifies the [p]'s together; indeed we may never have noticed their difference, but the [p] and [b] we consider to be altogether different. Now we are concerned with A and A′. The phonetician has distinguished between them since he writes them differently. What of the native speaker?

It is difficult to know just what question to ask. If a man in a pith helmet were to ask you, as a native speaker of English, to tell him whether there was any difference between two sounds and if he then painstakingly enunciated [p]'s, released and unreleased, you might well report the difference though noticing it for the first time. Any set that puts the informant on his mettle, that puts a premium on acuteness, is undesirable. What we want is his acculturated ear. We want a casual, habitual judgment, not an auditory difference limen.

Harris suggests that the phonetician produce A in its phonetic context (ABC) and then ask the native speaker whether A′BC is a repetition of ABC. In effect one asks if the utterances are the same but without focussing on the particular sound. If the utterances were "pan" and "ban" no speaker of English would accept them as equivalent. If the utterances were "nip" (unreleased) and "nip" (released) they would be accepted as equivalent so long as the informant did not feel that his powers of auditory discrimination were being tested. Alternatively the linguist might pronounce ABC and ask informants to repeat the utterances several times. If any of the "repetitions" were transcribed as A′BC we would know that the native speaker accepts A′ as equivalent to A. The parallel with coin classification is very close for the repetition procedure is a speech equivalent of giving and receiving change.

As an alternative to the repetition procedure the linguist might observe usage of ABC and A′BC to see whether they correlate with the same or different nonlinguistic circumstances. In the simplest case ABC and A′BC would be denotational words, used in pointing at members of identity categories. The informant would take one boy by the hand and say, "This is my son ABC and this," taking the other boy by the hand, "is A′BC." Of course this procedure is liable to serious misconstruction. A single pointing has no unequivocal meaning. Is this that I denote a glass, a glass of milk, milk, a container, or a thing? One pointing will not tell. By careful attention to positive and negative instances, however, the linguist may discover whether ABC and A'BC name different categories for native speakers. He fills here the role of a subject in the studies reported in this book, a subject who does not control the sequence of events but observes them.

Pike (1947) reports that one of his best checks on a phonemic analysis comes from the reaction of natives to his speech. If they roar with laughter when he is serious or if they are insulted when he is being pleasant, the inappropriate reaction can sometimes be traced to the pronunciation of A in a context that calls for A'.

Using several of these operations to check on one another the linguist obtains a set of phonetic categories. The phones within a category are mutually substitutable in a set of contexts. The members of a category are said to be in free variation with one another. They are free variants. Each category is given a symbol. These symbols have no exact phonetic value. They stand for classes of phones. The categorial [p] stands for both released and unreleased varieties. The original phonetic transcription made by the linguist was also necessarily categorial. The categories were his, rather than those of the native speakers, and they were smaller categories than the new variety. Still these new phonetic categories are not phonemes.

The coin parable offers no exact analogy for the second step in phoneme identification. Indeed, we can think of no close parallel for this procedure outside of linguistic analysis. What happens, essentially, is that some of the classes of freely varying phones can be classified together to yield a higher order category—the phoneme. Classes of phones that can be so united are called allophones (or varying forms) of a given phoneme. We are next concerned then with the criteria for discovering which classes of phones can be called allophones of one phoneme. There are two criteria: complementary distribution and articulational similarity. These are now described.

Among the categories of free variants are some that occur in complementary distribution; this is to say that the members of one class occur in phonetic contexts in which the members of the other class do not appear. In English the prolonged [o] is heard in "toad" and a shorter [o] is heard in "tote." When the [o] precedes a voiced consonant it is always longer than when it appears before a voiceless consonant ("poke-Pogo," "rope-robe," "moat-mode," etc.). These classes of [o] are in complementary distribution. The two [k] sounds of "keep cool" are similar but distinct. If you attend to your own articulation you will notice that the [k] of "keep" is farther forward (prevelar) than the mid-velar [k] of "cool." When classes of phones occur in complementary distribution the class can be predicted from phonetic context (e.g., shorter vowels before voiceless consonants, longer vowels before voiced consonants).

Among the phonetic categories that occur in complementary distribution are some that share distinctive features of articulation. This is true of the pre-velar and mid-velar [k]'s. Both are voiceless velar stops. In English the phonetic categories [h] (as in "hit") and [ŋ] (as in "sing") are also in complementary distribution. No English word begins with [ŋ] and none ends with [h]. The phonetic [h] should not be confused with the silent letter "h" which does occur in final position in English spelling. The categories [h] and [ŋ] do not have articulational similarity. Phonetic categories having articulational similarity and complementary distribution are *allophones* of a single phoneme. The categories [h] and [ŋ] cannot be allophones of the same phoneme since they lack articulational similarity. However, the two [k]'s satisfy both criteria for inclusion within a single phoneme.

The letters of an alphabet transcribe with more or less precision the segmental phonemes of speech but there are also suprasegmental phonemes that are not written alphabetically. These may appear as the printer's space (juncture) or as diacritics in a guide to pronunciation (stress) or in such end-of-sentence punctuation as the exclamation and question marks (intonation). In English the utterance "market" is not acceptable as a repetition of "mark it." The second utterance involves an external open juncture (symbolized #) which is lacking in the first. This phonemic difference signals a very great difference in meaning. In English also the utterance "pérmit" (stress on the first syllable) is not a repetition of permít (stress on the second syllable). The former word is a noun, the latter a verb. In many languages (Chinese, Mixteco, Navaho) there are tone phonemes. In Mixteco, for instance, a given sequence of segmental phonemes pronounced with a low tone means "mountain" while the same sequence means "brush" when pronounced with a medium tone. A syllable does not have a fixed lexical meaning unless its tone is specified. The absolute pitch of individual syllables is not a significant feature of English speech but the contour of relative pitch levels across an utterance is significant. We can change the utterance "Tom is here" from an exclamation of surprise to a statement of fact by altering the intonation contour. Pike (1945) has found that all the significant contrasts of English are accomplished with four levels of relative pitch. The secondary phonemes (juncture, stress, tone, intonation) together with the more familiar segmental phonemes comprise the total significant features of speech.

The phonemes of one community may be the allophones or free variations of another community. This fact has important implications for the teaching of languages. Particular problems of speech perception and production can be predicted from a knowledge of the phonology of the old and new languages. The English Language Institute at the University of Michigan has, under the direction of Charles Fries (1945), developed a training manual designed to teach English to students who natively speak Spanish and a quite different manual for students whose native language is Chinese. Each manual is based on a comparative study of the two languages concerned. With the Spanish speaker it is important to know that his language does not separate the phones [s] and [z] into separate phonemes. Consequently he will have trouble pronouncing and, especially, hearing the difference between such English words as "rice" and "rise" or "ice" and "eyes." Chinese speakers, especially those from the Yangtse River area, do not use [l] and [n] initially to contrast words and so confuse "light" with "night" and "line" and "nine." In general, where two languages give different categorial status to a phonetic distinction problems of perception and pronunciation can be anticipated. The English Language Institute lesson books contain pronunciation drills which contrast the sounds that will be difficult for the group of students for whom the book is designed.

What part does linguistic meaning play in the procedure for determining phonemes? An offhand characterization of the phoneme will sometimes describe it as the minimal speech element capable of signalling a difference of meaning. An equally offhand comparison of our English examples suggests that "pan" and "ban" differ in meaning while the two "nips" do not. Some of us, if pressed to define "a difference of meaning" might translate the phrase as any difference in an auditor's total response. This position is untenable since certain free variants and misplaced allophones will alter meaning in this sense. "Nip" with released [p] strikes me as rather jaunty while the unreleased "nip" is distinctly constricted and tight-lipped. This slight semantic shift would turn up in a sufficiently detailed record of my total responses to the' words. However, the difference does not prevent me from recognizing the two pronunciations as the same word. We have no use for total responses. Like Heraclitus' streams and the sounds of speech they probably do not repeat. We want the kind of categorial reaction elicited by the repetition procedure. The informant brings his own understanding of equivalence and difference of meaning to the task. There is no need in this procedure to specify any actual meaning. Nor is there any necessity to define the nature of meaning.

The practical purpose of a phonemic analysis is often the creation of an alphabet for a previously unwritten language. It would be possible to assign a letter to each category of free variants and thereby create a writing system that would differentiate all utterances the native speaker distinguishes. However, a simpler alphabet will accomplish the purpose. Because they are in complementary distribution a set of allophones can all be assigned the same letter. It is not necessary to assign different letters to the allophones since an allophonic difference is never the only feature differentiating utterances the native speaker finds different in meaning. The long and short [o] in English can be written with one symbol because there are no English words distinguished by vowel length. The differences between allophones are always redundant and so need not be represented alphabetically. However, not all categories in complementary distribution can be represented by a single letter. The native speaker of English will balk at using one letter for [h] and [ŋ] because they are too unlike in sound. Using the combined criteria of complementary distribution and articulational similarity, linguists have found that they obtain a set of speech elements for which an alphabet can be designed that will be acceptable to native speakers. The native speaker can learn his letters and spell at once. This means he finds it natural to use one symbol for all the allophones of a phoneme and that he recognizes the allophones as recurrences of one basic form. The feeling of the native speaker for all allophones is typified by the remark of a speaker of Spanish who said, with reference to his allophones, [z] and [s]), "Well, [z] is the way [s] sounds in some words." The ultimate criterion for including allophones within one phoneme is the acceptability to the native speaker of the assignment of a single symbol to these sounds in spelling his language.

The phoneme is a category of linguistic science. Phones belong to one phoneme when they have articulational similarity and are either mutually substitutable in the same contexts or else are in complementary distribution. Using these criteria the linguist is able to identify the particular phonemes of any given language. These individual phonemes are functioning categories for the naive speaker of the language although the phoneme as a concept of linguistic science is unknown to him. We speakers of English operate with /t/, /d/, /p/, and the like. What attributes do we naive speakers use in categorizing the phones we hear? What are the stigmata that mark phones for the /t/ category rather than the /d/, for /d/ rather than /p/? The specification of criterial attributes for particular phonemes is still a program rather than an accomplishment. However, the program is fairly clear. The attributes of individual phonemes are of two kinds, acoustic and functional, and procedures are available for studying the criteriality of both kinds of attribute.

The Acoustic Attributes of Individual Phonemes. The sound spectrogram pictures the distribution of energy among the constituent frequencies of a speech sound at any given time and so makes possible acoustic specification of individual phonemes. To determine the ecological validity of various acoustic attributes for the phonemes of English it would be necessary: 1. to sample adequately the populations of phones in each phoneme, and 2. to examine the spectrograms of these phones for attributes characteristic of each phoneme. To determine the criteriality of the acoustic attributes it would be necessary to sound phones of known acoustic properties for native speakers who would then categorize the phones into phonemes. This program has been well launched by people at the Haskins and Bell Telephone Laboratories. Most of the work so far has concentrated on the first three acoustic formants of single allophones of the English vowels. The full range of variation within a category, all the allophones pronounced by voices that range from adult bass to a child's soprano, remains to be studied. Trying to specify the acoustic attributes of English phonemes with available data would be rather like forming ideas about national character from a single interview with half a dozen foreigners. Even within this restricted range very complicated results have been obtained. Many allophones appear to be probabilistic categories but this picture may change when more acoustic features, beyond the first three formants, are studied. Very likely the phonemes of English will not all be the same kind of category. There may be simple conjunctive cases. There may also be probabilistic and disjunctive categories.

Perhaps the most ambitious program of phonemic fission is that initiated by Jakobson, Fant, and Halle with their publication *Preliminaries to Speech Analysis* (1952). Impressed with the binary computer as an analogue to the human nervous system, these authors have proposed that any phoneme can be uniquely characterized with a set of two-value attributes. An attempt has been made to describe these "distinctive features" in both acoustic and articulational terms. For example, the feature grave-acute has reference acoustically to the predominance of one half of the spectrum over the other. If the higher frequencies dominate, the feature is acute; where the lower frequencies dominate, it is grave. In articulational terms the grave feature is generated by a larger or less comparted mouth cavity, while the acute feature originates in a smaller or more divided cavity. The English phonemes /u/, /o/, and /f/ are grave, and /i/, /e/ and /s/ are acute. The features vocalic-nonvocalic, consonantal-nonconsonantal, compact-diffuse, grave-acute, flat-plain, nasal-oral, tense-lax, continuant-interrupted, and strident-mellow have been used to describe the phonemes of English. Each phoneme appears as a bundle of concurrent features. Many of these features are derived from more traditional articulational and acoustic studies. The idea that they all operate in a binary fashion is an added elegance. As yet this exciting proposal has not been widely enough tested to tell whether it will solve the problem of phoneme specification.

The potential criteriality of acoustic and articulational attributes follows the general rule of relativity. Criteriality must always be determined with respect to a particular category contrast. Using the descriptive terms of traditional phonetics we should describe the [p] of "pin" as an unvoiced bilabial stop since it is produced with a little explosion of breath at the two lips in the absence of voice. If [p] were to be distinguished from the [b] of "bin" the voiced-voiceless dimension would be important since [b] is a voiced bilabial stop. If, on the other hand, [p] were to be distinguished from the [t] of "tin" the position of articulation would be important since [t] is an unvoiced alveolar stop; it is produced at the alveolar ridge just behind the upper teeth rather than by the two lips. In the Jakobson system each phoneme is a unique bundle of a small number of distinctive features and the same features serve to characterize all the phonemes of a language. It follows that any given feature will have potential criteriality for some categorial distinctions and not for others.

The most important finding to come out of the work on phoneme specification is the reliable tendency for the phonemes of every language to fall into symmetrical groups. Thus, Jakobson can place the eight English stop consonants at the eight corners of a cube with each side of the cube labelled with one of the distinctive features. The fricatives of American English form another such cube. Within such a cube a given feature or attribute is criterial for four phonemic contrasts. It is nearly (but not quite) true in phonemics that an attribute which is criterial for one phonemic contrast will be criterial everywhere else in that language, i.e., where two phones could fall into different phoneme categories on the basis of this attribute they will usually do so. Once values of an attribute are distinguished there is evidently a tendency to distinguish them wherever they occur within a system of categories. By analogy we might say that if the radiator grill distinguishes Fords from Chevrolets it is likely that any two cars having different radiator grills will fall into different categories. This characteristic of the attributes of phonemes raises a most interesting problem for the developing speech perception of children. When a child learns to distinguish [p] from [b] (as in "pin" and "bin") does it follow that he will at once notice the distinction between all other consonant pairs that differ from one another in this same attribute? The attribute is traditionally that of voiced-voiceless though in Jakobson's terms it is lax-tense. More generally we should like to know whether speech perception develops by the orderly emergence of the attributes of phonemes (which may be the distinctive features) with each attribute bringing in a cluster of phonemic contrasts.

Functional Attributes of Individual Phonemes. When a subject is asked to identify a set of vowels all of which appear in the same phonetic context (e.g., "hid," "hud," "hod") he has only the stimulus attributes of the vowels to guide him. Ordinarily, however, our recognition of a speech sound is facilitated by the context in which it occurs. If the acoustic attributes do not enable us to choose between several possible vowels, the context may render one of them more probable than the others. Since the speech sound fills a position in a phonetic context, the context may be considered a functional attribute of the sound. The probability of finding one phoneme and no other in a given context describes the ecological validity and potential criteriality of the context for that phoneme. For some contexts in a language there are always some phonemes so improbable that the linguist has called them "impossible." If we treat these combinations as one extreme on a continuum of probabilities of occurrence, it is possible to bring together the descriptive linguist's work on phonemic structure with the information theorist's work on transition probabilities. Both of these have described functional attributes of specific sounds.

No system of speech makes use of all possible phoneme combinations in the manufacture of words and morphemes. No orthography puts its symbols together in all possible ways. There are always combinations that do not occur. Benjamin Whorf (1940) has constructed a formula describing phoneme combinations that are "possible" in the English monosyllabic word. The formula allows for a great variety of English monosyllables but it also clearly rules out many possibilities of which we can conceive. There is, for instance, no provision for syllables beginning with /zr/, /sr/, /vd/, or /ŋ/ because such syllables do not occur in English.

What is the status of the combinations that are not allowed? Whorf rules out any suggestion that the prohibited combinations are humanly unpronounceable with data showing that most of the things English will not allow are practiced in some language or other. In addition, he calls attention to the "unspeakable" combinations that we do manage: "sixths," "glimpsed," and the like. It seems that the formula summarizes cultural practice rather than human necessity.

However, Whorf writes as if there were a kind of necessity in this practice. Of course this necessity would be cultural rather than human. Whorf sees an imperative in the formula. "A new monosyllable turned out, say, by Walter Winchell or by a plugging adman concocting a name for a new breakfast mush, is struck from this mold as surely as if I pulled the lever and the stamp came down on his brain" (p. 82). Whorf allows that Winchell might coin the word "thrub," since it is tolerable by the formula, but that Winchell will not coin a word "srub." There is then a behavioral disposition created by familiarity with the combinational possibility structure of a set of phonemes or letters. We may suppose that there is also a perceptual disposition to hear "possible" morphemes and words.

The linguistic distinction between possible and impossible phoneme combinations can profitably be displaced by a continuum of more or less probable combinations. Whorf, at least, accomplished the "impossible" when he wrote "srub" and now we have done it also. I asked 30 native speakers of American English to invent new one-syllable English words. Most of these inventions were "possible," according to the Whorf formula, but two, "Bz" and "Zl," were not. In the comic strips an "impossible" word is occasionally created. My favorite example appears in Al Capp's *Li'l Abner*. There is, in this strip, a man who brings catastrophe wherever he goes. Capp draws him with a miniature cloud over his head, a cloud that follows him about dripping a perpetual rain. This character is an outcast. People flee at his approach. Capp has aptly named him Joe Btfsplk. "Joe" for the pitiable, human aspect; "Btfsplk" for the unspeakable fate he suffers. When phoneme combinations fall below a certain level of probability they fall under the linguist's ban as "impossible." Such combinations are more accurately described as highly improbable.

Shannon (1949) has introduced the "transition probability" in his book on the mathematical theory of communication. Any sequence of English letters (or phonemes) is followed by a variety of letters (or phonemes) with varying frequencies in English usage. The probability of various transitions can be calculated. In describing transi-

tion probabilities we will take English letters rather than phonemes
as our units. This is for convenience of presentation. What will be
said of letters applies also to phonemes.

Consider the letter "T." Suppose we know all the letters that follow "T" in written English and know also their relative frequencies
of occurrence. We might write each letter on slips of paper, making
the number of slips for a letter proportional to the frequency with
which the letter follows "T." Then if we were to add a second letter
to follow "T" by drawing at random from the slips of paper we should
be likely to draw "H," less likely to draw "R," and most unlikely to
draw "P, B, F, V, Z, M, N," etc. Suppose that "H" is drawn, we might
then use this new letter as context and again draw a letter to follow.
The drawing would, of course, be made from a new collection of slips
representing the relative frequencies with which "H" is followed by
various letters in written English. Proceeding in this way with each
successive letter we should construct a second-order approximation
to English which is a sequence of letters built on the transition probabilities for successive sequences of one letter.

As the amount of antecedent context used increases, one speaks of
third-order, fourth-order, nth-order approximations to English. A
first-order approximation would be constructed by drawing letters and
the printer's "space" according to their relative frequencies in ordinary text. The zero-order approximation is constructed by drawing
at random from the letters and space with no allowance for the relative frequencies of the language.

To make all the tabulations necessary to construct these various
orders is prohibitively laborious. The expedient used relies on the
behavioral disposition created in a person by his acquaintance with
the combinational probability structure of his native language. Several people co-operate to build the sequence a letter at a time. For
a third-order approximation one person would be asked to add a letter
to the first two. The next person would be given only the last two
and would again add a third. Each person, as a speaker of English,
is presumed to choose in accordance with the transition probabilities
of the language.

A variation on the method for determining transition probabilities
is the method by which context probabilities can be determined. A
subject is provided with surrounding context, rather than with antecedent context alone, and he is asked to provide as many letters as
are required to fill the context. Thus in CON-EXT the letter "T"
will have a very high probability of occurrence in English while all
other letters will have a very low probability. Speakers of English

might be expected to reveal their knowledge of the language's combinational probability structure in the responses they would make with this procedure. This same knowledge should affect the perception of speech whenever the audible pattern is somewhat ambiguous.

In an experiment described in the foregoing, native speakers of American English invented "new" English monosyllables. For another experiment we selected the first 15 of these monosyllables that contained exactly 4 phonemes. John Carroll, of the Harvard Graduate School of Education, kindly allowed us to use his table of first-order transition probabilities to calculate the average transition probability for each of these manufactured words. Carroll's table was constructed from a large sample of American English speech. It records the relative frequency with which every English phoneme is followed by every other English phoneme. One of the invented four-phoneme syllables was /guwp/. The average probability of transitions for this syllable was determined by noting first the frequency with which the space or juncture is followed by /g/ in the Carroll table and the frequency with which the transition from /g/ to /u/ occurs, and so on with the transition from /p/ to space completing the column of frequencies. The mean of these frequencies is the average transition probability with a single antecedent for this syllable. The 15 syllables varied widely with regard to this value.

The 15 syllables were then transmitted from one subject to another in a series of 15 successive repetitions. The 15 subjects, seated some distance apart in a line stretching across the room, covered their ears while I spoke the syllable to the first subject. This subject then spoke the syllable to the next man. Each participant uncovered his ears only while listening to the syllable. The final man in the row spoke the syllable to me and I recorded it in phonemic transcription.

Of the 15 syllables two returned to me unaltered. One of these had the highest average probability and the other was fifth highest. The remaining 13 syllables were changed in the course of successive reproduction. In only two cases did the final syllables have a lower average probability than the original syllables. The remaining 11 syllables changed into more probable combinations. The two that became less probable both ended as actual English words /koft/ (coughed) and /krak/ (crock). While these combinations had a lower average transition probability than the syllables from which they evolved (/awzt/ and /kræd/) they have, as total forms, a higher probability of occurrence.

Half of the 15 original syllables had slightly altered from the form in which they had been created. In each of seven syllables we interpolated one transition which is given zero frequency in the Carroll table. These included such improbable combinations as /pm/, /pn/, /zt/, etc. All but one of these was changed in the process of successive reproductions to a more probable combination. Thus the /z/ of /zt/ was displaced by its unvoiced equivalent consonant /s/, which frequently precedes /t/ in English. A syllable beginning with the velar nasal /ŋ/ changed from /ŋm/ to /dɪŋ/, putting that nasal where it belongs in English—the final position.

In general, this little demonstration shows that nonsense words change in successive reproductions, into more probable forms. The conditions for speaking and hearing were probably as good as they are in ordinary speech. Whatever stimulus ambiguity existed here probably exists also in ordinary speech. The auditor quite sensibly makes perceptual judgments in accordance with what he knows of English transition probabilities.

In listening to ordinary speech, knowledge of combinational probabilities must be a great help. When the speech is really English the most probable guess will most probably be correct. The ecological validity of each context attribute for a phoneme is the probability of finding the particular phoneme and no other in that context. The surrounding context /sk-æp/ ("sc-ap") predicts almost perfectly /r/). The context /t-n/ has a lower criteriality for a whole group of vowels since we have the words "ten," "tin," "tan," "ton," "tune," "tone," "teen." The context has some criteriality, however, since no consonant is likely to appear in the vacant position.

Phonetic context must ordinarily be an important factor in the identification of phonemes. Why, then, worry about the acoustic attributes of phonemes in isolation? The acoustic experiment is reminiscent of the visually reduced situations in which depth perception has sometimes been studied. Only when such monocular cues as superposition and relative size have been eliminated can the contribution of binocular disparity be studied. The acoustic experiments could be justified on the ground that their simplifications are essential if the role of acoustic attributes is to be determined. There is at least one very important reason for determining this role. To use contextual attributes in the identification of phonemes one must have learned something about the probabilities of various phonemic sequences. Probabilities cannot be learned until recurrences can be recognized. To learn the frequency with which a sequence occurs the sequence must be identified and distinguished from other sequences. It follows that the acoustic attributes of speech have priority over the contextual. The child must first learn something about the auditory characteristics of speech units.

In ordinary conversation, however, the functional attributes are important and may serve to convert some phonemes from probabilistic to certain categories. If the acoustic attributes admit of several alternative categorizations, the functional attributes are likely to provide a basis for choosing between these interpretations. In the stream of speech the functional and acoustic attributes combine to define phonemes and, in defining phonemes, they define the larger meaningful utterances.

The Attributes of Meaningful Utterances. The meaningful utterance is more easily defined by example than by principle. The word "pail" is meaningful but its constituent phones are not. Words, sentences, and paragraphs are all meaningful as are the linguist's morphemes and phrases. Allophones, phonemes, distinctive features, and phones are not meaningful. There is no semantic common denominator contributed by /p/ to "pull," "pig,' and "up." These few examples will bring us to an understanding about the meaningful utterance that is adequate for present purposes.

Linguistic analysis of meaningful units of speech is not so advanced as the analysis of speech elements. The sentence and paragraph are conventional units in some written languages but are not used in descriptive linguistics. The word has long defied precise definition. Of the units used by the linguist the morpheme is most important and nearest a clear operational definition. The postulates of morphemics are too involved and controversial to be discussed in detail but the main points can be described in a few words.

The morpheme is a unit reminiscent of the word but not to be identified with it any more closely than the phoneme is to be identified with the letter of the alphabet. The morpheme is the minimal semantic unit. The free morpheme can occur alone in the language. Speakers will sometimes pause after a free morpheme before continuing their discourse. The free morpheme is a word not susceptible of analysis into smaller semantic units. The words "dog," "house," and "man" are all free morphemes. However, a plural form like "dogs" is not a single morpheme word as it analyzes into the free form "dog" and the bound form "-s." A bound form like "-s" never occurs in isolation but it has a semantic content—in this case the idea of plurality.

Like phonemes, meaningful utterances have two kinds of attributes. Stimulus attributes include the segmental phonemes, the allophones, and the secondary phonemes—the whole substance of the utterance.

Functional attributes are the phonemic contexts in which an utterance may occur. The potential criterality of such a functional attribute is the probability of utterance occurrence in a given context. These two kinds of attributes are described now.

Stimulus Attributes of Meaningful Utterances. The first principle of systematic morphemics (Nida, 1949) is the statement that forms which possess a common semantic distinctiveness and an identical form in all their occurrences constitute a single morpheme. Identical form means the same phonemes in the same sequence (not necessarily contiguous). For phonemes are the attributes of morphemes and of all meaningful utterances. The individual morpheme, as also the word or phrase, is specified by the conjunction of particular phonemes in a particular sequence. The category can be changed by altering a phoneme or disturbing the sequence.

It is a little difficult to accept the phoneme as an attribute. We have grown accustomed to it in the role of concept. The internal complexity of the phoneme is now so clearly in mind that it is difficult to accord it the simplicity of an attribute. There is, of course, quite as much complexity in such familiar attributes as the color *red,* the form of the *circle,* the tactile experience of *hardness.* To be categorized as "red" a color must fall within critical ranges on the dimensions of hue, brightness, and saturation. Similarly an English consonant must satisfy conditions of energy placement and comparative intensity to be classified as [p]. As attributes of apples and of "apples" redness and [p] lose their internal differentiation. The morpheme, unlike the phoneme, is a category that is analyzed by the native speaker.

There is also a potential criterality in the particular allophone form assumed by a phoneme. Consider the English morphemes "need" and "neat." These two are distinguishable in speech by their distinct final consonants—a phonemic difference. In addition the vowels are different. Both are allophones of /i/ but the /i/ of "need" is more prolonged than that of "neat." The distinction is allophonic and therefore predictable from phonetic context. The long vowel always precedes a voiced consonant and the short vowel a voiceless consonant. It follows that any two words for which vowel length is a potentially criterial attribute are also distinguished by their final consonants. The consonants are predictable from the vowels. However, the converse is not true. There are pairs of words distinguished by the consonants /d/ and /t/ which are not distinguished by vowel length (e.g., "dill-till, drain-train"). We do not know what use is actually made of such allophonic variations in the identification of morphemes.

It seems likely, however, that this feature would be used where the final consonants were not clearly produced and the context gave no cue.

Functional Attributes of Meaningful Utterances. Phonemic equivalence does not guarantee that two utterances will have the same meaning. The English suffix "-er" in "runner," dancer," and "teacher" has not the same meaning as the "-er" of "taller," "older," and "stronger." The former is used to designate the performer of an action; the latter designates a higher degree of some quality. The difference of meaning that is not phonemically signalled is conveyed by functional attributes. The agentive "-er" is affixed to verbs while the comparative "-er" is attached to adjectives. This systematic difference in context keeps the meaning clear. The phonemic sequence "-er," appearing in isolation, is ambiguous.

In English some words are phonemically identical but distinct in meaning. Phonemic equivalence is not, of course, the same as identical spelling. Since stress is not represented in conventional print such pairs as "pérmit" and "permít," "présent" and "presént" look alike. However, they differ in the stress phoneme. The word "board" as in "board of wood" is a true homophone of "bored" as in "bored with psycholinguistics." These two are spelled differently but the difference between "board of wood" and "board of directors" is not marked in writing or in phonemic sequence. The two meanings have been distinguished by placing each word in a highly criterial context. Those are different boards that are likely to occur in the phrases "board of wood," board of directors," and "bored with psycholinguistics." The functional attributes sort out different meanings for phonemically identical words.

Transition probabilities can be computed for meaningful utterances by a method like that used with phonemes. One can treat any fraction of a context as a functional attribute of a morpheme, word, or phrase. The ecological validity of the context corresponds to the probability of finding one particular form in the context. Thus the sentence frame "Now is the time for all good ___ to come to the aid of the party" is so criterial for "men" that the acoustic attributes are really redundant. When utterances have identical stimulus attributes but different meanings, the importance of the functional attributes is especially clear. More usually, however, functional attributes join with stimulus attributes to identify the utterance.

Higher Order Functional Categories: Parts of Speech. If we were to record a very large sample of English speech we should find that there are some morphemes or words that occur in the same context.

In the linguistic frame "The ___ is good" we might find "book," "tree," "house," "speech," and many other words. Appearance in a given linguistic frame provides a basis for categorizing together a collection of words.

C. C. Fries (1952) uses the linguistic frame to define four large functional classes which correspond roughly to the conventional parts of speech: noun, verb, adjective, and adverb. Beginning with a large sample of telephone conversations he finds many words in the frame "(The)—is/was good." All of these are nouns. Fries goes on to define Form Class 1 as "a body of words that belong to the same part of speech by virtue of the fact that they can all fill this particular position" (p. 78). It is not necessary to find a word in this context to identify it as a member of Form Class 1. A native speaker of English can judge of any English word whether it is a possible entry in this test frame. This possibility has nothing to do with semantic suitability but rather with grammatical acceptability. Thus the utterance "The *devil* is good," is perverse in sentiment but quite possible grammatically.

The functional definition of the part of speech is, in some ways, an improvement on the older semantic definitions. According to these the noun, for instance, is the name of a person, place, or thing. Persons and places can be reliably identified but "thing" is clearly a word for whatever is neither person nor place and yet nominalized. It is difficult to find "thing" attributes in "virtue" and "truth" yet both are nouns. On the other hand, as Fries notes, "blue" is the name of a color but not a noun in "a blue tie." Functional rather than semantic attributes seem to provide the ultimate criteria for recognizing English parts of speech. It is even doubtful whether semantic common denominators exist for the parts of speech.

Functional classes sometimes have common stimulus attributes: a characteristic suffix or vowel. In English, however, nouns have no invariable phonemes nor have verbs, adjectives, or adverbs. With regard to acoustic attributes these are elaborately disjunctive categories. Some nouns end with "-al" ("arrival," "refusal," etc.); others with "-ure" ("departure," "failure," etc.); others with "-ance" ("acceptance," "acquaintance," etc. and there are many other common noun suffixes. In addition, there exist countless nouns that exhibit no characteristic suffixes, such as "house," "man," etc.

Both Harris (1951) and Fries (1952) think of word classes in terms of what can and cannot happen in the word combinations of a language. This is again a possibility-impossibility dichotomy, like that found in Whorf's formula of English phoneme combinations.

It may again be desirable to substitute a probability continuum for the linguist's dichotomy. The English speaker's judgment that "very" cannot possibly fill the gap in "The ___ is good" may derive from the very low frequency of such an occurrence. Members of a part of speech may be words that attain to a certain minimal probability of occurrence in a given language frame. I think, however, that something a little different is involved in these judgments of grammatical possibility or impossibility that define the parts of speech. The recognition that "The *devil* is good" constitutes a possible English utterance probably does not depend on actual experience of this utterance. The judgment would surely be made even if the word "devil" had never been heard in that frame. "Devil" will have been heard in such other frames as "The ___ is bad," or "The ___ visited them." In these frames such words as "man," "woman," "dog," "mayor," etc. have also appeared. The general functional equivalence of "devil," "man," "woman," "dog," and "mayor" would lead one to extend this equivalence to the frame "The ___ is good." If "man," "woman," "dog," and "mayor" have actually been heard in this frame then it will be consistent to believe that "devil" is able to occupy the same position. I might write "The *very* is good" 100 times and still it would not seem acceptable in the sense that "The *devil* is good" is acceptable. That is surely because "very" is organized into one functional class and "devil" into another on the basis of my total experience of the language rather than from a direct counting of occurrences in a particular sentence. The frame sentence is a useful test for part of speech membership but the judgment of possibility or impossibility on which the test depends is not founded simply on experience of the test sentence but on functional categories abstracted from total experience with the combinational probabilities of language.

The traditional parts of speech are not the only higher order functional categories. Utilizing the notion of contextual probabilities, it would be possible to categorize words or morphemes in infinitely various ways. One could put together all the words satisfying a particular level of probability for any set of contexts. In most cases these classes would have no semantic value for the native speaker. In other cases one might find that he had functionally isolated the names of living creatures or perhaps the class of proper nouns or the class of verbs of action or verbs of being. I should expect all such semantic categories to be susceptible of functional definition by the method of contextual probabilities. Indeed, I think functional categories are suggested to us by semantic categories. Proper nouns are names of identity categories. Living creatures have certain attributes separating them from nonliving objects. Even the parts of speech may have begun as semantic classes now grown fuzzy and inconsistent through historical change to the point where semantic attributes are only probabilistic in their association with the functional classes. All of this reminds us that language is more than a formal system. It is a system co-ordinated with the nonlinguistic world. The nature of these co-ordinations is our next concern.

THE RELATIONS BETWEEN LINGUISTIC AND NONLINGUISTIC CATEGORIES

Utterances are meaningful when they are co-ordinated with nonlinguistic or referential categories. We discuss first the classical suggestion that the meaning is an image of the referent, an image evoked by the utterance. We shall find that this proposal does not meet the requirements of a theory of linguistic meaning and we will desert image evocation in favor of the act of discriminatory naming of entities. This act is essentially the same as the operation accepted throughout this book as evidence that an individual has a category. A verbal discriminating response has important properties not found in other discriminating responses with which we shall be concerned later (cf. section on The Original Word Game, pages 284–295.

An experiment on verbal conditioning will introduce semantics into our discussion of language. In a study by Razran (1939) printed words were shown to subjects while they were eating. The words, of course, came to be conditioned stimuli eliciting the salivation response. Whenever a conditioned response is established the effects of the training generalize so that the response tends to be elicited by new stimuli to the degree that these resemble the original conditioned stimulus. In the present case new words were shown to the subjects; new words related to the original set as homophones, antonyms, or synonyms. One of the original conditioned words was "style." Among the new words were both "stile" and "fashion." In printed form "stile" closely resembles the original and in spoken form the two sound just alike. "Fashion," on the other hand, is quite unlike "style" in both appearance and sound. However, Razran found that the response was more likely to generalize from "style" to "fashion" than from "style" to "stile." If we are to continue to believe that generalization is determined by the degree of similarity between two stimuli we must assume that "style" and "fashion" are alike in some way that does not directly meet the eye or ear. Razran had used adult subjects. In a related study Riess (1946) showed that, with young children as subjects, the generalization to the homophone was greater than generalization to the synonym. The concealed, non-sensory similarity of "style" and "fashion" is learned and only overcomes the more direct similarity of sound after some experience with the language. For the adult, "style" and "fashion" resemble one another in meaning.

The experiments on linguistic conditioning suggest that when an utterance becomes meaningful it causes us to take account of something beyond itself. It has always seemed to be the central problem of a psychology of language to determine the nature of linguistic reference. Because utterances often acquire meaning through association with some referent object or event it has been easy to believe that a meaning is an image of such a referent. When the word "style" does not suggest "fashion" to a child it is merely because he has not learned that these words have similar meanings and so simply treats them as unlike sounds. For the adult these words have become transparent. Perhaps we may say that the adult sees through the words to their common referent image. For the child the words are still opaque.

The Generic Mental Image. The philosophers and psychologists who conceived linguistic meaning to be an image of a referent object used to worry a great deal about the kind of image that could give meaning to an abstract term, a class name. A proper noun, the name of a particular object, could be supposed to create a faint image of that object. But what image could one have of "triangle," "man," or "virtue"?

Suppose that the name "Ralph Jones" appears, as it usually would, in a verbal context that clearly determines its referent to be a particular man. Can we construct the imaginal idea that will be the meaning of this word? How shall Mr. Jones be clothed in this image? Which of the many hats and suits he has worn will he wear in the image that his name evokes? Will it be more suitable for the essential Mr. Jones to appear unclothed? Still this is the one mode in which he is not generally seen and association cannot account for the evocation of this image. If we have known Mr. Jones for some years his appearance may have changed greatly, his cellular substance has changed altogether, there is only a kind of structural-functional continuity. Clearly the name "Ralph Jones," though identified with a particular man, names a category of sensible appearances, an identity category. Our visual experience of the man is a vast collection of snapshots and we naturally wonder which of these is to represent him in the mind's eye when we hear his name. The fact is that concrete proper nouns involve the same difficulties for an imagery theory of meaning as do the class names ordinarily considered to be abstract. An utterance naming a completely specified referent would have to run on and on in this fashion: Ralph Jones on Christmas day at 9 in the morning seen in right profile under artificial light by eyes naturally 18/20 corrected to 20/20, etc., etc.

The difficulty that bedevils the imaginal meaning psychologist is that Ralph Jones the man can change many of his attributes without affecting the propriety of the designation "Ralph Jones." He is equally himself whether shaved or unshaved, bathed or unbathed. It would seem, however, that any visual representation of him must be either the one or the other. Since these are noisy attributes of the identity category "Ralph Jones," we do not know what value to give them in the generic representation. Other attributes if changed will alter the propriety of the designation "Ralph Jones." A certain relation of facial features, a narrow range of heights, weights, and skin colors, are attributes essential to Ralph Jones. Clearly these must appear in his essential image. But with which noisy attributes are they to be combined?

John Locke (1690) dealt with this problem in connection with the abstract term "triangle." The idea of triangle he thought must be "neither equilateral, equicrural, nor scalenon but all and none of these at once" (p. 509). The abstract idea might be a kind of average of the attributes associated with the individuals included within a genus. We can imagine this representation to be constructed like one of Galton's composite portraits. Galton obtained a generic photograph of epileptics using a single sensitive plate. Each subject sat at the same distance from the camera with his full face turned toward it. The same region of the plate was exposed for the same very brief time to each successive face. Lines and features common to all or many subjects grew dark with repetition while occasional attributes were scarcely noticed. The result was a composite portrait of many individuals. We can, on the other hand, imagine the generic idea to assume the modal attributes of the members of a class. If Ralph Jones has usually worn his brown suit he will so appear in his imaginal representation. If equilateral triangles are more common than any other variety then this will be the form of *the* triangle. It is possible, also, that certain attributes are salient for the class though not necessarily most frequent. The statue of Lincoln that appears in the Lincoln Memorial may, for mysterious reasons, be the most Lincolnesque posture we know though perhaps less frequent than some other representations.

Bishop Berkeley (1710) in his attack on abstract ideas thought of some very difficult cases. "The constituent parts of the abstract idea of animal are body, life, sense, and spontaneous motion. By body is meant body without any particular shape or figure, there being no one shape or figure common to all animals, without covering either of hair or feathers or scales, etc. nor yet naked; hair, feathers, scales and nakedness being the distinguishing properties of particular animals and for that reason left out of the abstract idea. Upon the same account the spontaneous motion must be neither walking, nor flying, nor creeping, it is nevertheless a motion, but what that motion is, it is not easy to conceive" (pp. 9, 10). A composite portrait of motion or animal—the mind reels. And what of virtue, justice, charity? They will not sit for their portraits. Berkeley again, "I readily agree with this learned author (Locke), that the faculties of brutes can by no means attain to abstraction. But then if this be made the distinguishing property of that sort of animals, I fear a great many of those that pass for men must be reckoned into their number" (p. 14).

Berkeley's substitute proposal is that ideas are always of some particular thing. When the word is generic the particular idea is supplemented with the knowledge that its accidental attributes are necessary and that it stands for all particular ideas of the same sort. Thus when something is predicated of triangles a particular triangle is pictured but it is understood that the predication applies to all triangles. Among the subjects of Francis Galton (1907) was a young lady who dealt in such specific images. Galton said to her, "I want to tell you about a boat," and stopping there, he asked for her images in connection with his remark. These came in a bubbling freshet. She had seen "a rather large boat, pushing off from shore, full of ladies and gentlemen, the ladies dressed in blue and white" (p. 51). Galton's philosopher friends were not so naive. Their images refused to be committed to whether the boat was a skiff, a wherry, a barge, launch, or punt. Their generic boat probably would not float but it was logically sound.

In thinking about abstract images I have been discouraged by a personal introspective blank. And yet I can recall such representations not as images but as percepts. In children's alphabet books "A" is for the essential, not the particular, apple. In dictionaries the illustrations of aardvark and zebra are of generic animals. In the illustrations of the dictionary we can see how it is possible to direct attention to essential attributes and to convey the information that certain attributes of the particular representation are accidental for the category. Looking at these pictures I find that I ignore the size, color, and texture values as well as the facial expressions of the animals. They are all alike with regard to these attributes. The gnat is as large as the gnu, as smooth, and as stolid. The illustrator means not to commit his representations with regard to these attributes. Those dimensions on which all his animals manifest the same values are thereby signalled to be not significant dimensions in this case. Consider, for example, the problem of representing the eyes of a generic animal. Should they be open or closed? In life the two conditions alternate with both a brief and prolonged periodicity. A composite portrait will be heavy-lidded but awake. If they are open in all the animals one pictures (as in the dictionary) then it will be understood that the attribute is of no use for distinguishing between them and may be overlooked. The wide-open eye of the picture now does not mean that this animal is commonly in that state but rather that this feature of his facial expression is not useful for identifying his generic membership. Other features of the animals pictured in the dictionary are significant; the number of legs, arms, and wings; the difference between hair, scales, and feathers; the total bodily contour. To these we attend. We expect these represented features to correspond to the actual features of the animals portrayed. Equating attributes in an array of images is probably not the only way of causing us to disregard their values. A feature sketched with conspicuous carelessness or perhaps only schematically described will also be understood to be insignificant. In any case Bishop Berkeley with a little help from the dictionary enables us to conceive of the abstract visual image. By one means or another attention is directed to the essential attributes of a particular image and withheld from those that are accidental.

There are two principal difficulties with an imaginal theory of linguistic meaning. The first of these is the total inability of many men, among them Binet, Watt, Bühler, and Woodworth, to find images for words they clearly understood. The second difficulty is that even those who report images as the meanings of all meaningful utterances often do not report images that properly represent the categories named in the utterance.

As all psychologists know, E. B. Titchener's (1909) consciousness was a flood of brightly colored, often audible, and sometimes scented imagery. No word, however abstract, failed to evoke an image. "Meaning," for instance, was "the blue-grey tip of a kind of scoop which has a bit of yellow about it (probably a part of the handle) and which is just digging into a dark mass of what appears to be plastic material" (p. 19). He suspected the origin of this image to be the numerous injunctions delivered to him in his youth to "dig out the meaning" of Latin or Greek phrases. There are many other delightful pictures from Titchener. Thus, "The stately heroine gives me a flash of a tall figure, the only clear part of which is a hand holding up a steely grey skirt" (p. 13). And, "Horse is to me a double curve and a rampant posture with a touch of mane about it; cow is a longish rectangle with a certain facial expression, a sort of exaggerated pout" (p. 18).

Titchener is one of the few men who has ever claimed to have an image of Locke's abstract triangle. The master imager describes it as "a flashy thing, come and gone from moment to moment: it hints 2 or 3 red angles, with the red lines deepening into black, seen on a dark green ground. It is not there long enough for me to say whether the angles join to form the complete figure or even whether all 3 of the necessary angles are given" (pp. 17, 18). But now we notice a startling thing about this image. It is not the particular image with essential attributes selected for attention that Bishop Berkeley had led us to expect, nor is it the generic image Locke proposed. The essential attributes of the triangle concept are not clearly represented. Titchener is uncertain whether the angles join and even whether there are three angles. This is no composite portrait of the population of triangles. It is a very personal Titchenerian triangle. Notice some of his other images: the horse that is a rampant posture, the cow that is a pouting rectangle. Titchener's is an existential psychology. He reports what he sees with his mind's eye, not what the word logically means. But have these images the properties we require of linguistic meanings?

Linguistic symbols are generally thought to acquire meaning by constant association with their referents. The mental reference aroused by the symbol should concentrate on the essential attributes of these referents, the attributes which experience has shown to be invariably present. The images reported by Titchener, and most of those reported in his laboratory, are not such clear distillations of experience. In some cases the image derives from a single accidental experience. Titchener's image of "but" was of the back of the head of a speaker who often used this word while Titchener sat behind him on a platform. In other cases it is a kind of physiognomic impression —the pout of the cow—having no relation to the functional importance of the referent and never mentioned in any definition of it. In fact, the images reported are connected with the eliciting words by what appears to be a capricious variety of associations. The image may assume any form whatsoever. Why are such images unacceptable as the meanings of words?

The meaning-image must be representative of the class of referents to which a word is applied in order to fill the function for which it is required. One of the things that may be confidently expected of the man who understands the word "triangle" is that he will be able to identify correctly actual triangles and will not confuse them with circles or squares. We can understand this process by analogy with a process of perceptual matching. If I am to meet at the railroad station someone whom I have never seen it will be useful to carry with me a picture of that person. I can recognize him by comparing the pictured face with the faces of the people leaving the train and will eventually find that correspondence of essential attributes that identifies my quarry. We can conceive that a man is able to name triangles in analogous fashion, by comparing the temporary image in his peripheral eye with the generic image in his mind's eye. If there is correspondence in essential points the percept will be labelled with the name of the type. What becomes of this explanation if the image is not an essential picture but is some sort of vagrant associate? With his image of the triangle Titchener must be expected never to apply the word to any percept for he will find none to agree with that mobile, flashing, and nontriangular triangle.

The accidental image is in every way inadequate to explain naming behavior. It is unlikely, for instance, that any of us will say that we "see" Titchener's image of the triangle and yet we will call the same entities by this name as he would have done. Accidental images are different from one individual to another and yet these individuals may agree perfectly in their denoting behavior. Students in Titchener's seminars agreed with him in finding imagery to be the contents of consciousness but they did not agree on the specific images. Where Titchener saw a colored scoop for "meaning" one student saw a great scroll unrolling and another saw a tangled skein being straightened out. These diverse images suggest no agreement at all on the meanings of words. Language is a cultural possession, shared by members of a society. The variable accidental image will never explain how we are able to agree in labelling the objects about us nor can it explain how we are able to communicate with one another.

For a large number of meaningful utterances the ultimate criterion of understanding is the ability to use the utterance to name entities of the category identified. Reports of imagery do not reliably predict this ability and so we abjure imaginal meaning and rely entirely on naming behavior as evidence of linguistic understanding. The act of naming certainly is not the only kind of evidence of linguistic understanding. It is my belief that when someone learns to understand an utterance his nervous system is partially "rewired" (in the sense of changes in synaptic resistance or neurone process growth) so that he is disposed to behave appropriately with regard to that utterance. The particular responses that are appropriate change with contingent circumstances. No single kind of response can be identified with language meaning but naming behavior is a salient element in the total population of responses to which one who understands is disposed. The present treatment of meaning is limited to this behavior because it is essentially the same as the behavior studied in all the experiments reported in this book.

There are two important things to say about naming behavior. For one who has already acquired a category the meaningful utterance of another can provide evidence that the speaker possesses the same category. For one who has not yet acquired a given category the meaningful utterance of another can function as an attribute of the category to be acquired. In the sections that follow, these two principles are expanded and then their interaction in first-language learning is described.

Speech as Evidence That the Speaker Has a Nonlinguistic Category. The concept has been defined in this book as "a way of grouping an array of objects or events in terms of those characteristics that distinguish this array from other objects or events in the universe." On the denotational level the evidence for "grouping an array of objects or events" is some kind of response elicited by the array and not elicited by entities outside the array. The dog gives evidence of knowing the difference between buzzers and bells by salivating to the one and not to the other. The rat shows that he can distinguish circles from triangles by jumping to the one in preference to the other. The human subject satisfies Bruner, Goodnow, and Austin that he has grasped their concept when he selects positive instances and avoids negative instances. A human subject can also give evidence that he has attained a concept by correctly patterning his naming behavior.

Grouping entities is not sufficient evidence that a subject has a concept. The dog may have been trained to salivate to particular buzzers, the rat to jump to particular triangles, the man to name only the Ford cars on his block. The authors of this book therefore add that a concept is considered to have been attained when a subject is able to "identify new instances of it without further training." Similarly a word cannot be said to be fully understood until it can be correctly extended to entities that one has not heard labelled.

It sometimes happens that we use the same words but do not have the same concepts. Consider the phrase "a great poem." A particular teacher of literature may have a subtle understanding of the meaning of this phrase. To convey this concept to his students he uses the denotational method. The teacher sets before his pupils a series of instances of the concept: the works of Shakespeare, Milton, Donne, etc. The pupils learn to refer to all of these as "great poems." They probably are not asked to identify new instances of the concept. When I. A. Richards (1929) asked Cambridge undergraduates to interpret and evaluate unfamiliar and untitled poems he tested their understanding of great poetry. They disagreed with him and with one another. Visual exposure to a set of poems cannot guarantee the abstraction of their qualities of greatness. One student might notice that most examples are in blank verse or that all involve some use of metaphor. Another student might recognize merit by the visceral disturbance it sets up, another would find nothing common to the lot but a suffocating dullness. Discovery of the common red quale in many long wave lengths seems to be fairly well guaranteed by a healthy visual apparatus but the defining attributes of great poetry do not arise from the visual system alone. They depend for their emergence on the experience, cultural membership, and intelligence of the individual. It is not surprising that individuals abstract quite different concepts from the same reading. Evidently this is very commonly the case in aesthetic matters. The general disagreement over contemporary art testifies to that. Many are discouraged by such elusive concepts and prefer to withhold judgment until an authoritative list of the great poems of the 20th century is published. "Time" magazine is very helpful about such things. Only a few years ago it referred to Artur Rubinstein as one of the four great pianists of the century and then in a footnote listed the other three in rank order. While we may not be able to agree on new instances in these areas we can all memorize a list.

How do we identify discriminating responses in the behavior of the Other One whose concepts are to be discovered? To begin with, the observer makes a judgment of equivalence; the "same" response is said to be generalized to a class of stimuli. We do not often think of the rat's successful jumps or lever pressings as a category and yet it is perfectly clear that no two jumps are identical. These categories are used in a molar psychology that takes the "act" for its response unit. Consequently the categories are not defined by the particular muscles activated but by a kind of functional equivalence determined by the character of the apparatus. All jumps sending the animal hurtling through the correct door, all pressures producing a pellet, these are the categories. The formal boundaries of the categories can be changed by altering the apparatus. Moving the jumping stand nearer the screen will reduce the force of the jumps; increasing the sensitivity of the lever will lower the resistance to be overcome by the animal's push. The ultimate functional significance of these responses is their ability to produce a food reward.

Where the subject is human and the responses are verbal it is again clear that the experimenter makes a judgment of response equivalence —an array of entities is called by the "same" name. The bounds of verbal categories are set by human beings. They are not built into the apparatus but are a cultural acquisition. Not all men everywhere will agree as to which utterances are the "same." The varying utterances categorized as one word have a kind of functional equivalence in that they will produce the same social effect. This effect in adults is very seldom the reduction of primary drives. Once we have gotten over crying to be fed, speech generally operates above the subsistence level. It is interesting to note, however, that when vocalization has a primary instrumentality this instrumentality is socially mediated. The child's cry of hunger is effective only because he is imbedded in a community concerned to interpret his utterances and to satisfy the needs they express. Speech responses are categorized in terms of the stimulus and functional attributes used in the linguistic community. These responses can give evidence that the speaker possesses a nonlinguistic category. The categorial response must appear in correlation with entities of a particular class and must be extended to new entities of that class.

Speech as an Attribute of a Category to Be Acquired. Treating speech as a selective response, we said that the experimenter will consider the Other One to have attained the concept when he is able to match the experimenter's identification of new instances. By this rule, however, we should never attribute to another a concept we ourselves do not possess, but in fact, of course, we often do. Leaving the role of behavior scientists and assuming that of standard adults, we look to see what circumstances will lead us to credit another with a concept we have not grasped.

We may look for a concept to explain any response that captures our attention and appears to have been deliberately produced. The presumption of a concept will be especially strong if the Other One manifests any communicative intent. Thus a stranger who stands in front of us and makes a motion with his hands is presumed to "mean something" thereby. The most likely response to take our attention and to suggest communication is vocalization. When this vocalization is recognizably a phoneme sequence from some foreign language or an unfamiliar sequence which could be English, the presumption of a concept approaches certainty. If a biology professor in his first lecture uses the word "coelenterate" he establishes an empty category to be filled in later. This is not the sense of empty category used earlier in the book: a category with known attributes but no known instances. We have here an empty category in the sense that nothing is signalled by the unfamiliar word except the existence of a category. The professor's "new word" functions as a lure to cognition. It attracts thought in a way that his other actions—wagging his head while he talks, stumbling against the platform—do not. It is not necessarily an invidious thing to say of a new study that "it is just a lot of new words." Chemistry, sociology, and psychology all have their own vocabularies. The words are handed out early in the term like empty containers to be filled with experience. The pejorative sense of the students' complaint is clear in a full translation, "This course is just a lot of new sounds for familiar concepts." It is a stupid nuisance to learn new names for old meanings. The value of a neologism is that it signals a new concept to be formed. This signal has so often proved misleading that some authors do not signal their new concepts with neologisms, preferring to alter the sense of familiar words. Perhaps it is a less frankly ambitious undertaking, a more modest rhetoric.

We take a new word as a lure for cognition because in a long experience of language we have learned that such utterances are attributes of nonlinguistic categories and that these categories are ordinarily worth learning. Of course, an utterance is a category in its own right, a category defined by functional and stimulus attributes within the speech system. But the semantic utterance is also a selective response elicited by some array of nonlinguistic stimuli. For a person who does not yet categorize this array the utterance he hears from another can function as an attribute of the nonlinguistic category. Ford cars produced in 1954 constitute an array of objects having certain visible attributes: a characteristic length, fender line, and distribution of chrome plate. Another attribute of this array is its ability to elicit the name "1954 Ford." This name is likely to be heard or seen when members of the category are in one's visual field.

The semantic utterance is a socially contingent attribute. It will not be heard unless someone is about who is disposed to name automobiles. In respect of this contingency the utterance is like many nonlinguistic attributes which are also contingent on particular circumstances. The characteristic front grill of the Ford is an attribute that cannot be used in categorizing automobiles unless one takes up a position from which the grill can be seen. If we face an array of automobiles at the Automobile Show their contrasting grills can be compared. If we are in the presence of an automobile-namer, contrasting names can also be compared. The utterance differs from nonlinguistic attributes in that it is not spatially localized with the car but emanates, instead, from a person. It is a functional attribute of the Ford to elicit a particular utterance from properly disposed and informed persons.

Since we are accustomed to thinking of color, size, and shape as attributes, it seems a little strange to call the name of a category an attribute. There is reason to believe that the name attribute has not always seemed so unlike the other attributes of a category. Vigotsky (1939) writes: "When children are asked whether it is possible to replace the name of one object with that of another, for instance to call a cow ink, and ink a cow, they answer that it is entirely impossible, because ink is used for writing and the cow gives milk. The exchange of a name means for them also the exchange of the qualities of the objects, so close and inseparable is the connection between the two" (p. 36).

The semantic utterance is only one variety of socially functional attribute. All sorts of discriminating responses are such attributes for the person who does not yet possess a concept but is concerned with learning it from the behavior of others and from the environment in which they behave. The biology professor will group his coelenterate specimens in one exhibition case. He will discuss the anatomies of the various coelenterates in the same week. Our kin are distinguished by more than kinship terminology. Categories are marked out by the price of Christmas gifts, the occasions for kissing, the likelihood of asking for a loan. And so with all categories. They may be marked out by winking, salivating, embracing, and—in all cases—by speech. Speech differs from these other selective responses in that it is a system constructed from a small set of recurrent elements, the phonemes. It differs also in its breadth of coverage. There is a distinctive utterance for practically every concept we possess and whenever there is not yet such an utterance the man who discovers the lack considers it his first civilizing duty to create one.

Because speech is a system providing attributes for the entire conceptual repertoire of a culture it would be possible to use the attributes of the utterances to represent the relations between concepts. Consider the categories of color vision. There are, as we know, millions of just noticeable differences obtainable from the color solid; $7\frac{1}{2}$ million is estimated in the Optical Society of America's book, *Science of Color* (1953). In American English, there are only about eight commonly used color names. Evidently we categorize colors. Suppose that a native speaker of English is presented with a large assortment of colors—the Holmgren yarns or the Munsell collection—and he is asked to group them according to hue, making piles of those that belong together and ranging the piles in order of similarity to one another. He would probably make a small number of piles, six or eight, and arrange these with the longer wave lengths at one end and the shorter at the other, possibly making a circle to suggest that the shortest wave lengths begin to resemble the longest.

Suppose this subject were next asked to give the common names for the various points in the color solid. We should find many of these called "red." The various pronunciations of "red" would vary but no phonemic boundaries would be crossed. Moving along the hue dimension in the solid we should eventually receive a "new" response, "orange." This is clearly a new morpheme varying in many phonemes at once. Taking another direction in the solid we should arrive at "pink," likewise a new morpheme. As each conceptual boundary is crossed there will be a phonemic change in speech. Within the concept only free variation in noncriterial attributes will occur in the subject's speech. The groupings of the nonlinguistic sorting are preserved in this labelling behavior but the distance between categories is not preserved. This could be accomplished by making the phonemic change proportional to the distance between the color groupings. For example, as we move from the longest wave lengths to those somewhat shorter, we ought not to squander phonemes on a great splurge of a word like "orange." Since this category is immediately adjacent to "red," let us give it a name in which only the vowel is changed, and that change to the vowel nearest on the vowel chart. Orange ought properly to be called [ræd]. We could then move through the vowel chart as we move through the groups of colors, keeping the phonemic change proportional to the cognitive remoteness of the categories. There would be time enough to change more than one phoneme when we moved into a new sense modality.

With very few exceptions the phonemic attributes of speech are not isomorphic with intercategorial relations. Jespersen (1922) reports a case in which two children invented a language that made limited use of this higher degree of isomorphism. They used the form "bal" for place and lengthened the vowel proportionally to the size of the place. So the vowel would lengthen as they moved from village to town to city. The Guarani Indians express the past tense with the suffix "-yma" pronounced more slowly as the temporal remoteness of the event increases. In English we have the word "brunch" phonemically between breakfast and lunch as the meal is temporally. These are rare exceptions. Speech, in general, does not use its phonemic attributes in this way. The phoneme ordinarily serves only to identify equivalent and nonequivalent stimuli.

Relations between categories are expressed by many different techniques. Consider, for instance, the sensory proximity and remoteness of hue categories. The sensory order could easily be reproduced in the word order "red, orange, yellow, green, blue, and violet." The chronological sequence of breakfast, lunch, and dinner is reproduced in this sentence. Word order is conventionally used in English to convey subject-object relations as in the familiar contrast: "Dog bites man" versus "Man bites dog." Word orders are easily revised to express a variety of relations. Perhaps the most common means of indicating intercategorial relations is the use of a free or bound morpheme naming the relation. The preposition "in" describes spatial containment in the phrase "the soup in the bowl." The affixed "-s" expresses possession in "dad's car." The stimulus attributes of a name do not present a category in any particular relation but leave it free to be presented in infinitely varied relations through the flexible combinational resources of the language.

It is necessary to remember that the semantic utterance, as a linguistic category, has functional as well as stimulus attributes. The sequence of phonemes comprising the word "stand" would be used by a speaker of English to label objects and events belonging to quite different categories. Music stands, vegetable stands, and a child who stands are functionally equivalent in their ability to elicit this word. Yet these are distinct nonlinguistic categories. Learning to recognize one array does not teach us either of the other arrays. The categories are not really equivalent in the names they are disposed to evoke. When "stand" is used to label one kind of stand, it functions as a noun in contexts concerned with music; for another kind of stand the word is a noun in contexts concerned with the sale of vegetables; and in a final case "stand' functions as a verb. If the three arrays were put in direct contrast and a subject asked to provide names he would probably use expanded names. These can be created by annexing a particularly characteristic bit of context as in "music stands," "vegetable stands," and "standing up." Distinctive phonemic sequences are likely to be used when a need exists to demonstrate the functional nonequivalence of these categories.

In the infant cries that are the precursors of speech there is a kind of innate isomorphism with the nonlinguistic circumstances that arouse the cries. This isomorphism makes the cries especially useful functional attributes. Something of their continuous isomorphism survives in intonation and, more particularly, in exclamations and in song. Sherman (1927) asked graduate students, medical students, and nurses to try to identify the causes of crying in children (three to seven days old) who were concealed behind a screen. It is well known that the adults were unable to judge correctly and this result has been taken as evidence of the random character of early vocalization. It is not as well known that Sherman equated the cries in intensity and duration. He did this because, in preliminary trials, these dimensions of the crying gave away the nature of the difficulty. The duration of the cry was proportional to the duration of the trouble causing the cry. Furthermore an abrupt stimulus gradient such as that caused by a pin prick resulted in an abrupt response gradient. A slower gradient such as that attending hunger resulted in a gradually intensifying cry. The loudness of the cry was generally proportional to the intensity of the discomfort. The rhythmicity of hunger and colic pains was preserved in a crying rhythm. In all these respects the cries of the child were isomorphic with his internal states. We do not ordinarily think of intensity and duration as semantic dimensions. However, the musical aspects of adult speech are often meaningful, not in the sense of presenting concepts but in the sense of expressing the speaker.

The earliest written symbols were representational. Such a symbol manifests some of the criterial attributes of the category of objects or events to which it refers. While a stick figure has not the color, size, or tridimensionality of a human being, there may be a rough equivalence of relations between the lines of the figure and the trunk and limbs of a man. Sketches of the moon and sun lack the luminosity of their originals but preserve the contours. Speech forms, also, are sometimes representational with the sound of the movements of articulation exemplifying attributes of the category signified. The onomatopoeic word is like the sound it names and the vocal gesture imitates movement that is not articulational.

When a name or a written symbol is representational it is possible to translate the name or symbol when one has not been given the specific rule of this translation. This is not to say that representational names or symbols can be translated quite without benefit of past experience. It is necessary, first of all, to possess the category that is the referent of the name. Perhaps this is sometimes the only prerequisite to a correct translation. It seems likely, however, that even line drawings of a buffalo or of the half moon will not be recognized unless one has learned that all such drawings preserve the contours of their referents while neglecting other, usually criterial, attributes. With this general rule, however, it would be possible to translate many representational symbols without specific prompting on each symbol. To discern the onomatopoeia in "cock-a-doodle-doo" and such foreign equivalents as *kikeriki* and *coquelico* it is necessary to realize that the call of the rooster does not contain these specific vowels and consonants but that it does fall into multiple acoustic divisions as do these polysyllabic words and that each division begins abruptly as do the plosive consonants of the words.

The ability to translate, with better than chance precision and without training on specific word-referent linkages, is to be found with some words that are neither onomatopoeic nor imitative of movement. The basis of such phonetic symbolism is difficult to determine. Sapir (1929) and Newman (1933) created nonsense syllables of the consonant-vowel-consonant variety and varied the vowels while keeping the consonantal environments the same (e.g., Mal-Mil). These syllables were put together in all possible pairs and subjects asked to say which of the two suggested the larger object, the brighter object, etc. They found that different syllables carried quite different implications (e.g., Mal seemed to most subjects to suggest something larger than Mil). Brown, Black, and Horowitz (1955) had English-speaking persons listen to antonymic pairs in such unfamiliar and unrelated languages as Chinese, Czech, and Hindi. They provided their subjects with the comparable English pair in each case and asked them to match the foreign word with its translation. Subjects agreed very closely among themselves; 91%, for example, matched *ch'ing* with "light" and *ch'ung* with "heavy." They evidently shared some conception of the likelihood of various meanings being attached to a given sequence of sounds. Phonetic symbolism, the usual name for this phenomenon, is inappropriate in so far as it implies that a definite meaning is suggested by unfamiliar speech. It is only rarely possible to make an absolute and unprompted translation of a morpheme from an unfamiliar language. Such sounds are not certainly linked in our minds with any concepts but we can judge the likelihood that a sound symbolizes something large rather than small, something dark rather than light, blunt rather than sharp. Members of a speech community agree very well on these semantic probabilities. This may be because their acquaintance with a common language has familiarized them with the sound-meaning correlations of that language. The fact that subjects in the study of Brown, Black, and Horowitz made *correct* translations with better than chance success suggests tantalizing alternative explanations. There may be in nature correlations between sounds and other sense data which impress themselves on men everywhere. Perhaps, for example, large waterfalls produce deeper sounds than small waterfalls. On the other hand, there may be attributes that have a natural intersensory application for all men—there is a volume of sound as of space. If either of the latter possibilities is correct subjects from unrelated-to-English speech communities should agree fairly closely with English subjects on the semantic probabilities of foreign words. If these probabilities are entirely a cultural matter we would expect little agreement. To decide between these interpretations the Brown, Black, and Horowitz study is being repeated with Chinese and Navaho monolinguals.

In summary, then, a name is itself a category—a category of sounds. It is furthermore an attribute of a nonlinguistic category since instances of the nonlinguistic category have the property of evoking the name. The name is never the only kind of distinctive response evoked by a category but names are peculiar among such responses in that they have a common structure. All the names of a given language are compounded of the same small number of phoneme attributes and there is a response of this type, a name, for practically every concept a man possesses. In general, names do not present concepts in any kind of fixed relationship; they simply indicate equivalence and nonequivalence. In some cases more than this is signalled. The meaning of a name can sometimes be guessed because it duplicates attributes of the referent category or because of systematic, though arbitrary, relationships in a language between the attributes of names and the attributes of referents.

The Original Word Game. In the Original Word Game one learns to speak a language. There must always be someone who knows the language (the tutor) and someone who is learning (the player). The movements of the game are, in outline form, as follows. The tutor speaks the language in accordance with the semantic and grammatical custom in his community. The player observes the performance of the tutor and learns to recognize equivalent utterances. The player forms hypotheses about the nonlinguistic categories eliciting particular utterances. In forming the categories of speech and the nonlinguistic categories that govern speech the player is seldom able to control the selection of instances. These are presented to him, sometimes in a random manner, sometimes in a systematic order determined by parent, teacher, or informant. The player is, therefore, concerned with reception strategies. He tests his hypotheses about the nonlinguistic categories by attempting to produce the utterance in appropriate circumstances. The tutor compares the player's utterances with his own anticipations of such utterances and, in this way, checks the goodness of fit of the player's concepts with his own. He improves the fit by correction. In simple concrete terms the tutor says "dog" whenever a dog appears. The player notes the equivalence of these utterances, forms a hypothesis about the nonlinguistic category that elicits this kind of utterance, and then tries naming a few dogs himself.

All of us have been players of the Original Word Game, as children, as students, or as anthropological linguists. The player with the greatest handicap is the child. He must learn the motor skill of producing linguistic utterances and must also learn to categorize both speech and nonlinguistic reality in conformity with the habits of the tutor. These part processes are the rudiments of the game. They can be picked up one at a time or all three can develop together. For the child this process of first-language learning is also the process of cognitive socialization. The categories of the parental tutors are, in large measure, the categories of the culture.

The Motor Skill. Speech as a response is an operant rather than a respondent. We cannot elicit utterances from a child but must wait for them to be emitted. For some reason children vocalize very frequently and this vocalization moves in the direction of the speech patterns of the family. This drift in the direction of language may be produced by selective reinforcement coming from adults. They will favor a vocalization to the degree that it approximates a recognizable speech pattern. Mowrer (1950), in his efforts to train birds to talk, found that it was necessary to nurture the bird while speaking to it. Under these circumstances, Mowrer reasons, the speech of the trainer becomes a secondary reinforcer. When the bird in isolation produces sounds it will be rewarded by those that most resemble human speech and this generalized secondary reinforcement will increase the probability of humanlike sounds until they dominate the bird's song. In similar fashion we may suppose the child's babbling will change in the direction of speech. Finally, control of speech is probably gained through some sort of imitation—both the matched dependent and copying behavior described by Miller and Dollard (1941). The contention of Miller and Dollard that imitation is a learned technique is supported by the many studies of speech acquisition which report that true imitation does not occur until the eighth month or later. It is not clear that even all of these mechanisms are adequate to explain the motor control of speech. Of one thing, however, we may be certain. The player of the game can practice speech sounds and the tutor can selectively reinforce without worrying about the patterning of the sound. Thus a child may practice saying "dog" as a response to the utterance of this word by his tutor rather than as a response to instances of the category. Or he may say it in response to one member of the category, never learning to identify new instances. Motor control is, then, just one of the rudiments of the game.

The Perception of Speech. Dorothea McCarthy (1946) in her review of the literature on acquisition of language by children concludes that speech comprehension precedes the ability to produce speech. The evidence for comprehension is usually the child's ability to designate some object or objects in response to a command. In most cases it seems not to have involved the identification of new instances and, on that account, we should hesitate to credit the child with the concept in question. The ability to respond to a command such as "Show me your book" by pointing to a particular book is not sufficient evidence that the child knows the meanings of these terms. The ability does, however, have important implications. It tells us little about speech comprehension but much about speech categorization. If the child can respond appropriately to a variety of commands then he must have learned to recognize certain utterances as equivalent and others as distinctive. He has made a beginning with the problem of perceiving speech as it is perceived by his community.

Even on this very simple level we are likely to make erroneous conclusions unless controlled observations are made. Meumann (as reported in Lewis, 1936) found that his child could respond to the question *"Wo ist das Fenster?"* by pointing to the object in question. He was tempted to conclude that the child understood the question but decided to follow it with *"Où est la fenêtre?"* To his amazement the child responded as before and did so again when asked "Where is the window?" It would have been unreasonable to conclude that the child was trilingual. In answer to a fourth question, *"Wo ist die Tür?"* the child again indicated the window. Evidently he had not been responding to phonemic patterns at all but to the interrogative pitch contour which was common to the four questions. Many observations suggest that children do not at first categorize speech in terms of the finicking phonemic contrasts the community insists upon but are at first disposed to attend to the pitch contours, the loudness patterns, and the emotional qualities of vocalization. Had Meumann instituted discrimination training the child would have revised his categories. When his response to *"Wo ist das Fenster?"* was reinforced and his response to *"Wo ist die Tür?"* not reinforced he would have re-examined these equivalent stimuli and eventually discovered at least one of their differences.

There are indications that considerable time is required for the speech categories to be apprehended in their full complexity. Joos (1948) estimates that this learning is not complete before puberty. Goldstein (1948) reports that aphasic patients sometimes retain the ability to understand the speech of the members of their immediate family though the speech of strangers, especially those with regional dialects or accents, is unintelligible. We have little information on the evolving perceptual categories of speech though it is clear that such information is of great importance to the psychology of language.

The infant can learn to categorize speech by learning to pattern his pointing responses to such commands as "Show me your nose; show me your eyes; show me your toes," etc. In this case the perception of speech is an isolated rudiment of the game. It can be combined with learning motor control in the process of copying speech. The player attempts to approximate the speech of his tutor. His efforts are approved or corrected and in that process he learns to recognize the equivalence or nonequivalence of the sounds his tutor produces and the sounds he produces. Even this complex process is not the complete word game. It leaves out the most critical aspect: the categorization of the nonlinguistic world, the formation of the concepts that pattern speech.

The Categorization of the Nonlinguistic World. We might learn to categorize the nonlinguistic world by testing hypotheses formed from sensory contact with that world. Presumably there are sensory attributes which have a kind of prepotency for the child. He might begin by categorizing in terms of these attributes. Perhaps he treats all shiny coins as equivalent and distinct from the array of dull coins. He reveals this concept to his tutor by giving some equivalent response to the shiny range and another response to the dull range. This response could be verbal or nonverbal. He might call one group dimes and the other pennies, or he might kiss the one group and throw the others away. His tutor could then correct this categorization and eventually the child would learn the proper designation for each kind of coin. Clearly this process would be an immensely complicated one. Nonlinguistic reality is categorized in terms of an enormously varied population of attributes. There is an economy available to us here in the fact that speech can provide a first-level categorization of all social reality in terms of a smaller number of attributes.

The experimenter in a concept-attainment study uses the responses of his subject to infer the concepts of that subject. An array of stimuli given an equivalent response is categorized together. Suppose, for a moment, that a child who is playing the game uses the responses of his tutors as a guide to equivalence and difference in nonlinguistic reality. He could have a cue to what is edible and what is inedible by noting what is eaten and what is not eaten. Mother might be distinguished from father by the fact that his uncle kisses the one and shakes the hand of the other. The categories "bed," "chair," and "floor" could be distinguished by noting which entities are lain upon, sat upon, and stood upon. In each realm of experience we have a different set of response categories giving evidence of concepts. Using the nonlinguistic responses of others as a guide to the categories of reality we should have to learn a set of response equivalents very nearly as complex as the stimulus equivalents in the world. This point is difficult to see because we are so familiar with such response categories as sitting, standing, or kissing. The point may be clearer if we imagine a community in which kin of one sort elicit a nod of the head in their direction while kin of another sort elicit a nod in the direction of the dwelling of the wife's family. We could not discover these kinship categories until we learned to classify properly the two kinds of nod and this might take considerable learning.

In a particular case the player might notice a response on the part of his tutor—a movement of head, of eyes, and hands. His problem is to discover the defining attributes of this response so that he can identify a recurrence and use this functional equivalence as an attribute of the governing nonlinguistic concept. The difficulty is that he does not have proper knowledge of the list of attributes of nonlinguistic discriminating responses. He is not in the position of the subjects of Bruner, Goodnow, and Austin who are told beforehand that attributes consist of the number, shape, and color of certain figures. The player has the problem of attribute analysis. He can scarcely use the wholist or focussing strategy since this would require him to hold all attributes of the first instance in mind and the attributes are not yet identified. He is more likely to use a part-scanning strategy, betting on one feature of the response and probably forced to revise his hypothesis a good many times.

With regard to linguistic responses the player is in a more favorable position. From a relatively small number of experiences of speech categories it is possible to discover all the defining attributes of any future utterances—the phonemes of the language. It is, furthermore, possible to learn that any semantic utterance will be a conjunctive category defined by phonemes in a particular sequence. Once the speech system has been grasped, then, there really is no problem of category attainment so far as linguistic utterances are concerned. A subject in the experiments reported by Bruner, Goodnow, and Austin knows in advance that there are three values for each of four attributes that may help to define the category in question. The subject does not, of course, know which of the attribute values present in an initial positive instance are defining of the category to be attained. To find that out is the experimental task. The player of the Original Word Game who hears /kæt/ knows that these three phonemes, in the sequence given, define the speech category. He has only to remember the response in these terms to recognize new instances. The player is not, of course, in this position when he first hears speech. The point is that his experience in forming the first speech categories can bring him great secondary benefits. Incidental learning of the structure of speech can teach him to perceive new utterances in proper categorial fashion. The study of nonlinguistic responses cannot yield such benefits since these responses do not constitute a system. It has been suggested to me by M. Wallach that a partiality for linguistic cues in the formation of concepts is itself a kind of strategy, a content selection strategy, since this partiality can maximize information, decrease cognitive strain, and regulate risk.

The Game is not complete when the player is able to categorize the speech of his tutor. He must discover the stimulus attributes governing the tutor's verbal behavior. The child's parent will not always be nearby to tell him what is "hot." He must learn to recognize hot things by their stimulus attributes.

Once we have learned what is distinctive and what is equivalent in a man's speech we have a key to his thought and to the culture he represents. Consider the categories "ball" and "strike" in baseball. These are extremely complex categories. In terms of stimulus attributes there is little likelihood that we would think of grouping together a pitch over the plate at the proper height, a swing that misses, and a hit that falls foul, yet all these are strikes. In terms of nonlinguistic response it might take some time for us to notice that the batter manifests some degree of chagrin after any one of these or that when three of these occur he leaves the plate and returns to the dugout. The response equivalences here are rather complicated. Walking forward in the right direction means four balls have occurred. Walking in the same direction with one's team means that enough strikes have accumulated to send them into the field. Consider how the umpire makes concept formation easier. He denotes each entity as a "Strike!" or a "Ball!" The shout locates the entity in space and time. It says, "Look here and now." The phonemic equivalence of his many shouts of "Strike" and their class difference from the cries of "Ball" tell us what entities go together and which are distinct. In speech we have a small number of highly available attributes providing a first approximation to all concepts. We have a common currency of cognition.

The utterance attribute will orient the player toward contemporaneous stimuli and will tell him when the important nonlinguistic stimuli recur. Even with these aids the categorization of nonlinguistic reality is a formidable problem. In the beginning there is no listing of attributes and no possibility of holding in mind the total nonlinguistic circumstances accompanying a given utterance and, therefore, no possibility of using a wholist reception strategy. With experience certain attributes, favored in the culture, will be noticed and can serve as a basis for first hypotheses. Because of its systematic character language can again be helpful. If, for instance, the parts of speech have a reliable semantic, then knowledge of the part of speech membership of an utterance could guide the player in his selection of attributes. If nouns usually name persons or places then a nominal utterance (recognized as such from its speech context or its phonemic structure) would suggest which kinds of nonlinguistic attributes were likely to be significant. Once a first language is learned it will strongly affect our attempts at translating a new language. If we hear a brief continuous utterance from a native who holds a coconut in his hand we will identify the utterance as a word and guess that it means coconut or hand or holding since these are nonlinguistic categories coded by words in our native speech. For many closely related languages one or another of these few hypotheses is likely to be correct. If the new language is a polysynthetic tongue in which the category "man-grasps-food-in-right-hand" can be expressed in a word we might guess wrongly for a very long time. Our conception of the kind of category that can elicit a word would lead us astray.

No brief treatment can do more than suggest the ways in which linguistic utterances are able to facilitate the acquisition of the concepts that one must possess to participate in a culture. Changing word order in English so as to reverse subject-object relations has a consistent meaning and so directs us to the nonlinguistic changes that may be expected to accompany this juggling of linguistic sequences. Appending "-ed" to an utterance identifies it as a verb in the past tense and, to one familiar with English, this is sufficient information to suggest the changes that have occurred in the nonlinguistic category eliciting the uninflected verb. In general, the systematic phonology and grammar of speech reduce the number of hypotheses about the nonlinguistic category to a relatively probable few.

In any case, however, the player must test his hypotheses. The beauty of the Game is that the player can now produce utterances as responses. The tutor can use the phonemic structure of the language to infer the categories of the player and can cause revision of these categories by correcting the player's usage of terms. The small boy who generalizes incorrectly from his father's naming behavior and calls any animal that goes on all fours a "dog" will be corrected until he learns to identify new instances correctly. To play this second part of the Game it is necessary to be able to produce approximations of speech sounds. Still, a parental tutor may allow considerable latitude here, tolerating "bow wow" until the child has grasped the category and then concentrating on changing the label to "dog." Both aspects may be worked on at once with the tutor correcting both usage and pronunciation. This Game may be played concurrently with many other activities. The child and his father can play as they walk along the street, father naming, child trying, father correcting. Concepts can be learned without direct contact with ultimate attributes that may have serious consequences. The child may be told by his father when it is "safe" to cross the street. After a while the child will tell when *he* thinks it "safe" and the father will correct his usage. When the child can pattern the word "safe" as the father patterns it in his mind the father will attribute to him the concept in question. He may then allow the child to cross streets alone. The whole process of trial and correction can be accomplished using the name as a surrogate for action that would have brought the child into perilous contact with the ultimate attributes of the traffic itself. The laboratory concept-attainment experiment is likely to differ from the usual situation in that the ultimate attributes of the concept will be the experimenter's verbal behavior. A subject learns the concept so that he can anticipate whether the experimenter will identify cards as instances of the concept. There is no purpose beyond this in the learning. In the child's learning, parental speech is not usually the ultimate attribute. Beyond this there will usually be physical or social attributes of the greatest importance.

We have conducted a little experiment to illustrate some features of the Word Game. Farnsworth has developed, with the Munsell Color Company, a series of 85 color chips equally spaced around the hue dimension. Saturation and brightness are constant. Eight alternate chips are drawn from the red-blue region of the series. There is the same very small perceptual gap between each adjacent pair of the series. The subject is shown this series of chips and told that the experimenter has a way of classifying them. It will be the subject's job to discover this classification. The experimenter moves the series behind a screen and then exposes them one at a time (in random order) naming each chip with a nonsense syllable. The subject simply watches this process until all eight have been named. He is then asked to group the chips as the experimenter has grouped them with his verbal behavior.

As Figure 15 shows there are four groups of two chips each. The groups are named [ma], [ma:], [mo], [mo:]. The difference between [a] and [o] is phonemic in English but the difference between the

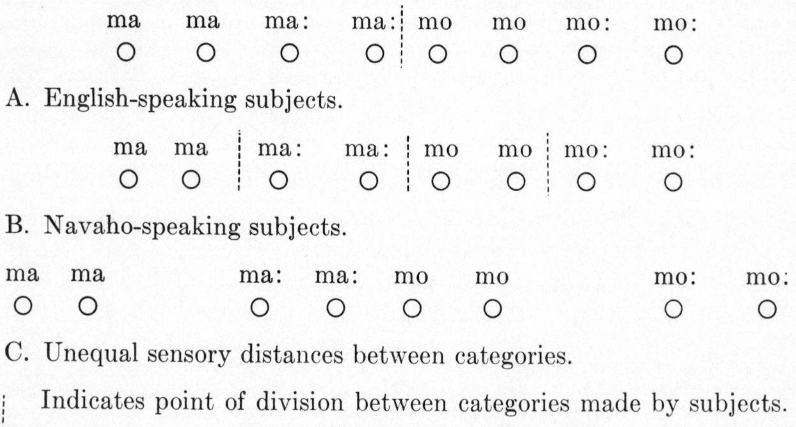

ma	ma	ma:	ma:	mo	mo	mo:	mo:
O	O	O	O	O	O	O	O

A. English-speaking subjects.

ma	ma	ma:	ma:	mo	mo	mo:	mo:
O	O	O	O	O	O	O	O

B. Navaho-speaking subjects.

ma	ma	ma:	ma:	mo	mo	mo:	mo:
O	O	O	O	O	O	O	O

C. Unequal sensory distances between categories.

¦ Indicates point of division between categories made by subjects.

Figure 15. Categorizations of eight color stimuli in terms of nonsense names varying in phonetic characteristics.

long and short forms of each vowel is not. To produce the proper length the experimenter thought of a voiceless consonant to follow the short form and a voiced consonant to follow the long form. Thus he pronounced [mo] by thinking "Mote" and [mo:] by thinking "Mode."

Fifteen Harvard students whose native language is English, after hearing one series, generally divided the colors into two groups of four chips each as in Figure 15. The line of division corresponds to the line of phonemic change. They do not make a line of division where the vowel changes in length. With four repetitions the subjects persisted in their two-group classification.

In the Navaho language vowel length is always a distinctive feature. Each vowel has a long and short form and these are different phonemes. Fifteen monolingual Navahos given the same problems of concept attainment by A. Horowitz generally divided the colors correctly into four classes of two colors each as in Figure 15 and persisted in this division through four repetitions.

We know that English subjects are able to distinguish the prolonged vowel from the short vowel, probably as easily as the Navaho. When we rejected their two-group classifications as erroneous they eventually discovered vowel length and the proper grouping of colors. Many then remarked that they had noticed some variations in the naming but assumed they were accidental. *We could have no better statement of the cognitive status of nonphonemic variations.* They are not purposeful and significant as are phonemic changes. The Navaho subjects did not assume that the variations in vowel length were accidental. Once the English subjects learned that this dimension was significant they made no errors in identification.

The groupings produced by both English and Navaho subjects were isomorphic with the groupings they heard in the tutor's speech. Having different sets of criterial attributes (phonemes) for speech they came up with rather different groupings. When the English-speaking subjects were corrected they re-examined the tutor's speech and discovered the attribute to which he gave significance.

Fifteen new English-speaking subjects were shown a different series of eight colors from the Farnsworth set. In this series there are four classes named as before, [ma], [ma:], [mo], [mo:]. However, the perceptual gap between the [ma-ma:] classes and [mo-mo:] classes was four times as great as the gap between [ma:] and [mo]. This situation is schematized by distance in Figure 15. When one looked at the series the two end classes were immediately seen as distinct from the four middle colors. There is a disproportionate change at the vowel-length boundary. The problem was to determine whether or not these autochthonous sensory categories would call attention to the change in vowel length and cause the subject to make four groups of the colors.

In Table 9 the results of all three groups are presented as the number of trials required to discover the categorizing of the colors into four classes. There were only four trials and the subjects who had not discovered the grouping after four trials have been tabulated under trial 5, the lowest score they could conceivably have obtained. The Navaho subjects, who appear first in the table, generally grouped the colors into four classes on the first trial. The English-speaking subjects who saw the eight equally spaced colors shown to the Navahos generally did not arrange the colors into four groups. The English-speaking subjects who saw eight Farnsworth colors with a disproportionate sensory gap at the points of change in vowel length show more variety of performance. Only two subjects divided the colors into four groups on the first trial. However, there were four others who did so on the second trial. Evidently the gaps in the series of eight colors help to call attention to the difference of vowel length. Even with this strong visual encouragement, however, there were six subjects who never did believe that a difference of vowel length could make two words different and so signal a categorial distinction in the nonlinguistic world.

TABLE 9

The Number of Subjects in Each of Three Groups, by Trial,
Who Arranged the Test Colors into Four Categories

Trial

Group	1	2	3	4	5 or More	N
Navaho subjects	11	1	—	2	1	15
English-speaking subjects, separated colors	2	4	2	1	6	15
English-speaking subjects, equally spaced colors	—	1	—	—	14	15

We used the median test to determine whether the first English-speaking group should be considered to have the same median as the Navaho group and also whether the two English-speaking groups were likely to have the same median. Using the chi-square test for independence (with Yates' correction) we found that there is a probability of less than 0.001 that English-speaking subjects of the first type have the same median as Navaho subjects. The two English-speaking groups are different with $P = 0.05$. These are very conservative tests since they give no credit for the prior prediction of order among the three groups.

The fact that some English-speaking subjects, who worked with unequally spaced colors, recognized the distinctiveness of the four classes after hearing them named only once is important. This result demonstrates a facet of the Word Game that we have not discussed. It is evidently possible for nonlinguistic reality to serve as a guide to the categorization of speech. The isomorphic relationship can be useful in either direction. An inescapable visual difference leads us to look for a speech difference. We may suppose that speech has less intrinsic importance than nonlinguistic reality, and it is therefore customary to describe speech as a map and the rest of the world as the region mapped. It is clear, however, that when a dirt road turns into a four-lane superhighway we may for the first time notice the difference between a thin and thick red line on an actual road map.

The method used in these experiments is a very simple model of the Word Game. There is at least one important difference from the Game as it is played with children. In our paradigm it is perfectly clear what entities are being named by the experimenter and it is also clear that hue is the only significant dimension for classifying these entities. When the child hears "things" named he usually will not know just where the "thing" is and which of its attributes are defining. He can use the name as an aid in forming hypotheses but these hypotheses will often require considerable refinement. Jespersen (1922) tells of a little girl shown a picture of a priest and given the word "priest." She then called her aunt a "priest" because that lady wore a collar like that of the man in the picture. A single denotation was not enough to form the category. It is this hypothesis-testing stage that is absent in our paradigm.

Speech as an Expression. A child may be trained to differentiate traffic conditions by means short of an ultimate and dangerous criterion. At first he can use the parental description "safe" or "not safe." Eventually he may rely on the visible aspects of the street itself. Should he mistakenly classify some hazardous situation as "safe" the action he bases on that categorization will acquaint him with the ultimate attributes of an unsafe situation. Sometimes the action one takes as a result of categorizing a situation leads to ultimate consequences which are not what we had anticipated. Consider the fable of the boy who cried "Wolf." This alarm ordinarily signified the presence of a wolf and the villagers acted on that assumption. They found no wolf but only an amused little boy. With several repetitions of this experience they recategorized the situation as one in which a shepherd boy was bored and in search of entertainment. When they acted on this judgment there were unhappy consequences for the boy. A man who habitually uses words so inaccurately that others are caused to form erroneous anticipations will eventually be classified as a liar. In these cases we do not respond to speech as a presentation of reality but rather as an expression of the speaker. His conversation does not lead us to conceive objects and events; it causes us to categorize the speaker himself—as liar, joker, coward, or gossip.

It often happens, of course, that a speaker means to present a self-categorization as when he says, "What a swine I am." To take him at his word is not to respond to his speech as an expression. He has presented himself as a swine. If, however, we interpret his speech as symptomatic of a pathetic need for reassurance then we are treating it as an expression. The behavioral difference is that the speaker will acknowledge that he has described himself as a swine but he will probably deny having asked for anybody's reassurance.

Parsons, Bales, and Shils (1953) are probably correct in holding that all gesture is in some degree taken to be expressive of the actor. We quite regularly react in this way to the nonphonemic, musical aspects of speech. The voice may "tremble" with fear or grow "cold" with anger. A woman irritated and made suspicious by her husband's late arrival may ask, with insinuating intonation, "Working *late?*" He may then react to the intonation rather than the morphemes and snap back, "That's right—working late!" She now has an option. If she likes she may be terribly hurt and say, "You needn't shout at me. I just asked if you had to work late." She is not responsible for what her speech expresses and can deny everything but the presentation. Alternatively she may continue the intonational conversation and with mock sympathy say, "You must find it very unpleasant doing so much *night* work." This can go on for any length of time with a set of more or less epiphenomenal morphemes.

It is certain that some individuals, at least, habitually respond to speech as an expression. The psychiatrist is one such. His patient's story about plots and threats does not move the doctor to phone the police. It causes him to diagnose the patient as paranoid. This categorization of the speaker predicts important ultimate attributes in a way that the categories he presents do not. Perhaps the most basic change in the thinking of Sigmund Freud was his realization that the complaints of incestuous seduction he received from the ladies of Vienna provided no information about the fathers of Vienna, but a great deal about the repressed desires of the ladies themselves. Speech from the couch ceased to be taken seriously as a presentation and became entirely an expression. When speech is used to infer latent dream content and repressed impulses we should say it is being treated as *revelation* rather than expression. The stronger word suggests the stronger resistance of the speaker to the interpretations of the auditor.

While speech is perhaps always taken to be an expression, there are circumstances in which this response is especially strong. In some cases this happens because the auditor has evidence that the presentation cannot be trusted. This is the story of the boy who cried "Wolf." In other cases the auditor does not check the ultimate attributes of the concepts presented but rejects them on the basis of some judgment of improbability. This is the story of the psychiatrist who diagnoses his patient as paranoid. We have no research on the determinants of this mode of reaction to speech—perhaps because it is our professional mode—but it would be interesting to learn something about the matter.

The Linguistic Environment. We have defined the semantic utterance as one which is selective in the nonlinguistic stimuli to which it is a response. This is not the only kind of stimulus-response selectivity that utterances manifest. They are also selective with regard to linguistic context. The contexts of an utterance have been treated as functional attributes of the utterance. It would seem that they must have also a role in the acquisition of linguistic meanings. For certainly many words are introduced to us without nonlinguistic reference. They are said to be verbally defined. How many schizophrenics do we see in our first course in abnormal psychology? About as many schizophrenics as unicorns. And yet we are supposed to learn the meaning of the term "schizophrenic" from reading and listening to many sentences in which the word occurs. How can this be?

Werner and Kaplan (1950) have done the only experimental study we know of this kind of language learning in children. They used a Word Context Test in which artificial words are embedded in sentences. The subject going from one context to another is expected to arrive finally at the meaning of the word. There were 12 series of six sentences each. Each sentence was presented on a separate card. It was made clear to the child that each word had only one meaning throughout its series of six sentences. After each sentence he was asked to tell what he thought the word might mean. Here are the first word and its six contexts.

I. Corplum:
1. A corplum may be used for support.
2. Corplums may be used to close off an open space.
3. A corplum may be long or short, thick or thin, strong or weak.
4. A wet corplum does not burn.
5. You can make a corplum smooth with sandpaper.
6. The painter used a corplum to mix his paints.

Werner and Kaplan gave their test to 125 children, 25 in each of 5 age groups between 8 and 13 years. Three judges derived 60 criteria (both linguistic and semantic) from a preliminary examination of the protocols and employed these criteria in the final analysis. They found a gradual improvement in performance with increasing age. Many of the dimensions (word syncresis, rigidity, holophrasis, etc.) are of great interest in the problems of genetic psychology. Our present concern is not with the interesting conclusions of Werner and Kaplan, but with the merits of their method as a paradigm for the acquisition of linguistic meanings without nonlinguistic reference.

The problem of the Word Context Test is not strictly a problem of concept formation or attainment but is rather concerned with concept identification. Each nonsense word has an equivalent already familiar to the subject; "stick" is the solution to the example we have given. Other nonsense words substitute for such familiar terms as "fault," "hope," "hole," etc. A word can usually be recognized by its phonemes. In the Word Context Test this class of attributes is meant to play no part. A nonsense sequence "stands in" for the sequence to be identified. The children of the Werner-Kaplan study did not always understand this condition. One child translated "lidber" as "leave." Another translated "hudroy" as "hurry." These children attempted to utilize the phonemic attributes which are of such great importance in the Original Word Game.

The familiar equivalents of the nonsense words can be discovered from the surrounding contexts in which the words appear. In effect, subjects are given a series of contextual attributes of the word to be recognized. For instance, the blank in the frame "A ___ is used for support" is filled in English by many words with various frequencies. The word "cane" is a likely choice in this context. This word, however, is a rather unlikely choice for the second sentence "___ may be used to close off an open space" and it is still less likely for the sixth sentence "The painter used a ___ to mix his paints." Still the word "cane" has some probability of occurrence in all the sentences. However, the word "stick" has a rather high probability for all six sentences. "A wet *stick* does not burn." "You can make a *stick* smooth with sandpaper." "The painter used a *stick* to mix his paints." We suggest that Werner and Kaplan's "solution" to each series is the word which has the highest probability across the series. The authors of the Word Context Test say that "as a child moves from one sentence to the next, the clues increase in definiteness." In our terms this means that the context probability of the word is higher for later sentences in a series than it is for earlier sentences.

It is interesting to speculate about the kinds of strategies that might be used on this problem. In this study the subject is not exposed to positive instances of the concept. He is given one attribute at a time and asked to guess the concept. As an analogue, suppose an experimenter is using the concept of the Boston Classified Telephone Directory and he means to give his subject one attribute at a time. "To begin with," he says, "it is yellow." The subject might think of everything in the world that is yellow and then eliminate concepts from this population as he is given additional attributes. This is an extreme of the simultaneous-scanning strategy, even more unlikely than that strategy ordinarily is. In the experiments of this book simultaneous scanning involves remembering all the concepts that might be exemplified in a single positive instance which manifests all the defining attributes. In the present case only one attribute is given. It might be combined with any number of other attributes to produce the concept the experimenter has in mind. To think of all these is impossible. It is likewise impossible to think of all the words that might fill the context "A ___ may be used for support." The simultaneous-scanning strategy would not always be impossible in the attribute-by-attribute recognition of a familiar concept. Certain highly criterial attributes are consistent with only a very few categories or even perhaps consistent with only a single category. Thus there is only one animal that has a trunk and only a few words that appear in the context "___ were some people at the door." Notice that if this attribute-by-attribute situation concerned the acquisition of arbitrary concepts rather than the recognition of familiar concepts it would never be possible to think of all the concepts that might exhibit a single attribute or any conjunction of attributes because the number of such concepts would be infinitely large.

Because the subject is to guess a familiar category that the experimenter has in mind he can form some shrewd hypotheses. Where the number of categories consistent with a given attribute is very large it is likely that a subject will think of only a few of the more probable cases. Perhaps butter and lemon for "yellow"; cane and pillar for "A ___ may be used for support."

In our analogue suppose that the subject guesses "banana" when told the object is yellow. This would be incorrect and so the experimenter might add a second attribute: "It weighs two pounds." One subject might think "Yellow and weighing two pounds" and guess, "Two cartons of butter." The subject we have imagined acts on the basis of the conjunction of all preceding attributes. We may wonder to what degree this is true in the Word Context Test. Alternatively, a kind of lazy scanning strategy might be used in which hypotheses would only be based on the immediate context attribute. The criteriality of some of the individual sentences, especially those last in their series, is so high that it may not be necessary to recall what has preceded. We have asked several people to try to guess the words from final sentences alone. On several they were always correct. With the sentence "Jimmy *lidbered* stamps from all countries" everyone guessed "collected."

There seem to be two extreme strategies that could be used. The subject might simply react to the immediate context, choosing the likeliest word for this case. When he finds a highly criterial context such as the one just mentioned for "collected," he has a strong suspicion that this is the answer and quickly glances back to see if it "fits" the earlier sentences. On the other hand, he might base each guess on the accumulation of previous attributes, selecting the word with the highest average probability in all earlier contexts. It should be possible to determine the degree to which previous attributes are kept in mind by comparing the guess offered when a sentence follows several other sentences with the guesses offered for this sentence in isolation. Some of the children's guesses were clearly based on single context attributes. Thus one child provided two different answers for two sentences in the same series. "Before the house is finished the walls must have *paint.*" "You can't feel or touch *air.*" The correct word in both cases is "holes." It has a lower probability than "paint" in the first context and a lower probability than "air" in the second context. However, "paint" will almost never occur in the second sentence and "air" will almost never occur in the first. If the first context were kept in mind "air" ought not to be offered for the second. In our inquiries with adults, however, we found evidence that the earlier sentences were kept in mind. When, for example, the sentence, "The painter used a *corplum* to mix his paints" was offered alone, a common suggestion was "palette." This never occurred when the sentence occurred in its proper serial position. We would suppose that "palette" is ruled out by such earlier sentences as "A *corplum* may be used for support."

Most of the guesses of the children in the Werner and Kaplan study likewise appear to be founded on probabilities generated by the entire series. It is our impression, however, that the easily solved series usually include at least one highly criterial context which will quite reliably evoke the correct word. Six sentences that call for the word with moderately high probability may be "solved" with a word possessing lower average probabilities. Where one sentence almost certainly calls for a word subjects feel confident that this word is a positive instance and will not easily relinquish it.

In the Werner-Kaplan study the older children found more correct solutions than the younger. The older children also showed less variability in the solutions offered. We may suppose them to be more like the adult-model computers (Werner and Kaplan) who designed the test. The younger children have not had enough experience of the English language to build in the context probabilities necessary to a "solution." Children frequently made grammatical errors because they had not learned that in the frame "A ＿＿＿ may be used for support" a noun is almost inevitably inserted. Furthermore, the child's subjective criteriality for a sentence attribute can be quite different from the potential criteriality based on adult usage. If one used young enough children to construct Shannon's approximations to English one would get something quite different from the approximation intended. One child used the word "cars" to replace the nonsense word in the sentence, "The way is clear if there are no *ashders*." This must be that very child we have postulated who is learning when it is safe to cross the street. In his experience "cars" was so predictable in this context that he persisted in using it in other sentences where we should say that it did not fit at all well.

The Werner-Kaplan test asks subjects to identify a familiar word with its phonemes changed and its contexts intact. This might conceivably be done without having the nonlinguistic categories named by any words. A knowledge of English word sequences could generate a solution quite independently of semantics. This is not a method for studying the acquisition of the nonlinguistic concepts named by words.

In second-language learning, however, we sometimes have problems like that posed in the Werner-Kaplan test. If, in reading German, I come upon an unfamiliar word, and am unable or unwilling to use a dictionary, the process by which I try to match this word with an English equivalent is like the process of deciphering "corplum." Suppose the context in which the German word occurs is one that I can translate. I then have an English sentence with a gap corresponding to the new word and am in a position to guess the English equivalent of the unfamiliar word from its single context attribute. As the new word recurs in different contexts the attributes multiply and the likelihood of identifying it increases. Successful use of this method depends, of course, on similarity of combinational probabilities in the first and second languages.

The Word Context Test might be improved as a model for the learning of word meanings (in the sense of co-ordinate nonlinguistic categories) if the critical term were totally unfamiliar. If it were a word we had never heard, standing for a concept we had not formed, there would be no reason to alter its phonemes. The psychiatric term "schizophrenic" once satisfied these conditions for most of us. Furthermore, it is usually introduced verbally rather than denotatively. Suppose our professor names some of the attributes of the schizophrenic. These might be attributes of physical appearance. If he can use words whose nonlinguistic concepts we have formed—"pale, trembling, unshaven"—we may be able to identify instances of the category without ever having had one pointed out. If the physical attributes are not denotatively familiar—"hypokinesis, waxy flexibility" —we may be unable to identify instances until these terms are reduced to something familiar. The professor may describe attributes of schizophrenic speech rather than schizophrenic appearance. If these attributes are familiar—"exceptionally slow, slurred pronunciation, small dynamic range"—we will be able to use them to identify schizophrenics. If the attributes are rather esoteric—"neologistic, autistic"— they will be of little use for identification until they are explicated.

In this example the concept is acquired from linguistic experience but the test of comprehension is still the denotative identification of new instances. The Werner-Kaplan test stays within the realm of verbal behavior. When a new word is used it is not possible to use their test of comprehension. What kind of verbal evidence can a subject give that convinces others he has attained a concept?

When someone has had nothing but direct sensory experience of concept instances there are verbal tests that can be applied. Suppose a child claims to have seen kangaroos at the zoo. His elders can question him about the physical traits of this animal to satisfy themselves that he has indeed seen a kangaroo. If he can separate the defining attributes from the noisy they will believe that he has learned the kangaroo concept. If, however, the child in question has heard kangaroos talked about it will be much harder to find out, by verbal means, whether or not he has learned to recognize kangaroos. He may simply be repeating what he heard in school and his appropriate talk may not predict the ability to identify instances of the category.

In this section we have held linguistic meaning close to a single operation: the act of discriminatory naming of referent entities. Of course, this operation does not exhaust the subject. Language function is in some ways like a game, such as bridge or chess. If someone watches others play bridge long enough he will eventually discover the rules of the game and become able to play bridge himself. In playing the game he will not have to restrict himself to the particular bids and plays others have been observed to make. He will be able to create novel plays that conform to the structure of the game. Games are systematic. From knowledge of a limited number of moves one learns to become a creative participant extending the game to new moves that are permitted by its rules. In a game like bridge, rules are legislated before play begins but, in the language game, play began long before anyone wrote down any rules and not all the rules are formulated yet. The grammarian, phonologist, logician, and psychologist watch the rest of us play to discover the norms of our game. Somehow those of us who play know more rules than anyone has yet formulated and we judge the speech of another to be meaningful when it stays within the rules. The laws of denotational semantics, governing the naming operation, are only one kind of rule in this complex game.

LANGUAGE AND CULTURE

It is popularly believed that reality is present in much the same form to all men of sound mind. There are objects like a house or a cat and qualities like red or wet and events like eating or singing and relationships like near to or between. Languages are supposed to be itemized inventories of this reality. They differ, of course, in the sounds they employ, but the inventory is always the same. The esthetic predilections of the Italian lead him to prefer euphonious vowels, while the German is addicted to harsh consonant groupings, but the things and events named are the same in both tongues. We are confirmed in this view by our first foreign language textbooks which present us with lists of French, German, or Latin words standing opposite their exact English equivalents.

There are, of course, poetic persons who claim to find in each language some special genius that peculiarly fits it for the expression of certain ideas. But the majority of us are at a loss to understand how this can be, since there is apparently a relationship of mutual translatability among the languages we learn. To be sure, we can see that one language might contain a few items more than another. If the Germans were to invent a new kind of automobile and we had not yet thought of such a machine, their dictionary would have one entry more than ours until we heard of the discovery and named it for ourselves. But these inequalities are in the lexical fringe. They do not disturb the great core of common inventory.

This glottocentric outlook will be seriously disturbed by the study of languages that lie outside the Indo-European group. It has not prepared us for finding that there is a language in which noun and verb categories apparently do not exist, or that there is another in which the colors gray and brown are called by the same name. Such data from the study of American Indian tongues have caused Whorf (1950), Sapir (1949), Lee (1938), Hoijer (1954), and others to reject the usual view of the relationship between language and thought. They suggest that each language embodies and perpetuates a particular world view. The speakers of a language are partners to an agreement to see and think of the world in a certain way—not the only possible way. The world can be structured in many ways, and the language we learn as children directs the formation of our particular structure. Language is not a cloak following the contours of thought. Languages are molds into which infant minds are poured. This view departs from the common-sense notion in *a.* holding that the world is differently experienced and conceived in different linguistic communities, and *b.* suggesting that language is causally related to these psychological differences.

In this extreme form the hypothesis seems to predict perfect correspondence of cultural and linguistic areas. It is embarrassed by the fact that the Finns who possess a European culture speak a language unrelated to the languages of most other European peoples. It is embarrassed by the fact that the Hopi and the Hopi-Tewan who share a general Puebloan culture (Hoijer, 1954) speak very divergent languages. Perhaps, however, these examples and others like them are not so damaging to the linguistic-relativity thesis as they first appear. It may be that the Finnish culture only very superficially resembles general European culture. A closer study of these people might show that their cognitive psychology is as unlike that of other European peoples as their language is unlike the Indo-European family. It is also possible that the assignment of Finnish speech to the Finno-Ugric rather than the Indo-European family is based on linguistic features that have little psychological importance. The Finnish language may resemble Indo-European languages in all major psychological aspects. Comparable questions can be raised with regard to every case in which linguistic and cultural boundaries do not coincide.

A good definition of culture is, "all those historically created designs for living, explicit and implicit, rational, irrational and non-rational, which exist at any time as potential guides for the behavior of men" (Kluckhohn and Kelly, 1945, p. 97). Culture will include such diverse systems as art, kinship, religion, etiquette, technology, fashions in clothes, and language. The question is whether the language system is a rather trivial fraction of the total culture or whether it has a special importance such that full comprehension of the language entails comprehension of all other cultural systems. We shall first examine the formal and then the semantic aspects of language to see how important each is to total culture.

It is certain that there are many features of language which may be studied without learning anything of religion, kinship, art, or the other major designs for living. In general these are the formal categories studied in abstraction from semantics. Languages differ, for instance, in the phonemes they use and in the relative frequency with which the same phonemes are used. Jespersen (1922) and Roback (1954) have suggested that the "phonetic preferences" of a language may be revealing of national character. According to one view vowels represent the feminine principle in speech and consonants the masculine. This leaves English and German more masculine in character than Italian or Hawaiian. No thesis is too exotic to test but this one is too exotic to take seriously without satisfactory test. What are the other formal features of language that might relate to total culture but probably do not?

Languages differ in the number of phonemes they employ. The range is from about 12 to 67 phonemes. Languages differ also in the complexity of their phonemes, in the number of allophones included within a phoneme. The complexity and number of phonemes are variables that we would expect, for theoretical reasons put forth earlier in this chapter, to be related to the ease of language acquisition. Where languages have identical phonemic repertoires they differ in the sequences used to name particular concepts. These names differ in representational value from one language to another and these differences should affect the ease with which the various names are learned. In general, then, linguistic differences on the level of phonology have implications for first-language learning but they have no clear implications for other cultural content. Languages might use very different sounds to say much the same things.

We shall use Morris' (1946) term "formator" for any linguistic device that expresses a relation between categories. Entwistle (1953) points out that relations of stems or words within the sentence may be shown by word order, auxiliary words, or affixes. Among the many relational concepts regularly expressed in English are possession, tense, and the subject-object relation. Possession is often expressed with a bound morpheme ("John's house"), tense with auxiliaries ("I will return"), the subject-object relation with word order ("Dog bites man"). It seems likely that most languages make some use of all three devices. They differ, however, in their partialities for particular devices. It is quite possible for languages to differ in the formators they use and yet to express the same relational concepts.

The "part of speech" is a functional category. Words are grouped together because they have the same functional relations with other forms in the language. The instances of the category do not necessarily have any phonemic common denominator. In English, nouns are such a functional category. There is some question whether these functional categories have any "shared" semantic value. Fries (1952) has convincingly demonstrated that the schoolteacher's semantic definitions of the parts of speech really do not cover all instances. However, the average speaker of English thinks of the parts of speech as representing the fundamental categories of reality. They are thought to stand for such abstract ideas as things, events, and qualities. It would be possible for languages to differ in the particular grammatical rules or contextual attributes defining their form classes and still to code the same higher order concepts into parts of speech.

Differences of phonology, of formators, and form classes are all used in comparative philology (together with historical, geographic, and other considerations) to decide on the degree of relationship between languages. Indeed it is on the basis of their methods of expressing relations that languages are classified into isolating, agglutinative, flexional, analytic, synthetic, and polysynthetic types and this classification has been a major factor in working out the language families. Yet all of these formal aspects—phonology, formators, and form classes —can be as irrelevant to the total culture as are differences in colored inks on two maps to the region represented. It is not surprising, therefore, that linguistic areas are not perfectly coincident with cultural areas.

When the semantics of speech is studied in conjunction with the formal characteristics we are likely to learn more about the total culture. Utterances can be analyzed as discriminating responses revealing the categories of the culture. Languages can be compared in terms of the nonlinguistic categories they reveal.

At the turn of the century Cambridge University sent a famous anthropological expedition to the Torres Straits. One member of that expedition, W. H. R. Rivers (1901), conducted some standard psychological tests with the native population. Among other things he used the Holmgren color yarns and asked subjects to group together colors that belonged together. Rivers found that they consistently made certain "odd" groupings which corresponded to lexical groupings for them. Within such a class the natives gave all the yarns a common name. Rivers decided that these colors did not really look alike but were put together because of the common name. This looks to us like a lingering remnant of culture bondage in the mind of this eminent scientist. One naturally hesitates on the threshold of believing that the categorization of physical reality is culturally relative. But what ground can there be for denying that these color groupings were perceptual categories? The subjects grouped the yarns with both lin-

guistic and nonlinguistic class responses. What more do we do with
our red, green, and blue?

In recent years Sapir (1949), Whorf (1950), and Lee (1938) have
provided us with examples of the following kind of linguistic difference. A range of experience is differentiated in the lexicon of one
language and undifferentiated in another. The color terminology of
the Torres Straits natives fits this pattern as do many Pacific island
languages that fail to distinguish blue and green, the Navaho word
that stands for both gray and brown, etc. The Wintu have names for
many varieties of cow; the Laplander distinguishes many snows; in the
Brazilian jungles lexicons are proliferated for palm trees and parrots.
We have more names for varieties of automobile than do most people.
Murdock (1949) has described kinship terminology in 250 societies
with respect to the biologically distinct varieties of "aunt;" mother's
sister, father's sister, mother's brother's wife, and father's brother's
wife. He found great variation, one lexicon having a distinct name
for each, others grouping them together in various ways. Most of the
areas of high lexical differentiation are of central importance to the
culture. The Wintu makes his living raising cattle. For the Laplander snow has a thousand household uses. I do not know what
Brazilian natives do with palm trees and parrots, but it is bound to be
important to them. It would be absurd to deny that the lexical differentiation of these items corresponds to a cognitive differentiation.
It remains, however, to wonder about the status of such distinctions
for people whose lexicon does not code them.

An extreme position would hold that the speakers of the language
with the relatively undifferentiated lexicon are unable to form the concepts named in the more differentiated language. This position is untenable. Too many travellers (among them the linguists who described the languages) have learned to see the Laplander's snows and
the Wintu's cows. Too many of us reading the reports of such travellers have grasped these concepts from a description—all in English.
All of us realize the differences between the four kinds of aunt, although
we seldom pay attention to them. Cultures differ in the *availability*
of the concepts in question. The low availability to the English
speaker of those we have mentioned is manifest in low *codability*.
They can be pinned with a phrase but not a word. We must speak
of "white spotted cows," "damp soft snow," and "father's brother's
wife." There is an unwieldy quality to our coding of the other man's
culture.

George K. Zipf (1935) has shown that there exists, in Peiping Chinese, Plautine Latin, and American and British English, a tendency for the length of a word to be correlated with its frequency of usage. There are many familiar examples of English words abbreviating as they increase in frequency. The "automobile" has become the "car." "Television" is now "TV." "Long-playing records" are "L.P.'s.' Following Doob (1952) we have suggested that the failure of such English phrases as "white spotted cow" and "damp soft snow" to abbreviate to a word means that they are less often used than the corresponding words among the Wintu and Laplanders. We go further and propose that these concepts are not only less frequently expressed but less frequently utilized in perception and thought. They are not habitual cognitive modes; they are less available to the English speaker and this is manifest in the fact that the concepts are not coded into single words.

Brown and Lenneberg (1954) have demonstrated a relationship between the availability of a concept and its codability. Their approach to this originally cross-cultural problem is peculiar in that they work within the English-speaking community. It is argued that the essential thing to be understood is the fact that experiences are more codable in one language than another. What is the cognitive significance of a difference of codability? Since there are differences of codability within a single language the authors hold that this question may be answered without recourse to cross-cultural data. Some colors can be named in English with a single word while others require a phrase. If one investigates the cognitive availability of these differentially codable colors for English subjects it seems reasonable to suppose that the results might be generalized to the cross-cultural case. They have compared differentially codable regions of experience within one language and extrapolated their conclusions to the case in which the same region of experience is differentially codable in two languages. The legitimacy of this extrapolation is supported by data of Lenneberg and Roberts (1955) collected from Zuni Indians using a field adaptation of methods developed for laboratory study.

The first step in the experiment with English-speaking subjects was to devise a method for measuring codability. The authors suspected that when a color required more than a single word to name it subjects would hesitate over their verbalizations, and disagree with one another and with themselves from time to time. Subjects were shown controlled exposures of single Munsell color chips (24 in all). They were asked to name each color as quickly as possible following its appearance. Five measures were drawn from these data. For each color they determined: 1. the length of the naming response in words;

2. the length of the naming response in syllables; 3. the average reaction time: 4. the degree of agreement among subjects in the naming response; 5. the degree of agreement on two occasions for the same subjects. These measures were all related to one another in the anticipated manner. Particularly interesting is the fact that semantic ambiguity within the community corresponds to inconsistency and hesitation in the individual. It is as though competing social tendencies are competing habits in the individuals; a nice example of interiorized social norms. The matrix of intercorrelations yielded a general factor which was called codability. The single index with the highest factor loading was item 4, the degree of agreement among subjects in the naming response, and this was used as the measure of codability in the second part of the experiment.

New subjects were given a recognition task which served as a first operation for getting at category availability. In the basic procedure 4 of the 24 colors, whose codability had been determined, were briefly and simultaneously exposed. After their removal subjects were asked to identify the 4 colors on a chart of 120 Munsell colors. The recognition score for a color was computed from the number of correct identifications. Codability was significantly related to availability as measured by the recognition score.

The basic procedure was modified so as to create conditions in which it should be easier to keep the colors in mind and also conditions in which it should be more difficult. For example, in one condition only a single color was exposed and the recognition immediately followed its removal, while in another case there were four colors and then a three-minute interval before recognition, during which the subject was occupied with unrelated tasks. As the recognition task was complicated the correlation with codability increased. This suggested to the authors that a single color might be briefly retained as an image but that a number of colors retained over a period of time would be "stored" as names. The ability to recover the color from the name would then depend on the unequivocality of its coding.

The reports of anthropological linguists make it clear that languages differ not only in the sounds they employ but also in the concepts they code. The experiment of Brown and Lenneberg suggests that the cognitive differences involved may be described in terms of the availability of concepts and that availability may be revealed in codability.

On the level of the formator, Whorf, Lee, and Hoijer have shown that languages differ not only in the nature of their formators but also in the relational concepts they employ. For example, Lee (1938) has described the conjugation of the Wintu verb as validity modes rather than tenses. They do not indicate the time of an action but rather the grounds for believing in it. One could report that "Harry is chopping wood" in several quite different ways. If we only know of the event by hearsay we use the verb form employed in relaying gossip and in describing one's own past drunken behavior. If we see the action another form is used. If we hear the action or see the chips fly there is another form. If we know that Harry is chopping wood because he does so every day at this time we conjugate the verb for a lawful regular occurrence. Whorf describes somewhat different validity modes for the Hopi verb. These reports suggest that quite different fundamental dimensions may characterize the thought of people in different cultures.

Among form classes there is one very familiar cultural difference. Gender is a functional category. Thus a class of French nouns is defined by the frame "Le __ est bon" and another class by "La __ est bonne." No one knows what the original semantic significance of gender may have been. Entwistle (1953) guesses that in Indo-European it originated as a distinction between animate and inanimate objects. It is not, of course, consistently sexual. The various western European languages do not group their morphemes into the same gender categories but it is doubtful that this difference has any cognitive significance since gender is an automatic appurtenance to speech.

Likelier to have cognitive implications is the observation of Whorf that the two Hopi parts of speech nearest our verb-noun categories divide neatly into words naming short-term events and words naming long-term events. Thus "spark" and "spasm" would be Hopi "verbs." Equally striking are the observations of Kluckhohn and Leighton (1946), and all students of Navaho, that that language employs object classes which make distinct grammatical categories of words for long thin objects, words for round objects, words for granular substances, etc. Actually there are exceptions in all these classes and the semantic definition is only a majority attribute. Still, when functional classes break along semantic lines it seems likely that the speakers of the language observe these lines in categorizing their world. Even with a semantically heterogeneous form class like our English noun there is a feeling that most instances name "things"—denotable objects. While "truth" and "beauty" are not such things it is possible that, as nouns, they are infected in our thought with the "thingness" that dominates the category. We will not know just how to interpret differences in form classes until the linguistic data are complemented with psychological experiments.

The vast differences in nonlinguistic culture which separate us from the Navaho, Wintu, and Hopi peoples are matched by great linguistic differences when the study of language includes semantics. Within the nations of the European community there are not such great cultural gaps, Neither are the linguistic gaps as great. Matched lexical items from the various European tongues are conventionally treated as semantic equivalents. While the Frenchman says *mère*, the German *mutter*, and the Italian *madre*, we know they all mean "mother." Such words are presented in elementary language courses as perfect synonyms but this they usually are not. The French word *amie*, for instance, is not quite the same as English "lady friend" or German *Freundin*. All three forms would be used to designate certain relationships but their categories do not exactly coincide. The word *amie* is more likely to designate a sweetheart than either of the Germanic expressions and yet it has a wider semantic range than English "sweetheart." Even the words *mère* and "mother" are not identical. "Mother" is replaced by "mom" or "ma" in certain circumstances and in certain social strata. It is unlikely that this precise pattern is duplicated in other languages. Slight differences in nonlinguistic reference are accompanied by differences in contextual probabilities. There will be French utterances containing *amie* for which "lady friend" is an unlikely English substitute.

It is probable that only the most subtle semantic studies will reveal cultural variations within the European community. A book could be written defining the full sense of the word *Vaterland* to the German and this book would be a description of German culture. Ruth Benedict (1946) has actually presented the Japanese culture by attempting to give the full meanings of a few Japanese words. The Japanese equivalent of "elder brother," for example, is partially identical with our term but a full definition involves a description of Japanese values, family life, law, etc. When the notion of language is expanded in this way it is a truism to identify language areas with culture areas. For language is nothing less than an inventory of all the ideas, interests, and occupations that take up the attention of the community. The study of semantics, in this extended sense, cannot be distinguished from the general study of culture.

The exotic cognitive modes discovered by anthropological linguists have usually been represented as totally foreign to our way of thinking. We have already presented arguments which show that we can learn to think in these unaccustomed ways but we will go further than this and claim that most of the conceptual oddities turned up by Whorf and others can be found in some group within our complex society. After all, small boys interested in making snowballs distinguish "good packing" snow from "poor packing." Skiers make still finer distinctions. Cattle breeders recognize many kinds of cattle. Experts on kinship terminology know all the kinds of aunts there are. A subject of Dr. Henry Murray's whose TAT protocols we have read habitually qualifies his statements by mentioning the source of his information. Scientists have developed the validity mode into the entire apparatus of statistics and experimental methodology. We conjugate our verbs with reliability coefficients and "T" ratios. Poets, schizophrenics, and scholars all cultivate deviant cognition. The strange conceptual habits of alien people may all be found in some minority of our population. They may be a professional habit, a flight into unreality, or a source of creativity.

In this appendix language has been described as a system of categories having important relations with the nonlinguistic categories of thought and culture. This "category analysis" points up some interesting continuities between language and the general psychology of cognition. In the last section, for example, it was proposed that the cognitive differences suggested by the data of anthropological linguistics may be differences of category availability. A less available category is not one we are unable to form but is, rather, a category we do not conventionally use. When the phoneme is treated as a category it is again possible to describe cognitive differences between societies in terms of availability. It is not that we are unable to categorize vowels by duration but we do not ordinarily so categorize them, whereas this is conventional practice for the Navahos. The Navaho's vowels and the Eskimo's snows appear to have the same kind of low availability for those not raised to them. Our method of analysis assimilates languages, in many ways, to general cognition. At the same time it has revealed something of the special role of the language system.

BIBLIOGRAPHY

Adkins D. C., & Lyerly, S. B.: 1951. Factor analysis of reasoning tests. Adjutant General's Office: PRS Rep. No. 878.

Adorno, T. W., Frenkel-Brunswik, E., Levinson, D. J., & Sanford, R. N.: 1950. *The authoritarian personality.* New York: Harper.

Adrian, E. D.: 1947. *The physical background of perception.* Oxford: Clarendon Press.

Allport, F. H.: 1955. *Theories of perception and the concept of structure.* New York: Wiley.

Allport, G. W.: 1954. *The nature of prejudice.* Cambridge, Mass.: Addison-Wesley.

Allport, G. W., & Postman, L.: 1947. *The psychology of rumor.* New York: Holt.

Ames, A., Jr.: 1955. *An interpretative manual: The nature of our perceptions, prehensions and behavior.* Princeton: Princeton Univ. Press.

Arrow, K. J.: 1951. Alternative approaches to the theory of choice in risk-taking situations. *Econometrica, 19,* 404–437.

Asch, S. E.: 1951. Effects of group pressure upon the modification and distortion of judgments. In H. Guetzkow (Ed.), *Groups, leadership and men.* Pittsburgh: Carnegie Press. Pp. 177–190.

Attneave, F.: 1953. Psychological probability as a function of experienced frequency. *J. exp. Psychol., 46,* 81–86.

Attneave, F.: 1954. Some informational aspects of visual perception. *Psychol. Rev., 61,* 183–193.

Austin, G. A., Bruner, J. S., & Seymour, R. V.: 1953. Fixed-choice strategies in concept attainment. *Amer. Psychologist, 8,* 314 (Abstract).

Bartlett, F. C.: 1932. *Remembering.* Cambridge, Eng.: Cambridge Univ. Press.

Bartlett, F. C.: 1951. Thinking. *Memoirs and Proceedings of Manchester Literary and Philosophical Soc., 93,* 31–44.

Benedict, R. F.: 1946. *The chrysanthemum and the sword; patterns of Japanese culture.* Boston: Houghton Mifflin.

Berkeley, G.: 1710. *A treatise concerning the principles of human knowledge.* Dublin: A. Rhames (printer).

Beritoff, J. S.: 1924. On the fundamental nervous processes in the cortex of the cerebral hemispheres. I. The principal stages of the development of the individual reflex: its generalization and differentiation. *Brain, 47,* 109–148.

Bexton, W. H., Heron, W., & Scott, T. H.: 1954. Effects of decreased variation in the sensory environment. *Canad. J. Psychol., 8,* 70–76.

Bloom, B. S., & Broder, L. J.: 1950. Problem-solving processes of college students. *Suppl. educ. Monogr.,* No. 73. Chicago: Univ. of Chicago Press.

Boring, E. G.: 1942. *Sensation and perception in the history of experimental psychology.* New York: Appleton-Century.

313

Bouthilet, L.: 1948. The measurement of intuitive thinking. Unpublished thesis, Univ. of Chicago.

Brown, D. R.: 1953. Stimulus-similarity and the anchoring of subjective scales. *Amer. J. Psychol., 66,* 199–214.

Brown, R. W., & Lenneberg, E.: 1954. A study in language and cognition. *J. abnorm. soc. Psychol., 49,* 454–462.

Brown, R. W., Black, A., & Horowitz, A.: 1955. Phonetic symbolism in natural languages. *J. abnorm. soc. Psychol., 50,* 388–393.

Bruner, J. S.: 1951. Personality dynamics and the process of perceiving. In R. R. Blake & G. V. Ramsey (Eds.), *Perception: An approach to personality.* New York: Ronald Press. Pp. 121–147.

Bruner, J. S., Matter, J., & Papanek, M. L.: 1955. Breadth of learning as a function of drive level and mechanization. *Psychol. Rev., 62,* 1–10.

Bruner, J. S., Miller, G. A., & Zimmerman, C.: 1955. Discriminative skill and discriminative matching in perceptual recognition. *J. exp. Psychol., 49,* 187–192.

Bruner, J. S., & Minturn, L.: 1955. Perceptual identification and perceptual organization. *J. gen. Psychol., 53,* 21–28.

Bruner, J. S., & Postman, L.: 1949. On the perception of incongruity: a paradigm. *J. Pers., 18,* 206–223.

Bruner, J. S., Postman, L., & Rodrigues, J.: 1951. Expectation and the perception of color. *Amer. J. Psychol., 64,* 216–227.

Brunswik, E.: 1939. Probability as a determiner of rat behavior. *J. exp. Psychol., 25,* 175–197.

Brunswik, E.: 1943. Organismic achievement and environmental probability. *Psychol. Rev., 50,* 255–272.

Brunswik, E.: 1947. *Systematic and representative design of psychological experiments, with results in physical and social perception.* Berkeley, Cal.: Univ. Cal. Press.

Brunswik, E.: 1952. *The conceptual framework of psychology.* Interntl. Encycl. Unif. Sci., 1, No. 10. Chicago: Univ. Chicago Press.

Brunswik, E., & Reiter, L.: 1938. Eindruckscharaktere schematisierter Gesichter. *Z. Psychol., 142,* 67–134.

Burma, B. H., & Mayr, E.: 1949. The species concept: a discussion. *Evolut.,* III, 4, 369–373.

Bush, R. R., & Mosteller, F.: 1955. *Stochastic models for learning.* New York: Wiley.

Cantril, H.: 1940. *The invasion from Mars.* Princeton: Princeton Univ. Press.

Cantril, H.: 1950. *The "why" of man's experience.* New York: Macmillan.

Cartwright, D.: 1941a. Decision-time in relation to the differentiation of the phenomenal field. *Psychol. Rev., 48,* 425–442.

Cartwright, D.: 1941b. Relation of decision-time to the categories of response. *Amer. J. Psychol., 54,* 174–196.

Cartwright, D., & Festinger, L.: 1943. A quantitative theory of decision. *Psychol. Rev., 50,* 595–621.

Cohen, J.: 1954. Conjecture and risk. *Advancement of Science, 11,* 333–339.

Crutchfield, R. S.: 1954. Conformity and character. Presidential address, Amer. Psychol. Assoc., New York, Div. Pers. & Soc. Psychol., Sept. 1954.

Curie, I., & Savitch, P.: 1938. Sur les radioéléments formé dans l'uranium irradié par les neutrons. II. *J. Phys. et Radium,* 7e Série, 9, 355–360.

Dollard, J., & Miller, N. E.: 1950. *Personality and psychotherapy.* New York: McGraw-Hill.

Doob, L. W.: 1952. *Social psychology.* New York: Holt.

Edwards, W.: 1954. The theory of decision making. *Psychol. Bull., 51,* 380–417.

Eidens, H.: 1929. Experimentelle Untersuchungen über den Denkverlauf bei unmittelbaren Folgerungen. *Arch. ges. Psychol., 71,* 1–66.

Entwistle, W. J.: 1953. *Aspects of language.* London: Faber & Faber.

Fellner, W.: 1943. Monetary policies and hoarding in periods of stagnation. *J. polit. Econ., 51,* 191–205.

Festinger L.: 1943a. Studies in decision. I. Decision-time, relative frequency of judgment and subjective confidence as related to physical stimulus differences. *J. exp. Psychol., 32,* 291–306.

Festinger, L.: 1943b. Studies in decision. II. An empirical test of a quantitative theory of decision. *J. exp. Psychol., 32,* 411–423.

Fisher, S. C.: 1916. The process of generalizing abstraction; and its product, the general concept. *Psychol. Monogr., 21,* No. 2 (Whole No. 90).

Frenkel-Brunswik, E.: 1949. Intolerance of ambiguity as an emotional and perceptual personality variable. In J. S. Bruner & D. Krech (Eds.), *Perception and personality: a symposium.* Durham, N. C.: Duke Univ. Press. Pp. 108–144.

Fries, C. C.: 1945. Teaching and learning English as a foreign language. Ann Arbor: Univ. Michigan Press.

Fries, C. C.: 1952. *The structure of English.* New York: Harcourt, Brace.

Galton, F.: 1907. *Inquiries into human faculty and its development.* London: Dent.

Goldstein, K.: 1940. *Human nature in the light of psychopathology.* Cambridge, Mass.: Harvard Univ. Press.

Goldstein, K.: 1948. *Language and language disturbances.* New York: Grune & Stratton.

Goldstein, K., & Scheerer, M.: 1941. Abstract and concrete behavior; an experimental study with special tests. *Psychol. Monogr., 53,* No. 2 (Whole No. 239).

Goodman, N.: 1947. The problem of counterfactual conditionals. *J. Phil., 44,* 113–128.

Goodnow, J. J.: 1955a. Determinants of choice-distribution in two-choice situations. *Amer. J. Psychol., 68,* 106–116.

Goodnow, J. J.: 1955b. Response sequences in a pair of two-choice probability situations. *Amer. J. Psychol.,* in press.

Goodnow, J. J., Bruner, J. S., Matter, J., & Potter, M. C.: 1955. Concept determination and concept attainment. In preparation.

Goodnow, J. J., & Pettigrew, T. F.: 1955. Effect of prior patterns of experience on strategies and learning sets. *J. exp. Psychol., 49,* 381–389.

Goodnow, J. J., & Postman, L.: 1955. Probability learning in a problem-solving situation. *J. exp. Psychol., 49,* 16–22.

Goodnow, R. E.: 1954. Utilization of partially valid cues in perceptual identification. Unpublished Ph.D. thesis, Harvard Univ.

Grant, D. A., Hake, H. W., & Hornseth, J. P.: 1951. Acquisition and extinction of a verbal conditioned response with differing percentages of reinforcement *J. exp. Psychol., 42,* 1–5.

Green, E. J.: 1955. Concept formation: a problem in human operant conditioning. *J. exp. Psychol.*, 49, 175–180.

Grether, W. F., & Wolfle, D. L.: 1936. The relative efficiency of constant and varied stimulation during learning. II. White rats on a brightness discrimination problem. *J. comp. Psychol.*, 22, 365–374.

Hahn, O., & Strassman, F.: 1939. Nachweis der Entstehung aktiver Bariumisotope aus Uran und Thorium durch Neutronenbestrahlung; Nachweis weiterer aktiver Bruchstucke bei der Uranspaltung. *Naturwiss.*, 27, 89–95.

Hake, H. W., & Hyman, R.: 1953. Perception of the statistical structure of a random series of binary symbols. *J. exp. Psychol.*, 45, 64–74.

Hallowell, A. I.: 1951. Cultural factors in the structuralization of perception. In J. H. Rohrer & M. Sherif (Eds.), *Social psychology at the crossroads.* New York: Harper. Pp. 164–195.

Hammond, K. R.: 1955. Probabilistic functioning and the clinical method. *Psychol. Rev.*, 62, 255–262.

Hanfmann, E., & Kasanin, J.: 1937. A method for the study of concept formation. *J. Psychol.*, 3, 521–540.

Hanfmann, E., & Kasanin, J.: 1942. Conceptual thinking in schizophrenia. *Nerv. ment. Dis. Monogr. Ser.*, No. 67.

Hardy, G. H.: 1940. *A mathematician's apology.* Cambridge, Eng.: Cambridge, Univ. Press.

Harris, Z. S.: 1951. *Methods in structural linguistics.* Chicago: Univ. Chicago Press.

Hayes, S. P., Jr.: 1950. Some psychological problems of economics. *Psychol. Bull.*, 47, 289–330.

Head, H.: 1926. *Aphasia and kindred disorders of speech.* New York: Macmillan.

Hebb, D. O.: 1949. *The organization of behavior.* New York: Wiley.

Heidbreder, E.: 1924. An experimental study of thinking. *Arch. Psychol.*, 11, No. 73.

Heidbreder, E.: 1945. Toward a dynamic psychology of cognition. *Psychol. Rev.*, 52, 1–22.

Heidbreder, E.: 1948. The attainment of concepts: VI. Exploratory experiments on conceptualization at perceptual levels. *J. Psychol.*, 26, 193–216.

Helson, H.: 1948. Adaptation-level as a basis for a quantitative theory of frames of reference. *Psychol. Rev.*, 55, 297–313.

Hilgard, E. R.: 1951. The role of learning in perception. In R. R. Blake & G. V. Ramsey (Eds.), *Perception: an approach to personality.* New York: Ronald Press. Pp. 95–120.

Hoijer, H.: 1954. *Language in culture.* Chicago: Univ. Chicago Press.

Hovland, C. I.: 1952. A "communication analysis" of concept learning. *Psychol. Rev.*, 59, 461–472.

Hovland, C. L., & Weiss, W.: 1953. Transmission of information concerning concepts through positive and negative instances. *J. exp. Psychol.*, 45, 175–182.

Hull, C. L.: 1920. Quantitative aspects of the evolution of concepts. *Psychol. Monogr.*, 28, No. 1 (Whole No. 123).

Humphrey, G.: 1951. *Thinking.* London: Methuen.

Humphreys, L. G.: 1939. Acquisition and extinction of verbal expectations in a situation analogous to conditioning. *J. exp. Psychol.*, 25, 294–301.

Irwin, F. W.: 1953. Stated expectations as functions of probability and desirability of outcomes. *J. Pers., 21,* 329–335.

Jakobson, C., Fant, G. M., & Halle, M.: 1952. Preliminaries to speech analysis; the distinctive features and their correlates. Cambridge, Acoust. Lab.: M.I.T., Tech. Rep. No. 13.

Janis, I. L., & Frick, F.: 1943. The relationship between attitudes toward conclusions and errors in judging logical validity of syllogisms. *J. exp. Psychol., 33,* 73–77.

Jarvik, M. E.: 1951. Probability learning and a negative recency effect in the serial anticipation of alternative symbols. *J. exp. Psychol., 41,* 291–297.

Jespersen, O.: 1922. *Language.* New York: Holt.

Johnson, D. M.: 1955. *The psychology of thought and judgment.* New York: Harper.

Katona, G.: 1953. Rational behavior and economic behavior. *Psychol. Rev., 60,* 307–318.

Katz, D.: 1935. *The world of colour.* London: Kegan Paul.

Keister, M. E.: 1943. The behavior of young children in failure. In R. G. Barker, J. S. Kounin, & H. F. Wright (Eds.), *Child behavior and development.* New York: McGraw-Hill. Pp. 429–440.

Keynes, J. M.: 1921. *A treatise on probability.* London: Macmillan.

Kluckhohn, C., & Kelly, W. H.: 1945. The concept of culture. In R. Linton (Ed.), *The science of man in the world crisis.* New York: Columbia Univ. Press. Pp. 78–106.

Kluckhohn, C., & Leighton, D.: 1946. *The Navaho.* Cambridge, Mass.: Harvard Univ. Press.

Klüver, H.: 1933. *Behavior mechanisms in monkeys.* Chicago: Univ. Chicago Press.

Knight, F. H.: 1921. *Risk, uncertainty, and profit.* Boston: Houghton Mifflin.

Köhler, W.: 1947. *Gestalt psychology; and introduction to new concepts in modern psychology.* New York: Liveright.

Korzybski, A.: 1951. The role of language in the perceptual processes. In R. R. Blake & G. V. Ramsey (Eds.), *Perception: an approach to personality.* New York: Ronald Press. Pp. 170–205.

Krech, D., Rosenzweig, M. R., & Bennett, E. C.: 1954. Enzyme concentrations in the brain and adjustive behavior-patterns. Radiation Lab.: Univ. Cal. Rep. No. 2673.

Krechevsky, I.: 1932. "Hypotheses" versus "chance" in the pre-solution period in sensory discrimination-learning. *Univ. Cal. Publ. Psychol., 6,* 27–44.

Laplace, P. S., Marquis de: 1825. *A philosophical essay on probabilities.* New York: Dover Publications. 1951.

Lashley, K. S.: 1938. Experimental analysis of instinctive behavior. *Psychol. Rev., 45,* 445–472.

Lawrence, D. H.: 1949. Acquired distinctiveness of cues: I. Transfer between discriminations on the basis of familiarity with the stimulus. *J. exp. Psychol., 39,* 770–784.

Lawrence, D. H.: 1950. Acquired distinctiveness of cues: II. Selective association in a constant stimulus situation. *J. exp. Psychol., 40,* 175–188.

Lawrence, M.: 1949. *Studies in human behavior.* Princeton: Princeton Univ. Press.

Lee, D. D.: 1938. Conceptual implications of an Indian language. *Phil. Sci.*, 5, 89–102.

Leeper, R.: 1951. Cognitive processes. In S. S. Stevens (Ed.), *Handbook of experimental psychology*. New York: Wiley. Pp. 730–757.

Lenneberg, E.: 1955. Personal communication.

Lenneberg, E., & Roberts, J.: 1956. *The language of experience.* Monogr. 13, Indiana Univ. Publ. in Anthr. and Linguistics.

Lewis, M. M.: 1936. *Infant speech.* London: Kegan Paul.

Locke, J.: 1690. *An essay concerning human understanding.* 1905 edition. London: G. Routledge, 1905.

Lorenz, K.: 1952. *King Solomon's ring.* New York: Crowell.

Luborsky, L. F.: 1945. Aircraft recognition: 1. The relative efficiency of teaching procedures. *J. appl. Psychol.*, 29, 385–398.

Luchins, A. S.: 1942. Mechanization in problem solving—the effect of Einstellung. *Psychol. Monogr.*, 54, No. 6 (Whole No. 248).

McCarthy, D.: 1946. Language development in children. In L. Carmichael (Ed.), *Manual of child psychology.* (1st ed.) New York: Wiley. Pp. 476–581.

McClelland, D. C.: 1951. *Personality.* New York: Sloane.

McDougall, W.: 1926. *Outline of Psychology.* New York: Scribner's.

MacLeish, A.: 1926. Ars Poetica. *In Collected Poems 1917–1952.* Boston: Houghton Mifflin. Pp. 40–41.

Maier, N. R. F.: 1930. Reasoning in humans, I. On direction. *J. comp. Psychol.*, 10, 115–143.

Maier, N. R. F.: 1931. Reasoning in humans. II. The solution of a problem and its appearance in consciousness. *J. comp. Psychol.*, 12, 181–194.

Maier, N. R. F.: 1945. Reasoning in humans. III. The mechanisms of equivalent stimuli and of reasoning. *J. exp. Psychol.*, 35, 349–360.

Marks, Rose W.: 1951. The effect of probability, desirability, and "privilege" on the stated expectations of children. *J. Pers.*, 19, 332–351.

Marschak, J.: 1941. Lack of confidence. *Soc. Research*, 8, 41–62.

Marschak, J.: 1950. Rational behavior, uncertain prospects, and measurable utility. *Econometrica*, 18, 111–141.

Marschak, J.: 1954. Scaling of utilities and probabilities. Cowles Commission Discussion Paper: Econ. No. 216.

Mayr, E.: 1952. Concepts of classification and nomenclature in higher organisms and microorganisms. *Ann. N. Y. Acad. Sc.*, 56, 391–397.

Mayr, E.: 1955. In *Proceedings of first conference on group processes.* New York: Josiah Macy Jr. Foundation.

Merton, R. K., & Kitt, A. S.: 1950. Contributions to the theory of reference group behavior. In R: K. Merton, & P. F. Lazarsfeld (Eds.), *Continuities in social research.* Glencoe, Ill.: Free Press. Pp. 40–105.

Michotte, A.: 1946. *La perception de la causalité.* (1st Ed.). Louvain et Paris: Vrin.

Michotte, A.: 1950. A propos de la permanence phénoménale: Faits et théories. *Acta Psychol.*, 7, 298–322.

Miller, G. A.: 1953. What is information measurement? *Amer. Psychologist*, 8, 3–11.

Miller, G. A., & Selfridge, J.: 1950. Verbal context and the recall of meaningful material. *Amer. J. Psychol.*, 63, 176–185.

Miller, N. E., & Dollard, J.: 1941. *Social learning and imitation.* New Haven: Yale Univ. Press.

Morgan, J. J. B., & Morton, J. T.: 1944. The distortion of syllogistic reasoning produced by personal convictions. *J. soc. Psychol., 20,* 39–59.

Morris, C. W.: 1946. *Signs, language and behavior.* New York: Prentice-Hall.

Mosteller, F., & Nogee, P.: 1951. An experimental measurement of utility. *J. polit. Econ., 59,* 371–404.

Mowrer, O. H.: 1950. *Learning theory and personality dynamics.* New York: Ronald Press.

Murdock, G. P.: 1949. *Social structure.* New York: Macmillan.

Newman, S. S.: 1933. Further experiments in phonetic symbolism. *Amer. J. Psychol., 45,* 53–75.

Nida, E. A.: 1949. *Morphology.* (2nd Ed.). Ann Arbor: Univ. Michigan Press.

North, A. J., & Leedy, H. B.: 1952. Discrimination of stimuli having two critical components when one component varies more frequently than the other. *J. exp. Psychol., 43,* 400–407.

Optical Soc. Amer., Committee on colorimetry: 1953. *The science of color.* New York: Crowell.

Parsons, T., Bales, R. F., & Shils, E. A.: 1953. *Working papers in the theory of action.* Glencoe, Ill.: Free Press.

Pettigrew, T. F.: 1955. A paper and pencil test of category width. Privately circulated by the author.

Piaget, J.: 1951. *Play, dreams and imitations in childhood.* New York: Norton.

Piaget, J.: 1953. "Experimental epistemology." Unpublished lecture at Harvard University.

Pike, K. L.: 1945. *The intonation of American English.* Ann Arbor: Univ. Michigan Press.

Pike, K. L.: 1947. *Phonemics.* Ann Arbor: Univ. Michigan Press.

Postman, L., & Bruner, J. S.: 1948. Perception under stress. *Psychol. Rev., 55,* 314–323.

Postman, L., Bruner, J. S., & Walk, R. D.: 1951. The perception of error. *Brit. J. Psychol., 42,* 1–10.

Preston, M. G., & Baratta, P.: 1948. An experimental study of the auction-value of an uncertain outcome. *Amer. J. Psychol., 61,* 183–193.

Pribram, K.: 1953. Paper read at annual AAAS meeting, Boston.

Ramsey, F. P.: 1926. Truth and probability. In F. P. Ramsey, *The foundations of mathematics and other logical essays.* New York: Harcourt, Brace, 1931.

Razran, G. H. S.: 1939. A quantitative study of meaning by a conditioned salivary technique (semantic conditioning). *Science, 90,* 89–90.

Reed, H. B.: 1946a. Factors influencing the learning and retention of concepts. I. The influence of set. *J. exp. Psychol., 36,* 71–87.

Reed, H. B.: 1946b. The learning and retention of concepts. IV. The influence of complexity of the stimuli. *J. exp. Psychol., 36,* 252–261.

Richards, I. A.: 1929. *Practical criticism.* New York: Harcourt, Brace.

Riess, B. F.: 1946. Genetic changes in semantic conditioning. *J. exp. Psychol., 36,* 143–152.

Rivers, W. H. R.: 1901. Vision. *Reports of the Cambridge anthropological expedition to Torres Straits, 2,* 1–132.

Roback, A. A.: 1954. *Destiny and motivation in language.* Cambridge, Mass.: Sci-Art Publishers.

Russell, B.: 1919. *Introduction to mathematical philosophy.* London: G. Allen & Unwin.

Sapir, E.: 1929. A study in phonetic symbolism. *J. exp. Psychol., 12,* 225–239.

Sapir, E.: 1949. Selected writing of Edward Sapir. D. G. Mandelbaum (Ed.). Berkeley: Univ. Cal. Press.

Savage, L. J.: 1954. *The foundations of statistics.* New York: Wiley.

Schachtel, E. G.: 1947. On memory and childhood amnesia. *Psychiatry, 10,* 1–26.

Senders, V. L.: 1953. Further analysis of response sequences in the setting of a psychophysical experiment. *Amer. J. Psychol., 66,* 215–228.

Senders, V. L., & Sowards, A.: 1952. Analysis of response sequences in the setting of a psychophysical experiment. *Amer. J. Psychol., 64,* 358–374.

Seymour, R.: 1954. Strategies in the utilization of information. Unpublished Ph.D. thesis, Dept. of Social Relation, Harvard. Available in Widener Library, Harvard Univ.

Shackle, G. L. S.: 1949. *Expectations in economics.* (1st Ed.). Cambridge, Eng.: Cambridge Univ. Press.

Shannon, C. E.: 1949. *The mathematical theory of communication.* Urbana, Ill.: Univ. Ill. Press.

Sheldon, W. H.: 1950. Personal communication.

Sherman, M.: 1927. The differentiation of emotional responses in infants. II. The ability of observers to judge the emotional characteristics of the crying of infants, and of the voice of an adult. *J. comp. Psychol. 7,* 335–351.

Silvestri, F.: 1929. The relation of taxonomy to other branches of entomology. *Fourth Interntl. Congr. Entomology, 2,* 52–54.

Simmel, M. L.: 1953. The coin problem: a study in thinking. *Amer. J. Psychol., 66,* 229–241.

Smedslund, J.: 1956. Multiple-probability learning. Oslo: *Akademisk Forlag.* In press, quotation from author's manuscript.

Smith, M. H.: 1949. Spread of effect is the spurious result of non-random response tendencies. *J. exp. Psychol., 39,* 355–368.

Smoke, K. L.: 1932. An objective study of concept formation. *Psychol. Monogr., 42,* No. 4 (Whole No. 191).

Smoke, K. L.: 1933. Negative instances in concept learning. *J. exp. Psychol., 16,* 583–588.

Stevens, S. S.: 1934. The attributes of tones. *Proc. nat. Acad. Sci., 20,* 457–459.

Stevens, S. S.: 1936. Psychology: the propaedeutic science. *Phil. Sci. 3,* 90–103.

Stigler, G. J.: 1950. The development of utility theory. *J. polit. Econ., 58,* 307–327, 373–396.

Tagiuri, R.: 1952. Relational analysis: an extension of sociometric method with emphasis upon social perception. *Sociometry, 15,* 91–104.

Thistlethwaite, D.: 1950. Attitude and structure as factors in the distortion of reasoning. *J. abnorm. soc. Psychol., 45,* 442–458.

Thurstone, L. L.: 1950. Creative talent. Psychometric Lab.: Univ. Chicago. Rep. No. 61.

Tinbergen, N.: 1948. Social releasers and the experimental method required for their study. *Wilson Bull.*, 60, 6–51.

Tinbergen, N.: 1951. *The study of instinct.* Oxford: Clarendon Press.

Titchener, E. B.: 1909. *Lectures on the experimental psychology of the thought processes.* New York: Macmillan.

Titchener, E. B.: 1915. *A beginner's psychology.* New York: Macmillan.

Todd, F. J.: 1954. A methodological analysis of clinical judgment. Unpublished Ph.D. thesis, Univ. Colorado.

Tolman, E. C.: 1932. *Purposive behavior in animals and men.* New York: Century.

Tolman, E. C.: 1951. A psychological model. In T. Parsons, & E. A. Shils (Eds.), *Toward a general theory of action.* Cambridge, Mass.: Harvard Univ. Press. Pp. 279–361.

Tolman, E. C., & Brunswik, E.: 1935. The organism and the causal texture of the environment. *Psychol. Rev.*, 42, 43–77.

Vigotsky, L. S.: 1939. Thought and speech. *Psychiatry*, 2, 29–54.

Vinacke, W. E.: 1951. The investigation of concept formation. *Psychol. Bull.*, 48, 1–31.

Vinacke, W. E.: 1952. *The psychology of thinking.* New York: McGraw-Hill.

von Neumann, J., & Morgenstern, O.: 1944. *Theory of games and economic behavior.* (1st Ed.) Princeton: Princeton Univ. Press.

Walk, R. D.: 1952. Effect of discrimination reversal on human discrimination learning. *J. exp. Psychol.*, 44, 410–419.

Walker, K. F.: 1946. The psychological assumptions of economics. *Econ. Rec.*, 22, 66–82.

Wallas, G.: 1926. *The art of thought.* New York: Harcourt, Brace.

Werner, H., & Kaplan, E.: 1950. Development of word meaning through verbal context: an experimental study. *J. Psychol.*, 29, 251–257.

Whitfield, J. W.: 1950. The imaginary questionnaire. *Quart. J. exp. Psychol.*, 2, 76–87.

Whorf, B. L.: 1940. Linguistics as an exact science. *Technol. Rev.* 43, 61–63.

Whorf, B. L.: 1950. *Four articles on metalinguistics.* Washington, D. C.: Foreign Inst., Dept. of State.

Wilkins, M. C.: 1929. The effect of changed material on ability to do formal syllogistic reasoning. *Arch. Psychol.*, No. 102.

Winder, C. L., & Wurtz, K. R.: 1954. Some effects of induced success and failure on judgment behavior. Dept. of Psych.: Stanford Univ. Tech. Rep. No. 5, Nonr. 225(01).

Wolfle, D. L.: 1936. The relative efficiency of constant and varied stimulation during learning. III. The objective extent of stimulus variation. *J. comp. Psychol.*, 22, 375–381.

Woodworth, R. S.: 1947. Reënforcement of perception. *Amer. J. Psychol.*, 60, 119–124.

Wyatt, D. F., & Campbell, D. T.: 1951. On the liability of stereotype or hypothesis. *J. abnorm. soc. Psychol.*, 46, 496–500.

Zipf, G. K.: 1935. *The psycho-biology of language.* Boston: Houghton Mifflin.

Index of Authors

323

Index of Subjects

24479